W9-CDI-717

Frommer's

4th
Edition

Seattle & Portland

by Karl Samson

Macmillan • USA

For my wife, Jane, who followed me down the Oregon trail.

ABOUT THE AUTHOR

Karl Samson chooses to make the Portland, Oregon, area his home. An inveterate traveler who was raised in Asia, he writes Frommer's guides to Arizona, Guatemala, Belize, and Nepal.

MACMILLAN TRAVEL

A Simon & Schuster Macmillan Company
1633 Broadway
New York, NY 10019

ISBN 0-02-860863-1
ISSN 1045-9308

Editor: Erica Spaberg
Map Editor: Douglas Stallings
Design by Michelle Laseau
Digital Cartography by John Decamillis and Ortelius Design

SPECIAL SALES

Bulk purchases (10+ copies) of Frommer's travel guides are available to corporations at special discounts. The Special Sales Department can produce custom editions to be used as premiums and/or for sales promotion to suit individual needs. Existing editions can be produced with custom cover imprints such as a corporate logo. For more information write to: Special Sales, Simon and Schuster, 1633 Broadway, New York, New York 10019.

Manufactured in the United States of America

Contents

List of Maps

AN INVITATION TO THE READER

In researching this book, I discovered many wonderful places—hotels, restaurants, shops, and more. I'm sure you'll find others. Please tell us about them, so we can share the information with your fellow travelers in upcoming editions. If you were disappointed with a recommendation, we'd love to know that, too. Please write to:

Karl Samson
Frommer's Seattle & Portland, 4th Edition
c/o Macmillan Travel
1633 Broadway
New York, NY 10019

AN ADDITIONAL NOTE

Please be advised that travel information is subject to change at any time—and this is especially true of prices. We therefore suggest that you write or call ahead for confirmation when making your travel plans. The authors, editors, and publisher cannot be held responsible for the experiences of readers while traveling. Your safety is important to us, however, so we encourage you to stay alert and be aware of your surroundings. Keep a close eye on cameras, purses, and wallets, all favorite targets of thieves and pickpockets.

WHAT THE SYMBOLS MEAN
✪ Frommer's Favorites
Hotels, restaurants, attractions, and entertainment you should not miss.

⑤ Super-Special Values
Hotels and restaurants that offer great value for your money.

The following abbreviations are used for credit cards:

AE	American Express	EU	Eurocard
CB	Carte Blanche	JCB	Japan Credit Bank
DC	Diners Club	MC	MasterCard
DISC	Discover	V	Visa
ER	enRoute		

Introducing Seattle

- **Relaxing Over a Latte in a Cafe:** When the rain and gray skies finally get to you, there is no better prescription (short of a ticket to the tropics) than a cup of frothy caffe latte in a cozy cafe. Grab a magazine and just hang out until it stops (maybe sometime in June).
- **Wandering Around Fremont:** This quirky neighborhood considers itself the center of the universe; it's really just a bit off center. Retro clothing and vintage furniture stores, cafes, a brewery, a great flea market, and the city's best public art make this hands-down the most fun neighborhood in Seattle.
- **Attending a Show at the Fifth Avenue Theatre:** This historic theater was designed to resemble the imperial throne room in Beijing's Forbidden City. Can you say ornate? Nothing else in Seattle compares, including the show on stage.
- **Going to the Spring Flower and Garden Show:** Each spring gardening madness descends on the Seattle Convention Center during the nation's third largest flower-and-garden show. There are more than five acres of garden displays and hundreds of vendors.
- **Riding the Monorail:** Though the ride is short and doesn't serve much purpose other than entertainment, it provides a totally new perspective on the city if your view has been from behind the wheel or strolling the city's sidewalks.
- **Hanging Out at an Oyster Bar:** New England may think it's got good oysters, but Seattleites will tell you that you can't beat the bivalves from the Northwest. Whether you say "oyster" or "erster," in the Northwest you order your bivalves by their first names— Kumamoto, Willapa Bay, Quilcene.
- **A Morning at Volunteer Park:** Whether the day is sunny or not, this park on Capitol Hill is a great spot to spend a morning. You can relax in the grass, study Chinese snuff bottles in the Seattle Asian Art Museum, marvel at the orchids in the park's conservatory, or simply enjoy the great view of the city from here.
- **A Day at the Zoo:** The cages are almost completely gone from this big zoo, replaced by spacious animal habitats that give the residents the feeling of being back at home in the wilds. Zebras gallop, brown

bears romp, river otters cavort, elephants stomp, orangutans swing. The levels of activity here make it clear that the animals are happy with their surroundings.

- **Strolling Through the Arboretum in Spring:** Winters in Seattle may not be long but they do lack color so, when spring hits, the sudden bursts of color it brings are reverently appreciated. There's no better place in the city to appreciate the spring floral displays than at the Washington Park Arboretum.

- **Browsing at Read All About It:** Located on the hectic corner by the main entrance to Pike Place Market, this bustling newsstand has magazines and newspapers from all over the world.

- **Walking, Biking, and Skating Along the Eastern Shore of Lake Washington:** A miles-long paved path runs along the shore of Lake Washington on the east side of Seattle and provides more than ample opportunities for skaters, joggers, cyclists, and walkers. There are even sandy beaches for summer visitors who want to cool off.

2   The City Today

Don't look now, but it's everywhere. It's in your computer, on your TV, on the big screen at your local movie theater, and in your cup of coffee. "It," of course, is Seattle, a city that has been propelled by geography, climate, and chance into the consciousness of the nation.

A few years back, Seattle was voted "America's most livable city," and this praise, along with other accolades, prompted a massive exodus of primarily Californians into the Seattle metropolitan area. About the same time that California refugees were discovering Seattle, the rock-music industry decided that Seattle's guitar-driven grunge rock was the next big sound to succeed, a sound that would supplant the music of Athens and Minneapolis. The youth of America discovered Seattle and headed for the city by the Sound (Puget, that is) with guitars in hand and dreams of Nirvana haunting their sleeping and waking hours. Today, the Seattle sound as played by such bands as Nirvana, Soundgarden, Alice in Chains, and Pearl Jam continues to dominate the airwaves.

Though Seattle's fortunes once rode on the wings of Boeing passenger jets, today the city has managed to diversify its economy enough so that it no longer must suffer the economic pendulum swings of the airline and aerospace industries. Once layoffs at Boeing could cripple the city, but today Boeing has slipped from the limelight as the new kid on the block has moved to center stage. Computer whiz kid Bill Gates, the richest man in America, and his Microsoft Corporation, which with its Windows software has become the most important software manufacturer in the world, have given the Seattle area a new economic diversity.

While people do move here to find work, most people came here because they love the outdoors. Few other cities in the United States are as immersed in the outdoors aesthetic as Seattle. The Cascade Range lies less than 50 miles to the east of downtown Seattle, and across Puget Sound stand the Olympic Mountains. It is to these lands that Seattleites head throughout the year. In the spring, summer, and fall, the forests and mountains attract hikers, mountain bikers, anglers, and campers, and in winter the ski areas of Snoqualmie Pass and Stephens Pass attract downhill and cross-country skiers.

Though mountains line the city's eastern horizon, a glance to the southeast on a sunny day will reveal the city's most treasured sight. Mount Rainier, a 14,410-foot-tall dormant volcano, looms so large and unexpected that it demands attention. When "the mountain is out," as they say here in Seattle, especially on a winter day, Seattleites head for the hills.

However, as important as The Mountain is to Seattle, it is water that truly defines the city's character. To the west lies Elliott Bay, an arm of Puget Sound; to the east is Lake Washington; and in the middle of the city there is Lake Union. Seattle claims the highest per capita private boat ownership of any city in America. These pleasure craft range in size from regally appointed yachts to slender sea kayaks. So popular is boating in this city that the opening day of boating season is one of Seattle's most popular annual festivals.

But more than anything, Seattle is perhaps best known as the coffee capital of America. To understand Seattle's coffee addiction, it is necessary to study the city's geography and climate. Seattle lies at almost 50 degrees north latitude, which means that winter days are short. The sun comes up around 7:30 and goes down as early as 4:30 and is frequently hidden behind leaden skies. A strong stimulant is almost a necessity to get people out of bed and through the gray days of winter. Seattleites love to argue over which coffee bar in town serves the best coffee, and the answer isn't always Starbucks, despite this company's massive expansion across the country.

When the sun finally does come out, Seattleites reach for their sunglasses to protect their eyes, which have become accustomed to the low levels of ambient light. When Seattleites misplace their shades, they simply buy another pair. And when next the sun comes out, the cycle begins anew—giving the city's residents the dubious honor of purchasing more sunglasses per capita than the citizens of any other city.

Seattle's popularity and rapid growth, though it has brought fine restaurants, a new art museum, rock-music fame, and national recognition of the city's arts scene, has not been entirely smooth. The streets and highways have been unable to handle the increased traffic load and commuting has become almost as nightmarish as in California, from whence so many of the city's recent transplants fled, partly due to the traffic congestion. Despite overpacked roadways, in 1995 the city once again voted not to build a light-rail mass transit system to alleviate congestion. Residents of the suburbs were unwilling to take on higher taxes in exchange for less congested roads. With roads growing ever more crowded and the cost of living continuing to rise, Seattle may not be the Emerald City it once was, but it remains a city of singularly spectacular setting. To stand in a park on Queen Anne Hill and gaze down at Puget Sound, the city skyline, and Mount Rainier in the distance is to understand why Seattleites love their city despite its flaws.

It is the Emerald City of the Northwest—the jewel in the crown of a land of natural beauty. The sparkling waters of Elliott Bay, Lake Union, and Lake Washington surround this city of shimmering skyscrapers. Forests of evergreens crowd the city limits. Everywhere you look, another breathtaking vista unfolds. Once a sleepy backwoods town, Seattle has become one of the key cities of the Pacific Rim, forging new trading links with Japan and the rest of Asia. In many ways, the city is similar to San Francisco: It is surrounded by water, was built on hills, and has a Chinatown, a large gay community, and even a trolley. What makes Seattle different are its people and their pace of life.

Things move more slowly up here, and although Seattle is growing more cosmopolitan by the minute, it is the wildness of the Northwest that has attracted many of the city's residents. With endless boating opportunities and beaches and mountains within a few hours' drive, Seattle is ideally situated for the active lifestyle that is so much a part of life in the Northwest. The city's rainy weather may be infamous, but the people of Seattle have ways of forgetting about the clouds. They either put on their rain gear or retreat to the city's hundreds of excellent restaurants, its dozens of theaters and performance halls, and its outstanding museums. They never let the weather stand in the way of having a good time—and neither should you. Although summer is the best time to visit Seattle, the city offers year-round diversions and entertainment.

3 A Look at the Past

Dateline

- **1792** Capt. George Vancouver of the British Royal Navy explores Puget Sound.
- **1841** Lt. Charles Wilkes surveys Puget Sound and names Elliott Bay.
- **1851** The first white settlers arrive in what will become West Seattle's Alki Point.
- **1852** These same settlers move to the east side of Elliott Bay from Alki Point, which

continues

Seattle got a late start in U.S. history, and to this day the city has been trying to make up for it. The first settlers didn't arrive until 1851, although explorers had visited the region much earlier. Captain George Vancouver of the British Royal Navy—who lent his name to both Vancouver, British Columbia, and Vancouver, Washington—had explored Puget Sound as early as 1792. However, there was little to attract anyone permanently to this remote region. Unlike Oregon to the south, Washington had little rich farmland, only acres and acres of forest. It was this seemingly endless supply of wood that finally enticed the first settlers.

The first settlement was on Alki Point, in the area now known as West Seattle. Because this location was exposed to storms, within a few years the settlers moved across Elliott Bay to a more protected spot, the present downtown Seattle. The new location for the village was a tiny island surrounded by mud flats. Although some early settlers wanted to name the town New York—even then Seattle had grand aspirations—the name Seattle was chosen as a tribute to Chief

Sealth, a local Native American who had be-friended the newcomers.

In the middle of town, on the waterfront, the first steam-powered lumber mill on Puget Sound was built by Henry Yesler. It stood at the foot of what is now Yesler Way—but what for many years was simply referred to as Skid Road, a reference to the way logs were skidded down from the slopes behind town to the sawmill. Over the years Skid Road developed a reputation for its bars and brothels. Some say that after an East Coast journalist incorrectly referred to it as Skid Row in his newspaper, the name stuck and was subsequently applied to derelict neighborhoods all over the country. But only Seattle can lay claim to the very first Skid Row. To this day, despite attempts to revamp the neighborhood, Yesler Way attracts the sort of visitors one would expect, but it is also in the center of the Pioneer Historic District, one of Seattle's main tourist attractions.

By 1889 the city had more than 25,000 inhabitants and was well on its way to becoming the most important city in the Northwest. On June 6 of that year, however, 25 blocks in the center of town burned to the ground. By that time the city—which had spread out to low-lying land reclaimed from the mud flats—had begun experiencing problems with mud and sewage disposal. The fire gave citizens the opportunity they needed to rebuild Seattle. The solution to the drainage and sewage problems was to regrade the steep slopes to the east of the town and raise the streets above their previous levels. Because the regrading lagged behind the rebuilding, the ground floor of many new buildings wound up below street level. Eventually these lower-level shops and entrances were abandoned when elevated sidewalks bridged the space between roadways and buildings. Today sections of several abandoned streets that are now underground can be toured (see section 4 of chapter 6 for details).

One of the most amazing engineering feats that took place after the fire was the regrading of Denny Hill. Seattle once had seven hills, but today has only six—nothing is left of Denny Hill. Hydraulic mining techniques, with high-powered water jets digging into hillsides, were used to level the hill, of which only a name remains—Denny Regrade, a neighborhood just south of Seattle Center.

is subject to storms.

- **1853** Washington Territory is formed.
- **1864** The transcontinental telegraph reaches Seattle, connecting it with the rest of the country.
- **1866** Chief Sealth, for whom Seattle is named, dies and is buried across Puget Sound at Suquamish.
- **1875** Regular steamship service begins between Seattle and San Francisco.
- **1889** The Great Seattle Fire levels most of downtown.
- **1893** The railroad reaches Seattle.
- **1897** The steamer *Portland* arrives from Alaska carrying more than a ton of gold, thus starting the Yukon gold rush.
- **1907** Pike Place Market is founded.
- **1916** William Boeing launches his first airplane from Lake Union, beginning an industry that will become Seattle's lifeblood.

continues

- **1940** The Mercer Island Floating Bridge opens.
- **1962** The Century 21 exposition is held in Seattle and the famous Space Needle is erected.
- **1977** Seattle is called the most livable city in America.
- **1982** Seattle ranked as the number-one recreational city.
- **1990** Metro bus tunnel, a sort of subway for buses, opens beneath downtown Seattle.
- **1992** Seattle Art Museum moves from Volunteer Park to a controversial new downtown building.

The new buildings went up quickly after the fire, and eight years later another event occurred that changed the city almost as much. The steamship *Portland* arrived in Seattle from Alaska, carrying a ton of gold from the recently discovered Klondike goldfields. Within the year Seattle's population swelled with prospectors ultimately headed north. Few of them ever struck it rich, but they all stopped in Seattle to purchase supplies and equipment, thus lining the pockets of Seattle merchants and spreading far and wide the name of this obscure Northwest city. When the prospectors came south again with their hard-earned gold, much of it never left Seattle, sidetracked by beer halls and brothels.

A very important event in Seattle history took place on Lake Union in 1916. William Boeing and Clyde Esterveld launched their first airplane, a floatplane, with the intention of flying mail to Canada. Their enterprise eventually became the Boeing Company, which has since grown to become the single largest employer in the area. Unfortunately, until recently Seattle's fortunes were so inextricably bound to those of Boeing that hard times for the aircraft manufacturer meant hard times for the whole city. In recent years, however, industry in the Seattle region has begun to diversify. There are now many computer-related companies in the area, including software giant Microsoft. Floatplanes still call Lake Union home, and if you should venture out on the lake by kayak, sailboard, or boat, be sure to watch out for air traffic.

The most recognizable structure on the Seattle skyline is the Space Needle. Built in 1962 for Century 21, the Seattle World's Fair, the Space Needle was, and still is, a futuristic-looking structure. Situated just north of downtown—in the Seattle Center complex that was the site of the World's Fair—the Space Needle provides stupendous views of the city and all its surrounding natural beauty.

The 1962 World's Fair was far more than a fanciful vision of the future—it was truly prophetic for Seattle. The emergence of the Emerald City as an important Pacific Rim trading center is a step toward a bright 21st century. The Seattle area has witnessed extraordinary growth in recent years, with the migration of thousands of

Impressions

Seattle is a comparatively new-looking city that covers an old frontier town like frosting on a cake.

—Winthrop Sargeant, *The New Yorker*, 1978

What Happened to Denny Hill?

"Hey, you've got steep hills here, especially that one coming up from First Avenue," commented an astute first-time visitor to Seattle as he checked into a downtown hotel. That's right, all through downtown Seattle the land slopes steeply up from the waterfront, making many first-time visitors glad they rented a car with an automatic transmission. San Francisco's streets, which must have their own agent and publicity director, may have landed all the great car chase scenes over the years, but Seattle's steep streets demand respect, too. Imagine San Francisco's streets covered with ice and you've got a good idea of a bad winter day in Seattle.

Supposedly there used to be seven Seattle hills, just as in Rome. However, the city fathers of Seattle were neither romantics nor cognizant of the potential cinematic value of their hills. To the people of Seattle at the turn of the 20th century, Seattle's hills were just big headaches, giant obstacles to transportation and construction.

Denny Hill was one of the steepest of all and by the 1890s, cable cars ran up and down the hill connecting downtown with the burgeoning neighborhood of Queen Anne, itself on a hill. Hang on, you say, consulting your map of Seattle. What hill between downtown and Queen Anne? Exactly. It's gone. Vanished. Blown to smithereens, to be precise. If you've ever taken your garden hose and turned the nozzle to that really powerful setting where the water comes blasting out so hard it hurts and then turned it against a dirt clod, then you have a pretty good picture of what happened to Denny Hill. They just used bigger hoses. This ambitious hydraulics project was begun in 1903 and not completed until 1930. When they were finally done hosing down the hill, Seattle had more flat land along the waterfront and no more Denny Hill to get in the way of commuters.

Today the Denny Regrade area, as it is known, is a flat and rather characterless area lying between downtown and the Seattle Center. It's that expanse of low-rise buildings over which the monorail soars. However, in recent years the Belltown area just north of Pike Place Market and in the center of the Denny Regrade has become one of Seattle's fastest growing neighborhoods. It's taken nearly a century, but Seattle is finally beginning to take advantage of its missing seventh hill.

people in search of jobs, a higher quality of life, and a mild climate. To keep pace with its sudden prominence on the Pacific Rim, Seattle has also been rushing to transform itself from a sleepy Northwest city into a cosmopolitan metropolis. New restaurants, theaters, and museums are cropping up all over the place as new residents demand more cultural attractions. Visitors to Seattle will immediately sense the quickening pulse of this awakening city.

2

Planning a Trip to Seattle

Seattle is becoming an increasingly popular destination for travelers, and as its popularity grows, so too does the need for previsit planning. Before leaving home, you should try to make hotel and car reservations. Not only will these reservations save you money, but you won't have to worry about finding accommodations when you arrive. Summer is the peak tourist season in Seattle and reservations are highly advisable, especially if you plan to visit during the Seafair festival in late July–early August, when every hotel in town can be booked up.

1 Information

The sources of information listed here can provide you with plenty of free brochures on Seattle, many with colorful photos to further tempt you into a visit.

If you still have questions about Seattle after reading this book, contact the **Seattle-King County Convention and Visitors Bureau,** 520 Pike St., Suite 1300, Seattle, WA 98101-9927 (☎ 206/461-5840). They'll be happy to send you more information on the city and the surrounding areas. They're open Monday through Friday from 8:30am to 5pm. To find their **Visitor Information Center,** walk up Union Street until it goes into a tunnel under the Washington State Convention and Trade Center. You'll see the information center on your left as you enter the tunnel. The exact address is 800 Convention Pl.

These helpful people also operate a **Visitor Information Center** at Seattle-Tacoma (Sea-Tac) International Airport (☎ 206/433-5218). You can't miss it—it's right beside the baggage-claim area (by carousel no. 8). They have brochures on many area attractions and can answer any last-minute questions.

For information on other parts of Washington, contact the **Washington State Tourism Office,** P.O. Box 42500, Olympia, WA 98504-2500 (☎ 206/586-2102, 206/586-2088, or 800/544-1800).

2 When to Go

CLIMATE

I'm sure you've heard about the climate in Seattle. Let's face it, the city's weather has a bad reputation. As they say out here, "The rain in Spain stays mainly in Seattle." Seattle can make London look like a

What Things Cost in Seattle	U.S. $
Taxi from the airport to the city center	27.00
Bus ride between any two downtown points	Free
Local telephone call	0.25
Double at Alexis Hotel (very expensive)	185.00
Double at Sixth Pacific Plaza Hotel (moderate)	74.00
Double at Kings Inn (inexpensive)	55.00
Lunch for one at Queen City Grill (moderate)	12.00
Lunch for one at Emmett Watson's Oyster Bar (inexpensive)	7.00
Dinner for one, without wine, at Chez Shea (expensive)	27.00
Dinner for one, without wine, at Ivar's Salmon House (moderate)	19.00
Dinner for one, without wine, at Wild Ginger Asian Restaurant (inexpensive)	14.00
Pint of beer	3.50
Coca-Cola	1.00
Cup of coffee (latte)	1.50
Roll of ASA 100 Kodacolor film, 36 exposures	5.25
Movie ticket	6.50
Theater ticket to Seattle Repertory Theater	13.50–34.00

desert. I wish I could tell you that it just ain't so, but I can't. It rains in Seattle—and rains and rains and rains. However, when December 31 rolls around each year, a funny thing happens: They total up the year's precipitation, and Seattle almost always comes out behind such cities as Washington, D.C., Boston, New York, and Atlanta. Most of the rain falls between September and April, so if you visit during the summer, you might not see a drop of rain the entire time. If July in Seattle is just too sunny for you, take a trip out to the Hoh Valley on the Olympic Peninsula. With more than 150 inches of rain a year, this is the wettest spot in the continental United States.

No matter what time of year you plan to visit Seattle, be sure to bring at least a sweater or light jacket. Summer nights can be quite cool, and daytime temperatures rarely climb above the low 80s. Winters are not as cold as in the East, but snow does fall in Seattle.

To make things perfectly clear, here's an annual weather chart:

Average Temperature & Days of Rain

	Jan	Feb	Mar	Apr	May	June	July	Aug	Sept	Oct	Nov	Dec
Temp. (°F)	46	50	53	58	65	69	75	74	69	60	52	47
Temp. (°C)	8	10	12	14	18	21	24	23	21	16	11	8
Rain (Days)	19	16	17	14	10	9	5	7	9	14	18	20

THE FESTIVAL CITY

Seattleites organize a festival at the drop of a rain hat. Summers in the city seem to revolve around the myriad festivals that take place every week. Check the "Tempo Arts and Entertainment" section of the *Seattle Times* on Friday or pick up a copy of *Seattle Weekly* to find out what special events will be taking place during your visit. Remember, festivals here take place rain or shine.

SEATTLE CALENDAR OF EVENTS

February

- **Chinese New Year,** International District. Date depends on lunar calendar (may be in January).
- **Northwest Flower & Garden Show,** Washington State Convention Center. Massive show for avid gardeners. Mid-late February (☎ 206/789-5333).
- **Mardi Gras,** Pioneer Square. Processions and events culminating on Fat Tuesday, the day before Lent and some seven weeks before Easter (☎ 206/682-4648).

April

- **Skagit Valley Tulip Festival,** Mt. Vernon and the Skagit Valley. Tulip fields in bloom an hour north of Seattle, plenty of entertainment on weekends. First two weeks of April (☎ 206/428-8547, or March 20 to April 30 800/4-TULIPS).
- **Cherry Blossom and Japanese Cultural Festival,** Seattle Center. Traditional Japanese spring festival. Late April (☎ 206/684-8582).

May

- **Opening Day of Boating Season,** Lake Union and Lake Washington. First Saturday in May (☎ 206/325-1000).
- **Seattle International Film Festival,** theaters around town (☎ 206/324-9996). Mid-May to mid-June.
- ✪ **Northwest Folklife Festival.** This is the largest folklife festival in the country, with dozens of national and regional folk musicians performing on numerous stages. In addition, craftspeople from all over the Northwest show and sell. Lots of good food and dancing too.
  Where: Seattle Center. **When:** Memorial Day weekend. **How:** Free (☎ 206/684-8582).
- **Pike Place Market Festival,** Pike Place Market. A celebration of the market, with lots of free entertainment. Memorial Day weekend (☎ 206/624-3570).

June

- **Seattle International Music Festival,** Meany Hall, University of Washington and other locations. Mid-June (☎ 206/233-0993).
- **Fremont Street Fair,** Fremont neighborhood. Food, arts and crafts, and entertainment in one of Seattle's favorite neighborhoods. Third weekend in June (☎ 206/548-8376).

July

- **Fourth of July fireworks,** Elliott Bay and Seattle waterfront. July 4.
- **Wooden Boat Festival,** Lake Union. Wooden boats, both old and new, from all over the Northwest. Races, demonstrations, food, and entertainment. First weekend in July (☎ 206/382-BOAT).
- **Chinatown International District Summer Festival,** International District. Features the music, dancing, arts, and food of Seattle's Asian district. Second weekend in July.
- **Bite of Seattle,** Seattle Center. Sample offerings from Seattle's best restaurants. Mid-July (☎ 206/684-8582).
- **King County Fair,** King County Fairgrounds, Enumclaw, south of Seattle. Starts the third Wednesday of the month (☎ 206/ 825-7777).
- ✪ **Seafair.** This is the biggest Seattle event of the year, during which festivities occur every day—parades, hydroplane boat races, performances by the Navy's Blue Angels, a Torchlight Parade, ethnic festivals, sporting events, and open house on naval ships. This one really packs in the out-of-towners and sends Seattleites fleeing on summer vacations.

   Where: All over Seattle. **When:** Third weekend in July to first weekend in August. **How:** Call for details on events and tickets (☎ 206/728-0123).
- **Pacific Northwest Arts and Crafts Fair,** Bellevue Square, Bellevue. The largest arts and crafts fair in the Northwest. Last weekend in July (☎ 206/454-4900).

August

- **Chief Seattle Days,** Suquamish. Celebration of Northwest Native American culture across Puget Sound from Seattle. Third weekend in August (☎ 206/598-3311).

September

- ✪ **Bumbershoot.** Seattle's second most popular festival derives its peculiar name from a British term for umbrella—an obvious reference to the rainy weather. Lots of music and other events packs Seattle's youthful set into Seattle Center and other venues. You'll find plenty of arts and crafts on display too.

   Where: Seattle Center. **When:** Labor Day weekend. **How:** Phone 206/684-7200 for schedule.
- **Out to Lunch,** locations throughout Seattle. Free lunchtime music concerts. Phone 206/623-0340 for a schedule. Beginning in mid-September.

3 Tips for Special Travelers

FOR SENIORS

Be sure to ask about senior discounts when making hotel reservations. Also, museums, theaters, gardens, and tour companies usually offer senior-citizen discounts. These can add up to substantial savings, but you have to remember to ask for the discount.

When making airline reservations, always mention that you are a senior citizen. Many airlines offer discounts. Also, if you aren't already a member, consider joining the **American Association of Retired Persons (AARP),** 601 E. St. NW, Washington, D.C .20049 (☎ 800/ 424-3410). One of the many benefits of belonging to this organization is the 10 percent discount offered at many motels and hotels. If you are looking for someone to travel with, **Travel Companions Exchange,** P.O. Box 833, Amityville, NY 11701-0833 (☎ 516/454-0880), provides listings of possible travel companions (mostly older travelers). It costs $99 for a six-month membership and subscription to the service. It is also possible to subscribe to the organization's bimonthly newsletter without becoming a member. The newsletter costs $48 per year.

FOR SINGLES

There's no doubt about it, single travelers are discriminated against by hotels and motels. A lone traveler often has to pay the same room rate as two people, and if you want to spend time at an expensive hotel, this can make a vacation a very costly experience. Unless you are dead set on staying at a particular hotel, you might be able to save some money by finding a comparable hostelry that offers separate rates for single and double rooms.

FOR FAMILIES

Many of the less expensive hotels outside the city center allow kids to stay free in their parents' room. Be sure to check the listings or ask when you contact a hotel.

At mealtimes, keep in mind that many of the larger restaurants, especially along the waterfront, offer children's menus. If you want to keep the kids entertained all day long, spend the day at **Seattle Center.**

FOR STUDENTS

See "For Students" in Section 4 of Chapter 3.

4 Getting There

BY PLANE

Seattle-Tacoma International Airport (☎ 206/431-4444), known as **Sea-Tac,** is located about 14 miles south of Seattle. It's connected to the city by I-5.

The Major Airlines   Sea-Tac Airport is served by about 30 airlines. The major carriers include **Alaska Airlines** (☎ 206/433-3100, or 800/426-0333); **American Airlines** (☎ 800/433-7300); **America West** (☎ 800/235-9292); **Continental** (☎ 800/525-0280); **Delta** (☎ 800/221-1212); **Horizon Air** (☎ 800/547-9308); **Northwest** (☎ 800/225-2525); **Southwest** (☎ 800/435-9792); **TWA** (☎ 800/221-2000); **United** (☎ 206/441-3700 or 800/241-6522); and **USAir** (☎ 800/428-4322).

In addition to air service at Sea-Tac Airport, there are several small airlines offering seaplane flights between Seattle and the San Juan Islands and British Columbia. **Kenmore Air** (☎ 206/486-1257 or 800/543-9595) is one airline that offers regular flights.

BY TRAIN

Amtrak trains stop at King Street Station, Third Avenue South and Jackson Street (☎ 206/382-4125), near the Kingdome. Several trains run daily between Seattle and Portland, Oregon (reservations are required). The trip takes about four hours and costs between $24 and $36 one way. These trains continue south to San Francisco and Los Angeles. There are also daily trains heading east by way of Spokane and Boise, Idaho. For Amtrak reservations, call 800/872-7245.

BY BUS

From the **Greyhound** bus station, Eighth Avenue and Stewart Street (☎ 206/628-5508, or 800/231-2222), buses can connect you to almost any city in the continental United States.

BY CAR

Interstate 5 is the main artery between Seattle and Portland and points south, stretching as far as the Mexican border. I-5 also continues north between Seattle and the Canadian border. **I-90** comes into Seattle from Spokane and from the east—all the way from Boston. **I-405** bypasses downtown Seattle on the east side of Lake Washington, passing through the city of Bellevue instead.

Here are some driving distances from selected cities (in miles):

Los Angeles	1,190
Portland	175
Salt Lake City	835
San Francisco	810
Spokane	285
Vancouver, B.C.	110

BY SHIP

Seattle is a major port. The city is served by the **Washington State Ferries** (☎ 206/464-6400, or 800/84-FERRY in Washington State), the most extensive ferry system in the United States. Ferries travel between Seattle and Vashon Island, Bainbridge Island, and the Olympic Peninsula. In addition, there is service north of Seattle between Anacortes and the San Juan Islands and between Edmonds and Kingston.

For high-speed passenger service between Seattle and Victoria, B.C., there is the **Victoria Clipper,** Pier 69, 2701 Alaskan Way, Seattle, WA 98121 (☎ 206/448-5000 or 800/888-2535). The trip aboard this speedy catamaran takes only 2¹/₂ to 3 hours. Round-trip fare for adults is between $69 and $89; for senior citizens, between $69 and $79; and for children ages 1 to 11, between $41.50 and $44.50. Round-trip tickets are substantially cheaper if purchased in advance.

3

Getting to Know Seattle

Water, water, everywhere—that's Seattle. This rapidly growing city has water on three sides. Sailboats, seaplanes, kayaks, and sailboards are permanent fixtures of the cityscape and one of the main reasons why many people live here. Any visit to Seattle should include some manner of waterborne activity, and even if you never leave dry land, you'll find your visit affected by water. There are drawbridges all over the Seattle area, and if you're in a hurry, you can bet that the one you have to cross will be delaying traffic. If you happen to be driving across Lake Washington, you might notice that the bridge you are on is rather close to the water; in fact, it's floating on the water. Seattle has some of the only floating bridges in the world.

In between Elliott Bay, Lake Union, and Lake Washington, there are hills—not gentle hills, but the same kind that San Francisco is famous for. There used to be seven hills, just as in Rome, but one of them (now known as the Denny Regrade) was leveled shortly after 1900 to permit commercial construction and to provide fill for the waterfront. This combination of hills and water makes for spectacular views, so be sure to take extra care when driving: Don't let the natural beauty of the city's surroundings distract you. Unfortunately, Seattle has been busy erecting huge skyscrapers in recent years, and many excellent views have been lost to development. The city is trying to put some controls on growth in order to preserve its unique character.

Seattle is a city of neighborhoods. People identify with their neighborhood even more than they identify with the city itself. Although the best way to explore the different neighborhoods is by car, there is an excellent public bus system that will get you in from the airport and all over the city.

1 Orientation

ARRIVING

By Plane   **Seattle-Tacoma (Sea-Tac) International Airport** (☎ 206/431-4444) is located about 14 miles south of Seattle and is connected to the city by I-5. Generally, allow 30 minutes for the trip between the airport and downtown, and more during rush hour. See "Getting There" in Chapter 2 for information on airlines serving Seattle.

   Gray Line Airport Express (☎ 206/626-6088) provides service between the airport and downtown Seattle daily from 5am to midnight.

This shuttle van stops at the Stouffer Madison, Holiday Inn-Crowne Plaza, Best Western Executive Inn, Days Inn Town Center, Four Seasons Olympic, Seattle Hilton, Sheraton Seattle, Westin Hotel Seattle, Warwick, Quality Inn, Loyal Inn, Downtown Travel Lodge, and WestCoast Roosevelt. Rates are $7 one way and $12 round-trip.

Shuttle Express (☎ 206/622-1424 or 800/487-RIDE) provides 24-hour service between Sea-Tac and the Seattle area. Their rates vary from $18 to $23. You need to make a reservation to get to the airport, but to leave the airport, just give them a call when you arrive. Push 48 on one of the courtesy phones outside the baggage-claim areas.

Metro Transit (☎ 206/553-3000) operates three buses between the airport and downtown. It's a good idea to call for the current schedule when you arrive in town. At this writing, **no. 174** and **no. 184** operate every 15 to 30 minutes around the clock; they makes local stops and the trip takes about an hour. On Saturday and Sunday the first buses leave between 6 and 6:30am. **No. 194**, an express taking only 30 minutes, also departs every 30 minutes and operates between about 4:30am and 7:30pm Monday through Friday; Saturday from about 6:30 am. The fare is $1.10 during off-peak hours and $1.60 during peak hours. Nos. 174 and 184 operate to Ninth Avenue and Stewart Street. No. 194 operates to either Third Avenue and Union Street or the Convention Place Station of the Bus Tunnel, depending on the time of day.

A **taxi** into downtown Seattle will cost you about $27. Graytop Cab (☎ 206/282-8222) has a special rate of $20 from Sea-Tac to downtown Seattle. Around Seattle, their rates tend to run a little less than the two previous companies. There are usually plenty of taxis around, but if not, call **Yellow Cab** (☎ 206/622-6500) or **Farwest Taxi** (☎ 206/622-1717). The flag-drop charge is $1.80; after that, it's $1.80 per mile.

By Train   If you arrive in Seattle on an Amtrak train, you will find yourself at the **King Street Station** (☎ 206/382-4125), right across the parking lot from the Kingdome. The heart of downtown Seattle is only a few blocks north.

By Bus   The **Greyhound bus station,** Eighth Avenue and Stewart Street (☎ 206/628-5508), is slightly northeast of downtown Seattle.

By Car   I-5 is the main north-south artery through Seattle, running south to Portland and north to the Canadian border. **I-90** comes to Seattle from Spokane, in the eastern part of Washington, and ends just after 23rd Avenue. **Washington Hwy. 99,** the Alaskan Way Viaduct, is another major north-south highway through downtown Seattle; it passes through the waterfront section of the city.

By Ship   **Washington State Ferries** (☎ 206/464-6400, or in Washington State 800/84-FERRY) dock at Pier 52. The *Victoria Clipper,* which connects Victoria, British Columbia, with Seattle (☎ 206/448-5000 or 800/888-2535), docks at Pier 69.

VISITOR INFORMATION

Visitor information on Seattle and the surrounding area is available by contacting the **Seattle-King County Convention and Visitors**

Bureau, 520 Pike St., Suite 1300, Seattle, WA 98101-9927 (☎ 206/ 461-5840). The bureau is open Monday through Friday from 8:30am to 5pm. You can stop by their office located at the Washington State Convention and Trade Center, 800 Convention Place, Galleria Level, at the corner of Eighth Avenue and Pike Street (☎ 206/461-5840). To find this information center, walk up Union Street until it goes into a tunnel under the Convention Center. You'll see the information center on your left as you enter the tunnel. This office operates one other **Visitor Information Center** in the baggage-claim area at Sea-Tac Airport. It's across from carousel no. 8 (open daily from 9:30am to 7:30pm; ☎ 206/433-5218).

For information on the rest of Washington State, call the **Washington State Tourism Office,** at 206/586-2102, 206/586-2088, or 800/544-1800.

CITY LAYOUT

Although downtown Seattle is fairly compact and can easily be navigated on foot, finding your way through this area by car can be frustrating. The Seattle area has been experiencing phenomenal growth in the past few years, and this has created traffic-congestion problems that must be anticipated. Here are some guidelines to help you find your way around.

Main Arteries & Streets   There are three interstate highways serving Seattle. **I-90** comes in from the east and ends downtown. **I-405** bypasses the city completely, traveling up the east shore of Lake Washington through Bellevue. The main artery is **I-5,** which runs through the middle of Seattle. Take the James Street exit west if you're heading for the Pioneer Square area; take the Seneca Street exit for Pike Place Market; or the Olive Way exit for Capitol Hill.

Downtown is roughly defined as extending from **Yesler Way** on the south to **Denny Way** on the north and from Elliott Bay on the west to **Broadway** on the east. Within this area avenues are numbered, whereas streets have names. The exceptions to this rule are the first two roads parallel to the waterfront. They are Alaskan Way and Western Avenue. Spring Street is one way eastbound, and Seneca Street one way westbound. Likewise, Pike Street is one way eastbound, and Pine Street, one way westbound. First Avenue and Third Avenue are two-way streets, but Second and Fifth are one way southbound. Fourth Avenue and Sixth Avenue are one way northbound.

Finding an Address   After you become familiar with the streets and neighborhoods of Seattle, there is really only one important thing to remember to find an address: Pay attention to the compass point of the address. Downtown streets have no directional designation attached to them, but when you cross I-5 going east, most streets and avenues are designated "East." South of Yesler Way, which runs through Pioneer Square, streets are designated "South." West of Queen Anne Avenue, streets are designated "West." The University District is designated "NE" (Northeast); the Ballard, "NW" (Northwest). Therefore, if you are looking for an address on First Avenue South, head south of Yesler Way.

Greater Seattle Orientation

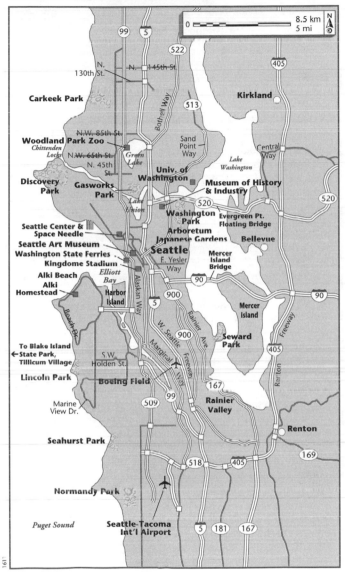

Another helpful hint is that odd-numbered addresses are likely to be on the west and south sides of streets, whereas even-numbered addresses will be on the east and north sides of streets. Also, in the downtown area, address numbers increase by 100 as you move away from Yesler Way going north or south, and as you go east from the waterfront.

The Bridges of King County

Ever wish you had the perfect excuse for those mornings when you just can't get out the door in time to make it to work on time? Seattleites have got just the excuse—"The bridge was open." With water on three sides, Seattle is a collection of neighborhoods connected by bridges, many of which are drawbridges that open at particularly inconvenient times. At times it seems as though the city has a love-hate relationship with its bridges. Bridges are the object of derision, curses, humor, and affection.

"Welcome to the center of the universe," reads a sign on the Fremont Bridge as you drive from the north side of Queen Anne hill across the Lake Washington Ship Canal and into the funky neighborhood of Fremont. You might just get plenty of time to contemplate this lighthearted sign; this is the busiest drawbridge in the United States. Two blocks away, under the Aurora Avenue Bridge, the Fremont Troll, a huge cement sculpture, attacks a real Volkswagen Beetle.

Seattle likes to boast that its Evergreen Point Bridge, which connects Seattle to Bellevue and Kikland on the east side of Lake Washington, is the longest floating bridge in the world. What the city doesn't like to tell visitors is that the I-90 Bridge, also across Lake Washington, sank in a storm just a few years back.

Further afield (and not actually in King County), there are the Hood Canal Bridge and the Tacoma Narrows Bridge, both of which have had their own problems over the years. The former, which connects the Kitsap Peninsula with the Olympic Peninsula, is another of the Northwest's floating bridges. It, too, once sank in a storm. The Tacoma Narrows Bridge spans a southern arm of Puget Sound and, at 2,800 feet long, is one of the largest suspension bridges in the world. Since it doesn't float it shouldn't have any problems, right? Wrong. The original bridge here bucked itself apart back in 1940, only four months and seven days after it opened. It seems the suspension cables resonated in the high winds that blow through the narrows. This resonance caused the main suspension cables to sway up and down until the entire bridge collapsed. In souvenir shops around Seattle, you can even find film clips of "Galloping Gertie," as the bridge was dubbed.

Street Maps   Even if the streets of Seattle seem totally unfathomable to you, rest assured that even longtime residents sometimes have a hard time finding their way around. Don't be afraid to ask directions. You can obtain a free map of the city from the Seattle-King County Convention and Visitors Bureau or at its other Visitor Information Center (see above).

If you want to obtain a more detailed map of Seattle, stop by **Metsker Maps,** 702 First Ave. (☎ 206/623-8747).

If you happen to be a member of AAA, you can get free maps of Seattle and Washington State from them, either at an office near you or at the Seattle office, 330 Sixth Ave. N. (☎ 206/448-5353). They're open Monday through Friday from 8:30am to 5pm (Wednesday until 6:30pm).

2   Getting Around

BY PUBLIC TRANSPORTATION

Bus   Seattle's **Metro bus system** has been voted the best in the country, so be sure to avail yourself of it while you're in town. The best part of riding the bus in Seattle is that as long as you stay within the downtown area, you can ride for free between 4am and 9pm. The **Ride Free Area** is between Alaskan Way in the west, Sixth Avenue in the east, Battery Street in the north, and South Jackson Street in the south. Within this area are Pioneer Square, the waterfront attractions, Pike Place Market, and all major hotels. Two blocks from South Jackson Street is the Kingdome, and six blocks from Battery Street is Seattle Center. Keeping this in mind, you can visit nearly every tourist attraction in Seattle without having to spend a dime on transportation. For more information, phone 206/553-3000.

The Metro's latest innovation is the **Bus Tunnel,** which allows buses to drive underneath downtown Seattle, thus avoiding traffic congestion. The tunnel extends from the International District in the south to the Convention Center in the north, with three stops in between. Commissioned artworks decorate each of the stations, making a trip through the tunnel more than just a way of getting from point A to point B. In fact, the tunnel is becoming a regular tourist attraction. It's open Monday through Friday from 5am to 7pm, on Saturday from 10am to 6pm (closed on holidays). When the Bus Tunnel is closed, buses operate on surface streets. Because the tunnel is within the Ride Free Area, there is no charge for riding through it, unless you are traveling to or from outside of the Ride Free Area.

If you travel outside the Ride Free Area, fares range from 85¢ to $1.60, depending on the distance and time of day. Keep in mind that you pay when you get off the bus when traveling out of the Ride Free Area. When traveling into the Ride Free Area, you pay when you get on the bus. Exact change is required.

Discount Passes   On Saturday, Sunday, and holidays, you can purchase an **All Day Pass** for $1.70; it's available on any Metro bus or the Waterfront Streetcar.

Ferry   Washington State Ferries is the most extensive ferry system in the United States and serves numerous cities and towns in the area such as Bremerton, Edmonds, and Bainbridge Island; Vashon Island; Victoria, British Columbia; and the San Juan Islands. At press time, fares from Seattle to Bremerton via car ferry (a 60-minute crossing) were car and driver one way, $5.90, passengers, $3.50; children and senior citizens, $1.75; eastbound from Bremerton to the mainland, there was no charge for passengers. Fares to Bainbridge Island (a 35-minute crossing) were the same.

For ferryboat schedule and rate information, call the ferry system at 206/464-6400 or 800/84-FERRY within Washington State.

Monorail   If you are planning a visit to Seattle Center, there is no better way to get there from downtown than on the monorail. It leaves from Westlake Center shopping mall (Fifth Avenue and Pine Street). The once-futuristic elevated trains cover the 1.2 miles in 90 seconds and provide a few nice views along the way. The monorail leaves every 15 minutes daily from 9am to midnight during the summer; the rest of the year, Sunday through Thursday from 9am to 9pm, on Friday and Saturday until midnight. The one-way fare is only 90¢ for adults, 35¢ for senior citizens and the handicapped, and 70¢ for children 5 to 12.

Waterfront Streetcar   Old-fashioned streetcars run along the waterfront from Pier 70 to the corner of Fifth Avenue South and South Jackson Street on the edge of the International District, providing another unusual means of getting around in downtown Seattle. The trolley operates Monday through Friday from around 7am to around 6:30pm, departing every 20 to 30 minutes; on Saturday, Sunday, and holidays from just after 10am to almost 7pm, departing about every 20 minutes. One-way fare is 85¢ in off-peak hours and $1.10 in peak hours. If you plan to transfer to a Metro bus, you can get a transfer good for 70 minutes. Streetcars are wheelchair accessible.

BY TAXI

If you decide not to use the public-transit system, call **Yellow Cab** (☎ 206/622-6500) or **Farwest Taxi** (☎ 206/622-1717). Taxis can be difficult to hail on the street in Seattle, so it's best to call or wait at the taxi stands at major hotels. The flag-drop charge is $1.80; after that, it's $1.80 per mile.

Graytop Cab (☎ 206/282-8222) charges $1.20 for the flag-drop and $1.40 per mile.

BY CAR

Before you venture into downtown Seattle in your own car, remember that traffic congestion is severe, parking is limited, and streets are almost all one way. Be forewarned that you're better off leaving your car outside the downtown area.

Car Rentals   For the very best deal on a rental car, make your reservation at least one week in advance. It also pays to shop around and call the same companies a few times over the course of a couple of weeks; the last time I visited Seattle, I was quoted different rates each time I called the major car-rental agencies. If you decide on the spur of the moment that you want to rent a car, check to see whether there are any weekend or special rates available. If you are a member of a frequent-flier program, be sure to mention it: You might get mileage credit for renting a car. Currently, daily rates for a subcompact are around $25 to $35, with weekly rates at around $130 to $150.

All the major car-rental agencies have offices in Seattle, and there are also plenty of independent companies. I recommend that you try to rent a car from: **Budget Rent A Car** (☎ 800/527-0700).

Parking   On-street parking is very expensive, extremely limited, and rarely available near your destination. Downtown parking decks (either above or below ground) charge from $7 to $16 per day. Many lots offer early bird specials that, if you park by a certain time in the morning (around 9 or 10am), allow you to park all day for $6 to $7. With the purchase of $20 or more, many downtown merchants offer Easy Streets tokens that can be used toward parking fees in many downtown lots. Look for the black and yellow signs.

You'll also save money by parking nearer the Space Needle, where parking lots charge around $6 per day. If you don't mind a bit of a walk, try the south lot at the Kingdome, where all-day parking costs about $2 (best deal in town).

Driving Rules   A right turn at a red light is permitted after coming to a full stop. A left turn at a red light is permissible from a one-way street onto another one-way street. If you park your car on a sloping street, be sure to turn your wheels to the curb—you may be ticketed if you don't. When parking on the street, be sure to check the time limit on parking meters; it ranges from 15 minutes to 4 hours. Also be sure to check whether or not you can park in a parking space during rush hour. Don't leave your keys in the ignition and walk away from your car—you might get a ticket.

BY BICYCLE

Downtown Seattle is congested with traffic and is very hilly. Unless you have experience with these sorts of conditions, I wouldn't recommend riding a bicycle downtown. However, there are many bike paths that are excellent for recreational bicycling, and some of these can be accessed from downtown by routes that avoid the steep hills and heavily trafficked streets. See "Outdoor Activities" in Section 5 of Chapter 6 for details.

ON FOOT

Seattle is a surprisingly compact city. You can easily walk from Pioneer Square to Pike Place Market. Remember, though, that the city is also very hilly. When you head in from the waterfront, you will be climbing a very steep hill. If you get tired of walking around downtown Seattle, remember that between 4am and 9pm you can always catch a bus for free as long as you plan to stay within the Ride Free Area. Cross streets only at corners and only with the lights in your favor. Jaywalking, especially in the downtown area, is a ticketable offense.

3   Neighborhoods in Brief

Seattle is a city of neighborhoods, partly because it is divided by bodies of water.

International District   The most immediately recognizable of Seattle's neighborhoods, the International District is home to the city's Asian population. It's just south of Yesler Way.

Pioneer Square   Just northwest of the International District is the Pioneer Square Historic District, known for restored old buildings. It's full of shops, galleries, restaurants, and bars.

Downtown   This is Seattle's main business district and can roughly be defined as the area from Pioneer Square in the south to just north of Pike Place Market and from First Avenue to Seventh Avenue. It's characterized by high-rise office buildings and steep streets, and also offers the city's greatest diversity of retail shops.

Belltown   Located in the blocks north of Pike Place Market primarily along Western and First avenues, this area once held mostly warehouses, but now is rapidly gentrifying and contains lots of restaurants and nightclubs.

First Hill   Known as Pill Hill by Seattleites, this hilly neighborhood, just east of downtown across I-5, is home to several hospitals as well as the Frye Art Museum.

Capitol Hill   To the northeast, centered along Broadway near Volunteer Park, Capitol Hill is Seattle's cutting-edge shopping district and gay community.

Queen Anne Hill   This neighborhood is where you'll find some of Seattle's oldest homes, several of which are now bed-and-breakfast inns. Queen Anne is located just northwest of Seattle Center and offers great views of the city. This is one of the most prestigious Seattle neighborhoods.

Ballard   In northwest Seattle, bordering Puget Sound, you'll find Ballard, a former Scandinavian community now known for its busy nightlife, but with remnants of its past still visible.

University District   As the name implies, this neighborhood surrounds the University of Washington in the northeast section of the city. The U District, as it's known to locals, provides all the amenities of a college neighborhood.

Wallingford   This neighborhood is one of Seattle's up-and-comers. Just west of University District and adjacent to Lake Union, it's filling with small, inexpensive-but-good restaurants. There are also interesting little shops.

Fremont   Home to Seattle's best-loved piece of public art—*Waiting for the Interurban*—Fremont is located north of the Lake Washington Ship Canal between Wallingford and Ballard. It's a neighborhood of eclectic shops, ethnic restaurants, and artists' studios.

Madison Park   One of Seattle's more affluent neighborhoods, it fronts on the western shore of Lake Washington, northeast of downtown. The centerpiece is the University of Washington Arboretum, including the Japanese Gardens.

Impressions

. . . on a famous ferry going into famous Seattle, dusk on a November night, the sky, the water, the mountains are all the same color: lead in a closet. Suicide weather. The only thing wrong with this picture is that you feel so happy.   —*Esquire* magazine

FAST FACTS: Seattle

Airport   Seattle-Tacoma International Airport (Sea-Tac) is located about 14 miles south of Seattle; for information call 206/431-4444.

American Express   In Seattle, the Amex office is in the Plaza 600 building at 600 Stewart St. (☎ 206/441-8622). The office is open Monday through Friday from 9am to 5pm.

Area Code   The telephone area code in Seattle is 206.

Babysitters   Check at your hotel first if you need a sitter. If they don't have one available, contact **Best Sitters** (☎ 206/682-2556).

Business Hours   **Banks** are generally open weekdays from 9am to 5pm, with later hours on Friday; some have Saturday morning hours. **Offices** are generally open weekdays from 9am to 5pm. **Stores** typically open Monday through Saturday between 9 and 10am and close between 5 and 6pm. Some department stores have later hours on Thursday and Friday evenings until 9pm and are open on Sunday from 11am to 5 or 6pm, and stores in malls may be open until 9pm most nights. **Bars** stay open until 1am; **dance clubs** and **discos** often stay open much later.

Car Rentals   See "By Car" in Section 2 of this Chapter.

Climate   See "Climate" in Section 2 of Chapter 2.

Dentist   If you need a dentist while you are in Seattle, contact the **Dentist Referral Service,** the Medical Dental Building, Fifth Avenue and Olive Way (☎ 206/448-CARE).

Doctor   To find a physician in Seattle, check at your hotel for a reference, or call the Medical Dental Building line (☎ 206/448-CARE).

Drugstores   Conveniently located downtown, **Peterson's Pharmacy,** 1629 Sixth Ave. (☎ 206/622-5860), has been serving Seattle for more than 50 years. It's open weekdays from 8:30am to 5:45pm, on Saturday from 9am to 1pm. **Pacific Drugs,** 822 First Ave. (☎ 206/624-1454), another convenient choice, is open Monday through Friday from 7am to 6:30pm, on Saturday from 10am to 5pm.

Emergencies   For police, fire, or medical emergencies, phone 911.

Hospitals   One of the hospitals most convenient to downtown Seattle is the **Virginia Mason Hospital and Clinic,** 925 Seneca St. (☎ 206/583-6433 for emergencies or 206/624-1144 for information). There is also the **Virginia Mason Fourth Avenue Clinic,** 1221 Fourth Ave. (☎ 206/223-6490), open Monday through Friday from 7am to 5pm, Saturday from 10am to 1:45pm, which provides medical treatment for minor ailments without an appointment.

Information   For information on Seattle and the surrounding area, call or write to **Seattle-King County Convention and Visitors Bureau,** 520 Pike St., Suite 1300, Galleria Level, Seattle, WA 98101-9927 (☎ 206/461-5840); their office is located at Eighth Avenue and Pike Street. For information on the state of Washington, contact the **Washington State Tourism Office** at 206/586-2102, 206/586-2088, or 800/544-1800.

Liquor Laws   The legal minimum drinking age in Washington is 21.

Lost Property   If you left something on a Metro bus, call 206/553-3090, if you left something at the airport, call 206/433-5312.

Luggage Storage/Lockers   There is a luggage-storage facility at Amtrak's King Street Station. It costs $1.50 per day. The Greyhound bus station, 811 Stewart St., has luggage lockers.

Newspapers/Magazines   *SeattlePost-Intelligencer* is Seattle's morning daily, and the *Seattle Times* is the evening daily. The arts and entertainment weekly for Seattle is *Seattle Weekly.*

Photographic Needs   **Cameras West,** 1908 Fourth Ave. (☎ 206/622-0066), is the largest-volume camera and video dealer in the Northwest. Best of all, it's right downtown and also offers 1-hour film processing. It's open Monday through Saturday from 10am to 6pm, and on Sunday from noon to 6pm.

Police   For police emergencies, phone 911.

Post Office   Besides the main post office, Third Avenue and Union Street (☎ 206/442-6340), there are also convenient postal stations in Pioneer Square at 91 Jackson St. S. (☎ 206/623-1908), and on Broadway at 101 Broadway E. (☎ 206/324-2588). All stations are open Monday through Friday with varying hours; the Broadway station is open Saturday from 9am to 1am as well.

Radio   For National Public Radio (NPR), tune to 94.9 FM or 88.5 FM.

Restrooms   There are public restrooms in Pike Place Market and the Convention Center.

Safety   Although Seattle is rated as one of the safest cities in the United States, it has its share of crime. Take extra precautions with your wallet or purse when you're in the crush of people at Pike Place Market—this is a favorite spot of pickpockets. Whenever possible try to park your car in a garage, not on the street, at night.

Taxes   The state of Washington makes up for its lack of an income tax with its heavy **sales tax** of 6.5 percent; King County adds another 1.7 percent for 8.2 percent total. **Hotel-room tax** is 15.2 percent in Seattle.

Taxis   To get a cab, call **Yellow Cab** at 206/622-6500, **Farwest Taxi** at 206/622-1717, or **Graytop Cab** at 206/282-8222. See also "By Taxi" in Section 2 of this chapter.

Television   The six local television channels are 4 (ABC), 5 (NBC), 7 (UPN), 9 (PBS), 11 (CBS), and 13 (Fox).

Time   Seattle is on **Pacific Time (PT),** and **Daylight Saving Time,** depending on the time of year, making it three hours behind the East Coast.

Transit Information   For 24-hour information on Seattle's **Metro bus system,** call 206/553-3000. For information on the **Washington State Ferries,** call 206/464-6400 or 800/84-FERRY. For **Amtrak information,** call 800/872-7245. To contact the **King Street Station** (trains), call 206/382-4125. To contact the **Greyhound bus station,** call 206/628-5508.

Useful Telephone Numbers   For police, fire, or medical emergencies, phone 911. The local rape hotline is 206/632-7273. If you have a touch-tone phone, you'll want to call the **Seattle Times Info Line** at 206/464-2000; this service provides a wealth of information on topics that range from personal health to business news, from entertainment listings to the weather report and marine forecast.

Weather   If you can't tell what the weather is by looking out the window, or you want to be absolutely sure that it's going to rain the next day, call 206/526-6087.

4 Networks & Resources

FOR STUDENTS

The **University of Washington,** located in northeast Seattle, is the largest state university in Washington and also happens to have the second-largest student bookstore in the country. The university's **Visitors Information Center** is located at 4014 University Way NE (☎ 206/543-9198), and the bookstore is at 4326 University Way NE (☎ 206/634-3400). **Seattle Pacific University,** 3307 Third Ave. W. (☎ 206/281-2000), is a Methodist liberal arts university, and **Seattle University,** Broadway and Madison Street (☎ 206/296-6000), is affiliated with the Roman Catholic church.

If you don't already have one, get an **official student ID** from your school. Such an ID will entitle you to discounts at museums and on performances at different theaters and concert halls around town.

Seattle's **AYH youth hostel** is at 84 Union St. (☎ 206/622-5443). Besides being a place to stay, this hostel has a bulletin board with information on rides, other hostels, camping equipment for sale, and the like.

FOR GAY MEN & LESBIANS

Seattle's large gay community is centered around Capitol Hill. In this chic shopping and residential district, you can find gay restaurants, bars, bookstores, and more. For a guide to Seattle's gay community, get a copy of the *Greater Seattle Business Association (GSBA) Guide Directory.* Their mailing address is 2033 Sixth Ave., Suite 804, Seattle, WA 98121 (☎ 206/443-4722). The *Seattle Gay News* is the community's newspaper. Their offices are at 1605 12th Ave., No. 31., Seattle, WA 98122 (☎ 206/324-4297).

The **Lesbian Resource Center,** 1808 Bellevue Ave., Suite 204 (☎ 206/322-3953), is a community resource center providing housing and job information, therapy, and business referrals. **Thumpers Restaurant and Bar,** 1500 E. Madison St. (☎ 206/328-3800), is a long-time favorite Seattle gay bar located in the Capitol Hill area. **The Connection** and **Brass Connection,** 722 E. Pike St. (☎ 206/322-7777), are a popular restaurant and disco in the heart of Capitol Hill. Although not strictly a lesbian establishment, **Wildrose,** 1021 E. Pike St. (☎ 206/324-9210), is a tavern primarily for women, with a full menu, pool tables, and a wide selection of nonalcoholic beverages. **Beyond the Closet,** 1501 Belmont Ave. (☎ 206/322-4609) is a gay and lesbian bookstore. **Gaslight Inn** is a bed-and-breakfast in the Capitol Hill area; see Section 4 of Chapter 4 for details.

FOR WOMEN

Seattle is a large city, and all the normal precautions that apply in other cities hold true here. The Pioneer Square area is particularly unsafe for either sex late at night.

Wildrose, 1021 E. Pike St. (☎ 206/324-9210), is a women's tavern with a friendly atmosphere and a good menu.

The local **rape hotline** is 632-7273.

FOR SENIORS

Be sure to carry some form of photo ID with you when touring Seattle. Most attractions, some theaters and concert halls, and the Washington State Ferries all offer senior-citizen discounts. Also, if you aren't already a member, you should consider joining the **American Association of Retired Persons (AARP),** 601 E. St. NW, Washington, DC 20049 (☎ 800/424-3410). One of the many benefits of belonging to this organization is the discount of about 10 percent offered at many motels and hotels.

4

Seattle Accommodations

1 Best Bets

Best Grand Old Hotel (or Best Lobby for Pretending You're Rich):
So you've got a Napoleon complex and have always dreamed of sub
letting Versailles; if things haven't yet worked out for you, spend the
day lounging in the lobby of the Four Seasons Olympic Hotel. This
place has all the same architectural ingredients as any old palace
(☎ 206/621-1700).

Best for Business Travelers: Maybe you're in Seattle to get serious
about your work, but why not do it with a view? At the Westin
Hotel Seattle, work desks in deluxe rooms face out to views, and the
phones all have modem ports built in. If you're here on Microsoft
business, do anything you have to to stay at the Woodmark Hotel at
Carillon Point. Rooms have two phones, computer hookups, and
most have water views (☎ 206/728-1000).

Best for a Romantic Getaway: Though Seattle has quite a few hotels
that do well for a romantic weekend, the Inn at the Market gets my
vote for its Elliott Bay views, European atmosphere, and proximity to
lots of great and romantic restaurants (☎ 206/443-3600).

Best for Families: The Seattle Marriott Hotel, down by the airport,
is your best bet if you have the family along. In addition to the
huge atrium with a pool, waterfall, and model train going round in
circles, there's a game room. Turn the kids loose and relax (☎ 206/
241-2000).

Best Value: With a fabulous location right in Pike Place Market, views
of Elliott Bay, great hotel restaurants, and excellent service, the Inn at
the Market offers the best hotel value in Seattle (☎ 206/443-3600).

Best Moderately Priced Hotel: The Sixth Avenue Inn is a low rise
motel just a few blocks from Pike Place Market and the heart of
Seattle's shopping district. For these reasons, it's a good deal (☎ 206/
441-8300).

Best Exercise Facilities: So, you're on the road again, but you don't
want to give up your circuit training. Don't worry, bring your sweats
and book a room at the Sheraton Seattle Hotel and Towers
where you'll find a great assortment of exercise machines, indoor pool,

whirlpool tub, and sauna. Best of all, these facilities are on the top floor with a view of the city (☎ 206/621-9000).

Best Eastside Hotel: If you happen to be in the area on high-tech business, or you just want to stay outside the city, there is no better choice than the Woodmark Hotel at Carillon Point. This place has views, a waterfront location, and services and amenities that just don't quit (☎ 206/822-3700).

Best Hotel Pool: The Seattle Marriott Hotel is down by the airport, which isn't too convenient for exploring the city, but the hotel makes up for it by providing a big pool in a huge tropical greenhouse complete with totem poles and waterfalls (☎ 206/241-2000).

Best Views from Guest Rooms: If you're not back in your room at The Edgewater by sunset it won't turn into a pumpkin, but you will miss the smashing sunsets over the Olympic Mountains on the far side of Puget Sound (☎ 206/728-7000).

Best View from a Hotel Pool: Most center-city hotels stick their swimming pool (if they have one at all) down in the basement or on some hidden-away terrace, but at the Sheraton Seattle, you can do laps up on the top floor with the lights of the city twinkling all around (☎ 206/621-9000).

Best Hotel Art Collection: Stay at the Sheraton Seattle, and you'll be bumping into original works of contemporary art every time you turn around. The main exhibit is an impressive collection of art glass that includes works by Dale Chihuly and other artists from the Pilchuck School (☎ 206/621-9000).

Best Complimentary Service: Washington state is close on the heels of California when it comes to winemaking, and to introduce guests to the joys of Washington wines, the Hotel Vintage Park hosts complimentary evening wine tastings (☎ 206/624-8000).

Best Hotel Restaurant: Despite changes in chefs over the years, Fuller's, in the Sheraton Seattle, has continued to maintain its impeccable standards and perfectly prepared cuisine. And, all without pretense (☎ 206/621-9000).

Best Room Decor: Even if your eyes are closed most of the time you're in your hotel room, you just might sleep easier at the Hotel Vintage Park knowing you'll wake up to a draped canopy curtain over your headboard and stylish Italianate decor touches (☎ 206/624-8000).

Best Suite: The Hotel Vintage Park knows how to do things right, and applies this talent especially to its Château St. Michele suite. Named for Washington's largest winery, it is extravagantly decorated with contemporary furnishings and art. A fireplace visible from both the bedroom and the sitting room and a Japanese soaking tub make it the perfect weekend cocoon (☎ 206/624-8850).

Best Room Service: If you stay at the Inn at the Market, you can order room service from Campagne, the inn's excellent French restaurant (☎ 206/443-3600).

Seattle's largest concentrations of hotels are in downtown and near the airport, with a few good hotels in University District and over in the Bellevue/Kirkland area. If you don't mind high prices, the downtown hotels are the most convenient for many visitors. However, if your budget won't allow for a first-class business hotel, you'll have to stay near the airport or elsewhere on the outskirts of the city.

In the following listings, **very expensive** hotels are those generally charging more than **$125 per night** for a double room; **expensive** hotels, about **$90 to $125 per night** for a double; **moderate** hotels, about **$60 to $90 per night** for a double; and **inexpensive** hotels, less than **$60 per night** for a double. These do not include the state and local sales and room taxes, which add up to 15.2 percent (slightly less at airport hotels). A few hotels include breakfast in their rates; others offer complimentary breakfast only on certain deluxe floors.

Keep in mind that room rates are almost always considerably lower from October through April, and downtown hotels often offer substantially reduced prices on weekends.

Make reservations as far in advance as possible, especially if you plan a visit during Seafair or another Seattle festival (see "Seattle Calendar of Events" in Chapter 2 for dates of festivals).

There are a number of fine bed-and-breakfast establishments in Seattle, and I have listed a few of my favorites. In addition, the **Pacific Reservation Service,** 701 NW 60th St., Seattle, WA 98107 (☎ 206/784-0539; fax 206/782-4036), offers many accommodations, mostly in bed-and-breakfast homes, in the Seattle area; rates range from $45 to $95 for a double and a small booking fee may be charged. They charge $5 for a directory of members.

Most all hotels in the Seattle area now offer no-smoking rooms, and, in fact, most bed-and-breakfast inns are exclusively no-smoking establishments. Most hotels also offer wheelchair-accessible rooms.

Toll-free telephone numbers for the major chain motels are as follows (Motel 6 does not have a toll-free number): **Best Western,** 800/528-1234; **Comfort Inns,** 800/221-2222; **Days Inns,** 800/329-7466, (800/DAYS-INN); **Econo Lodges,** 800/424-4777; **Hampton Inns,** 800/426-7866, (800/HAMPTON); **La Quinta Inns,** 800/531-5900; **Quality Inns,** 800/221-2222; **Rodeway Inns,** 800/424-4777; **Super 8 Motels,** 800/800-8000; **Travelodge,** 800/578-7878.

2 Downtown

VERY EXPENSIVE

✪ Alexis Hotel & Arlington Suites

1007 First Ave. (at Madison St.), Seattle, WA 98104 ☎ **206/624-4844** or 800/426-7033 (outside Washington). Fax 206/621-9009. 54 rms, 43 suites. A/C TV TEL. $185–$205 double (including continental breakfast and service); $220–$350 suite. AE, CB, DC, MC, V. Parking $15.

Unbelievable as it sounds, this elegant little hotel was once a parking garage. Now listed in the National Register of Historic Places, the 90-year-old building is a sparkling gem. The hotel also has an enviable

Seattle Accommodations—Downtown

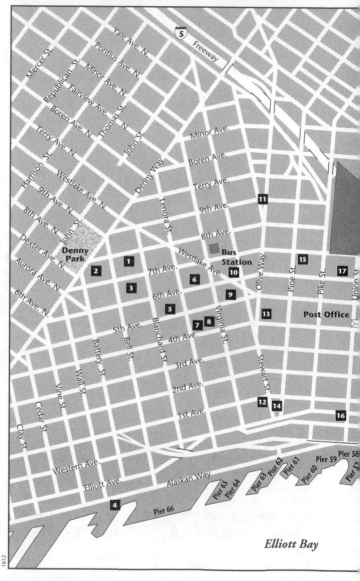

location halfway between Pike Place Market and Pioneer Square and only two blocks from the waterfront.

Throughout the hotel there is a pleasant mix of old and new, contemporary and antique, giving the Alexis a very special atmosphere. The cheerful service—from doormen to chambermaids, none of whom you need to tip—will make you feel as if you are visiting old friends.

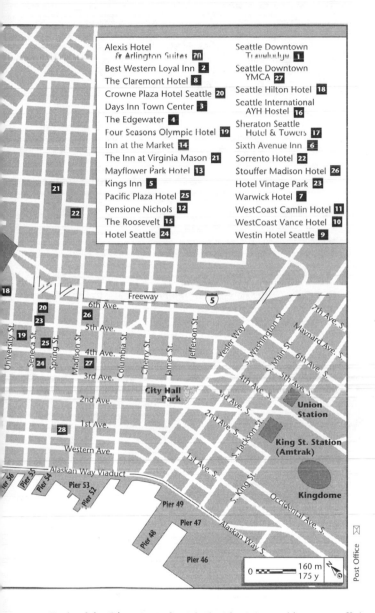

Alexis Hotel
& Arlington Suites **20**

Best Western Loyal Inn **2**

The Claremont Hotel **8**

Crowne Plaza Hotel Seattle **20**

Days Inn Town Center **3**

The Edgewater **4**

Four Seasons Olympic Hotel **19**

Inn at the Market **14**

The Inn at Virginia Mason **21**

Mayflower Park Hotel **13**

Kings Inn **5**

Pacific Plaza Hotel **25**

Pensione Nichols **12**

The Roosevelt **15**

Hotel Seattle **24**

Seattle Downtown
Travelodge **1**

Seattle Downtown
YMCA **27**

Seattle Hilton Hotel **18**

Seattle International
AYH Hostel **16**

Sheraton Seattle
Hotel & Towers **17**

Sixth Avenue Inn **6**

Sorrento Hotel **22**

Stouffer Madison Hotel **26**

Hotel Vintage Park **23**

Warwick Hotel **7**

WestCoast Camlin Hotel **11**

WestCoast Vance Hotel **10**

Westin Hotel Seattle **9**

Each of the 54 rooms is furnished with antique tables, overstuffed chairs, and brass reading lamps. There are four pillows on every bed, with chocolates on them in the evening. In the black-tiled bath, you'll find a marble counter, luxurious terry-cloth robes, a shaving mirror, a telephone, and a basket of special toiletries. Each room is a little different, but the nicest by far are the fireplace suites, which have raised king-size beds, whirlpool baths, and wet bars.

If you need that extra bit of space that only a suite can provide, you might want to stay at the hotel's adjacent Arlington Suites, where all the suites have fully equipped kitchens.

Dining/Entertainment: You'll enjoy highly creative but moderately priced meals at The Painted Table, which is the hotel's main dining room. This informal restaurant takes its name from the colorful, handmade ceramic plates that frame the meals (see listing in Section 3 of Chapter 5 for details). Just off the lobby, the Bookstore Bar serves light lunches as well as drinks, and is filled with books, magazines, and newspapers for browsing. The Cajun Corner, another casual restaurant run by the hotel, is just down Madison Street.

Services: Room service, concierge, valet/laundry service, morning paper, evening turn down, complimentary evening sherry, shoeshine service.

Facilities: Steamroom, privileges at two sports clubs.

The Edgewater

Pier 67, 2411 Alaskan Way, Seattle, WA 98121-230. ☎ **206/728-7000** or 800/ 624-0670. Fax 206/441-4119. 230 rms, 3 suites. A/C TV $119–$210 double; $300 suite. AE, CB, DC, DISC, MC, V. Parking $6.

The Edgewater, Seattle's only waterfront hotel, has the feel of a deluxe fishing lodge, albeit with all the amenities you'd expect from a luxury hotel. A vaulted open-beamed ceiling, deer-antler chandelier, and riverstone fireplace greet you as you enter the lobby, where a wall of windowpaned glass looks out on ships and sailboats on Elliott Bay. With such a lodgelike atmosphere, it's difficult to believe that the crowded streets of downtown Seattle are only steps away.

The mountain-lodge theme continues in the rooms, which feature rustic lodge-pole pine furniture. Half the rooms have minibars and balconies over the water, and all have clock radios and remote-control TVs. In each bright red-and-green bathroom, you'll find a basket of soaps and a shoeshine kit.

Dining/Entertainment: Ernie's Bar and Grill is a woodsy retreat that could have been designed by Eddie Bauer or Ralph Lauren. You'll find Northwest cuisine featured on the menu and a stunning view of the harbor from all the tables. In the pine-walled Lobby Lounge, there is live piano music in the evenings and a fireplace to warm your toes in winter.

Services: Room service, concierge, same-day laundry/valet service, courtesy shuttle to downtown locations, in-room movies.

Facilities: Gift shop, access to athletic club.

✪ Four Seasons Olympic Hotel

411 University St., Seattle, WA 98101. ☎ **206/621-1700**, 800/332-3442, 800/ 821-8106 (in Washington State), or 800/268-6282 (in Canada). Fax 206/682-9633. 450 rms, 200 suites. A/C MINIBAR TV $225–$255 double; $245–$1,150 suite. Weekend available. AE, CB, DC, ER, JCB, MC, V. Valet parking $15.

Old-fashioned grandeur fit for kings is what you'll find when you step through the doors of this Italian Renaissance palace. Gilt-and-crystal chandeliers hang from the high-arched ceiling; ornate cornices and moldings grace the glowing hand-burnished oak walls and pillars. A huge floral arrangement sits in the middle of the expansive lobby, surrounded by new and antique furnishings and subdued pink-and-gray carpets. At either end, curving stairways lead to the mezzanine level.

Guest rooms are all quite spacious and tastefully appointed with modern furnishings. Remote-control TVs and minibars are standard here, as are hairdryers, plush bathrobes, and large baskets of scented toiletries.

Dining/Entertainment: The Georgian Room is the most elegant restaurant in Seattle. Marble stairs and carpeted terraces lead from the lobby to its doors, and inside, luxurious drapes, a marble floor, antique chairs, and the same ornate moldings that grace the lobby all contribute to the strong feeling of courtly elegance. The menu combines creative Northwest and continental cuisines. (See listing in Section 3 of Chapter 5 for details.) Downstairs from the lobby is Shuckers, an English pub featuring fresh seafood. In the spacious skylighted Garden Court, more Northwest International cuisine is served—but at lower prices than meals served in The Georgian Room.

Services: 24-hour room service, concierge, same-day valet/laundry service, 1-hour pressing, complimentary shoeshine, valet parking, massage available.

Facilities: Indoor pool, whirlpool spa, sauna, sundeck, health club, exclusive shopping arcade.

Crowne Plaza Hotel Seattle

1113 Sixth Ave., Seattle, WA 98101 ☎ **206/464-1980,** 800/521-2762, or 800/858-0511 (in Washington). Fax 206/340-1617. 415 rms, 28 suites. A/C TV $140–$160 double; $250–$500 suite. AE, CB, DC, DISC, JCB, MC, V. Valet parking $13.

This 34-story tower in the heart of downtown is popular with businesspeople attending conventions at the nearby Washington State Trade and Convention Center. Almost all the rooms offer views of Puget Sound or the Cascade Mountains through large picture windows; ask for an even-numbered room on one of the higher floors for the best views. The oversized guest rooms all have spacious sitting areas, and come with two phones and an iron and ironing board. On the executive floors, guests receive a complimentary breakfast and afternoon hors d'oeuvres, use of the concierge lounge, and upgraded room amenities.

Dining/Entertainment: The City Views Restaurant offers American and Northwest meals and informal dining in a mezzanine-level atrium. There is also a lounge area on the mezzanine.

Services: Room service, concierge, valet/laundry service, in-room movies.

Facilities: Whirlpool spa, sauna, exercise facilities, gift shop.

✪ Inn at the Market

86 Pine St., Seattle, WA 98101. ☎ **206/443-3600** or 800/446-4484. 65 rms, 9 suites. A/C MINIBAR TV $115–$190 double; $205–$245 suite. AE, CB, DC, DISC, MC, V. Parking $14.

French country decor is the theme of this inconspicuous little hotel in the middle of Pike Place Market. There is no grand entrance, no large sign—only a plaque on the wall to indicate that this simple brick building in fact houses a very elegant hotel. A small lobby with a fireplace,

Sleepless in Seattle

Travel can play havoc with your internal clock. Insomnia strikes, you toss and turn in your bed. That's right, you're sleepless in Seattle. Don't turn on that mindless talk radio; there are better things to do. The first thing you might think of is a nightclub. At live-music clubs, shows usually start at 9pm, with the main act coming on around 10 or 10:30. Dance clubs usually don't get cranking until some time after 11 and may keep going until 2 or 3am. Of course there are also midnight movies: campy classic *The Rocky Horror Picture Show* plays Saturday nights at the Varsity, 4329 University Way NE (206/632-3131), which also does other cult classics on Fridays at midnight. Pike Street Cinema, 1108 Pike St. (☎ 206/682-7064), also does midnight movies on Saturdays.

But would you think of live theater if you were looking for something to do at midnight? Seattleites do. A few local theaters stage late-night shows, usually pretty outrageous stuff. The Empty Space Theater, 3509 Fremont Ave. N. (☎ 206/547-7500), and AHA Theatre, 2222 Second Ave. (☎ 206/728-1375), both do weekend late-night shows that start at 11pm. The Velvet Elvis Arts Lounge Theatre, 107 Occidental Ave. S. (☎ 206/624-8477), also does the occasional 10pm show.

If you're suddenly struck with a craving for pasta at 1am, head for Trattoria Mitchelli, 84 Yesler Way (☎ 206/623-3883). If nothing else will do at 3am but a filet mignon, 13 Coins, 125 Boren Ave. N. (☎ 206/682-2513) or 18000 Pacific Highway S. (☎ 206/243-9500), is the place for you.

antique tables, and carved-wood display cabinets will make you think you've stepped into the living room of a French country home. A roof-top deck overlooking the harbor provides a tranquil spot to soak up the sun on summer afternoons.

In the guest rooms, wide bay windows overlook Puget Sound and can be opened to let in refreshing sea breezes. Antiqued furniture, stocked minibars and refrigerators, coffeemakers with complimentary coffee, and well-lit writing desks are amenities that will make you feel right at home here. The huge bathrooms are equipped with telephones and feature baskets of special toiletries from the market.

Dining/Entertainment: Bacco, the hotel's little bistro, serves juices, simple-but-tasty breakfasts, and lunches. Café Campagne offers French country-style meals and take-out. The hotel's formal dining room is Campagne, an excellent southern French restaurant located across the courtyard from the lobby (see listing in Section 3 of Chapter 5 for details).

Services: Limited room service, concierge, valet/laundry service, complimentary limousine service in downtown Seattle.

Facilities: Health spa, privileges at athletic club, hair salon.

Mayflower Park Hotel

405 Olive Way, Seattle, WA 98101. ☎ **206/623-8700**, 800/426-5100, or 800/562-4504 (in Washington). Fax 206/382-6997. 173 rms, 22 suites, A/C TV $120–$150 double; $165 suite. Children under 18 stay free in parents' room. AE, CB, DC, DISC, MC, V. Parking $9.

If shopping is your favorite sport, you'll really like this hotel. The Mayflower Park is connected by covered walkway to the shops of Westlake Center, and two department stores are within a block. Built in 1927, the Mayflower Park provides subdued elegance. In the high-ceilinged lobby an antique Chinese screen, Chinese cabinet, grandfather clock, and skylights complement the deep-green carpets and aquamarine overstuffed chairs. Floral arrangements add a colorful touch.

Most rooms are furnished with an eclectic blend of contemporary Italian and traditional European furnishings and Chinese accent pieces. Some rooms have bathrooms that are old-fashioned, small, and lack counter space but have large old tubs that are great for soaking. If you crave space, ask for one of the large corner rooms or a suite. Rooms with two queen beds and two baths, a roomy closet and full-length mirror are good for two women traveling together.

Dining/Entertainment: Clippers restaurant features fresh seafood and French and Italian cuisine. The intimate bilevel restaurant is bright and airy, with marble tables and brass rails. Oliver's lounge provides another cheerful spot for light lunches or drinks and conversation. The room once housed a pharmacy, in which the floor-to-ceiling windows were completely painted over.

Services: 24-hour room service, valet/laundry service.

Facilities: Privileges at private athletic club.

Seattle Downtown-Lake Union Marriott Residence Inn

800 Fairview Ave. N., Seattle, WA 98109. ☎ **206/624-6000** or 800/331-3131. 234 suites. A/C TV $140–$210 studio suite; $120–$210 one-bedroom suite; $200–$600 two-bedroom suite; (all including complimentary breakfast). AE, DC, DISC, JCB, MC, V. Parking $9.

Located at the north end of downtown Seattle and just across the street from Lake Union, this Marriott Residence Inn is the sort of place that usually is built in the suburbs. A seven-story atrium floods the hotel's plant-filled lobby court with light, while the sound of a waterfall soothes traffic-weary nerves. All accommodations here are suites, so you'll buy quite a bit more space for the money. You'll also have use of a full kitchen, complete with dishes, so you can fix your own meals if you like, though the buffet breakfast down in the lobby shouldn't be missed.

Though the suites here are generally quite spacious, they don't have much in the way of character. However, they do have phones and televisions in bedrooms and living rooms and there are large desks as well.

Dining/Entertainment: Though the hotel has no restaurant of its own, there are three restaurants across the street that will bill meals to your room.

Services: Complimentary cookies and coffee, valet/laundry service.

Facilities: Indoor lap pool, children's pool, steam room, sauna, whirlpool spa, exercise room.

Seattle Hilton Hotel

Sixth Ave. and University St., Seattle, WA 98101. ☎ **206/624-0500,** 800/426-0535, or 800/542-7700 (in Washington). Fax 206/682-9029. 237 rms. 6 suites. A/C TV $137–$167 single; $154–$177 double; $295–$395 suite. Weekend packages available. AE, CB, DC, DISC, MC, V. Parking $11.

When you step into the street-level lobby of the Seattle Hilton, you won't find the check-in desk, no matter how hard you look, because the main lobby is actually up on the 13th floor, though the elevator labels it the lobby floor or second floor. When you finally do reach the lobby, you'll find an attractive pink-marble floor, black-wood pillars, and lots of pink tones and black accents. The overall effect is Art Deco, with a grand piano and frosted-glass windows further adding to the elegance.

Unfortunately, you won't find a swimming pool here, but you will find very comfortable rooms. Blond woods and pastel walls and carpets give the place a stylish and contemporary feeling. In the small bathroom you'll find plenty of fragrant toiletries on hand.

Dining/Entertainment: Macaulay's Restaurant and Lounge is a casual spot serving good old-fashioned American food. Up on the top floor at Asgard Restaurant, there is Continental cuisine with a Northwest accent. The views are superb.

Services: 24-hour room service, concierge, valet/laundry service, car-rental desk.

Facilities: Gift shop, small exercise room.

Sheraton Seattle Hotel & Towers

1400 Sixth Ave., Seattle, WA 98101. ☎ **206/621-9000** or 800/325-3535. Fax 206/621-8441. 840 rms, 42 suites. A/C TV $168–$230 double; $195–$625 suite. Weekend available. AE, CB, DC, DISC, ER, JCB, MC, V. Parking $13, $15 valet.

This 35-story tower is the largest hotel in Seattle, and you'll almost always find the building buzzing with activity. However, don't let convention crowds prevent you from appreciating the hotel's superb collection of art glass from the Pilchuck School. Also be sure to note the unusual string sculpture that hangs from the ceiling near the lobby lounge. It is this emphasis on contemporary art, which can be seen throughout the hotel, that makes the Sheraton the most interesting of the city's convention hotels. Art aside, though, if you don't want to deal with crowds, consider staying at a smaller hotel.

The standard-size rooms are not quite as luxurious as the lobby would suggest, but they do have hairdryers, irons and ironing boards, plenty of bathroom counter space, and good lighting. The king rooms are quite spacious and include a worktable with telephone, a minibar, and a couch with a second phone beside it. On the other hand, if you book a room in the Towers, the hotel's club floors, you'll get the kind of attention and service you would expect only from a small luxury hotel. Whichever type of room you stay in, make sure it's as high as possible to take advantage of the great views.

Dining/Entertainment: The subdued elegance and outstanding meals at Fuller's continue to win this restaurant awards and recommendations. The very finest and most innovative Northwest cuisine is what has the critics raving (see listing in Section 3 of Chapter 5 for details).

The Pike Street Cafe is a less formal restaurant with a 27-foot dessert bar. Gooey's, named for a gigantic local clam, is the hotel's popular lounge. The Gallery Lounge is a quiet spot near the entrance to Fuller's and serves light meals as well as drinks. Across the driveway from the main entrance is Andiamo Presto serving espresso and pizzas.

Services: 24-hour room service, concierge, valet/laundry service tour desk, American Airlines desk.

Facilities: Indoor pool, whirlpool spa, sauna, exercise room, business center, gift shop.

Stouffer Madison Hotel

515 Madison St., Seattle, WA 98104. ☎ **206/583-0300** or 800/468-3571. Fax 206/624-8125. 553 rms, 78 suites. A/C MINIBAR TV $129–$185 double; $159–$194 suite. Weekend packages and super-saver available. AE, CB, DC, DISC, JCB, MC, V. Parking $13.

Despite its size, the Stouffer Madison provides friendly service and attention to detail. A spacious lobby graced by attractive Japanese prints is only the beginning of the comforts and amenities here.

All rooms are larger than average and many have views of either Puget Sound or the Cascade Range. Separate seating areas, remote-control TVs, contemporary art, and soft color schemes make every room a winner. In the bath you'll find plenty of counter space and a nice selection of toiletries. On the Club Floors, you'll find slightly more luxurious accommodations and a lounge in which complimentary continental breakfast and afternoon hors d'oeuvres are served.

Dining/Entertainment: Prego, way up on the 28th floor, serves northern Italian cuisine amid eye catching views of Seattle. (See Section 5 of Chapter 5 for details.) Down on the second floor, Maxwell's serves American food in a casual cafe atmosphere; Sunday brunch here is very popular. The lobby court is a convivial lounge, and when the weather permits, tables spill out onto an outdoor terrace complete with waterfall. There's live piano music here in the evenings.

Services: 24-hour room service, concierge, complimentary morning coffee and newspaper, valet/laundry service, complimentary shoeshine, in-room movies, turn-down service on club floors, massage available.

Facilities: Indoor pool, whirlpool tub, fitness room, gift shop.

✪ Hotel Vintage Park

1100 Fifth Ave., Seattle, WA 98101. ☎ **206/624-8000** or 800/624-4433. Fax 206/623-0568. 126 rms, 1 suite. A/C TV $185–$215 double; $370 suite. AE, CB, DC, DISC, JCB, MC, V. Valet parking $16.

Small and classically elegant is the best way to describe the Vintage Park. In the lobby, a black-marble fireplace flanked by shelves full of old books beckons you to sit and relax a while amid Italianate furnishings. To further help you unwind, there are complimentary evening wine tastings featuring Washington wines.

To continue the wine theme, the hotel has named each of its rooms after a Washington winery, and throughout the hotel, you'll likely spot other homages to the grape. Rooms vary quite a bit here, and if you are willing to spend a little more for a deluxe room, you'll experience luxury rarely found in this price range. You'll want to spend your days luxuriating in bed when you see the Arabesque-patterned comforters, pillows, and canopy draperies of deep plum, hunter green, and gold. A minibar is stocked with Washington wines, and there is a large basket of snacks. The bathrooms, though small, feature attractive granite counters, hairdryers, and telephones. Standard rooms, though smaller and less luxuriously appointed, are still very comfortable. Many of these smaller rooms have a wall of mirrors to give the room the feeling of space, and surprisingly the bathrooms in these rooms are larger than in the deluxe rooms. If you're feeling like a splurge, the Château St. Michele suite will surround you with a stunningly contemporary decor that includes a four-poster bed, pass-through fireplace, Japanese soaking tub, compact disc stereo piped throughout the suite, and lots of artistic furnishings.

Dining/Entertainment: The adjacent Tulio Restaurant serves Italian meals based on the food of Tuscany. A small bar adjoins the restaurant.

Services: Room service, concierge, use of in-room exercise equipment, access to health club, complimentary daily newspaper and morning coffee, valet/laundry service.

Warwick Hotel

401 Lenora St., Seattle, WA 98121. ☎ **206/443-4300** or 800/426-9280. Fax 206/448-1662. 229 rms, 4 suites. A/C TV $165–185 double; from $350 suite. Children under 18 stay free in parents' room. Weekend available. AE, CB, DC, DISC, MC, V. Parking $9.50.

Located in the heart of downtown Seattle, only six blocks from Pike Place Market and two blocks from the monorail terminal, the Warwick offers European charm and exceptional service. A sunken lobby with a copper fireplace provides a quiet setting for relaxing conversation. Black mirrored walls, spotlighted bouquets of flowers, and Asian art offer just the right touch of sophistication. The owner formerly owned a marble quarry, so you'll notice marble making many appearances here.

Rooms come with either two double beds or a king-size bed, and rooms on the tenth floor and above have stocked minibars; all have minirefrigerators. Modern furnishings in greens and warm beiges, a desk for working, and a couch or an easy chair for relaxing complete the amenities that will help you settle in. On all floors, a marble bath with a basket of toiletries and a terry-cloth robe assure you of a fresh start each day, and a telephone in the bath lets you keep in touch.

Dining/Entertainment: Liaison is the hotel's distinctive eatery, serving Northwest-influenced Mediterranean cuisine that uses only the freshest local ingredients. The menu here changes daily, and there is live piano music weekends in the adjacent lounge.

Services: 24-hour room service, concierge, valet/laundry service, complimentary limousine service in downtown Seattle.

Facilities: Indoor pool, whirlpool spa, sauna, fitness room.

Westin Hotel Seattle

1900 Fifth Ave., Seattle, WA 98101. ☎ **206/728-1000** or 800/228-3000. Fax 206/728-2259. 822 rms, 43 suites. A/C MINIBAR TV $180–$205 double; from $225 suite. Children 18 and under stay free in parents' room. Third person in room $25. AE, CB, DC, DISC, JCB, MC, V. Parking $13, valet $17.

The hallmark cylindrical towers of the Westin chain rise above the downtown Seattle skyline like a pair of honeycombs. Within, you'll find a veritable beehive of activity as tour groups assemble and conventioneers register, and although the hotel has the amenities you'd expect, service can be impersonal and the crowds overwhelming.

Although all the rooms now have irons and ironing boards and hairdryers, the standard rooms are rather worn and feature dated furnishings and color schemes. However, the remodeled deluxe rooms, which feature an Italianate decor, are everything you would expect and more. These latter rooms include work desks facing the window and the Seattle views, a bit of art in the bathrooms, and safes for your valuables. The rooms on the upper floors offer fine views of Seattle and Puget Sound.

Dining/Entertainment: The Palm Court is the Westin's premier, award-winning purveyor of Northwest cuisine. This restaurant sparkles with wide windows, large mirrors, and bright lights. Nikko is one of Seattle's finest Japanese restaurants. Unusual decor here melds traditional Japanese with high-tech contemporary. (See listings in Section 3 of Chapter 5 for details.) The Market Café is a casual place done up to look as if it belongs in Pike Place Market.

The quiet lobby court and the much more lively Fitzgerald's on Fifth provide two different ambiances in which to enjoy a drink.

Services: Concierge, 24-hour room service, 1-day valet/laundry service, in-room movies.

Facilities: Indoor pool, exercise room, whirlpool spa, sauna, gift shops, barber, beauty salon.

EXPENSIVE

Ⓢ WestCoast Camlin Hotel

1619 Ninth Ave., Seattle, WA 98101. ☎ **206/682-0100** or 800/426-0670. 136 rms, 12 suites. TV $83–$114 double; $175 suite. AE, DC, DISC, MC, V. Parking $9.

The high-ceilinged lobby, with its ornate trim and marble floors and walls, speaks of a past elegance. However, there is often a disquieting feeling of emptiness that hangs over this once grand room.

The hotel seems to be getting a bit worn around the edges, but guest rooms are still a good deal, especially compared with the prices charged at nearby convention hotels. There are many different floor plans, so you may get a room that is quite spacious or one that just isn't big enough for your tastes.

Located only a block from the Washington State Convention and Trade Center, the WestCoast Camlin has the feel of a classic European hotel. Sophisticated without being pretentious, small without sacrificing amenities, the Camlin provides personal service at reasonable rates.

Dining/Entertainment: The Cloud Room Restaurant and Lounge, on the top floor, serves a varied menu, with an emphasis on fresh seafood. Great views!

Services: Room service, laundry service, in-room movies.

Facilities: Outdoor pool.

The Roosevelt

1531 Seventh Ave., Seattle, WA 98101. ☎ **206/621-1200** or 800/426-0670. Fax 206/233-0335. 151 rms, 12 suites. A/C TV $95–$170 double; $135–$220 suite. AE, DC, DISC, MC, V. Parking $9.75.

Though The Roosevelt hints at the elegance of times gone by, it is surprisingly expensive for what you get unless you stay in the off-season. The lobby is decorated to look like a library in an old mansion. To one side is a baby grand piano. Around the fireplace are shelves full of old books.

In the guest rooms there are king-size beds, couches, wet bars, and recessed lighting. The queen rooms are rather small, but the king deluxe rooms have good layouts. Most rooms have cramped bathrooms with little counter space. If you choose to stay in one of the suites, you can also enjoy your own private whirlpool bath, honor bar, hairdryer, shoeshine machine, and soft terry-cloth robes.

Dining/Entertainment: Just off the lobby is Von's Grand City Café and Martini Manhattan Memorial bar. The restaurant, which can trace its history back 80 years, dedicates itself to preparing juicy steaks, lamb, veal, chicken, and salmon cooked over apple wood. Be sure to have one of the special desserts that are prepared at your table. In the bar you'll be fascinated by the wild array of "objets d'junk" that hangs from the ceiling.

Services: Room service, concierge, valet/laundry service, in-room movies.

Facilities: Exercise room.

⑤ WestCoast Vance Hotel

620 Stewart St., Seattle, WA 98101. ☎ **206/441-4200** or 800/426-0670. Fax 206/441-8612. 165 rms. A/C TV $95–$115 double. Children under 17 stay free in parents' room. 15 percent discount for AAA and AARP. AE, DC, DISC, MC, V. Parking $7.

Built in the 1920s by lumber baron Joseph Vance, the Vance underwent a $7 million restoration in 1990 and reopened as a WestCoast hotel. Typically, the high-ceilinged lobby is very elegant—wood paneling, marble floors, Oriental carpets, tapestry-cloth upholstered chairs and couches, and ornate plaster work moldings. Accommodations vary in size and style and some are quite small; the corner rooms compensate with lots of windows. Furniture, in keeping with the style of the lobby, includes an armoire for the TV. Some bathrooms have pedestal sinks and windows.

Dining/Entertainment: Salute in Citta Ristorante is a bright and popular Italian restaurant.

Services: Valet/laundry service.

MODERATE

Best Western Loyal Inn

2301 Eighth Ave., Seattle, WA 98121. ☎ **206/682-0200** or 800/528-1234. Fax 206/467-8984. 91 rms, 12 suites. A/C TV $85–$95 double (including continental breakfast); $180 suite. AE, DC, DISC, MC, V. Free parking.

A recent remodeling has turned this place into a very attractive city-center accommodation. The deluxe rooms have wet bars, coffeemakers, remote-control TVs, king-size beds, and two sinks in the bathrooms. Even the standard rooms come with remote-control TVs. There's no restaurant on the premises, but because the Loyal Inn is only five minutes' walk from Seattle Center, it makes a good choice for families.

Facilities: 24-hour sauna, whirlpool spa.

The Claremont Hotel

2000 Fourth Ave., Seattle, WA 98121. ☎ **206/448-8600** or 800/448-8601. Fax 206/441-7140. 110 rms, 10 suites. TV $79–$99 double; $89–$129 suite. Children under 16 stay free in parents' room. Discounts for extended stays. AE, MC, V. Parking $9.

This 1920s downtown hotel was recently remodeled and is now a perfectly adequate and very reasonably priced choice for budget travelers who want to be close to the action. Most rooms include small kitchens, which makes them a great idea for families trying to save on meal expenses. Groups of young travelers may also find these rooms a welcome respite from hostels. The rooms combine old-fashioned touches such as glass doorknobs and modern furnishings.

In the suites, bathrooms have been updated, but other bathrooms are small and tend to show their age. Otherwise these accommodations are perfectly acceptable. Rooms on the upper floors have good views.

Dining/Entertainment: Assaggio Ristorante is an Italian bistro just off the lobby that has received kudos for its cuisine.

Facilities: Coin-operated laundry, free local phone calls.

Days Inn Town Center

2205 Seventh Ave., Seattle, WA 98121. ☎ **206/448-3434** or 800/648-6440. Fax 206/441-6976. 91 rms. A/C TV $65 $90 double (discount card good for 9 percent off regular is available). AAA, senior discount. AE, CB, DC, DISC, MC, V. Free parking.

Conveniently located close to Seattle Center and within walking distance (or a free bus ride) of the rest of downtown Seattle, this three-story hotel offers large, clean accommodations. Modern furniture and pastel color schemes make every room comfortable and attractive.

Dining/Entertainment: The Greenhouse Café and Bar—as its name implies—is a sunny, cheerful place serving breakfast, lunch, and dinner. In the lounge you can sit by the fire or watch the big-screen TV.

Services: Valet/laundry service.

Hotel Seattle

315 Seneca St., Seattle, WA 98101. ☎ **206/623-5110**, 800/426-2439 or 800/421-6662 (in Washington). 89 rms, 4 suites. A/C TV $72–$76 double; $80–$98 suite. AE, CB, DC, DISC, JCB, MC, V. Parking not available.

The 11-story Seattle has seen better days but is still worth considering, since it's one of the least expensive city-center hotels that's still acceptable. Rooms are small but clean. The hotel seems to be very popular with young Japanese travelers, and I'd recommend it primarily for young people who don't expect everything to be perfect. If you want convenience and economical rates, this is the place for you.

Seattle Accommodations—North & Northeast

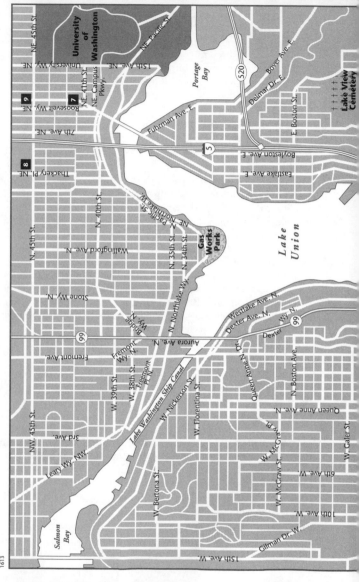

Dining/Entertainment: Bernard's on Seneca serves inexpensive German and American food in large portions.

Facilities: Hair salon.

Ⓢ Pacific Plaza Hotel

400 Spring St., Seattle, WA 98104. ☎ **206/623-3900** or 800/426-1165. Fax 206/623-2059. 160 rms. A/C TV $70–$97 double (including continental breakfast). AE, DC, DISC, MC, V. Parking $9.

Econo Lodge Seattle Downtown **1**

Gaslight Inn **5**

Meany Tower Hotel **9**

The M.V. Challenger **3**

Roberta's Bed & Breakfast **4**

Salisbury House **6**

Seattle Downtown-Lake Union Marriott Residence Inn **2**

University Inn **7**

University Plaza Hotel **8**

Built in 1928, this old hotel was renovated a few years back and offers attractive rooms and excellent value. The building, in the heart of the financial district, is now dwarfed by some of the surrounding skyscrapers. However, you're halfway between Pike Place Market and Pioneer Square, and just about the same distance from the waterfront. Rooms are small and sometimes cramped, but they come with such amenities as ceiling fans and alarm clocks. Wingback chairs and cherry-wood finishes on the furnishings give each guest room an elegant touch. Bathrooms are small and dated, but luckily they still have their old-fashioned porcelain shower knobs.

Dining/Entertainment: A Red Robin Restaurant serving gourmet hamburgers is on the lower level of the hotel.

Services: Valet/laundry service.

Seattle Downtown Travelodge

2213 Eighth Ave., Seattle, WA 98121. ☎ **206/624-6300** or 800/578-7878. Fax 206/233-0185. 72 rms. A/C TV $49–$99 single; $6 extra per person. AE, CB, DC, DISC, MC, V. Free parking.

This conveniently located and moderately priced downtown motel is located about midway between the Washington State Convention and Trade Center and Seattle Center, so it's convenient whether you are here on business or pleasure. The rooms are attractive and some even have balconies. There are clock radios in all rooms, and some baths and rooms are large, with a basket of toiletries on the counter.

Dining/Entertainment: Behind the Travelodge there is a 24-hour restaurant (the Hurricane Café) serving straightforward meals at economical prices.

Services: Complimentary coffee, in-room movies.

✪ Sixth Avenue Inn

2000 Sixth Ave., Seattle, WA 98121 ☎ **206/441-8300** or 800/648-6440. 166 rms. A/C TV $80–$99 double (lower are for off-season). Children under age 17 stay free in parents' room. AE, CB, MC, V. Free parking.

You won't have to wonder what time it is here: The huge railway clock behind the front desk takes up an entire wall. Royal-blue carpeting and oversize wicker chairs provide an interesting contrast of casualness and sophistication in the lobby. The deep-blue color scheme is continued throughout the hotel, from the awning over the entrance to the bedspreads and draperies in every guest room. And if you haven't already realized that this is more than your standard moderately priced hotel, one look at your room will convince you: On a small wall shelf is a selection of old hardcover books, and old photos of Seattle provide a glimpse into the city's past. Wicker furniture and a large potted plant give the room the feeling of a tropical greenhouse. There are even brass beds.

Dining/Entertainment: The Sixth Avenue Bar and Grill serves breakfast, lunch, and dinner, and is located on the second floor, looking out to a Japanese garden that makes dining a tranquil experience. Steak, pasta, and seafood are featured on the menu. In the lounge, warm dark-wood paneling and a fireplace are part of the cozy environment.

Services: Room service, valet/laundry service.

INEXPENSIVE

Econo Lodge—Seattle Downtown

325 Aurora Ave. N., Seattle, WA 98109. ☎ **206/441-0400** or 800/446-6900. Fax 206/448-3353. 58 rms. A/C TV $59–$84 double. AE, CB, DC, DISC, JCB, MC, V.

Located on a busy road only two blocks from the Space Needle, this basic motel is among the least expensive, acceptable places to stay in downtown Seattle. Rooms were recently redone and are clean and

> ### ⓘ Family-Friendly Hotels
>
> **Sheraton Seattle Hotel & Towers** *(see pg. 36)* The VIK (very important kids) program provides four hours of supervised activities on Saturdays for kids aged 5 to 12: There is a cooking class in Fuller's restaurant, a behind-the-scenes tour of the hotel, a special lunch, and a movie.
>
> **Seattle Marriott Hotel** *(see pg. 47)* With a huge jungly atrium containing a swimming pool and whirlpool spas, kids can play Tarzan and never leave the hotel. There is also a game room that will keep the young ones occupied for hours if need be.
>
> **Seattle Downtown YMCA** *(see below)* This Y welcomes families and has rooms with or without private baths. You get to use all of the athletic facilities here; for facilities like these, you'd have to stay at the most expensive hotel in Seattle.

comfortable. Amenities include a small outdoor pool, a coin laundry, complimentary coffee and weekday newspaper.

Kings Inn

2106 Fifth Ave., Seattle, WA 98121. ☎ **206/441-8833** or 800/546-4760. Fax 206/441-0730. 68 rms, 21 suites. A/C TV $55–$70 double $65–$95 suites. AE, CB, DC, DISC, MC, V. Free parking.

You'll find this economical motel in the shadow of the monorail (about midway between Westlake Center and the Space Needle). Rooms are a bit small and show their age, but new carpets and wallpaper do a lot to make them feel more comfortable. Suites have various sleeping arrangements that can fit several people.

No-smoking rooms and complimentary coffee are available, and perhaps best of all, there's free parking. You just won't find an acceptable room in downtown for less. I suggest that finicky travelers ask to see a room here before committing to one, however.

Y'S AND HOSTELS

Seattle Downtown YMCA

909 Fourth Ave., Seattle, WA 98104-1194. ☎ **206/382-5000.** 185 rms. $39–$43 double ($1 discount to YMCA members). Weekly available. MC, V.

This YMCA welcomes men women, and families, and has rooms without private baths (only three have private baths). If you want, you can get a room with a TV or just walk down the hall to the TV lounge. The rooms are basic and fairly clean. The best part of staying here is that you will have use of all the athletic facilities. You'd have to stay at the most expensive hotel in the city for facilities like these.

Amenities include free local phone calls, baggage storage, indoor pool, running track, weight room with Nautilus machines, racquetball and squash courts, TV lounges, coin-operated laundry, tailor, and barbershop.

Seattle International AYH Hostel

84 Union St., Seattle, WA 98101-2084. ☎ **206/622-5443.** Fax 206/682-2179
126 beds. $16.25 for members. JCB, MC, V.

This conveniently located hostel is housed in the former Longshore-
man's Hall, which was built in 1915. To find it, walk down Post
Alley, which runs through and under Pike Place Market, to the corner
of Union Street. If you don't provide your own sheets, you can rent
them for $2 for the duration of your stay. If you plan to stay for three
nights or less, you need not be an American Youth Hostel (AYH)
member, but you'll have to pay a $3 surcharge each night (which later
could be applied toward membership). After your first three nights and
any time between June and September, you must buy a membership
for $25. There's a kitchen and a self-service laundry.

BED & BREAKFASTS

Pensione Nichols

1923 First Ave., Seattle, WA 98101. ☎ **206/441-7125** or 800/440-7125. 8 rms
(none with private bath). 2 suites (both with private bath). $85 double; $160 suite;
(all including breakfast). AE, DISC, MC, V.

If you have ever traveled through Europe on a budget, you have probably stayed at bed-and-breakfast lodgings that started on the second or
third floor of a building. This city-center bed-and-breakfast is just such
a European-style lodging, and you'll find it up two flights of stairs.
Located only a block from Pike Place Market, Pensione Nichols is a
touch expensive for what you get, though it is hard to beat the location. Only two of the guest rooms have windows (the two rooms
facing the street), but all the rest have skylights. High ceilings and
white bedspreads brighten the rooms and make them feel spacious.

The two suites on the other hand are huge and have full kitchens as
well as large windows overlooking the bay. These also have the occasional antique here and there, as does the inn's living room, which also
overlooks the water.

✪ The M. V. *Challenger*

1001 Fairview Ave. N., Seattle, WA 98109. ☎ **206/340-1201.** Fax 206/621-9208.
8 rms (5 with private bath). $75–$160 double (including full breakfast). Children by
reservation only. AE, CB, DC, MC, V. Free parking. Directions: Yale Street Landing on
Chandler's Cove, at the south end of Lake Union.

This has to be the most unusual bed-and-breakfast I've ever seen, but
if you need lots of space, this place is definitely not for you. However,
if you love ships and the sea and don't mind cramped quarters, don't
pass up this opportunity to spend the night on board a restored and
fully operational 45-year-old tugboat. (The only other waterfront
hotel in Seattle is the much pricier Edgewater.) You're welcome to visit
the bridge for a great view of Lake Union and the Seattle skyline, or
delve into the mechanics of the tug's enormous diesel engine. A
conversation pit with granite fireplace fills the cozy main cabin, and in
each of the guest cabins you'll find lots of polished wood.

3   Near Sea-Tac Airport

VERY EXPENSIVE

Red Lion Hotel/Seattle Airport

18740 Pacific Hwy. S., Seattle, WA 98188. ☎ **206/246-8600** or 800/547-8010. Fax 206/242-9727. 850 rms. 13 suites. A/C TV $134–$154 double; $175–$495 suite. Weekend packages available. AE, CB, DC, DISC, MC, V. Free parking.

You'll find Red Lions throughout the Northwest, and they're almost all like this one—big, sprawling, glitzy, with lots of amenities. However, a shake-shingle roof and a Northwest Coast Native American design on the portico are reminders that you're in the Pacific Northwest now. Built on the banks of a small lake, this Red Lion has seven wings and a 14-story tower. With so many rooms, it isn't surprising that the hotel frequently plays host to conventions and often feels crowded and chaotic.

Take a room in the tower and a glass elevator will whisk you up to your floor, providing a great view of the airport all the way. Red Lion rooms are consistently large, and whether you book one with two double beds, a queen-size bed, or a king-size bed, you'll have plenty of space to move around.

Dining/Entertainment: Maxi's, up on the 14th floor, is a very elegant large restaurant and serves good Northwest cuisine. The adjacent lounge is on three levels so that you can enjoy the view no matter where you're sitting. Down on the first floor you'll find Seaports, a seafood restaurant open for lunch and dinner. The Coffee Garden is a very casual lobby coffee shop and is open for breakfast, lunch, and dinner.

Services: Room service, concierge, free airport shuttle, car-rental desk, valet/laundry service.

Facilities: Outdoor pool, exercise room, gift shop, business center, beauty salon, barbershop.

EXPENSIVE

⑤ Seattle Marriott Hotel

Seatac 3201 S. 176th St., Seattle, WA 98188. ☎ **206/241-2000** or 800/228-9290. 459 rms, 5 suites. A/C TV $104–$139 double; $195–$350 suite. AE, CB, DC, DISC, MC, V. Free parking.

With its soaring atrium garden full of tropical plants, a swimming pool, and two whirlpool tubs, this resort hotel may keep you so enthralled you won't want to leave. There are even waterfalls and totem poles for that Northwest outdoorsy feeling. Best of all, it's always sunny and warm in here, unlike in the real outdoorsy Northwest. In the lobby, there is a huge stone fireplace that will make you think you're at some remote mountain lodge. You can't pick a better place to stay in the airport area.

Although all rooms are relatively large and attractively decorated, the concierge-level rooms are particularly appealing. In the bathroom, there are scales, a hairdryer, and a basket of elegantly bottled toiletries. And, of course, there's a concierge on hand to help you and a special lounge with complimentary coffee.

Dining/Entertainment: Yukon Landing Restaurant will have you thinking you're in the middle of the gold rush. Stone pillars; rough-hewn beams and wooden walls; moose, deer, and elk heads on the walls; and deer-antler chandeliers—all make this rustic restaurant very popular. For that gold-rush high life, enjoy the Sunday champagne brunch. The Lobby Lounge is a greenhouse that looks into the atrium.

Services: Room service, free airport shuttle, car-rental desk, valet/laundry service, in-room movies, complimentary coffee.

Facilities: Indoor swimming pool, whirlpool spa, health club, sauna, game room.

MODERATE

Holiday Inn, Sea-Tac Airport

17338 Pacific Hwy. S., Seattle, WA 98188. ☎ **206/248-1000** or 800/465-4329. Fax 206/242-7089 260 rms. A/C TV $74–$134 double. AE, CB, DC, DISC, JCB, MC, V. Free parking.

Although the halls and elevators are getting a bit battered, this hotel is still a good choice if you are looking for a full-service hotel. The best features here are the indoor pool and rooftop restaurant. The lobby is also quite attractive, with lots of slate and marble and a decor that gives the room the feel of a small European hotel.

Guest rooms, especially those with a single king bed, are designed with the business traveler in mind, but lack sufficient closet space or bathroom counter space for a stay of more than a night or two.

In rooms on the executive floors, there are comfortable easy chairs with hassocks for relaxing after a long business day. Rooms on the higher floors also offer good views (ask for a room on the Mount Rainier side of the hotel). The King Leisure rooms come with sofas, desks, king-size beds, and a bit more room than the standard accommodations.

Dining/Entertainment: In its rotating dining room on the 12th floor, the Top of the Inn features a sweeping vista of the airport and the surrounding area, plus Continental and American fare prepared with fresh local ingredients. To entertain you while you dine, there are singing waiters and waitresses, a pianist, and a violinist. The lobby lounge is a dark and lively place.

Services: Room service, courtesy airport shuttle, valet/laundry service, in-room movies.

Facilities: Indoor pool, exercise room, whirlpool spa, coin-operated laundry.

⑤ WestCoast Sea-Tac Hotel

18220 Pacific Hwy. S., Seattle, WA 98188. ☎ **206/246-5535** or 800/426-0670. Fax 206/246-0459. 146 rms, 2 minisuites. A/C TV $93–$102 double; $150 minisuite. AE, CB, DC, DISC, MC, V. Free parking.

Step into this WestCoast hotel and you enter a world of European styling, comfort, and service. The simple, elegant lines of the lobby—done in subtle pastels and shades of gray—are accentuated by a grand piano, this hotel chain's trademark. Feel free to play whenever the urge strikes.

The spacious, elegantly furnished guest rooms have queen- or king-size beds, writing table, and Art Deco–style chairs. In superior king rooms, you get special service, including coffee and a newspaper in the morning, plush terry-cloth robes, hairdryers, and an honor bar.

Dining/Entertainment: Gregory's Bar and Grill is across the parking lot from the main hotel facility. Five nights a week, there is karaoke music in the lounge, which features an aeronautical theme. Meals in the restaurant are in the $8 to $13 range.

Services: Room service, free airport shuttle, valet/laundry service, in-room movies.

Facilities: Outdoor pool, whirlpool spa, sauna.

INEXPENSIVE TO MODERATE

Among the better and more convenient inexpensive chain motel choices are **Motel 6** (Sea-Tac South), 18900 47th Awe. S., Seattle, WA 98188 (☎ 206/241-1648), charging $36 to $40; **Motel 6** (Sea-Tac Airport), 16500 Pacific Hwy. S., Seattle, WA 98188 (☎ 206/246-4101), charging $36 to $40 for a double; **Super 8 Motel,** 3100 S. 192nd St., Seattle, WA 98168 (☎ 206/433-8188), charging $57 to $62 for a double; and **Travelodge Seattle Airport,** 3900 S. 192nd St., Seattle, WA 98188 (☎ 206/241-9292), charging $39–$70 double.

4   First Hill & Capitol Hill

VERY EXPENSIVE

✪ Sorrento Hotel

900 Madison St., Seattle, WA 99104-9742. ☎ **206/622-6400** or 800/426-1265. Fax 206/343-6155. 76 rms, 42 suites. A/C MINIBAR TV $160–$180 double; $185–$1,000 suite. AE, DC, DISC, MC, V. Parking $12.

Sit by the tiled fireplace in the lobby of the Sorrento and try to imagine all these dark mahogany-paneled walls painted white and the beautiful fireplace hidden, covered over with plywood. That's the state this building was in before it was renovated. Today an old-fashioned European atmosphere reigns at this small hotel. From the wrought-iron gates and palm trees of the courtyard entrance to the plush seating of the octagonal lobby, the Sorrento whispers style and grace, and the service here is as fine as you can expect anywhere in town.

When the Sorrento opened in 1909, there were 150 rooms. Today there are only 76. What this means is that your room will be spacious and unique. No two rooms are alike, but all have remote-control TVs and stereos hidden inside large armoires, minibars and mini-refrigerators, plush terry-cloth robes, and dual-line telephones. A couch or easy chair and hassock let you put your feet up and relax after a hard day of touring or working. In the bathroom you'll find a basket of toiletries, including a small sachet to keep your wardrobe smelling fresh. You even have a choice of down or fiber-filled pillows, and in colder months, you'll slip into a bed that has been warmed with an old-fashioned hot-water bottle.

Dining/Entertainment: The Hunt Club, a dark and intimate restaurant with exposed brick walls and louvered doors that can be closed to create private dining areas, serves superb Northwest cuisine (see Section 5 of Chapter 5 for details). In the adjacent Fireside Room bar, where meals are lighter and less expensive, dark-wood paneling continues the clublike, old-world atmosphere. Several nights a week a pianist provides musical atmosphere in this lounge. Afternoon tea and weekend meals are served in the lobby and Fireside Room.

Services: Room service, concierge, valet/laundry service, complimentary limousine service in downtown Seattle, morning paper, in-room movies.

Facilities: Health-club privileges.

MODERATE

⑤ The Inn at Virginia Mason

1016 Spring St., Seattle, WA 98104. ☎ **206/583-6453** or 800/283-6453. Fax 206/223-7545. 79 rms, 3 suites. A/C TV. $77–$135 double; $125–$190 suite. Senior-citizen, AAA discounts available. Children under 18 stay free in parents' room. AE, CB, EC, DISC, MC, V. Parking $4.

You may think I've sent you to a hospital rather than a hotel when you first arrive at this small European-style hotel on Pill Hill. It takes its name from the Virginia Mason Hospital, which is next door; in fact, the two buildings are connected. The location is slightly removed from the hustle and bustle of downtown Seattle.

The lobby is small but elegant, with a little brick courtyard just outside. Room sizes vary a lot, since this is an old building, but most have large closets, modern bathrooms (some with windows), and wing-back chairs. The larger deluxe rooms and suites are quite large, and some have whirlpool baths, fireplaces, dressing rooms, hairdryers, and minirefrigerators.

Dining/Entertainment: The Rhododendron Restaurant serves Northwest and traditional cuisine. There is live piano music several nights per week.

Services: Valet/laundry service, concierge, room service, massages, in-room movies.

Facilities: Privileges at nearby fitness center.

BED & BREAKFASTS

✪ Gaslight Inn

1727 15th Ave., Seattle, WA 98122. ☎ **206/325-3654.** 9 rms (5 with private bath), 3 suites (all with private bath). TV $62–$118 double; $92–$103 suite; (all including continental breakfast). AE, MC, V. Parking on street.

Anyone who is a fan of arts-and-crafts movement of the early 20th century will enjoy a stay at this 1906 vintage home. Throughout the inn, there are numerous pieces of Stickley furniture, and everywhere you turn, oak trim frames doors and window. The common rooms are spacious and attractively decorated with a combination western and northwestern flare. A library filled with interesting books and magazines makes a comfortable spot for a bit of free time or, if it's cold out, take a seat by the fireplace. In summer, guests can swim in the backyard pool or lounge on the deck. Guest rooms continue the design themes of the common areas with lots of oak furnishings and heavy, peeled-log beds in some rooms.

An annex next door has three suites with kitchens and dining areas, as well as separate bedrooms and living rooms. These suites also include off-street parking.

Roberta's Bed & Breakfast

1147 16th Ave. E., Seattle, WA 98112. ☎ **206/329-3326.** 5 rms (4 with private bath). $85–$105 double (including full breakfast). MC, V.

Bibliophiles will be certain to develop an instant rapport with this B&B's namesake innkeeper. Roberta is, to say the least, fond of books and has filled shelves in nearly every room with books both old and new. On a rainy Seattle day, I can think of no better way to spend an afternoon than curled up at Roberta's with a good book. This turn-of-the-century home is on a beautiful tree-lined street just around the corner from Volunteer Park. A big front porch stretches across the front of the house, while inside there are hardwood floors and a mix of antique and modern furnishings. My favorite room is the attic hideaway, which has angled walls, painted wood paneling, lots of skylights, and a claw-foot bathtub. The overall effect of this room is that of a ship's cabin. Breakfast starts with tea or coffee left at your door and continues downstairs in the dining room with a hearty meal that includes home-baked treats.

Salisbury House

750 16th Ave. E., Seattle, WA 98112. ☎ **206/328-8682.** Fax 206/720-1019. 4 rms (all with private bath). $70–$105 double (including full breakfast). AE, MC, V.

This grand old house on tree-lined 16th Avenue East has a wide porch that wraps around two sides. Sit down in one of the white Adirondack chairs and enjoy one of Seattle's prettiest streetscapes. Inside there's plenty to admire as well. Two living rooms (one with a wood-burning fireplace) and a second-floor sun porch provide plenty of spots for relaxing and meeting other guests. On sunny summer days, breakfast may even be served in the small formal garden in the backyard. Guest rooms all have queen-sized beds with down comforters, and one even has a unique canopy bed hung with pink satin. One of the other rooms has an old claw-foot tub in the bathroom. Breakfasts here are deliciously filling and might include fresh fruit, juice, quiche, fresh-baked muffins or bread, or oatmeal pancakes. Cathryn and Mary Wiese, mother and daughter, are the friendly innkeepers.

5 The University District

Meany Tower Hotel

4507 Brooklyn Ave. NE, Seattle, WA 98105. ☎ **206/634-2000** or 800/648-6440. 155 rms. A/C TV $79–$90 double. AE, DC, MC, V. Free parking.

If you need to be near the University of Washington and want a view of downtown Seattle and the surrounding hills and water, book a room in this moderately priced high-rise. There is no swimming pool but there is a fitness room here, and the views are superb. Every room is a corner room, and all are pleasingly appointed in peach and deep-green tones. You'll also find an extremely large TV in each room, as well as a clock radio. Though the tiled combination baths are small, they do have baskets of toiletries.

Dining/Entertainment: The Meany Grill features prime rib, steak, and fresh seafood in an elegant atmosphere of deep greens and soft pinks. Brass rails and exposed ceiling beams give it the feeling of an old-fashioned club.

Services: Room service, valet/laundry service, complimentary newspaper.

Facilities: Exercise room.

✪ University Inn

4140 Roosevelt Way NE, Seattle, WA 98105. ☎ **206/632-5055** or 800/733-3855. Fax 206/547-4937. 102 rms, 12 junior suites. A/C TV $86–$106 double (including continental breakfast). AE, DC, DISC, MC, V.

Located within easy walking distance of the university, this hotel offers very attractive rooms, many of which have views of Lake Union. The standard rooms have only showers in their bathrooms, but these rooms compensate for this lack with small balconies. The deluxe rooms are more spacious and have double vanities. For even more room, opt for one of the junior suites, which have large windows, microwaves, small refrigerators, coffeemakers, and telephones in the bathrooms. Facilities include a heated outdoor pool, whirlpool spa, and a tiny exercise room. Along with your simple breakfast, you can grab a free copy of the paper.

University Plaza Hotel

400 NE 45th St., Seattle, WA 98105. ☎ **206/634-0100** or 800/343-7040. Fax 206/633-2743. 135 rms, 2 suites. A/C TV $80–$94 double; $125–$165 suite. AE, CB, DC, DISC, MC, V. Free parking.

You'll think you've been transported to Merrie Olde England when you step through the front door of this hotel. The walls in the lobby and along an adjacent hall are done in scaled-down half-timbered cottage facades. Alas, the guest rooms do not continue the English-village theme. They were, however, remodeled a few years ago in soothing pastels with blond-wood accents. There are comfortable chairs and a remote control for the TV.

Dining/Entertainment: Excalibur's Restaurant and Lounge is a baronial dining room that completes the English-village theme. There is live vocal and piano entertainment in the lounge nightly.

Services: Room service, valet/laundry service.

Facilities: Outdoor pool, fitness room, hair salon.

6 Bellevue & Kirkland

Across Lake Washington from Seattle, in the area known as Eastside, are two of Washington's fastest-growing cities—Bellevue and Kirkland—which are at the heart of the region's high-tech industrial growth. These two cities also are bedroom communities with many attractive and wealthy neighborhoods. Should you be out this way on high-tech business or visiting friends, you may find an eastside hotel more convenient than one in downtown Seattle. It's only 15 minutes to downtown Seattle if it isn't rush hour.

VERY EXPENSIVE

Hyatt Regency Bellevue

900 Bellevue Way NE, Bellevue, WA 98004. ☎ **206/462-1234** or 800/233-1234. Fax 206/646-7567. 382 rms, 21 suites. A/C TV $175–$200 double; $185–$800 suite. Weekend rates available. Parking $7, valet $11.

Located across the street from the Northwest's largest shopping mall and connected to a smaller and more exclusive shopping center, the Hyatt Regency Bellevue is a sure bet for anyone who likes to shop. This high-rise also offers from its upper floors some good views of Lake Washington and the Seattle skyline. Decor in the public areas is a mixture of traditional European styling and Oriental art and antiques. Guest rooms are done in a pale powder gray with yellow accents and include a marble-top desk and rattan chairs. Tile bathrooms have lots of counter space and an assortment of soaps and lotions. In rooms on the Regency Club floors, you'll also find robes, an iron and ironing board, a hairdryer, extra soaps, a bathroom scale, mineral water, and a jar of candies. These latter rooms also have the best views and include access to a concierge lounge.

Dining/Entertainment: Eques, the hotel's main dining room, is located just off the lobby and serves primarily Mediterranean cuisine. The decor, as the name implies, incorporates various horse images. An adjacent lounge provides a quiet spot for a drink. Chadfield's Sports Pub features green-marble counters, hardwood floors, and plenty of televisions for monitoring the big game. Light snacks and sandwiches are served in the pub.

Services: 24-hour room service, valet/laundry service, evening turndown.

Facilities: Adjacent health club ($7 per day), with lap pool, steam room, sauna, whirlpool spa, weight room, aerobics room.

✪ The Woodmark Hotel at Carillon Point

1200 Carillon Point, Kirkland, WA 98033. ☎ **206/822-3700** or 800/822-3700. 100 rms, 25 suites. A/C TV MINIBAR $155–$195 double; $225–$900 suites. Weekend rates available. AE, CB, DC, ER, JCB, MC, V. Parking $8.

If you're willing to stay on the east side of Lake Washington in Kirkland, you can stay at the most luxurious waterfront hotel in the metropolitan area. Surrounded by a luxury residential community and shopping center, the Woodmark looks over a wide lawn to the waters of the lake. In the lobby a cosmopolitan sophistication prevails, and the overall effect is of being in the living room of a well-traveled friend. Off to one side a wide staircase leading down to the lounge and restaurant curves past a wall of glass that frames the lake beyond.

Guest rooms are no less impressive. When this hotel was planned, they must have asked frequent travelers what they would most like to find in the perfect hotel room. The answers are all here: a VCR, floor-to-ceiling windows that open, terry-cloth robes, oversized towels, a tiny television and a hairdryer in the bathroom, a large work desk, two telephones, computer hookup, complimentary coffee and a coffeemaker, and a stocked minibar. In addition there are views of the lake from most rooms, so sit back and enjoy.

Dining/Entertainment: The Carillon Room serves a combination of Northwest and continental cuisines at fairly high prices. Decor is an eclectic mix of rustic antiques and classical lines. Sunday brunch is lavish and delicious. The Carillon Room Lounge is a casual place more evocative of a library than a bar.

Services: Room service, concierge, courtesy local shopping van, complimentary newspaper, shoeshine service, laundry/valet service, complimentary late-night snacks, video lending library, complimentary use of laptop computer, cellular phone, pager.

Facilities: Exercise room, business center.

MODERATE

Best Western Bellevue Inn

11211 Main St., Bellevue, WA 98004. ☎ **206/455-5240** or 800/421-8193. Fax 206/455-0654. 179 rms. $85–$100 double. AE, DC, DISC, JCB, MC, V. Free parking.

The Bellevue is one of the few hotels in the Seattle area that captures the feel of the Northwest in design and landscaping. The sprawling two-story hotel is roofed with cedar-shake shingles and lushly planted with rhododendron, fir, fern, and azalea. Try to book a poolside first-floor room. These rooms, though a bit dark, have sunken, rock-walled patios. Bathrooms include plenty of counter space, and there are built-in hairdryers. There are also clock radios and minirefrigerators in all rooms.

Dining/Entertainment: Jonah's Restaurant and Bistro Bar serves a mix of American and Continental dishes, with the occasional touch of Northwest creativity.

Services: Complimentary passes to local athletic club, complimentary local van service, in-room movies, rental-car desk.

Facilities: Outdoor pool, exercise room, newsstand.

5

Seattle Dining

1 Best Bets

Best Spot for a Romantic Dinner: Ask for a table at Chez Shea that looks out on the waterfront, where you can see the ferry lights go by at night. Tasteful, subdued lighting heightens the experience. Go ahead—gaze into the eyes of your companion, and slice into the walnut encrusted loin of lamb with pear bourbon sauce—it doesn't get much better than this (☎ 206/467-9990).

Best Spot for a Business Lunch: The Hunt Club at the Sorrento Hotel has mahogany paneled walls and louvered doors that can be closed for privacy, and a creative menu (☎ 206/343-6156).

Best View: There's no question here, the Space Needle Restaurant and Emerald Suite have the best views in Seattle—360 degrees of them. Sure it's expensive, and it's not the best food Seattle has to offer, but there's no other place in town with such a view (☎ 206/443-2100).

Best Wine List: Canlis has been around for four decades and has had plenty of time to develop an extensive and well-thought-out wine list (☎ 206/283-3313).

Best Value: Café Campagne offers creative and delicious house specialties such as pork tenderloin on foccacia with apricot mustard ($6.95 at lunch, $7.95 at dinner), and a great wine list, in an atmosphere that feels surprisingly like turn-of-the-century Paris (☎ 206/728-CAFE).

Best for Kids: Built to resemble a Northwest Coast longhouse, Ivar's Salmon House is filled with artifacts kids will find interesting, and on the floating patio outside they can watch boats go by (☎ 206/632-0767).

Best Italian: Serafina focuses on rustic Italian, with dishes such as braised rabbit with fennel and kalamata olives. A bonus is that it's also very romantic, with live music and an outside garden (☎ 206/323-0807).

Best Northwest Cuisine: Chef Thierry Rautureau at Rovers combines his love of Northwest ingredients with his classic French training to produce his own distinctive take on Northwest cuisine (☎ 206/325-7442).

Best Desserts: With a baby grand piano and white table linens, the Famous Pacific Dessert Company is a sophisticated place to fulfill your fantasies of sweetness. Gratify yourself with a slice of chocolate raspberry Victorian soufflé cake or espresso truffle torte (☎ 206/328-1950).

Best Espresso: Torrefazione serves its brew in hand-painted Italian crockery, and has delectable pastries to go with your espresso (Occidental Ave. S., ☎ 206/624-5773; Olive Way, ☎ 206/624-1429).

Best Espresso Milkshake: Squeeze into the Western Coffee Shop, plunk yourself on a stool, and order one (☎ 206/682-5001).

Best Crab Cakes: Dungeness crab cakes with roasted bell pepper and garlic aioli at Queen City Grill melt in the mouth (☎ 206/443-0975).

Best Burger: Peppered bacon, kasseri cheese, and grilled onions on a thick, juicy burger all inside a chewy Italian roll—this is the combination that makes the Belltown pub burger the best in my book (☎ 206/728-4311).

Best Juices: After you've indulged in caloric eating and want to improve your habits, visit the Gravity Bar, where you can get concoctions like the Dennis Hopper, with carrot, beet, garlic, and wheatgrass (☎ 206/448-8826).

Best Vegetarian: Interesting and diverse preparations with vegetables and their friends—grains, legumes, nuts, and pasta—come out of the kitchen at Café Flora. Their Thanksgiving feast includes nary a turkey (☎ 206/325-9100).

Best Seafood: With a wall of glass that overlooks a canal, Ponti Seafood Grill is elegant and modern. Favorites that keep people coming back are appetizers such as smoked salmon with a corn pancake, vodka crème fraîche, chives, and caviar (☎ 206/284-3000).

Best Oysters: Choose from the many varieties of fresh oysters you'll see piled up on the oyster bar at the Brooklyn Seafood, Steak, & Oyster House (☎ 206/224-7000).

Best Paddle-Up Restaurant: If you're out on Lake Union in a kayak and you get hungry, just paddle up to the Kayak Lakefront Grill where you can order fish, Cajun, and pasta dishes for additional carbohydrates (☎ 206/284-2535).

Best Steaks/Beef: The Metropolitan Grill in downtown Seattle serves corn-fed, aged beef grilled over mesquite wood (☎ 206/624-3287).

Best Pizza: It looks gooey, crusty, and tempting, and tastes even better at Pizzeria Pagliacci, with several different locations around Seattle (☎ 206/324-0730).

Although it has been only a few years since Northwest cuisine seemed to be on the cutting edge of culinary trends, familiarity seems to have dulled the edge. Today it is almost as difficult to find a dinner of salmon in raspberry buerre blanc as it is to find a parking space in downtown Seattle. This is not to say that Northwest cuisine's innovative combinations of regional ingredients have lost their power to two-step across your tastebuds, but, as in the rest of the country,

Italian food, whether solo or jointly packaged as Mediterranean cuisine, is enjoying a renaissance in Seattle. If ever there were a city prime to embrace the sunny flavors of the Mediterranean, it is Seattle, where gray skies and cool weather predominate for much of the year. Also, unlike many eastern cities, Seattle never had a very large Italian immigrant population, and consequently the city was never, until now, inundated with Italian restaurants. So, Seattleites today are reveling in their rosemary and noshing on gnocchi. So, my recommendation is to keep an eye out for any characteristically northwestern culinary combination (hazelnut-crusted salmon, Dungeness crab cakes with raspberry salsa, wild mushrooms with anything, you get the picture), but enjoy your *pizza rustica* and keep an eye on how much olive oil you soak up with that crusty bread—those calories add up and your salad hasn't even arrived.

One Seattle dining trend that has been unchanged by the passing of time has been the city's near obsession with seafood. You may be aware that wild salmon in the Northwest are rapidly disappearing from the region's rivers, but this doesn't prevent salmon from showing up on nearly every menu in the city. Much of it is now hatchery fish, or imported from Canada or Alaska. However, there are also nearly a dozen varieties of regional oysters available—the best of which come from Quilcene or Willapa Bay. Dungeness crabs are another Northwest specialty, which though not as large as king crabs, are quite a bit heftier than the blue crabs of the eastern United States. You may also run across such unfamiliar clams as the razor clam or the geoduck (pronounced "gooey duck"). The former is shaped like a straight razor and can be chewy if not prepared properly, and the latter is a bivalve of prodigious proportions (as much as 12 pounds) that usually shows up only in stews and chowders.

Pricing categories are as follows: **expensive, over $25; moderate, $15 to $25; inexpensive, under $15.** These prices are in most cases based on a meal of two or more courses and do not include the cost of beer, wine, or cocktails.

2 Restaurants by Cuisine

AMERICAN

Canlis (Queen Anne &
the Lake Union Area, E)
Merchants Café
(Downtown, M)
Western Coffee Shop
(Downtown, IE)

CHINESE

Hing Loon (Downtown, IE)

CHINESE/SOUTHEAST ASIAN

Wild Ginger Asian Restaurant
& Satay Barn (Downtown, IE)

CONTINENTAL

Café Sophie (Downtown, M)
Canlis (Queen Anne &
the Lake Union Area, E)

The Georgian Room
(Downtown, E)

13 Coins Restaurant
(First Hill, Capitol Hill &
East Seattle, M)

DESSERTS

The Crumpet Shop
(Downtown, IE)

The Famous Pacific Dessert
Company (First Hill, Capitol
Hill & East Seattle, IE)
The Green Room Café (North
Seattle, IE)

EASTERN EUROPEAN
Labuznik (Downtown, M)

FRENCH
Café Campagne
(Downtown, M)
Campagne (Downtown, E)
Maximilien in the Market
(Downtown, M)
Le Gourmand (The University
District, Fremont &
Wallingford, M)
The Painted Table
(Downtown, M)

GEORGIAN/MEDITERRANEAN
Pirosmani (Queen Anne &
the Lake Union Area, E)

INTERNATIONAL
Belltown Pub
(Downtown, IE)
Café Lago (The University
District, Fremont &
Wallingford, M)
Cyclops (Downtown, IE)
Kamon on Lake Union
(Queen Anne & the
Lake Union Area, E)
Kaspar's (Queen Anne &
the Lake Union Area, E)
La Buca (Downtown, M)
Marco's Supperclub
(Downtown, M)
The Pink Door (Downtown, M)
Queen City Grill
(Downtown, M)
Shea's Lounge (Downtown, M)
Trattoria Mitchelli
(Downtown, M)
Triangle Café (The University
District, Fremont &
Wallingford, IE)

ITALIAN/EUROPEAN
Serafina (Queen Anne &
the Lake Union Area, M)

JAPANESE
Kamon on Lake Union
(Queen Anne & the Lake
Union Area, E)
Nikko (Downtown, E)

MEDITERRANEAN
Adriatica (Queen Anne &
the Lake Union Area, E)

NATURAL FOODS
Gravity Bar (Downtown, IE)

NEW MEXICAN
Cactus (First Hill, Capitol Hill
& East Seattle, M)

NORTHWEST
Chez Shea (Downtown, E)
Dahlia Lounge (Downtown, E)
The Emerald Suite and
Space Needle Restaurant
(Seattle Center, E)
Fuller's (Downtown, E)
The Georgian Room
(Downtown, E)
The Hunt Club (First Hill,
Capitol Hill &
East Seattle, E)
Kaspar's (Queen Anne &
the Lake Union Area, E)
Le Gourmand
(The University
District, Fremont &
Wallingford, M)
The Painted Table
(Downtown, M)
The Palm Court
(Downtown, M)
Rover's (First Hill,
CapitolHill &
East Seattle, E)
Shea's Lounge
(Downtown, M)

PIZZA

Pizzeria Pagliacci (First Hill,
Capitol Hill & East
Seattle, IE)

SEAFOOD

The Brooklyn Seafood,
Steak & Oyster House
(Downtown, E)
Emmett Watson's Oyster Bar
(Downtown, IE)
Ivar's Salmon House
(The University District,
Fremont & Wallingford, M)
Kayak Lakefront Grill
(Queen Anne & Lake
Union Area, M)
McCormick & Schmick's
(Downtown, M)
McCormick's Fish House
and Bar (Downtown, M)
Ponti Seafood Grill
(The University
District, Fremont &
Wallingford, E)

Ray's Boathouse
(The University District,
Fremont &
Wallingford, M)

STEAK

Ray's Boathouse
(The University District,
Fremont & Wallingford, M)
Metropolitan Grill
(Downtown, M)

THAI

Siam on Broadway (First Hill,
Capitol Hill & East Seattle, IE)

VEGETARIAN

Cafe Flora (First Hill, Capitol
Hill & East Seattle, M)

VIETNAMESE

Café Hue (Downtown, IE)
Vietnam's Pearl (First Hill,
Capitol Hill & East
Seattle, IE)

---

3 Downtown

EXPENSIVE

Campagne

Inn at the Market, 86 Pine St. ☎ **206/728-2800.** Reservations required. Main dishes $14–$26. AE, MC, V. Daily 5:30–10pm (cafe dining until midnight). FRENCH.

On the far side of the fountain that bubbles in the courtyard of the Inn at the Market, French country decor continues inside the aptly named Campagne. Large windows let in precious sunshine and provide a view of Elliott Bay over the top of Pike Place Market. Cheerful and unpretentious, Campagne is one of the most enjoyable French restaurants in Seattle.

Il Bistro

93-A Pike St. and First Ave. (inside Pike Place Market). ☎ **206/682-3049.** Reservations recommended. Pastas $10–$16, main dishes $16–$26.50. AE, CB, DC, MC, V. Lunch Mon–Sat 11:30–3pm; dinner Sun–Thurs 5:30–10pm, Fri–Sat 5:30–11pm; bar nightly until 2am. ITALIAN

You'll find Il Bistro to the left of the famous Pike Place Market sign. The entrance is from the ramp that leads into the bowels of the market, and once inside you'll have the feeling that you're dining in a wine cellar. Il Bistro takes Italian cooking very seriously and puts the Northwest's bountiful ingredients to good use. The region is damp most of the year and brings forth excellent crops of wild and cultivated mushrooms. Watch for them on the menu; they're always a treat.

The menu lists such mouthwatering starters as calamari sautéed with fresh basil, garlic vinegar, and white wine. Pasta can be a genuine revelation when served with the likes of shiitake mushrooms, hot pepper flakes, vodka, and tomato cream. Long before you arrived, the choice of which main dish to order was decided by the hundreds of loyal fans who insist that the rack of lamb with wine sauce is the best in Seattle. Don't take their word for it—decide for yourself.

The Brooklyn Seafood, Steak & Oyster House

1212 Second Ave. ☎ **206/224-7000.** Reservations recommended. Main courses $12–$24; lunches $7–$13. AE, DC, DISC, MC, V. Lunch Mon–Fri 11am–3pm; dinner Mon–Fri 5–10pm, Sat–Sun 4:30–10:30pm. SEAFOOD.

Designed to look as if it's been here for decades, The Brooklyn is housed in one of the city's oldest buildings. The specialty here is definitely oysters, with about 10 different types piled up at the oyster bar on any given night. If oysters on the half shell don't appeal to you, there are plenty of other tempting appetizers ranging from grilled salmon sausages to roasted garlic and goat cheese. Alder-planked meats and fishes are another specialty here. This type of cooking is similar to smoking or grilling and originated with the Native Americans of the Northwest. In addition, there are simply prepared grilled steaks, and such dishes as seafood pasta in parchment grilled vanilla prawns. There are even a couple of vegetarian dishes on the menu. After 5pm, there is free valet parking.

Chez Shea

94 Pike St., Suite 34, Pike Place Market. ☎ **206/467-9990.** Reservations highly recommended. Appetizers $6; main dishes $21; fixed-price four-course dinner $36. AE, MC, V. Dinner only, Tues–Sun 5:30–10pm; late night menu until 1:30am. NORTHWEST.

It's hard to believe that there could be a quiet corner of Pike Place Market, but here it is. Quiet, dark, and intimate, Chez Shea is one of the finest restaurants in Seattle. A dozen candlelit tables, with views across Puget Sound to the Olympic Mountains, are the perfect setting for a romantic dinner. The ingredients used in preparing the meals here come from the market below, and they are always the freshest and finest. Dinner is strictly fixed price on weekends—four courses with a choice of five or six main dishes, but on weeknights there are also à la carte dinners available.

The menu changes to reflect the season and on a recent wintry night included filet of salmon seared with braised savoy cabbage, tarragon, and a red butter sauce; and a succulent loin of lamb roasted in walnut crust with a pear bourbon sauce. The meal started with grape leaves stuffed with couscous, currants, and mint, and served with citrus chutney. Though dessert is à la carte, you'll find it impossible to let it pass you by.

✪ Dahlia Lounge

1904 Fourth Ave. ☎ **206/682-4142.** Reservations highly recommended. Appetizers $6–$9; main dishes $12–$20. AE, DC, DISC, MC, V. Lunch Mon–Fri 11:30am–2:30pm; dinner Mon–Thurs 5:30–10pm, Fri–Sat 5:30–11pm, Sun 5–9pm. NORTHWEST.

The neon chef holding a flapping fish may suggest that the Dahlia is little more than a roadside diner, but a glimpse inside at the stylish decor will likely have you thinking otherwise. One look at the menu, one bite of any dish, will convince you that this is one of Seattle's finest restaurants. Mouth-watering and succulent Dungeness crab cakes, a bow to Douglas's Maryland roots, are the house specialty and should not be missed. Menu influences also extend to the far side of the Pacific Rim, from which the Dahlia special fried rice with grilled prawns, shiitake mushrooms, and daikon originates. The house-made gnocchi is always dense and delicious, while the Tuscan bread salad is a meal in itself. The lunch menu features many of the same offerings at slightly lower prices. You can even get half an order of the crab cakes.

✪ Fuller's

Sheraton Seattle Hotel & Towers, 1400 Sixth Ave. ☎ **206/447-5544.** Reservations recommended. Main dishes $17.25–$24.50; prix-fixe dinner $40; lunches $8–$13. AE, CB, DC, DISC, JCB, MC, V. Lunch Mon–Fri 11:30am–2pm; dinner Mon–Sat 5:30–10pm. NORTHWEST.

Fuller's, named for the founder of the Seattle Art Museum, is dedicated to both the culinary and the visual arts of the Northwest. Each dish is as artfully designed as it is superbly prepared, and surrounding you in this elegant dining room are works of art by the Northwest's best artists. The service is gracious and attentive.

You never know what influences might show up on Fuller's menu, which changes seasonally, though Mediterranean flavors seem to be predominating of late. A recent menu included an appetizer of Northwest oysters with starfruit mignonette and such main dishes as grilled pork loin with apple cider–mustard sauce and pan-seared kasu cod with soy-ginger vinaigrette. This latter dish is a Fuller's specialty and is made with a flavorful by-product of sake rice-wine brewing. Lunch, with its lower prices, is especially popular. The wine list reflects the seasonal changes on the menu.

The Georgian Room

Four Seasons Olympic Hotel, 411 University St. ☎ **206/621-1700.** Reservations recommended. Main dishes $19–$30. AE, CB, DC, MC, V. Breakfast Mon–Fri 6:30–11am, Sat 6:30am–noon, Sun 7am–1pm; dinner Mon–Thurs 5:30–10pm, Fri–Sat 5:30–10:30pm. CONTINENTAL/NORTHWEST.

Nowhere in Seattle is there a more elegant restaurant—to dine at The Georgian Room is to dine in a palace. The soaring ceiling is decorated with intricate moldings, and the huge windows are framed by luxurious curtains. The excellent service will convince you that your table is the only one being served.

Seattle Dining—Downtown

The menu offerings are a mingling of Northwest and Continental cuisines, but veal or New York tenderloin with mushrooms and aged Black Angus steak are the signature dishes. As you would expect, the wine list is well suited to both the food and the restaurant's ambience.

Nikko

Westin Hotel Seattle, 1900 Fifth Ave. ☎ **206/322-4641.** Reservations strongly recommended. Dinners $16.50–$35; lunch $6.75–$15. AE, CB, DC, MC, V. Dinner only, Mon–Sat 5:30–10pm. JAPANESE.

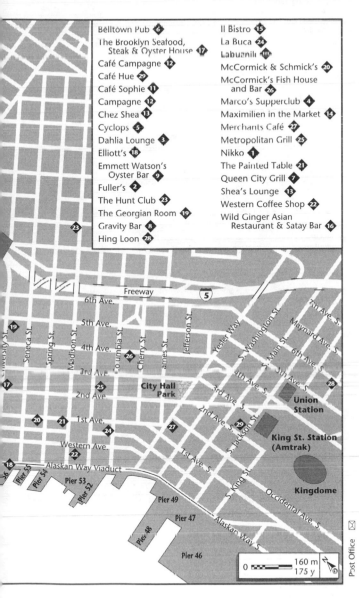

Belltown Pub **6**

The Brooklyn Seafood,
  Steak & Oyster House **17**

Café Campagne **12**

Café Hue **29**

Café Sophie **11**

Campagne **12**

Chez Shea **13**

Cyclops **5**

Dahlia Lounge **3**

Elliott's **18**

Emmett Watson's
  Oyster Bar **9**

Fuller's **2**

The Hunt Club **23**

The Georgian Room **19**

Gravity Bar **8**

Hing Loon **28**

Il Bistro **15**

La Buca **24**

Labuznik **10**

McCormick & Schmick's **20**

McCormick's Fish House
  and Bar **26**

Marco's Supperclub **4**

Maximilien in the Market **14**

Merchants Café **27**

Metropolitan Grill **25**

Nikko **1**

The Painted Table **21**

Queen City Grill **7**

Shea's Lounge **13**

Western Coffee Shop **22**

Wild Ginger Asian
  Restaurant & Satay Bar **16**

Traditional Japanese styling meets contemporary Euro-styling at this stunningly trendy Japanese restaurant. Black-slate floors, blond shoji-screen walls, indirect and subtle lighting, and original art on the walls are just some of the details that make Nikko an attractive place for a meal. Expert sushi chefs, a display teppan–grill bar, and an extensive menu that makes the most of the Northwest's abundance of seafood assure you that Nikko is more than just a pretty place to assuage a hunger. For entertainment and value, I recommend such one-pot dinners as shabu-shabu or sukiyaki. There are even family-style dinners that allow you to sample a wide assortment of dishes, if you dine in a group of four or more.

MODERATE

✪ Café Campagne

1600 Post Alley. ☎ **206/728-CAFE.** Reservations not accepted. Main courses $8–$15; lunches $6–$10. AE, MC, V. Mon–Sat 8am–10pm, Sun brunch 8am–3pm. FRENCH.

This cozy little café is an offshoot of the Inn at the Market's popular Campagne, and though it is located in the heart of the Pike Place Market neighborhood, it is a world away from the market madness. Glass cases just inside the door display roast chickens, luscious tarts, and plenty of other delicacies. The menu changes with the season but might include a hearty country-style pate or baked marinated goat cheese on the appetizer menu. Entrées include filling sandwiches such as the popular lamb burger with aioli or roast pork tenderloin on foccacia with apricot mustard. Main courses are served à la carte, so if you're particularly hungry, peruse the list of side dishes, which might include baby artichokes stewed in olive oil with lemon and garlic. The café also doubles as a wine bar and has a good selection of reasonably priced wines by the glass or by the bottle.

✪ Café Sophie

1921 First Ave. ☎ **206/441-6139.** Reservations highly recommended. Main dishes $13–$20; desserts $5–$10. MC, V. Lunch Mon–Sat 11:30am–2:30pm; dinner Mon–Thurs 5:30–9:30, Fri–Sat 5:30–10:30; late night menu until 1am. CONTINENTAL.

A self-consciously stylish restaurant for self-consciously stylish patrons, Café Sophie hearkens back to the grand old days of supper clubs on the Continent. It used to be a mortuary, and now has a grand salon with dark green walls covered with mirrors and paintings, and very romantic booths. A library room overlooks the bay and is a good spot for viewing the moon or ferry lights on Elliot Bay at night. The menu pulls its gastronomic references from all over the world and changes frequently to keep the loyal patrons returning. On a recent evening, straight-forward coq au vin shared the menu with pork Schitzel with artichoke-lemon aioli. The extravagant desserts are the main reason most people come here. On Friday and Saturday nights, live jazz puts the finishing touch on this romantic setting.

La Buca

102 Cherry St. ☎ **206/343-9517.** Reservations recommended on weekends. First courses $7–$12; main courses $12–$16; lunch main courses $6–$9.50. AE, DC, MC, V. Lunch Mon–Fri 11:30am–2:30pm; dinner Mon–Thurs 5–11pm, Fri–Sat 5pm–midnight, Sun 5–10pm. ITALIAN.

Turn off of Pioneer Square onto Cherry Street, walk down a flight of steps, and you'll be dining in the Seattle underground. Dark and cavernous with brick arches supporting the ceiling, La Buca is reminiscent of a huge wine cellar. The menu is primarily southern Italian, but goes far beyond spaghetti and meatballs. A house-made sausage is braised with red wine, garlic, peppers, and tomatoes, and served on a bed of polenta, while the saddle of lamb is served with fresh rosemary, figs, port, and Gorgonzola. Appetizers and first courses of risottos and pastas are equally creative and flavorful. Such dishes as pan-roasted quail with aromatic vegetables and fresh herbs; polenta with pecorino cheese and a topping of lamb ragout; and rigatoni with roasted chicken and roasted pepper sauce show off the mouth-watering fare that comes out of La Buca's kitchen.

Labuznik

1924 First Ave. ☎ **206/441-8899.** Reservations recommended. Main dishes $12.50–$25. AE, DC, DISC, MC, V. Dinner only, Tues–Sat 4:30–11pm. EASTERN EUROPEAN.

These days when we think of ethnic food we tend to think of Thai, Moroccan, Caribbean, and other exotic cuisines. But before all of these began to appear on the American scene, there was a very different sort of ethnic cuisine—Eastern European. Well, at Labuznik, the meat-and-potatoes meals of Eastern Europe have never been forgotten. Instead, they have been perfected. In Czech, *labuznik* means "lover of good food." Dine here and you'll be a happy labuznik when you leave.

The tasty but tongue-twisting *vepro knedlo zelo* translates into a filling plate of roast pork with sauerkraut and dumplings. The veal Orloff is deliciously rich with mushrooms, capers, pickles, and cream. A meal here would not be complete without the Sacher torte. A lighter and less expensive menu is served in the bar.

McCormick & Schmick's

1103 First Ave. ☎ **206/623-5500.** Reservations recommended. Main dishes $10–$19.60; box lunches $6.95. AE, DC, DISC, MC, V. Mon–Fri 11:30am–11pm, Sat–Sun 5–11pm. SEAFOOD.

Force your way past the crowds of business suits at the bar and you'll find yourself in a classic fish house. From the cafe curtains on the windows to the highly polished brass to the sparkling leaded glass to the dark-wood paneling, everything about this restaurant shines. Waiters wearing black bow ties will help you find your way through the exhaustingly long sheet of daily specials and equally long wine list.

The well-prepared seafood, lamb, veal, and steak have made McCormick and Schmick's extremely popular with executives from Seattle's surrounding financial community. You, too, can hobnob with the wheelers and dealers for the price of such dishes as blackened Canadian lingcod with tomato-ginger chutney; yellowfin tuna with soy, wasabi, and ginger; or halibut stuffed with crab, shrimp, and brie. From 3 to 6pm and 10 to closing daily, you can get appetizers in the bar for only $1.95, and if you're in the mood for a downtown picnic, they also prepare box lunches. Weekdays between 5 and 6pm, a limited menu is available for between $5 and $6.

McCormick's Fish House and Bar

722 Fourth Ave. (at Columbia St.) ☎ **206/682-3900.** Reservations recommended. Main dishes $8.65–$23.20. AE, CB, DC, DISC, MC, V. Mon–Thurs 11:30am–11pm, Fri 11:30am–midnight, Sat 5pm–midnight, Sun 5–10pm. SEAFOOD.

A recent menu here listed more than 30 different seafoods from such far-flung locations as Massachusetts, Chile, Hawaii, Idaho, and, of course, Washington—to give you some idea of how committed McCormick's is to bringing you the very best. However, most of the listed seafoods were from the Northwest, and this was noted for those who insist that the freshest is always local. It is immediately apparent that McCormick's is determined to please. The ambiance is old-fashioned, with dark-wood booths and a tile floor around the long bar, and the service is fast. The crowds are large; the clientele tends to be very upscale, especially in the bar after the financial offices let out. Both traditional and imaginative Northwest-style cuisine is served, with the menu broken into categories based on how the seafood is cooked.

Marco's Supperclub

2510 First Ave. ☎ **206/441-7801.** Reservations highly recommended. Main courses $10–$15. AE, MC, V. Lunch Mon–Fri 11:30am–2pm; dinner daily 5:30–10pm; Sun brunch 10am–2pm. INTERNATIONAL.

With it's thrift-store crockery and reupholstered yard-sale furnishings, Marco's has a casual ambiance that belies the high-quality meals that emanate from the kitchen. Perhaps it is this eclectic attitude toward decor that helps keep the prices here so reasonable. The menu draws on cuisines from around the world for inspiration, so even jaded gourmands may find something new to try here. A recent menu included such unexpected and unusual offerings as fried sage leaves with a medley of dipping sauces, butternut squash samosas, and tempura-fried oysters on the appetizer list. Among the entrées, you're likely to find such memorable dishes such as a pork loin marinated in juniper berries and herbs, cumin-marinated rack of lamb, or lobster risotto. If you enjoy creative cookery at reasonable prices, be sure to check this place out.

Maximilien in the Market

81A Pike St. ☎ **206/682-7270.** Reservations recommended. Mon–Thurs fixed-price dinners $13.50–$22.95; Main dishes $10.50–$22. AE, MC, V. Mon–Sat 7:30am–10pm; brunch Sun 9:30am–4pm. FRENCH.

Located in Pike Place Market to the left of the main market entrance, Maximilien is not your usual highbrow French restaurant. Dark-green walls and old, well-used tables speak volumes about the ambiance here. It is country French, the sort of place you might find in a small village. And the fare is as no-nonsense as the decor, especially on weeknights, when the meals are fixed price. On Friday and Saturday evenings, however, dinner is a bit more formal, with such standards as beef tenderloin with béarnaise sauce; escargots bourguignons; and broiled rack of lamb with mint-butter sauce. If you're at the market early, you might stop by for breakfast or lunch, which are less expensive than dinner.

Merchants Café

109 Yesler Way. ☎ **206/624-1515.** Reservations not necessary. Main dishes $7–$12. CB, DC, MC, V. Sun–Mon 10am–3pm, Tues–Thurs 10am–7pm (winter, 10am–4pm), Fri–Sat 10am–9pm. AMERICAN.

Merchants Café is Seattle's oldest restaurant and looks every bit of its 100-plus years. A well-scuffed tile floor surrounds the bar, which came around the Horn in the 1800s. An old safe and gold scales are left over from the days when Seattle was the first, or last, taste of civilization for those bound for, or returning from, the Yukon goldfields. This bar/restaurant has had a long and colorful history. At one time the basement was a card room and the upper floors were a brothel. In fact, this may be the original Skid Row saloon, since Yesler Way was the original Skid Road down which logs were skidded to a sawmill. Straightforward sandwiches and steaks are the mainstays of the menu, though a few more imaginative main dishes also appear.

Metropolitan Grill

818 Second Ave. ☎ **206/624-3287.** Reservations recommended. Main dishes $11–$30. AE, CB, DC, DISC, JCB, MC, V. Lunch Mon–Fri 11am–3:30pm; dinner Mon–Sat 5–11pm, Sun 5–10pm. STEAK.

Another reliable restaurant for aspiring financial whiz kids and their mentors, this one is dedicated to meat eaters rather than to seafood lovers. Green-velvet booths, bar stools, and floral-design carpets are the keynote of the sophisticated atmosphere at the Metropolitan. Mirrored walls and a high ceiling trimmed with elegant plaster work make the dining room feel larger than it actually is, while historic photos depicting scenes from Seattle history make the local movers and shakers feel secure that one day they, too, will be part of Seattle history.

Perfectly cooked steaks are the primary attraction here, and you'd be foolish not to order one of them. They're considered the best steaks in Seattle by those in the know. A baked potato and a pile of crispy onion rings complete the perfect steak dinner.

⑤ The Painted Table

Alexis Hotel, 92 Madison St. ☎ **206/624-3646.** Reservations recommended. Main dishes $12–$20; lunch main dishes $7–$15.50. AE, CB, DC, DISC, MC, V. Breakfast Mon–Fri 6:30–10am, Sat–Sun 7am–noon; lunch Mon–Fri 11:30am–2pm; dinner daily 5:30–10pm. NORTHWEST/FRENCH.

Artistically presented meals are *de rigueur* these days at expensive restaurants, but here at The Painted Table it isn't just the main dishes that are works of art, it's the plates as well—and the prices are relatively moderate! Every table is set with colorful hand-painted plates done by West Coast ceramic artists. Should you take a fancy to your plate, you can take it home with you for around $65. Though the restaurant's atmosphere and service are casual, every dish is beautifully arranged. The pasta with tea-smoked duck, glazed turnips, roasted walnuts, and dried cherries is one of my favorites. Herb crusted lamb fillet with grilled eggplant and fennel polenta is another winner. For dessert, I order the espresso-flavored crème brûlée.

The Palm Court

Westin Hotel Seattle, 1900 Fifth Avenue. ☎ **206/728-1000.** Reservations recommended. Main dishes $14.50–$22.75; lunch main dishes $9. AE, DC, MC, V. Lunch Mon–Fri 11:30am–2pm; dinner Mon–Thurs 5:30–10pm, Fri–Sat 5:30–10:30pm. NORTHWEST.

Life in the Espresso Lane

"I'll take a double half-caf tall skinny latte with a shot of hazelnut syrup, hold the foam." It may sound like a foreign language to you, but it doesn't take long to decipher the complexities of espresso. The following primer should soon have you speaking (and understanding) coffeespeak like a Seattle native.

First, a little background. Coffee originated centuries ago in the highlands of east Africa in the region that is today Ethiopia. Legend has it that a goatherd noticed that his goats acted differently after eating the berries of particular bush. Trying the berries himself, the goatherd found that they did indeed have an effect, they made him more alert, definitely an attribute in the goatherding business, what with lions, and tigers, and hyenas stalking the flock.

Coffee consumption has changed radically over the ages. The Italians introduced espresso, the French rounded things off with milk, and Seattle raised it to an American obsession transmuting espresso in much the same way that pizzas were transfigured when they crossed the Atlantic to the new world. Where else but in the United States would you find such bizarre concoctions as Milky Way coffee (espresso, chocolate milk, and caramel syrup)? However, despite the occasional cookie-coffee aberrations, coffee-making today is a fine art that may have reached its zenith in the coffee bars, cafés, coffee carts, and drive-thru coffee windows of Seattle.

There are two basic types of coffee beans—robustus and arabica. The former are the cheaper, lower quality beans and are used primarily in standard American supermarket coffees. The latter are the higher quality beans, with richer flavor and are used for gourmet coffees and espresso. Flavor in either of these beans is determined in large part by the way the raw bean is roasted. Most regular coffees are given a light to medium roasting that produces a rougher, less complex flavor. A dark or espresso roast provides a dark oily looking bean that produces a well-rounded, rich, deep flavor. Roasting coffee beans is an art that produces immense variations in flavors and, which in turn causes educated coffee drinkers to develop loyalties to different coffee roasters.

Espresso isn't quite ubiquitous throughout the United States, so, for those of you who are not yet cruising in the espresso lane, here are some important definitions and examples of how to order coffee Seattle-style:

Espresso—a specially roasted and ground coffee that has hot water forced through it to make a small cup of dense, flavorful coffee. Straight espresso is definitely an acquired taste. Espresso developed in Italy, where today it is often drunk with a twist of lemon.

European shots of espresso are smaller than American shots. Different coffeehouses serve different size shots, which means you might get more or less coffee flavor in your drink.

Latte—a shot of espresso topped off with steamed milk at roughly a three-to-one ratio. The correct term for this drink is *caffe latte* (with the accent on the final *e*'s). This translates as coffee milk, but in the Northwest, folks just say, "I'll have a latte (pronounced *lah* tay)," which really means, "I'll have a milk." Oh well, so much for learning a second language.

Single—one shot of espresso. You say, "I'll have a single latte."

Double—two shots of espresso. You say, "I'll have a double latte."

Tall—a latte with extra milk. A tall usually comes with one shot of espresso, but you can also get two shots. You say, "I'll have a double tall latte."

Grande—a 16-ounce latte with two shots of espresso. This is pretty high-test, so leave it to the pros until you've worked your way up the latte ladder.

Skinny—skimmed milk. You say, "I'll have a tall, skinny latte." You can also get lattes made with 2 percent milk or with whole milk.

Half-caf—a drink made with half decaffeinated coffee. You say, "I'll have a double tall, skinny, half-caf latte." They say, "Why bother?"

Foam—formed by steaming milk, this is the topping on a latte. Some people want it and some people don't.

Flavorings—sweet syrups with different flavors for giving your latte a bit more complexity. Sort of the wine cooler of the espresso lane. You can get everything from caramel to mango.

Cappuccino—espresso with hot milk and usually a sprinkling of cinnamon on top. A cappuccino's color is same as that of a Capuchin monk's habit and thus the name.

Macchiato—an espresso with a dollop of foamed milk on top to keep the coffee hotter just a little bit longer.

Mocha—espresso, steamed milk, and chocolate. Slap some whipped cream on top and you've got the ultimate high-octane, high-calorie pick-me-up.

Americano—a single shot of espresso topped off with water to make an approximation of traditional American-style coffee but with more flavor.

Café au lait—regular brewed or drip-filter coffee mixed with hot or steamed milk. These don't have the intense flavor of a latte and aren't readily available in Seattle.

The Palm Court's gardenlike dining rooms are the antithesis of those of other highly acclaimed local hotel restaurants such as Fuller's and the Hunt Club—bright and well lit. Walls of glass and sparkling lights turn it into a giant jewel box. Despite the glimmer and glitz, service is friendly and the atmosphere is always relaxed and casual. The Palm Court's menu these days is primarily Northwest with overtones of Mediterranean here and there. A recent menu included some excellent examples of this melding of flavors from opposite sides of the world: a cold appetizer of calamari salad with lime and ginger over spinach leaves; a Caesar sald with Dungeness crab, and roasted veal with forest mushrooms and juniper berry spatzle.

The Pink Door

1919 Post Alley. ☎ **206/443-3241.** Reservations recommended. Pastas $7.50–$9.50; main dishes $9.50–$12. AE, MC, V. Tues–Sat 11:30am–midnight. ITALIAN.

If I didn't tell you about this one, you'd never find it. There is no sign out front, only the pink door for which the restaurant is named (watch for a pale-gray wall with flower boxes in the windows between Stewart and Virginia streets). Open the door and you step into a cool, dark room with a high ceiling, hanging Chianti bottles, and a fountain in the middle of the floor. Tuesday through Thursday, there's a tarot card reader working the tables so you can find out before your meal whether you're going to enjoy your evening or not. There are also cabaret singers in the evening, and on the weekend there's an accordion player. In summer the action moves outside to the back deck where there is a magnificent view of the harbor and downtown Seattle. Be sure to start your meal with the fragrant roasted garlic and ricotta-Gorgonzola spread. I can never get enough seafood when I'm in Seattle, so I highly recommended the cioppino, a flavorful seafood stew.

✪ Queen City Grill

2201 First Ave. ☎ **206/443-0975.** Reservations recommended. Main dishes $8–$20; lunch main dishes $9–$14. AE, DC, DISC, MC, V. Lunch Mon–Fri 11:30am–4:30pm; dinner Sun–Thurs 4:30–11pm, Fri–Sat 4:30pm–midnight. INTERNATIONAL.

Battered wooden floors that look as if they were salvaged from an old hardware store and high-backed wooden booths give the new Queen City Grill the look of instant age. If you didn't know better, you'd think this place had been here since the Great Fire of 1889.

The spare decor and sophisticated lighting underscore an exciting menu. Some people come here just for the crab cakes (with just the right amount of roasted pepper/garlic aioli) but everything else is just as inspired.

Seafood is the specialty, so you might start with tuna carpaccio accompanied by a lime, ginger, and mustard sauce. The chicken wild rice gumbo is an unusual and tasty soup. There are several daily seafood specials. Dungeness crab cakes and Szechuan prawns are always on the menu.

⊗ Shea's Lounge
94 Pike St., Suite 34, Pike Place Market. ☎ **206/467-9990.** Reservations for 6 or more people only. Main courses $10–$12. AE, MC, V. Tues–Sun 4:30pm–10 or 11pm. NORTHWEST/INTERNATIONAL.

This is the lounge for the ever-popular Chez Shea, one of the Pike Place Market's hidden treasures, and is one of the most sophisticated little spaces in Seattle. Romantic lighting and a view of the bay make this a popular spot with couples, and whether you just want a cocktail and an appetizer or a full meal, you can get it here. The menu features gourmet pizzas, sandwiches, combination appetizer plates, a few soups and salads, and four nightly specials such as chicken saltimboca or lasagne with hazelnuts and winter squash. The desserts, though pricey, are divinely decadent. This is a great spot for a light meal.

INEXPENSIVE

✪ Belltown Pub
2322 First Ave. ☎ **206/728-4311.** Reservations not accepted. Sandwiches $6.50–$7. AE, MC, V. Sun–Thurs 11:30am–midnight, Fri–Sat 11:30am–2am. INTERNATIONAL.

Slide into one of the huge wooden booths, order from one of almost 20 microbrew taps, and take a look at the menu. Though this is basically just a neighborhood pub, the menu offers much more than your standard pub grub. The appetizers list might include Penn Cove mussels sautéed with fennel sausage, shallots, garlic, tomatoes, and herbs in a wine sauce or a zesty tapenade made with three kinds of olive as well as capers and garlic. The soups can be quite memorable as was a full-bodied mushroom soup on one occasion and the Belltown burger just might be the best burger in Seattle. You'll find this pub just a few blocks north of Pike Place Market.

⊗ Café Hue
312 Second Ave. S. ☎ **206/625-9833.** Reservations not necessary. Main dishes $4.50–$19.50. MC, V. Mon–Fri 11am–10pm, Sat noon–10pm, Sun 5–10pm. VIETNAMESE.

For inexpensive Southeast Asian food in a mildly elegant atmosphere, Café Hue is a good bet. The proprietors are Vietnamese refugees and very pleasant—Quy Phi and Kieutuy Nguyen turn out Vietnamese dishes with a French flair. Try the appetizer of escargots stuffed with pork and ginger. Each little snail comes with its own lemongrass pull tab. Other unexpected and equally succulent dishes are stuffed crab, roast quail, and the soups. Kieutuy is trained as a French pastry chef and for dessert creates such pasties as napoleons and kiwi tarts. The location is convenient to both Pioneer Square and the International District.

Cyclops
2416 Western Ave. ☎ **206/441-1677.** Reservations not accepted. Breakfast $4–$6; lunch $4–$7; dinner $7–$10. MC, V. Mon–Fri 11am–11pm, Sat–Sun 9am–11pm. INTERNATIONAL.

🙂 Family-Friendly Restaurants

Ivar's Salmon House *(see pg. 80)*   This restaurant is built to resemble a Northwest Coast Native American longhouse and is filled with artifacts that kids will find fascinating. If they get restless, they can go out to the floating patio and watch the boats passing by.

Gravity Bar *(see below)*   If you're traveling with teenagers, they'll love this place where Seattle's young and hip and health-conscious crowd comes to dine. The decor is postmodern neoindustrial and the food is wholesome, with juices called Martian Martini and 7 Year Spinach.

Merchants Café *(see pg. 66)*   Seattle's oldest restaurant may be the original Skid Row saloon. This bar/restaurant looks every bit of its 100 years. The kids will go for the straightforward sandwiches and steaks.

A neighborhood restaurant just a few blocks from Pike Place Market, Cyclops offers a bit of 1950s retro funk. You can't miss the building as you walk north from Pike Place market on Western Avenue—the exterior is painted purple. The people who eat here are always interesting, and you never know what kind of artwork will be up on the walls. Along with the interesting art, Cyclops serves breakfast fare (weekends only) and lunch and dinner items such as a roasted eggplant sandwich, a savory onion and chewy mozzarella tart, Greek salad, and chile rellenos. The menu is primarily vegetarian, but chicken and fish appear as well.

Emmett Watson's Oyster Bar

1916 Pike Place No. 16. ☎ **206/448-7721.** Reservations not accepted. Soups $1.75–$6; main dishes $3–$6. No credit cards. Mon–Thurs 11:30am–8pm, Fri–Sat 11:30am–9pm. In winter, Sun 11:30am–5pm, and closes 1 hour earlier the other nights. SEAFOOD.

Tucked away in a rare quiet corner of Pike Place Market (well, actually, it's across the street in the market overflow area), Emmett Watson's looks like a fast-food place, but the service here in fact is infamously slow. The booths are tiny, so it's best to come here on a sunny afternoon when you can sit in the courtyard. The restaurant is named for a famous Seattle newspaper columnist, and there are clippings and photos all over the walls. Oysters on the half shell are the raison d'être for this little place, but the fish dishes are often memorable as well. Check the blackboard for specials.

✪ Gravity Bar

113 Virginia St. ☎ **206/448-8826.** Reservations not necessary. Meals $4–$7; juices $2–$4.75. MC, V. Downtown—Mon–Thurs 11am–9pm, Fri 11am–10pm, Sat 10am–10pm, Sun 10am–8pm; Broadway—Mon–Thurs 9am–10pm, Fri–Sat 9am–11pm, Sun 9am–9pm (later in summer). NATURAL.

If you're young and hip and concerned about the food that you put into your body, this is the place you frequent in Seattle. The postmodern neoindustrial decor (lots of sheet metal on the walls, bar, and menus) is the antithesis of the wholesome juices and meals they serve here. The juice list includes all manner of unusual combinations, all with catchy names like Martian Martini or 7 Year Spinach. Be there or be square. Another Gravity Bar is at 415 E. Broadway (☎ 206/325-7186), although this branch accepts neither credit cards nor reservations and is open slightly different hours.

Hing Loon

628 S. Weller St. ☎ **206/682-2828.** Reservations not necessary. Main dishes $5.25–$9. Sun–Thurs 10am–midnight, Fri–Sat 10am–2am. CHINESE.

No atmosphere, bright fluorescent lighting, big Formica-top tables. This is the sort of place you would walk by if you were aimlessly searching for a restaurant in the International District. With so many choices in a few square blocks, it is easy to be distracted and attracted by fancy decor. Forget the rest and take a seat in Hing Loon. Seafood is the house specialty and none is done better than the oysters with ginger and green onion on a sizzling platter. For a veggie dish, don't miss the eggplant in Szechuan sauce. If you're feeling really daring, try the cold jellyfish; it's not at all the way you'd imagine it to be. Be careful of the pork dishes, which tend to have Chinese style pork that is mostly fat. The restaurant makes all its own noodles, so you can't go wrong ordering chow mein or chow funn (wide noodles).

✪ Western Coffee Shop

911½ Western Ave. ☎ **206/682-5001.** Reservations not accepted. Complete meal $3–$6. No credit cards. Mon–Fri 7am–2:15pm, Sat–Sun 8am–3pm. AMERICAN.

This place is so narrow that you'll probably walk right past it the first time, and once you do find it, you won't be able to get past that big guy on the first counter stool. Persevere and you'll be treated to a real Seattle experience. The Western is a very casual coffee shop sporting a Western theme—toy horses on the counter, cowboy hats here and there, cowboy music on the stereo. The cooking is good old-fashioned home cooking, no Northwest fruit-and-meat combos here. Don't miss the espresso milk shake.

✪ Wild Ginger Asian Restaurant & Satay Bar

1400 Western Ave. ☎ **206/623-4450.** Reservations not necessary. Satay $1.50–$7.50; main dishes $7–$18. AE, DC, DISC, MC, V. Lunch Mon–Sat 11:30am–3pm; dinner Mon–Thurs 5–11pm, Fri 5pm–midnight, Sat 4:30pm–midnight, Sun 4:30–11pm. Satay until 1am. CHINESE/SOUTHEAST ASIAN.

With sushi bars old hat these days, the satay bar may be a worthy replacement. Pull up a comfortable stool around the large grill and watch the cooks grill little skewers of anything from fresh produce to fish to pork to prawns to lamb. Each skewer is served with a small cube of sticky rice and a dipping sauce. Order three or four satay sticks and you have a meal. If you prefer to sit at a table and have a more traditional dinner, Wild Ginger can accommodate you. Try the pungent Prawns Assam—tiger prawns in a curry of tamarind, turmeric, candlenuts, chiles, and lemongrass. Accompany your meal with a pot of jasmine tea or a beer from China or Thailand for a real Southeast Asian experience. As in Asia, the lunch menu leans toward noodle dishes.

4   Seattle Center & the Lake Union Area

EXPENSIVE

Adriatica

1107 Dexter Ave. N. ☎ **206/285-5000.** Reservations recommended. Appetizers $6–$10.50; pastas $13.50–$18.50; entrées $15.50–$24. AE, DC, MC, V. Sun–Thurs 5–10pm, Fri–Sat 5–11pm. MEDITERRANEAN.

Go up a long flight of stairs, and once inside, you'll find the warm glowing walls, candlelight, white linens, and dark wood trim provides a suitable ambiance for savoring this widely hailed Mediterranean cuisine. An appetizer of garlic roasted with olive oil and rosemary and served with eggplant, goat cheese, and nicoise olives is a mélange of classic Mediterranean ingredients, while more "nouvelle" Mediterranean dishes include pork tenderloin marinated in olive oil and thyme with a cranberry sauce, a mixed grill with lamb in lemon and oregano, or red-pepper sausage wrapped in grape leaves. The atmosphere is elegant, but not stuffy, and the staff is very accommodating. A bar and dining room for smokers are upstairs, and tables both inside and outside on the tiny balcony are well situated for viewing Lake Union below.

Canlis

2576 Aurora Ave. N. ☎ **206/283-3313.** Reservations highly recommended. Jacket required for men. Appetizers $7.50–$10.50; main dishes $19.50–$30. AE, DC, MC, V. Dinner only, Mon–Sat 5:30–10pm. AMERICAN/CONTINENTAL.

Peter Canlis opened his first restaurant at Waikiki in 1947. It proved very popular with Seattleites fleeing Northwest damp, and they wished they had a Peter Canlis restaurant of their own. In 1950 they got their wish, and the restaurant has enjoyed unflagging popularity for more than 40 years now. The reason? It could be the perfectly prepared steaks and seafood, or it could be the excellent service by kimono-clad waitresses, or it could be the view across Lake Union from high on a hillside. Why not find out for yourself? This is the perfect place to close a big deal or celebrate a very special occasion. The perfect meal? Filet mignon with the restaurant's legendary baked potato, plus a salad tossed at your table, finished off with a Grand Marnier soufflé.

The Emerald Suite and Space Needle Restaurant

Seattle Center, 219 Fourth Ave. ☎ **206/443-2100.** Reservations required. Lunch $18–$20; main dishes $22–$31. Sun brunch $16.50–$19.50. AE, CB, DC, MC, V. Breakfast Mon–Sat 7–10:30am; lunch Mon–Sat 11am–3:30pm; dinner Mon–Sat 4–10:45pm, Sun 5–11pm; Sun brunch 8am–2:45pm. NORTHWEST.

There may not be a more difficult restaurant in Seattle to get into than The Emerald Suite at the Space Needle. With seating for only 50, the attractively decorated restaurant is cozy, elegant, and almost always booked solid. Both the prices and the views are some of the highest in the city, and this 500-foot high dining room rotates, assuring you a new vista with each course. The Space Needle Restaurant offers the same views in a more casual setting. Menus at both restaurants are almost identical.

Kamon on Lake Union

1177 Fairview Ave. N. ☎ **206/622-4665.** Reservations recommended. Main dishes $11–$19; lunch $6–$13. AE, JCB, MC, V. Lunch Mon–Fri 11:30am–2:30pm; dinner Sun–Thurs 5–9:30pm, Fri–Sat 5–10pm. JAPANESE/INTERNATIONAL.

Of the many big waterfront restaurants at the south end of Lake Union, Kamon is still my favorite. There are, of course, the views across the lake to the sunset sky and later the twinkling lights of the city, but there are also Asian-inspired dishes both traditional and contemporary. Sushi fans can take a seat at the long sushi bar, but, if it's summer, I'd much rather be sitting out on the deck. If you prefer a bit more lively entertainment with your meal, try a teppanyaki dinner and watch the chef cook your meal right at your table. Japanese, Chinese, Thai, and Indonesian dishes all show up on the menu, and forthose with a more nouvelle leaning, there are such dishes as pasta with smoked scallops in a ginger cream sauce, as well as raspberry teriyaki chicken.

⊕ Kaspar's

19 W. Harrison St. ☎ **206/298-0123.** Reservations recommended. Main courses $13–$19. AE, MC, V. Vintners dinners $55; chef's table dinners $50 for 5-course and $75 for 8-course. Tues–Thurs 5–9:30pm, Fri–Sat 5–10pm. INTERNATIONAL/ NORTHWEST.

Though Kaspar's has been around for years, the restaurant moved in 1994 to a new setting in a large sunny building in the Lower Queen Anne neighborhood. The main dining room is elegant yet spare, with dramatic lighting illuminating the tables, while in the lounge, there are long walls of glass that take in great summer sunsets. Kaspar's offers many dining options depending on your hunger and pocketbook. For the connoisseur and oenophile there are vintner's dinner. For the ultimate in personal service, try a chef's table dinner and dine in the kitchen with chef Kaspar Donier. For light meals, drinks and desserts, there's the lounge. The menu here draws on worldwide influences and produces such dishes as an Asian antipasto plate that includes a crab sushi roll, smoked ahi, and a vegetable spring roll. Pasta might be flavored with a fragrant and flavorful hazelnut-and-rosemary pesto, and mussels might be scented with lemongrass and curry. However, it is the scallops in spicy bacon sauce that has become the restaurant's signature dish.

✪ Pirosmani

2220 Queen Anne Ave. N. ☎ **206/285-3360.** Reservations recommended, especially on weekends. Entrées $16–$22. AE, DC, MC, V. Tues–Thurs 5:30–10pm, Fri–Sat 5:30–10:30pm. GEORGIAN/MEDITERRANEAN.

Named after the Georgian Republic's most famous artist, Pirosmani is a small, informal restaurant in a Victorian home in the Queen Anne district. The chef pulls her uncommon gastronomic references both from Georgia and the sunny Mediterranean. For starters, you may whet your appetite with such dishes as juicy traditional Georgian pork and beef dumplings seasoned with mint, onion, green pepper and paprika, or chicken breast stuffed with olives, bulgur and wrapped in grape leaves. The detail and attention given to each dish—lamb, duck, rabbit, and fresh fish—makes each one distinctively different, but I most recommend the tuna wrapped in grape leaves with an unexpected tart and savory sauce containing pomegranate, walnuts, and roasted red peppers. Save room for one of the light and unusually flavored desserts.

MODERATE

Kayak Lakefront Grill

1200 Westlake Ave. N. ☎ 206/284-2535. Reservations recommended. Main dishes $7.50–$16. AE, DC, JCB, MC, V. Lunch Mon–Fri 11:30am–2:15pm; dinner Sun–Thurs 5–9pm, Fri–Sat 5–10pm. Light meals served 3:30pm–2am. SEAFOOD.

The marina in front of Kayak brings a very upscale yachting crowd to this large seafood restaurant on Lake Union, but the prices are extremely reasonable. Overhead fans turn languidly, and through the floor-to-ceiling windows you can watch sailboats drift slowly past the looming skyscrapers of downtown. It's all very casually sophisticated.

The Kayak is best known for its grilled fish, but the extensive menu also lists steak, pasta, and chicken, as well as daily specials. Cajun preparations are a staple here, and so are Northwest, Italian, and French dishes. To accompany your meal, there is an excellent selection of wines by the glass or by the bottle.

✪ Serafina

2043 Eastlake Ave. E. ☎ 206/323-0807. Reservations recommended. Pastas $8–$13; entrées $10–$15. MC, V. Lunch Mon–Fri 11:30am–2pm; dinner Sun–Thurs 5:30–10pm, Fri–Sat 5:30–11pm. ITALIAN/EUROPEAN.

The atmosphere is rustic and serves to underscore the earthy Italian country dishes here. It's one of my favorite dining spots, with just a touch of sophistication in an oversize floral arrangement, a casual ambiance in the stacked wine bottles and loaves of bread. In the summer, there's dining in the romantic garden courtyard. For starters, try the antipasti or fresh mussels smoked in a leek, vermouth and lime broth. Among the pastas you'll find are penne pasta with artichokes and spinach in a leek and gorgonzola cream sauce, and linguine with prawns in a spicy sauce of olives, tomatoes, anchovies, and capers. For a main dish try a classic that will conjure up dreams of Italy— Italian sausages sautéed with grapes and onions and served with soft polenta. Nearly every evening there is jazz and Latin-influenced live music.

5 First Hill, Capitol Hill & East Seattle

EXPENSIVE

✪ The Hunt Club

Sorrento Hotel, 900 Madison St. ☎ **206/343-6156.** Reservations recommended. Main dishes $19–$26. AE, DC, MC, V. Breakfast Mon–Fri 7–10am, Sat–Sun 7am–noon; lunch Mon–Fri 11am–2:30pm; dinner Sun–Thurs 5:30–10pm, Fri–Sat 5:30–11pm. NORTHWEST.

The Hunt Club is just the sort of place its name would indicate—dark, intimate, well suited to business lunches and romantic celebrations. Mahogany paneling lines the walls, and deep rose upholstery adds rich color. If you need a little privacy, folding louvered doors can create private dining areas.

Menus balance French, Italian, and Asian influences and flavors while stirring in a generous helping of Northwest ingredients. Whether you are having a quick meal in the lounge, a light lunch, or a four-course dinner, you'll find creativity a keystone of the menu. You might start a meal with dungeness crab risotto with wild mushrooms or butternut squash raviolis with rock shrimp, and then move on to grilled king salmon with succotash or alderwood and rosemary–smoked rack of lamb. For dessert, you can choose from creme brule, tiramisu, or raspberry roulade.

✪ Rover's

2808 E. Madison St. ☎ **206/325-7442.** Reservations required. Main dishes $22.75–$26.95; five-course menu degustation $44.50–$54.50. AE, DC, MC, V. Dinner only, Tues–Sat 5:30–11pm. NORTHWEST.

Tucked away in a quaint clapboard house behind a chic little shopping center is one of Seattle's most talked about restaurants. Chef Thierry Rautureau received classic French training before falling in love with the Northwest and all the wonderful ingredients it had to offer an imaginative chef.

Voilà! Northwest cuisine with a French accent. Or is it French cuisine with a Northwest accent? Find out for yourself. If the salad of wild greens and edible flowers is on the daily changing menu, don't pass it by; the flavors are delicately Northwest. Perennial appetizer favorites include warm foie gras salad, sometimes served with wild greens and a balsamic vinegar sauce, and vegetable flans with caramelized turnips and a red burgundy sauce. Among main dishes you will likely encounter salmon or halibut, with pomme mousseline, an ocean salad, and one of Rautureau's imaginative sauces with dry vermouth; or roasted squab with green lentils and a black peppercorn sauce.

In summer, don't miss the raspberry desserts—or, for that matter, the desserts at any time of year.

MODERATE
Cactus
4220 E. Madison St. ☎ **206/324-4140.** Reservations recommended for 6 or more. Main dishes $9–$12; lunch $6–$8.50. DISC, MC, V. Lunch Mon–Sat 11:30am–2:30pm; dinner Mon–Thurs 5–9:30pm, Fri–Sat 5–10pm, Sun 5–9pm. NEW MEXICAN.

Northwesterners seem constantly to shuttle back and forth between Northwest and Southwest. Perhaps it is the lack of light in winter that sends them winging southward to sunnier states. Now, however, it is not necessary to go any farther than Madison Park to fire up your life with a bit of New Mexican cooking. At Cactus the decor is straight out of Santa Fe, with strings of chiles hanging from the ceiling, stucco walls, and Mexican *ranchera* music on the stereo. How about a plate of cactus salad to start—no spines, guaranteed. A selection of tapas such as empanadas or Spanish style tortillas also make good starters.

You can assemble your own fajitas with tender marinated beef, or try a couple of soft tacos. The pork steak adobo, made with smoky chipotle peppers and orange juice is a medley of powerful flavors that shouldn't be missed. For dessert, try the three-milk flan.

⊛ Café Flora
2901 E. Madison St. ☎ **206/325-9100.** Reservations taken for 8 or more. Main dishes $7.25–$14. MC, V. Tues–Fri 11:30am–10pm, Sat 5–10pm; brunch Sat–Sun 9am–2pm. VEGETARIAN.

Big and bright and airy, this cafe will dispel any ideas about vegetarian food being boring. This is meatless gourmet cooking and it's delicious. The menu changes weekly and might include a sauté of shiitake mushrooms, onion, peppers, carrots, and celery, seasoned with lemongrass, basil, ginger, lime, and coconut milk, and served with basmati rice and fruit chutney. Unusual pizzas typically are on the menu. A recent artichoke pesto pizza camewith artichoke heart pesto, fried Yukon gold potatoes, radicchio, and goat cheese.

The roasted eggplant sandwich is especially popular at lunch. The dessert tray brought to your table always has plenty of temptations, such as a chocolate mousse pie with whole strawberries inside. In the summer, you can sit on the patio.

13 Coins Restaurant
125 Boren Ave., N. ☎ **206/682-2513.** Reservations recommended for parties of six or more. Main dishes $9.75–$39.95. AE, MC, V. Daily 24 hours. CONTINENTAL.

The name comes from a Peruvian legend about a poor boy who had only 13 coins in his pocket to offer for the hand in marriage of the girl he loved. Embedded in each of the tables at these two restaurants you will find 13 coins. The star attraction here is the exhibition cooking, but what keeps fans loyal are the gargantuan portions. Every meal is enough for two people! The menu offers all the standard continental favorites. The second 13 Coins is at 18000 Pacific Highway S. (☎ 206/243-9500).

INEXPENSIVE

Pizzeria Pagliacci

426 Broadway E. ☎ **206/324-0730.** Reservations not accepted. Pizza $7.50–$16.50. AE, MC, V. Sun–Thurs 11am–11pm, Fri–Sat 11am–1am. PIZZA.

Pagliacci's pizza was voted the best in Seattle, and they now have three popular locations. Although you can order a traditional cheese pizza, there are much more interesting pies on the menu, like pesto pizza or the sun-dried tomato primo. It's strictly counter service here, but there are plenty of seats at each of the bright restaurants. For those in a hurry or who just want a snack, there is pizza by the slice. Pagliacci is also at 550 Queen Anne Ave. N. (☎ 206/285-1232) and at 4529 University Way NE (☎ 206/632-0421).

Siam on Broadway

616 Broadway E. ☎ **206/324-0892.** Reservations recommended on weekends. Main dishes $5.75–$8.25; lunches $5–$8.25. AE, MC, V. Mon–Thurs 11:30am–10pm, Fri 11:30am–11pm, Sat 5–11pm, Sun 5–10pm. THAI.

All the way at the north end of the Broadway shopping district in trendy Capitol Hill is one of Seattle's best inexpensive Thai restaurants. In fact, the food's generally as good as you'll get in Thailand, and that's saying a lot when you can't always come up with all the necessary ingredients. Siam on Broadway is small and very casual. The tom yum soups, made with either shrimp or chicken, are the richest and creamiest I've ever had—also some of the spiciest. If you prefer your food less fiery, let your server know; the cooks will prepare any meal with one to four stars, depending on how much fire you can handle. But remember that they mean it when they say superhot. The phad Thai (spicy fried noodles) is excellent, and the muu phad bai graplau (spicy meat and vegetables, one of my all-time favorites) is properly fragrant with chiles and basil leaves.

A second, and much larger, restaurant, Siam on Lake Union, is located at 1880 Fairview Ave. E. (☎ 206/323-8101).

Vietnam's Pearl

708 Rainier Ave. S. ☎ **206/726-1581.** Reservations recommended. Main dishes $4.25–$15. AE, CB, DC, MC, V. Sun–Thurs 11am–10pm, Fri–Sat 10am–midnight. VIETNAMESE.

Located in an unremarkable neighborhood about a mile or two from Pioneer Square, Vietnam's Pearl is very popular with local Vietnamese. You'll also find plenty of other folks from all over the Seattle area descending on the restaurant's Spartan dining room. What has people driving across town to a neighborhood eatery is great food at budget prices. The menu is long and only shrimp and some fish dishes will run you more than $7. If you are willing to order adventurously, you are certain to encounter several new tastes and flavor combinations. The ginger chicken is a particular standout. One of my favorite dishes is minced shrimp wrapped around sugarcane.

6   North Seattle

EXPENSIVE

Ponti Seafood Grill

3014 Third Ave. N. ☎ **206/284-3000.** Reservations recommended. Main courses $14–$23.50; early dinners $13.95. AE, MC, V. Lunch Mon–Sat 11:30am–2:30pm; dinner Sun–Thurs 5:30–10pm, Fri–Sat 5:30–11pm; Sun brunch 10am–2:30pm. SEAFOOD.

Situated at the south end of the Fremont Bridge and overlooking the Lake Washington Ship Canal, Ponti is one of Seattle's most elegant and sophisticated restaurants. The menu here has an international flavor, though it also offers some solidly northwestern creations. On a recent evening, the appetizers list included a decadent dish of smoked salmon served with a corn pancake, vodka crème fraîche, chives, and caviar. Oysters on the half shell came with a choice of mignonette, cilantro pesto, or pickled ginger. For a pleasing twist on a classic, try the Caesar salad with smoked prawns. The pasta menu always includes some highly creative dishes such as Dungeness crab ravioli with herbs and champagne buerre blanc, and the daily listing of fresh seafoods might include such tempting entrées as macadamia nut crusted marlin with Chinese plum-wine sauce and pineapple salsa. The early dinners are served between 5 and 6pm.

MODERATE

Café Lago

2305 24th Ave. E. ☎ **206/329-8005.** Reservations not accepted. Main courses $9–$12.50. AE, DISC, MC, V. Sun–Thurs 5–9:30pm, Fri–Sat 5–10pm. ITALIAN.

This casual trattoria is located in the Montlake district just south of the University of Washington, and bakes some of the best *rustica*-style pizzas in Seattle. These gourmet pizzas are as visually appealing as they are delicious and include such ingredients as *bresaola,* an air-dried beef, and *coppa,* a peppered pork shoulder. If you're here with a few friends, by all means, start with the big antipasto plate, which comes with roast garlic, *crostini,* and several different cheeses among other things. The lasagnes and raviolis may be even more popular than the pizzas. The menu changes weekly.

Ivar's Salmon House

401 NE Northlake Way. ☎ **206/632-0767.** Reservations recommended. Main dishes $10.45–$19; fish bar $4–$7. AE, MC, V. Main restaurant—lunch Mon–Fri 11:30am–2:30pm; dinner Mon–Thurs 4:30–10pm, Fri 4:30–11pm, Sat 4–11pm, Sun 4–10pm; Sun brunch 10am–2pm. Fish bar—Sun–Thurs 11:30am–10pm, Fri–Sat 11am–11pm. SEAFOOD.

This Ivar's commands an excellent view of the Seattle skyline from the north end of Lake Union. Floating docks out back act as magnets for weekend boaters who abandon their own galley fare in favor of the restaurant's clam chowder and famous alder-smoked salmon. The theme here is Northwest Coast Indian, and the building has even won an award from the Seattle Historical Society for its replica of a tribal longhouse. Inside are many artifacts, including long dugout canoes and historic photographic portraits of Native American chiefs. Kids, and adults, love this place.

⑤ Le Gourmand

425 NW Market St. ☎ **206/784-3463.** Reservations required. Three-course fixed-price dinners $18–$28. AE, CB, DC, MC, V. Dinner only, Wed–Sat 5:30–midnight. FRENCH/NORTHWEST.

On an otherwise forgettable corner in the Ballard neighborhood of north Seattle stands a tiny building that looks as if it might once have been a laundry or dry cleaner. Chefs Bruce Naftaly and Robin Sanders, former music students who came to Seattle to study voice, have converted this aging storefront into a memorable French restaurant. With only a handful of tables, service is very personal and the atmosphere is very inviting, with a woodland mural in airy colors that wraps around the walls and silk pillows and bolsters as accents.

On the back of the menu you'll find a list of all the ingredients used at the restaurant, from hand-made cheeses to line-caught fish to organically grown herbs and vegetables, and where they come from (neighborhood gardens, in the case of some of the herbs). A nice touch. On my last visit the menu included a pâté of rabbit livers flavored with cognac, port, and thyme for a starter. There was a choice of eight different main dishes, but the roast rack of lamb with a sauce of homemade mustard flavored with roasted and pickled red peppers was perfect for a cold winter's night. A choice from the tempting pastry tray is not included in the fixed-price dinner.

Ray's Boathouse and Cafe

6049 Seaview Ave. NW. ☎ **206/789-3770.** Reservations downstairs, recommended on weekends; upstairs not necessary. Appetizers $4–$9; main dishes $11–$27; prices slightly lower upstairs; early dinners $13. AE, CB, DC, MC, V. Lunch Mon–Fri 11:30am–2pm; dinner Mon–Thurs 5–10pm, Fri 5–10:30pm, Sat 4:30–10:30pm, Sun 4:30–10pm. Early dinners served 5–6pm. SEAFOOD/STEAK.

Upstairs at Ray's, where you'll find the lounge, thecrowd of sun-tanned boating types can get pretty rowdy. The restaurant compensates by reducing the price of the food here, but waits of up to an hour for a table are not unusual. Downstairs, everything is quiet, cozy, and sophisticated.

Luckily, everyone gets fine meals. As at other Seattle restaurants, fresh herbs make bold appearances on the menu in dishes such as manila clam fettucine with peppered bacon and fresh herbs in garlic lemon cream. There are many delicious reasons why this is considered one of the best restaurants in Seattle.

Trattoria Mitchelli

84 Yesler Way. ☎ **206/623-3883.** Reservations not taken. Appetizers $3.25–$6.25; pastas $6.85–$8; main dishes $8.25–$10; lunches $4.50–$7.50. AE, DC, MC, V. Tues–Fri 7am–4am, Sat 8am–4am, Sun 8am–11pm, Mon 7am–11pm. ITALIAN.

Located only a few steps toward the water from Pioneer Square, Trattoria Mitchelli is a cozy place with a friendly old-world atmosphere. The white tiled waiting area has large windows that let in the warm summer air and salty breezes. An old circular bar in the counter

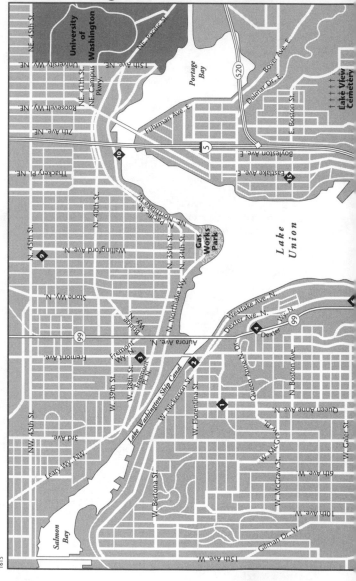

room is a popular after-work and late-night gathering spot; candles flicker in Chianti bottles, and conversation is lively. There is a selection of chicken and veal dishes, all of which are worth trying. The pizza kitchen and bar features pizza and calzone baked in a wood oven. If you're a night owl, keep Mitchelli's in mind—they serve full meals right through to 4am.

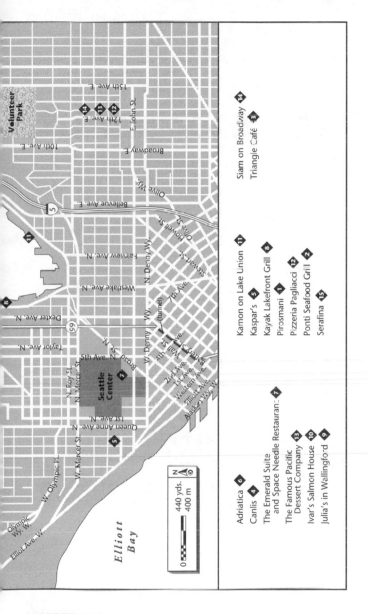

Siam on Broadway 14
Triangle Café 3

Kamon on Lake Union 11
Kaspar's 5
Kayak Lakefront Grill 8
Pirosmani 1
Pizzeria Pagliacci 12
Ponti Seafood Grill 2
Serafina 15

Adriatica 6
Canlis 4
**The Emerald Suite
and Space Needle Restauran:** 7
**The Famous Pacific
Dessert Company** 13
Ivar's Salmon House 10
Julia's in Wallingfo·d 9

Elliott Bay

Volunteer Park

Seattle Center

INEXPENSIVE

Triangle Café

3507 Fremont Place N. ☎ **206/632-0880.** Reservations not accepted. Entrées
$7.25–$9. MC, V. Lunch daily 11:30am–3pm; dinner Mon Thurs 5–10pm,
Fri–Sat 5–11pm. INTERNATIONAL.

Located in the middle of the Fremont neighborhood, this relaxed restaurant, with both a cafe and a bar/lounge area, is a local hang-out. The restaurant serves cheap and imaginative sandwiches from grilled eggplant to char-broiled steak, pasta, pizzas, fish, and a selection of draft beers. Look around for triangle images—on the wall there's a Superman logo, a map of the Bermuda triangle, and a pyramid.

7 Cafés, Coffee Bars & Tea Rooms

Unless you've been on Mars the past few years, you're likely aware that Seattle has become the espresso capital of America. Seattleites are positively rabid about coffee. Coffee isn't just a hot drink or a caffeine fix anymore, it's a way of life. Espresso and its creamy cousin latte (made with one part espresso to three parts milk) are the stuff that this city runs on, and you will never be more than about a block from your next cup. There are espresso carts on the sidewalks, drive-through espresso windows, espresso bars, espresso milk shakes, espresso chocolates, even eggnog lattes at Christmas. The ruling coffee king is **Starbucks,** a chain of dozens of coffee bars where you can buy your java by the cup or by the pound. They sell some 36 types and blends of coffee, and you can find their shops all over the city. **SBC,** formerly Stewart Brothers Coffee and also known as Seattle's Best Coffee, doesn't have as many shops as Starbucks, but it does have a very devoted clientele.

Coffee bars and cafes are rapidly overtaking bars as the most popular places to hang out and visit with friends. Among my favorite Seattle cafés are the following:

Counter Intelligence, 94 Pike St., Pike Place Market (☎ 206/ 622-6979). This cozy, quiet place is hidden away on the second floor of building across Pike Street from the Pike Place Market information booth.

The Crumpet Shop, 1503 First Ave. (☎ 206/682-1598). If coffee isn't your cup of tea, check out this tea shop in Pike Place Market. As the name implies, crumpets are the specialty.

The Famous Pacific Dessert Company, 516 Broadway E. (☎ 206/ 328-1950). In this spiffy spot near Capitol Hill with white linen–covered tables, you can indulge in one of more than 30 cakes and tortes. Several nights a week, there's live piano and jazz music.

The Green Room Café, 4026 Stone Way N. (☎ 206/632-6420). In an old house on a nondescript street, the Green Room is a warren of cozy little rooms decorated in a funky college style. The fireplace is great on a cold rainy night. Great desserts.

110 Espress + Panini Bar, 110 Union St. (☎ 206/343-8733). The very contemporary decor and artwork in this bright little downtown cafe make this a popular spot. Good soups and sandwiches.

Still Life in Fremont Coffeehouse, 709 N. 35th St. (☎ 206/ 547-9850). Fremont is Seattle's most eclectic neighborhood, and Still Life reflects this eclecticism. It's big and always crowded. Good vegetarian meals.

Torrefazione, 320 Occidental Ave. S. (☎ 206/624-5773), and also at 622 Olive Way, (☎ 206/624-1429). With its hand-painted Italian crockery, Torrefazione has the feel of a classic Italian cafe. The one in the Pioneer Square area has much more atmosphere. Great pastries.

Zio Rico, 1415 Fourth Ave. (☎ 206/467-8616). This is the most elegant cafe in Seattle, with big, comfortable easy chairs and lots of dark, wood paneling. A great place to sit and read the *Wall Street Journal.*

6

What to See & Do in Seattle

Seattle is a relatively new city, and until recently it was considered a
cultural backwater rich in natural beauty. Things have changed on
the cultural front, but the city's natural surroundings are still one of
the city's primary attractions. You can easily cover all of Seattle's
museums and major sights in two or three days. With the help of the
itineraries below, you should have a good idea of what not to miss.
After that, rent a car and head for the great outdoors. You have your
choice of islands, ocean beaches, or mountains, all of which can be
enjoyed in any season.

The itineraries outlined here will give you an understanding of the
history, natural resources, and cultural diversity that have made Seattle
the city it is today.

SUGGESTED ITINERARIES

If You Have 1 Day

Day 1   Start your day in the historic Pioneer Square District and take
the earliest Seattle Underground Tour you can. You'll have fun and get
a good idea of Seattle's early history. From Pioneer Square, walk down
to the waterfront and head north. You'll pass numerous seafood restaurants, all quite good. Stop in at the Seattle Aquarium and learn about
the sea life of the region. At Pier 55 you can get a one-hour harbor tour
cruise. Continue along the waterfront until you reach the signs for Pike
Place Market, which is on the far side of the elevated highway and up
a hill. In the market, you can buy fresh salmon and Dungeness crabs
packed to go and much more. From Pike Place Market, walk to the
monorail station in Westlake Center, which is at the corner of Pine
Street and Fourth Avenue. The monorail will take you to Seattle Center, where you can ride an elevator to the top of the Space Needle.
Seattle's best-known landmark. Finish the day with dinner at one of
the city's many restaurants serving seafood or Northwest cuisine.

If You Have 2 Days

Day 1   Start your first day in Pioneer Square, as outlined above. After
the Seattle Underground Tour, head over to the nearby International
District (Chinatown) and have lunch in a Chinese restaurant. Hing

Loon is my favorite. After lunch, head over to the waterfront for a harbor cruise, a stop at the aquarium and Ye Olde Curiosity Shop, and dine at one of the seafood restaurants.

Day 2   Start your second day at Pike Place Market, and be sure to arrive early to get the freshest fish (they'll pack it to take on the plane). From here it is only two blocks to the new Seattle Art Museum. After touring the museum, take the lunch tour to Tillicum Village. You'll see Northwest Native American dances while dining on alder-smoked salmon. When you return to Seattle, head for Seattle Center and the Space Needle.

If You Have 3 Days

Days 1–2   Follow the two-day strategy outlined above.
Day 3   Take a trip out of the city to the Olympic Peninsula, the San Juan Islands, or the Mount Rainier area. All these trips can be turned into overnighters or longer, but if you plan on a day trip, leave early.

If You Have 5 Days or More

Days 1–2   Follow the two-day strategy, as outlined above.
Days 3–4   Stay a night or two somewhere like Port Townsend on the Olympic Peninsula or at a bed-and-breakfast in the beautiful San Juan Islands. Or better yet, take the ferry from the San Juans to the Olympic Peninsula and then back to Seattle. This makes a great loop.
Day 5   Visit Mount St. Helens and stop at the Museum of Flight on your way south.

1   The Top Attractions

✪ Museum of Flight

9404 E. Marginal Way S. ☎ **206/764-5720.** Admission $6 adults, $3 ages 6–15, under age 6 free. Free first Thursday from 5 to 9pm. Daily 10am–5pm (until 9pm Thurs). Closed Christmas. Bus: 174. Directions: Take exit 158 off I-5.

Located right next door to busy Boeing Field, 10 minutes south of downtown Seattle, is one of the world's best museums dedicated to the history of flight. Aviation buffs will be walking on air when they visit this cavernous repository of some of history's most famous planes. A six-story glass-and-steel building holds most of the collection, and a viewing area lets you watch planes take off and land at the adjacent airport. There is a replica of the Wright brothers' first glider to start things off, and then the exhibits bring you right up to the present state of flight. Suspended in the Great Hall are 20 planes, including a DC-3 and the first air force F-5 supersonic fighter. You'll also see the Blackbird, the world's fastest jet; a rare World War II Corsair fighter rescued from Lake Washington and restored to its original glory; and an exhibit on the U.S. space program featuring an Apollo command module. Other planes have been grounded and can be examined up close. See Chapter 6, Section 3, below, for information on a tour of the Boeing plant.

Museum of History & Industry

2700 24th Ave. E. ☎ **206/324-1126.** Admission $5.50 adults, $3 senior citizens and ages 6–12, $1 for ages 2–5, under age 2 free. Tuesday by donation. Daily 10am–5pm. Closed Thanksgiving, Christmas, and New Year's Day. Bus: 25, 43, or 48.

You can learn about the history of Seattle and the Northwest in this museum at the north end of Washington Park Arboretum. There is a Boeing mail plane from the 1920s, plus an exhibit on the 1889 fire that leveled the city. If the Seattle Underground Tour's vivid description of prefire life has you curious about what the city's more respectable citizens were doing back in the 1880s, you can find out here, where re-created storefronts provide glimpses into their lives. This museum also hosts touring exhibitions that address Northwest history.

Omnidome Film Experience

Pier 59, Waterfront Park. ☎ **206/622-1868.** Admission $6 adults, $5 senior citizens and ages 13–18, $4 ages 3–12, under age 3 free. Sun–Thurs 10am–9pm, Fri–Sat 10am–11pm. Bus: 15 or 18; then walk down Pike Place hill climb. TROLLEY: To Pike Place Market stop.

This huge wraparound theater is located adjacent to the Seattle Aquarium, and on my last visit was showing a film about the eruption of Mount St. Helens. The Omnidome, for those who have never experienced it, is a movie theater with a 180° screen that fills your peripheral vision and puts you right in the middle of the action. People with hangovers or who get motion sickness should stay away!

Pacific Science Center

200 Second Ave. N., Seattle Center. ☎ **206/443-2001** or 206/443-2880. Admission $6 adults, $5 ages 6–13 and senior citizens, $3.50 ages 2–5, under 2 free. IMAX $5.50 adults, $4.50 ages 6–13 and senior citizens, $3.50 ages 2–5. Laser show $6 for evening performances ($3 on Tuesday), $2 for matinee performances as add-on to general-admission ticket only. June–Sept, daily 10am–6pm; Oct–May, Mon–Fri 10am–5pm, Sat–Sun 10am–6pm. Closed Christmas. Bus: 1, 2, 3, 4, 6, 13, 15, 16, 18, 19, 24, or 33. Monorail: To Seattle Center station.

Although exhibits are aimed primarily at children, the Pacific Science Center is fun for all ages. The main goal of this sprawling complex at Seattle Center is to teach kids about science and to instill a desire to study it. To that end, there are dozens of fun hands-on exhibits addressing the biological sciences, physics, and chemistry. Kids learn how their bodies work, blow giant bubbles, and experiment with robots. There is a planetarium for learning about the skies, plus laser shows. Even more interesting are the many special exhibits. There are also special events, including a bubble festival. An IMAX theater has daily showings of short films on its huge $3^1/_2$-story-high screen. (For map of Seattle Center, see below.)

✪ Pike Place Market

Between Pike St. and Pine St. (at First Ave.). ☎ **206/682-7453.** Free admission. Mon–Sat 9am–6pm, Sun 11am–5pm. Closed New Year's Day, Easter, Memorial Day weekend, July 4, Labor Day, Thanksgiving, Christmas. Any downtown bus. Waterfront Trolley: To Pike Place Market stop.

Pike Place Market, a farmers' market, was founded in 1907 when housewives complained that middlemen were raising the price of

Seattle Attractions

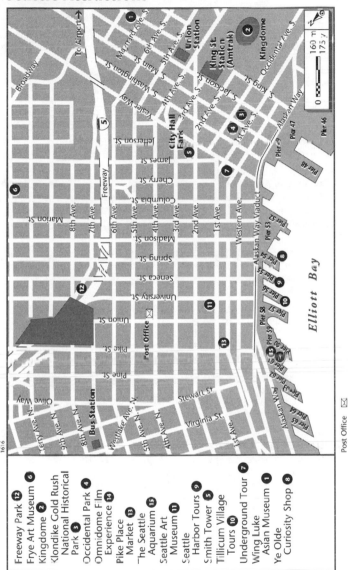

Freeway Park **12**

Frye Art Museum **6**

Kingdome **2**

Klondike Gold Rush National Historical Park **3**

Occidental Park **4**

Omnidome Film Experience **14**

Pike Place Market **13**

The Seattle Aquarium **15**

Seattle Art Museum **11**

Seattle Harbor Tours **9**

Smith Tower **5**

Tillicum Village Tours **10**

Underground Tour **7**

Wing Luke Asian Museum **1**

Ye Olde Curiosity Shop **8**

produce too high. The market allowed shoppers to buy directly from producers, and thus save on grocery bills. By the 1960s, however, the market was no longer the popular spot it had once been. World War II had deprived it of nearly half its farmers when Japanese Americans were moved to internment camps. The postwar flight to the suburbs almost spelled the end for the market, and the site was being eyed for a major redevelopment project. However, a grassroots movement to save the 9-acre market culminated in its being declared a National Historic District.

Today it is once again bustling, but the 100 or so farmers and fishmongers who set up shop here are only a small part of the attraction. More than 200 local craftspeople and artists can be found selling their creations throughout the year. There are excellent restaurants, and hundreds of shops fill the market area. Street performers—including mimes, sitar players, and hammered-dulcimer players—serenade milling crowds. There is an information booth almost directly below the large Pike Place Market sign where you can pick up a free map and guide to the market. Watch for the flying fish and Rachel the giant piggy bank.

✪ The Seattle Aquarium

Pier 59, Waterfront Park. ☎ **206/386-4320.** Admission $6.95 adults, $5.50 senior citizens, $4.50 ages 6–18, $2.25 ages 3–5. Labor Day–Memorial Day, daily 10am–5pm; Memorial Day–Labor Day, daily 10am–7pm. Bus: 15 or 18; then walk down Pike Place.

The highly acclaimed Seattle Aquarium, in the heart of the waterfront, is a fascinating place to spend a few hours learning about marine and freshwater life in the Northwest. From the underwater viewing dome, you'll get a fish's-eye view of life beneath the waves. A salmon ladder is particularly exciting when the salmon return to the aquarium to spawn (autumn). There is a beautiful large coral-reef tank, as well as many smaller tanks that exhibit fish from local and distant waters. A telling exhibit on the pollution of Puget Sound shows the effect of human population expansion not only on the Sound but also on the area's salmon-spawning streams.

One of the aquarium's most popular exhibits is an interactive tide pool and discovery lab that re-creates Washington's wave-swept intertidal zone. As part of the exhibit, a video microscope provides a magnified glimpse of the seldom-seen world of plankton.

Seattle Asian Art Museum

Volunteer Park, 14th Ave. E. and E. Prospect St. ☎ **206/654-3100.** Admission $6 adults, $4 students and senior citizens, ages 12 and under free. Free to all on first Tuesday of each month. Admission ticket also valid at Seattle Art Museum if used within two days. Tues–Sun 10am–5pm (Thurs until 9pm; first Tues of each month until 7pm). Closed Thanksgiving, Christmas, and New Year's Day. Bus: 10.

The Seattle Art Museum's extensive Asian collection finally got the space it deserved when this museum opened in 1994. Housed in the renovated Art Deco building that once served as the city's main art museum, the Asian art collection has an emphasis on Chinese and Japanese art but also includes pieces from Korea, Southeast Asia, South Asia, and the Himalayas. The Chinese terra-cotta funerary art, snuff bottles, and Japanese *netsukes* (belt decorations) are among the more notable collections. One room is devoted almost exclusively to Japanese screens and painting while another holds Japanese folk art, including several old kimonos. The central hall is devoted to the stone religious sculptures of South Asia (primarily India). Special exhibits change every six months.

Seattle Art Museum

100 University St. ☎ 206/654-3100. Admission $6 adults, $4 senior citizens and students, ages 12 and under free. Free to all on first Tuesday of each month. Admission ticket also valid at Seattle Asian Art Museum if used within two days. Tues–Sun 10am–5pm (Thurs until 9pm; first Tues of each month until 7pm). Closed Thanksgiving, Christmas, and New Year's Day. Bus: 10, 12, 15, 18, 21, 22, or 23 or any bus using the bus tunnel.

Despite the controversy that surrounded the opening of the Seattle Art Museum, this is the city's premier museum and a point of civic pride. Out front, Jonathon Borofsky's *Hammering Man*, a giant black silhouette of a steel sculpture, toils unceasingly, while inside, a grand staircase leads from the main entrance to rooms devoted to special exhibits. One floor higher, you'll find one of the nation's premier collections of Northwest Coast Native American art and artifacts and an equally large collection of African art. These displays juxtapose cultures rich in expressive religious and decorative art. Also on this floor is an extensive collection of Asian art. On the top floor, you'll find the museum's collection of European and American art, covering the ancient Mediterranean to the medieval, Renaissance, and Baroque periods in Europe. A large 18th-century collection and a smaller 19th-century exhibition lead up to a large 20th-century collection that includes a room devoted to Northwest contemporary art.

Space Needle

203 Sixth Ave. N., Seattle Center. ☎ 206/443-2100. Admission $7 adults, $6.50 senior citizens, $3.50 ages 5–12, ages 4 and under free. Memorial Day–Labor Day, daily 7am–midnight; day after Labor Day–day before Memorial Day, daily 8am–midnight. Bus: 1, 2, 3, 4, 6, 13, 15, 16, 18, 19, 24, or 33. Monorail: To Seattle Center station.

From a distance it resembles a flying saucer on top of a tripod, and when it was built it was meant to suggest future architectural trends. Erected for the 1962 World's Fair, the 600-foot-tall tower is the most popular tourist sight in Seattle. At 518 feet above ground level, the views from the observation deck are stunning, and there are displays identifying more than 60 sites and activities in the Seattle area. High-powered telescopes let you zoom in on things. You'll also find a history of the Space Needle, a lounge, and two very expensive restaurants. If you don't mind standing in line and paying quite a bit for an elevator ride, make this your first stop in Seattle so you can orient yourself.

2 More Attractions

MUSEUMS

Burke Museum

17th Ave. NE and NE 45th St. ☎ 206/543-5590. Donation, $3 adults, $2 students and seniors, $1.50 ages 6–18. Daily 10am–5pm. Closed July 4, Thanksgiving, Christmas, and New Year's Day. Bus: 70, 71, 72, 73, or 74.

Located in the northwest corner of the University of Washington campus, the Burke Museum features exhibits on the natural and cultural heritage of the Pacific Rim. It is noteworthy primarily for its Northwest

Native American art collection and an active schedule of special exhibits. Down in the basement, there is a large collection of minerals and fossils. In front of the museum stand replicas of totem poles carved in the 1870s and 1880s. There is also an ethnobotanical garden displaying plants used by northwestern tribes. Campus parking is very expensive on weekdays and Saturday mornings, so try to visit on a Saturday afternoon or a Sunday.

Frye Art Museum

704 Terry St. (at Cherry St.). ☎ **206/622-9250.** Free admission. Mon–Sat 10am–5pm, Sun noon–5pm. Closed Thanksgiving and Christmas. Bus: 3, 4, or 12.

This small museum on First Hill exhibits the extensive personal collection of Charles and Emma Frye. The collection focuses primarily on late 19th-century painters, but also includes quite a few works by American artists. There are works by Thomas Hart Benton, Edward Hopper, Albert Bierstadt, and Pablo Picasso, as well as a large collection of engravings by Winslow Homer. There are special exhibits that change monthly. The museum will be closed for renovation until October 1996.

✪ Henry Art Gallery

University of Washington, 15th Ave. NE and NE 41st St. ☎ **206/543-2280.** Admission $3.50 adults, $2 students and senior citizens, ages 12 and under free. Thurs by donation. Tues–Sun 11am–5pm (Thurs until 9pm). Closed Thanksgiving, Christmas, and New Year's Day. Bus: 7, 43, 70, 71, 72, 73, or 74.

This small museum on the University of Washington campus mounts interesting temporary exhibits throughout the year. The focus is primarily on contemporary art with retrospectives of individual artists, as well as exhibits focusing on specific themes or media. Call for information on the current show.

Klondike Gold Rush National Historical Park

117 S. Main St. ☎ **206/553-7220.** Free admission. Daily 9am–5pm. Closed Thanksgiving, Christmas, and New Year's Day. Bus: 15, 18, 21, 22, or 23. Waterfront Trolley: To Occidental Park stop.

It isn't in the Klondike (which isn't even in the United States) and it isn't really a park (it's a single room in an old store), but it is a fascinating little museum. "At 3 o'clock this morning the steamship *Portland,* from St. Michaels for Seattle, passed up [Puget] Sound with more than a ton of gold on board and 68 passengers." When the *Seattle Post-Intelligencer* published that sentence on July 17, 1897, they started a stampede. Would-be miners heading for the Klondike goldfields in the 1890s made Seattle their outfitting center and helped turn it into a prosperous city. When they struck it rich up north, they headed back to Seattle, the first outpost of civilization, and unloaded their gold, making Seattle doubly rich. It seems only fitting that this museum should be here. Film buffs can catch a free screening of Charles Chaplin's great film *The Gold Rush* the first Sunday of each month at 3pm. Another unit of the park is centered in Skagway, Alaska.

Wing Luke Asian Museum

407 Seventh Ave. S. ☎ **206/623-5124.** Admission $2.50 adults, $1.50 students and senior citizens, 75¢ ages 5–12, under 5 free. Free to all on Thursday. Tues–Fri 11am–4:30pm, Sat–Sun noon–4pm. Closed New Year's Day, Easter, July 4, Veteran's Day, Thanksgiving, Christmas eve, and Christmas day.

Asian American culture, art, and history are explored at this museum in the heart of the International District. The emphasis is on the life of Asian immigrants in the Northwest, and special exhibits are meant to help explain customs to non-Asians. Asians, primarily Chinese and Japanese, played an integral role in settling the Northwest, and today the connection of this region with the far side of the Pacific is opening up many new economic and cultural doors.

✪ Ye Olde Curiosity Shop

Pier 54, Alaskan Way. ☎ **206/682-5844.** Free admission. Mon–Thurs 9:30am–6pm, Fri–Sat 9am–9pm, Sun 9am–6pm. Closed Thanksgiving, Christmas, and New Year's Day. Bus: 15, 18, or 91; then walk down Pike Place stairs.

It's a museum. It's a store. It's weird! It's tacky! If you have a fascination with the bizarre—and I think we all do—shoulder your way into this crowded shop and erstwhile museum. See Siamese-twin calves, a natural mummy, the Lord's Prayer on a grain of rice, a narwhal tusk, shrunken heads, walrus and whale oosiks (the bone of the male reproductive organ)—in fact, all the stuff that fascinated you as a kid. The collection of oddities was started in 1899 by Joe Standley, who had developed a more-than-passing interest in strange curios.

NEIGHBORHOODS

International District

Fifth Ave. S. to Eighth Ave. S. (between S. Main St. and S. Lane St.).

Seattle's large and prosperous Asian neighborhood is called the International District rather than Chinatown because so many Asian nationalities call this area home. This has been the traditional Asian neighborhood for 100 years or more and you can learn about its history at the Wing Luke Museum (see above). There are of course lots of restaurants and import and food stores, including the huge Uwajimaya (see "Markets" in Section 2 of Chapter 8 for details). Both the Nippon Kan Theatre, 628 S. Washington St. (☎ 206/467-6807), and the Northwest Asian-American Theater, 409 Seventh Ave. S. (☎ 206/340-1049), feature performances with an Asian flavor.

Fremont District

North end of Freemont Bridge around the intersection of Freemont Ave. N. and N. 36th St.

"Welcome to the Center of the Universe" reads the sign on the Fremont Bridge, and from that point onward, you know you are in a very different part of Seattle, maybe even a different dimension. This funky neighborhood also goes by the name Republic of Fremont, and has as its motto "De Libertas Quirkas," which roughly translated means "free to be peculiar." At this crossroads business district, you'll find unusual outdoor art, the Fremont Sunday Market, several vintage clothing and furniture stores, a brew pub, and many more unexpected and unusual shops, galleries, and cafes. In summer, there's the wacky Solstice Parade, and on summer Saturday nights there are outdoor B movies. Among the public artworks in the neighborhood are *Waiting for the Interurban* (at the north end of the Fremont Bridge), the *Fremont Troll* (under the Aurora Bridge on N. 36th Street), and *The Rocket at the Center of the Universe* (at the corner of Evanston Ave. N. and N. 35th Street).

TOTEM POLES

Totem poles are the quintessential symbol of the Northwest, and although this Native American art form actually comes from farther north, there are quite a few totem poles around Seattle. The four in Occidental Park at Occidental Avenue South and South Washington Street were carved by local artist Duane Pasco. The tallest is 35-foot-high *The Sun and Raven,* which tells the story of how Raven brought light into the world. Next to this pole is the *Man Riding a Whale.* This type of totem pole was traditionally carved to help villagers during their whale hunts. The other two figures that face each other are symbols of the Bear Clan and the Welcoming Figure.

A block away, in the triangular park of Pioneer Place, you can see Seattle's most famous totem pole.

The one you see now is actually a copy of the original that stood here, which arrived in Seattle in 1890 after a band of drunken men stole it from a Tlingit village up the coast. In 1938 the pole was set afire by an arsonist. The Seattle city fathers sent a $5,000 check to the Tlingit village requesting a replacement. Supposedly, the response from the village was, "Thanks for paying for the first totem pole. If you want another, it will cost another $5,000." The city of Seattle paid up, and so today Pioneer Square has a totem pole and the city has a clear conscience.

Up near Pike Place Market, at Victor Steinbrueck Park, which is at the intersection of Pike Place, Virginia Street, and Western Avenue, are two 50-foot-tall totem poles. To see the largest concentration of authentic totem poles, visit the University of Washington's Burke Museum (see above for details).

PANORAMAS

If you want to take home a drop-dead photo of the Seattle skyline at sunset, head up to Kerry Viewpoint on Queen Anne Hill. To reach the park, head north from Seattle Center on Queen Anne Avenue N. and turn left on W. Highland Drive. When you reach the park, you'll immediately recognize the view—it's on the cover of virtually every Seattle tourist booklet available.

For a less familiar view of the city, you can visit the following old skyscraper:

Smith Tower

508 Second Ave. ☎ **206/682-9393.** Admission $2 adults, $1 children and senior citizens. Daily 10am–10pm. Bus: 15, 18, 21, 22, 23, 39, 70, 136, or 137.

Despite all the shiny glass skyscrapers crowding the Seattle skyline these days, you can't miss the Smith Tower. It sits off all by itself, a tall white needle on the edge of the Pioneer Square District. At 42 stories, it was the tallest building west of the Mississippi for many years after being built in 1914. It isn't nearly as popular as the Space Needle, but there is an observation platform way up near the top. You should call ahead if you are going out of your way, since the observation floor is sometimes closed due to special functions.

PARKS & GARDENS

Freeway Park

Sixth Ave. and Seneca St. Free admission. Daily dawn to dusk. Any bus that goes to the downtown bus tunnel; Washington State Convention and Trade Center stop.

What do you do when a noisy interstate runs right through the middle of your fair city and you haven't got enough parks for all the suntanners and Frisbee throwers? You could tear up the whole darn thing and turn it into a park, as Portland did with its riverfront freeway, or you could put a roof on the highway and build a park over all the rushing cars and trucks, as Seattle did. Terraced gardens, waterfalls, grassy lawns—they're all here, and they're all smog resistant. They have to be to survive in this environment. You'd never know there's a roaring freeway beneath your feet.

Hiram M. Chittenden Locks

3015 NW 54th St. ☎ 206/783-7059. Free admission. Park and locks, daily 7am–9pm; visitors center June–Sept daily 10am–7pm, Oct–May Thurs–Mon 11am–5pm. Closed Thanksgiving, Christmas, and New Year's Day. Bus: 17 or 46.

These locks connect Lake Washington and Lake Union to Puget Sound and allow boats to travel from the lakes onto open water. The difference between the water levels of the lakes and the Sound varies from 6 to 26 feet, depending on the tides and lake levels. Mostly used by small boats, the locks are a popular spot for salmon watching. People watch salmon jumping up the cascades of a fish ladder as they return to spawn in the stream where they were born, and windows below the waterline give an idea of what it's like to be a salmon. The best months to see salmon are July and August.

Japanese Gardens

Washington Park Arboretum, Lake Washington Blvd. E. (north of E. Madison St.). ☎ 206/684-4725. Admission $2 adults; $1 senior citizens, the disabled, and ages 6–18. Mar 1–last Sat in Apr, daily 10am–6pm; last Sun in Apr–May 31, daily 10am–7pm; June 1–Aug 31, daily 10am–8pm; Sept 1–fourth Sat in Oct, daily 10am–6pm; fourth Sun in Oct–Nov 30, daily 10am–4pm. Closed Dec–Feb. Bus: 11 or 84.

Situated on 3½ acres of land, the Japanese Gardens are a perfect little world unto themselves. Babbling brooks, a lake rimmed with Japanese irises and filled with colorful koi (Japanese carp), and a cherry orchard for spring color are peaceful any time of year. Unfortunately, noise from a nearby road can be distracting at times. A special Tea Garden encloses a Tea House, where, between April and October, on the third Saturday of each month at 1:30pm, you can attend a traditional tea ceremony.

On the Trail of Dale Chihuly

In the past few years, Northwest glass artist Dale Chihuly, one of the founders of the Pilchuck School for glass art north of Seattle, has been garnering nationwide media attention for his fanciful and color-saturated contemporary glass art. From tabletop vessels to massive window installations that capture and transform the sun, his creations in glass have a depth and richness of color that have captured the attention of collectors across the country. Sensuous forms include vases within bowls that are reminiscent of Technicolor birds' eggs in giant nests. His ikebana series, based on the traditional Japanese flower-arranging technique, are riotous conglomerations of color that twist and turn like so many cut flowers waving in the wind.

So where do you go to see the works of this master of molten glass? There's no one place in Seattle to see a collection of his work, but there are numerous public displays around the city. In the lobby of the Sheraton Seattle Hotel, 1400 Sixth Ave., there are works by Chihuly and other Northwest glass artists. The Stouffer Madison Hotel, 515 Madison St., also has a piece on display in the lobby. In the U.S. Bank Centre (formerly the Pacific First building), between Fourth and Fifth avenues on Pike Street, there is an extensive exhibit. The City Centre shopping arcade, 1420 Fifth Ave., has displays by numerous glass artists, including Chihuly. Up on the third floor of the Washington State Convention and Trade Center, there is a case with some smaller, but beautifully lighted, vases.

If you're willing to drive to Chihuly's home town of Tacoma, 32 miles south Seattle, you can see the largest museum exhibit of Chihuly's work at the Tacoma Art Museum, 1123 Pacific Ave. Just up the street from here, at Tacoma's restored Union Station (now the federal courthouse), some of the artist's larger pieces have been installed.

If after tracking down Chihuly's works you decide you must have some for yourself, stop in at the Foster-White Gallery, 311 Occidental Ave., which represents Chihuly here in Seattle.

Volunteer Park

E. Prospect St. and 14th Ave. E. ☎ **206/684-4743.** Free admission (park and conservatory). Daily dawn to dusk. Conservatory May 1–Sept 15, daily 10am–7pm; Sept 16–Apr 30, 10am–4pm. Bus: 10.

Volunteer Park is surrounded by the elegant mansions of Capitol Hill and is a popular spot for suntanning and playing Frisbee. A stately conservatory houses a large collection of tropical plants, including palm trees, orchids, and cacti. The Seattle Asian Art Museum (see above) is also here.

Washington Park Arboretum

2300 Arboretum Dr. E. ☎ **206/543-8800.** Free admission. Daily dawn to dusk; visitors center Mon–Fri 10am–4pm, Sat–Sun noon–4pm. Bus: 11, 43, or 84.

Acres of trees and shrubs stretch from the far side of Capitol Hill all the way to the Montlake Cut, a canal connecting Lake Washington to Lake Union. Within the arboretum, there are quiet trails that are most beautiful in spring, when azaleas, cherry trees, rhododendrons, and dogwoods are all in flower. There are more than 5,000 varieties of plants in the 200-acre park. The north end, a marshland that is home to ducks and herons, is popular with kayakers and canoeists (see below for where you can rent a canoe or kayak).

✪ Woodland Park Zoo

5500 Phinney Ave. N. ☎ **206/684-4800.** Admission $6 adults; $5.25 senior citizens, college students and disabled; $4.50 children ages 6–17; $2.25 ages 3–5; ages 2 and under free. Mar 15–Oct 14 daily 9:30am–6pm; Oct 15–Mar 14 daily 9:30am–4pm. Parking $1. Bus: 5.

This big, sprawling zoo in north Seattle has outstanding new exhibits focusing on such bioclimatic zones as Alaska, tropical Asia, the African savanna, and the tropical rain forest. The brown bear enclosure is an amazing reproduction of an Alaskan stream and hillside, and in the savanna, zebras gambol as antelopes and giraffes graze contentedly. An elephant forest provides plenty of space for the zoo's pachyderms. The tropical nocturnal house has fascinating exhibits that allow visitors to see nocturnal creatures when they are at their most active. Gorilla and orangutan habitats also are memorable. For the little ones, there is a farm animals area.

3 Especially for Kids

Look under "The Top Attractions" and "More Attractions," above, for the following Seattle attractions for kids: **Pacific Science Center, The Seattle Aquarium, Ye Olde Curiosity Shop,** and **Woodland Park Zoo.**

The places listed in this section are also great for kids. They'll be interested in the arcades and rides at **Seattle Center,** as well as their very own museum, the **Seattle Children's Museum.**

Also look under "Children's Theater Companies" in Chapter 9 for The Children's Theatre and the Northwest Puppet Center.

Or you can take them to a sports event. Seattle supports professional football, basketball, and baseball teams (see Section 6 below). And what could be more fun than exploring the **Seattle Underground** (see Section 4 below)!

Enchanted Village & Wild Waves

36201 Enchanted Pkwy. S., Federal Way. ☎ **206/661-8000.** Enchanted Village, $11 adults, $9 children ages 3–9, free for children 2 and under; Enchanted Village and Wild Waves together, $18.50 adults, $16.50 children ages 3–9, free for children 2 and under. Easter–late May Sat–Sun 11am–5pm (Enchanted Village only);

late May–mid-June Mon–Fri 9:30am–5pm, Sat–Sun 11am–6pm; mid June–Labor Day daily 11am–7pm. Directions: By car from Seattle, take I-5 south to Exit 142-B, Puyallup.

The littlest kids can watch the clowns and ride on miniature trains, merry-go-rounds, and the like at Enchanted Village. The older kids, teenagers, and adults will want to spend the hot days of summer riding the wild waves, tubing down artificial streams, and swooshing down water slides.

Seattle Center

305 Harrison St. ☎ **206/684-7200.** Free admission; pay per ride or game. June 2–Labor Day, daily noon–midnight; Labor Day–mid-March, weekends noon–6pm; mid-March–June 2, Fri 7pm–midnight, Sat noon–11pm, Sun noon–8pm. Bus: 1, 2, 3, 4, 6, 13, 15, 16, 18, 19, 24, or 33.

This 74-acre amusement park and cultural center was built for the Seattle World's Fair in 1962 and stands on the north edge of downtown at the end of the monorail line. The most visible building at the center is the Space Needle (see above), which provides an out-standing panorama of the city from its observation deck. However, of much more interest to children are the rides (a roller coaster, log flume, merry-go-round, and Ferris wheel) and arcade games. This is Seattle's main festival site, and in the summer months hardly a weekend goes by without some festival or another filling its grounds. (See map above.)

The Children's Museum

Center House, Seattle Center. ☎ **206/298-2521.** Admission $3.50 adults or children. Tues–Sun 10am–5pm. Closed Thanksgiving, Christmas, and New Year's Day. Bus: 1, 2, 3, 4, 6, 13, 15, 16, 18, 19, 24, or 33.

Seattle's Children's Museum is located in the basement of the Center House at Seattle Center and recently tripled in size. The museum includes plenty of hands-on cultural exhibits, a child-size neighbor-hood, an imagination station, a mountain wilderness area, and other exhibits to keep the little ones busy learning and playing for hours.

4 Organized Tours

BUS TOURS

Gray Line of Seattle

☎ **206/626-5208** or 800/426-7532. Half-day tour $19.50 adults, $9.75 children; full-day tour $28 adults, $14 children.

If you'd like an overview of Seattle's main tourist attractions, or if you're pressed for time during your visit, you can pack in a lot of sights with one of Gray Lines' half-day or full-day tours. Tours outside the city are also available.

BOAT TOURS

In addition to the boat tours and cruises mentioned below, you can do your own low-budget cruise simply by hopping on one of the ferries operated by Washington State Ferries. Try the Bainbridge Island or

Bremmerton ferries out of Seattle for a two-hour round-trip. For a longer and more scenic trip, drive north to Anacortes and ride the ferries through the San Juan Islands, perhaps spending a few hours in the town of Friday Harbor before returning. It's also possible to take the first ferry of the day from Anacortes, ride all the way to Sidney, British Columbia, and then catch the next ferry back to Anacortes.

Argosy

Pier 55. ☎ **206/623-4252**. Seattle Harbor Cruise, $12.70 adults, $6 children ages 5–12; Locks Cruise, $19.90 adults, $10.65 children ages 5–12; $15.50 adults, $5.80 children ages 5–12.

Seattle is a city surrounded by water, and if you'd like to see it from various aquatic perspectives, take one of the cruises offered by this company. There's a Seattle harbor cruise (departs from Pier 55), a cruise through the Hiram Crittenden Locks to Lake Union (departs from Pier 57), and a cruise around Lake Washington (departs from downtown Kirkland).

Clipper Navigation

Pier 69. ☎ **206/206/448-5000** or 800/888-2535. One way, $36 adults, $31 senior citizens, $18 children; round-trip, $59 adults, $52 senior citizens, $29.50 children.

From mid-February through early September, you can explore the mazelike waterways of the Puget Sound on an all-day cruise aboard the *San Juan Explorer.* This cruise heads up the east side of Whidbey Island and through Deception Pass before reaching the San Juan Islands. You then get three hours in the town of Friday Harbor before starting the return trip to Seattle.

Spirit of Puget Sound

Pier 70. ☎ **206/443-1442**. Cruise $14.95–$45.25.

If you'd like a bit of dining and dancing with your cruise around Puget Sound, book a cruise on this big sleek yacht. They do lunch, dinner, and moonlight party cruises.

WALKING TOURS

Chinatown Discovery Tours

☎ **206/236-0657**. Tours $24.95–$39 adults; $12.95–$25 children ages 5–11.

If you'd like an insider's glimpse of life in Seattle's International District, book a tour with this company. On these walking tours, you'll learn the history of this colorful and historic neighborhood. Tours also include a traditional Chinese meal such as dim sum, tea, or an eight-course banquet.

City Hunt

322 Occidental Ave. S. ☎ **206/625-0607**. Hunt $8.50–$59.50.

Sort of a combination self-guided tour and scavenger hunt, these tours have you solving riddles and searching for clues that will help you learn about different aspects of Seattle. There's a downtown hunt, an art hunt, a microbrew hunt, a restaurant hunt, and a bicycle hunt. All are lots of fun and start from the Pacific NW Brewing Co. pub.

Seattle's Best Walking Tour
☎ **206/226-7641.** Tour $15–$25.

If you'd like to explore downtown Seattle with a knowledgeable guide, join one of these informative walking tours. The half-day tour visits Pike Place Market, the waterfront, and the Pioneer Square District, and the full-day tour continues on to the International District and Freeway Park.

Underground Tour
610 First Ave. ☎ **206/682-4646.** Tour $5.50 adults, $4.50 senior citizens, $4 students ages 13–17, $2.50 children ages 6–12. Tours held daily.

If you have an appreciation of off-color humor and are curious about the seamier side of Seattle history, this tour will likely entertain and enlighten. The tours lead down below street level in the Pioneer Square area where vestiges of Seattle businesses built before the great fire of 1889 still remain. This is Seattle's most popular tour.

BEHIND-THE-SCENES TOURS
Market Classroom Tours
85 Pike Place Market. ☎ **206/682-7453.** Tour $5.

On these tours, you'll go behind the scenes at the famous Pike Place Market, learn the market's history, learn the ins and outs of shopping here, and maybe meet restaurant chefs as they shop for fresh market ingredients. Call for information on scheduled tours.

OTHER TOURS
Spirit of Washington Dinner Train
625 S. Fourth St., Renton. ☎ **206/227-RAIL** or 800/876-RAIL. Tour $57–$69.

Great scenery and good food are the appeal of this scenic railway excursion. Running from Renton, at the south end of Lake Washington, to the Columbia Winery near Woodinville, at the north end of the Lake, this train rolls past views of the lake and Mount Rainier. Along the way, you're fed a tasty and filing lunch, dinner, or brunch. At the turn-around point, you get to tour a winery and taste some wines.

Tillicum Village Tours
Pier 56. ☎ **206/443-1244.** Tours $46.50 adults, $43 senior citizens, $30 ages 13–19, $18.50 ages 6–12, $9.25 ages 4–5. Daily May–Oct; other months schedule varies.

Northwest Native American culture comes alive at Tillicum Village, across Puget Sound from Seattle at Blake Island Marine State Park. Totem poles stand vigil outside a huge cedar longhouse fashioned after the traditional dwellings of Northwest Indians. You'll enjoy a meal of alder-smoked salmon while watching traditional masked dances. All around stand the carved and painted images of fanciful animals, and you can see the park's resident wood-carver create more of these beautiful works of art. After the dinner and dances, you can explore the deep forest that surrounds the clearing in which the lodge stands. There are even beaches on which to relax.

5 Outdoor Activities

BEACHES

Alki (rhymes with sky) **Beach,** on Puget Sound, is the nearest beach to downtown Seattle. It stretches for $2^1/_2$ miles down the west side of the Alki Peninsula, which is the promontory you see across Elliott Bay from Seattle's waterfront. This is a busy beach, and the views across the sound to the Olympic Mountains can be stunning on a clear day.

BICYCLING

Gregg's Green Lake Cycle, 7007 Woodlawn Ave. NE (☎ 206/ 523-1822); the **Bicycle Center,** 4529 Sand Point Way NE (☎ 206/ 523-8300); and **Sammamish Valley Cycle,** 8451 164th Ave. NE, Redmond (☎ 206/881-8442)—all rent bikes by the hour and by the day, as well as by the week. Rates range from $4 to $7 per hour and $15 to $32 per day. These three shops are all convenient to the **Burke-Gilman Trail** and the **Sammamish River Trail.** The former is a $12^1/_2$ mile trail created from an old railway bed. It starts at **Gasworks Park** and continues to **Kenmore Logboom Park** at the north end of Lake Washington by way of the University of Washington. Serious riders can then connect to the Sammamish River Trail, which leads to Lake Sammamish. There are lots of great picnicking spots along both trails.

DAY SPAS

If you prefer being pampered to paddling a kayak, facials to fishing, or massages to mountain climbing, consider spending a few hours at a day spa. These facilities offer such treatments as massages, facials, seaweed wraps, mud baths, and the like. Seattle day spas include Le Salon Paul Morey, Rainier Square Concourse, 1301 Fifth Ave. (☎ 206/ 624-4455), and Ummelina, 1523 Sixth Ave. (☎ 206/624-1370). A half day will run you between $125 and $150 and a full day will cost between $250 and $300.

FISHING

As you might have guessed from the plethora of seafood restaurants in Seattle, the waters around here are brimming with fish. You can fish the rivers for salmon and steelhead trout, or try the saltwater of Puget Sound for salmon or bottom fish.

GOLF

There are more than a dozen public golf courses in the Seattle area. **Jackson Park Municipal Golf Course,** 1000 NE 135th St. (☎ 206/363-4747); **Jefferson Park Municipal Golf Course,** 4101 Beacon Ave. S. (☎ 206/762-4513); and **West Seattle Municipal Golf Course,** 4470 35th Ave. SW (☎ 206/935-5187)—these are three of the most convenient courses. Greens fees are $19.50 if you're not a King County resident, $15 if you are.

HIKING

The areas surrounding Seattle are a hiker's paradise, and hiking, backpacking, and camping are some of the most popular activities in the region. Within an easy drive of the city are three national parks, Mount St. Helens National Volcanic Monument, and numerous national forests, all of which offer hikes of varying lengths and degrees of difficulty.

Mount Rainier National Park, Tahoma Woods/Star Route, Ashford, WA 98304 (☎ 206/569-2211), is the easiest to reach from Seattle. **Olympic National Park,** 600 E. Park Ave., Port Angeles, WA 98362 (☎ 360/452-0330), is the most varied of the national parks in this region. There are long stretches of isolated beaches, snow-capped mountains, lush rain forests, and hot springs. The **North Cascades National Park,** 2105 State Route 20, Sedro Woolley, WA 98284 (☎ 360/856-5700), is adjacent to the Canadian border northeast of Seattle.

Mount St. Helens National Volcanic Monument, 42218 N.E. Yale Bridge Rd., Amboy, WA 98601 (☎ 360/750-3900), has been left as a monument to the power of a volcanic eruption and is an amazing site that should not be missed. A limited number of hikers are allowed to climb the peak each day, but you have to make reservations far in advance.

HORSEBACK RIDING

Down at the south end of Lake Washington near the airport you can rent horses at **Aqua Barn Ranch,** 15227 SE Renton-Maple Valley Hwy., Renton, WA (☎ 206/255-4618), which offers guided rides at the rate of $19.50 per hour; reservations are required.

IN-LINE SKATING

You can rent in-line skates at **Greg's Green Lake Cycle,** 7007 Woodlawn Ave. NE (☎ 206/523-1822) or **Seattle Ski & Skate,** 907 NE 45th St. (☎ 206/548-1000) for about $12 per day or $4 per hour. The trail around Green Lake and the Burke-Gilman trail (see the description under "Bicycling," above) are both good places for skating.

KAYAKING/CANOEING

Northwest Outdoor Center, 2100 Westlake Ave. N. (☎ 206/281-9694), is located on Lake Union and will rent you a sea kayak for only $8 to $12 per hour. You can also opt for guided paddles lasting from a few hours to several days, and there are plenty of classes available for those who are interested. From April to September, the center is open Monday through Friday from 10am to 8pm, on Saturday, Sunday, and holidays from 9am to 6pm; from October through March, Wednesday through Monday from 10am to 6pm.

The **University of Washington Waterfront Activities Center,** on the university campus behind Husky Stadium (☎ 206/543-9433), is open to the public and rents canoes and rowboats for $4 per hour. Rentals are available from February to October, daily from 10am to about an hour before sunset.

SAILBOARDING

Sailboarding is one of Seattle's favorite sports. The local waters are ideal for learning—the winds are light and the water is flat. **Urban Surf,** 2100 N Northlake Way (☎ 206/545-WIND), will rent you a board and give you lessons if you need them. Rates are $35 per day for a board. Private lessons are $35 per hour, and a four-hour group class is $59. The shop is open Monday through Friday from 10am to 6pm, Saturday from 10am to 5pm, and Sunday from noon to 5pm.

SAILING

The **Center for Wooden Boats,** 1010 Valley St. (☎ 206/382-BOAT), a museum that rents classic boats, is at Waterway 4 at the south end of Lake Union. Dedicated to the preservation of historic wooden boats, the center is unique in that many exhibits can be rented and taken out on Lake Union. There are rowboats and large and small sailboats. Rates range from $6 to $15 per hour. Individual sailing instruction is also available. From June 1 to Labor Day, the center is open daily from 11am to 7pm; the rest of the year, Wednesday through Monday from noon to 6pm.

SKIING

One of the reasons Seattleites put up with long, wet winters is because they can go skiing within an hour of the city, and with many slopes set up for night skiing, it's possible to leave work and be on the slopes before dinner, ski for several hours, and be home in time to get a good night's rest. The ski season in the Seattle area generally runs from mid-November to the end of April.

Equipment can be rented at the ski areas listed below, and at **REI,** 1525 11th Ave. (☎ 206/323-8333).

CROSS-COUNTRY SKIING

In the Snoqualmie Pass area, less than 50 miles east of Seattle on I-90, **Ski Acres Cross-Country Center,** (☎ 206/434-6646), offers rentals, instruction, and many miles of groomed trails. Ski Acres even has lighted trails for night skiing. The trail fee runs $5 to $9.

Stevens Pass Nordic Center (☎ 360/973-2441 for general information, or 206/634-1645 for snow conditions) is 83 miles east of Seattle on U.S. 2 and is open Friday through Sunday and holidays. There are 30 kilometers of groomed trails here. Use of the trails costs $7.50 for adults and $6.50 for children.

When renting skis, be sure to get a **Sno-Park permit.** These are required in parking areas near ski trails. They are available at ski shops.

DOWNHILL SKIING

Alpental, Ski Acres, Snoqualmie, and Hyak ski areas (☎ 206/232-8182, or 206/236-1600 for snow conditions) are all located less than 50 miles east of Seattle off of I-90. These four ski areas offer more than 60 ski runs, rentals, and lessons. Adult lift ticket prices range from $14 to $16 for midweek night skiing to $29 for a weekend all-day pass. Call for hours of operation.

Crystal Mountain Resort (☎ 206/663-2265 for general information or 206/634-3771 for snow conditions) is 76 miles southeast of Seattle off of Wash. 410. Many Seattle skiers prefer this ski area over the Snoqualmie Pass ski areas. Lift ticket prices range from $16 for night skiing to $32 for a weekend all-day pass. Call for hours of operation.

Stevens Pass (☎ 360/973-2441 for general information or 206/634-1645 for snow conditions) is 78 miles east of Seattle on U.S. 2. A little more than half the runs here are for intermediate skiers. Adult lift ticket prices range from $10 for midweek night skiing to $31 for a weekend all-day pass. Call for hours of operation.

TENNIS

Seattle Parks and Recreation operates dozens of outdoor tennis courts all over the city. The most convenient are at **Volunteer Park,** 15th Ave. East and East Prospect St., and at **Lower Woodland Park,** West Green Lake Way North. If it happens to be raining and you had your heart set on playing tennis, there are indoor public courts at the **Seattle Tennis Center,** 2000 Martin Luther King Jr. Way S. (☎ 206/684-4764). Rates here are $12 for singles and $16 for doubles for 1¼ hours.

WHITE-WATER RAFTING

Seattle is surrounded by water, but it's flat water. For more thrilling boating experiences you have to head to the Olympic Mountains or Cascade Range. **Olympic Raft and Guide Service,** 239521 U.S. 101 W., Port Angeles, WA 98363 (☎ 206/452-1443), offers trips down the Olympic Peninsula's Elwha and Hoh rivers. The rate is $35 per person. Another outfit that runs trips down rivers all over the state is **River Riders** P.O. Box 1299 Monroe, WA 98272 (☎ 800/448-RAFT). They charge $45 to $75 for a four-hour trip.

6 Spectator Sports

BASEBALL

The American League's **Seattle Mariners** (☎ 206/628-3555) are Seattle's major-league baseball team, and they play in the Kingdome from April to October. Prices range from $6 to $15. Tickets are available at the Kingdome box office or by calling TicketMaster (☎ 206/628-0888). Parking is next to impossible, so plan to leave your car behind.

BASKETBALL

The NBA's **Seattle SuperSonics** (☎ 206/281-5800) play professional basketball in the Seattle Center Coliseum from November to about May. Games start at 7pm, and tickets are $7 to $60. Tickets are available through Ticketmaster (☎ 206/628-0888).

FOOTBALL

The **Seattle Seahawks** (NFL) play in the Kingdome from September to December. Games are on Sunday at 1pm, and tickets, at $19 to $38, are very difficult to get. Call for schedule and ticket information (☎ 206/827-9777). Parking in the Kingdome area is nearly impossible during games, so take the bus.

MARATHON

The **Seattle Marathon** takes place in November. There's a runners' hot line in Seattle that you can call for more information on this and other races in the area (☎ 206/524-RUNS).

7

Strolling Around Seattle

Downtown Seattle is easy to explore on foot. Foremost, of course, are the Pike Place Market and the waterfront, which together form the busiest neighborhood in Seattle. You really don't need a guided tour of this area: Just follow the hoards of people. The historic Pioneer Place neighborhood is a different story. This area has interesting buildings and history that you will probably not want to miss. *Note:* For additional information on some stops, see Chapter 6.

WALKING TOUR
PIONEER SQUARE AREA

Start: Pioneer Place at the corner of Yesler Way and First Avenue.
Finish: Washington Street Public Boat Landing.
Time: Approximately two hours, not including shopping, dining, and museum and other stops.
Best Times: Weekdays, when Pioneer Square and the Seattle Underground Tour are not so crowded.
Worst Times: Weekends, when the area is very crowded.

The buildings surrounding Pioneer Square were erected after the fire of 1889, and today this small section is all that remains of old Seattle. You will probably notice a uniformity of architectural style—this is because many of the buildings were designed by one architect, Elmer Fisher.

Start your tour of this historic neighborhood at the corner of Yesler Way and First Avenue on:

1. **Pioneer Place,** the triangular park in the middle of Pioneer Square. The totem pole here is a replacement of one that burned in 1938. The original pole had been stolen from a Tlingit village up the coast in 1890. Legend has it that after the pole burned the city fathers sent a check for $5,000 requesting a new totem pole. The Tlingit response was, "Thanks for paying for the first one. Send another $5,000 for a replacement." The cast-iron pergola in the park was erected in 1905 as a shelter for a large underground lavatory. Facing the square is the:

2. **Pioneer Building,** one of the architectural standouts of this neighborhood. It houses an antiques mall and several bars, including:

3. **Doc Maynard's** (610 First Ave.), a nightclub featuring live rock bands, which is also the starting point of the Underground Tour, which takes a look at the Pioneer Square area from beneath the sidewalks. Forming the south side of Pioneer Square is:

4. **Yesler Way,** the original Skid Row. In Seattle's early years, logs were skidded down this road to a lumber mill on the waterfront, and the road came to be known as Skid Road. These days it's trying hard to live down its reputation, but there are still quite a few people down on their luck here.

☕ **TAKE A BREAK**   Across Yesler Way from the pergola is **Merchants Café** (109 Yesler Way), the oldest restaurant in Seattle. If it happens to be time for lunch or dinner, this makes a good place to stop. Meals are moderately priced and well prepared.

Glance up Yesler Way past the triangular parking deck and you'll see:

5. **Smith Tower,** which was the tallest building west of the Mississippi for a long time. There's a great view of the city from an observatory near the top. This 1914 building is worth a visit just to view the ornate lobby and elevator doors.

Walk down Second Avenue (take the right fork, not Second Avenue Extension) to Main Street and you'll find the shady little:

6. **Waterfall Park,** with a roaring waterfall that looks as if it had been transported here straight from the Cascade Range. The park was built by United Parcel Service (UPS) and makes a wonderful place for a rest or a picnic lunch. Two more blocks down Main Street toward the water is cobblestoned:

7. **Occidental Park,** with four totem poles carved by a northwestern artist. This shady park serves as a gathering spot for homeless people. On the west side of the park is the:

8. **Grand Central Arcade,** a shopping and dining center created from a restored brick building. Inside, you can watch craftspeople at work in their studios. Across Main Street from Occidental Park is a unit of:

9. **Klondike Gold Rush National Historical Park** (117 S. Main St.). The small museum is dedicated to the history of the 1897–98 Klondike gold rush, which helped Seattle grow from an obscure town into a booming metropolis. A couple of doors toward the water from this museum is:

10. **The Elliott Bay Book Company,** on the corner of Main Street and First Avenue. This is one of Seattle's most popular bookstores and has an extensive selection of books on Seattle and the Northwest.

Walking Tour—Pioneer Square Area

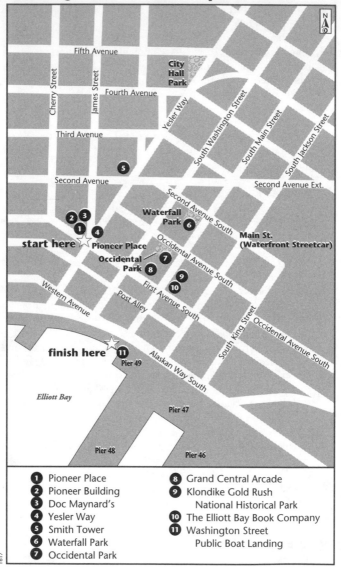

1. Pioneer Place
2. Pioneer Building
3. Doc Maynard's
4. Yesler Way
5. Smith Tower
6. Waterfall Park
7. Occidental Park
8. Grand Central Arcade
9. Klondike Gold Rush
   National Historical Park
10. The Elliott Bay Book Company
11. Washington Street
    Public Boat Landing

Continue down Main Street to the water and turn right. In one block you will come to the:

11. **Washington Street Public Boat Landing.** This iron open-air building was erected in 1920 and today serves as a public dock where people can tie up their boats while they are in Seattle.

8

Seattle Shopping

Seattle is a Northwest shopping mecca, and you too are welcome to join the pilgrims as they wander from grand old department stores to tiny specialty shops in search of bargains, great values, one-of-a-kind purchases, and memorable shopping experiences. Whether shopping is your passion or merely an activity in which you occasionally indulge, you should not miss Pike Place Market. Once the city's main produce market, this sprawling building is today filled with hundreds of unusual shops, including quite a few produce vendors' stalls. Just west of Pike Place Market is the Seattle waterfront, where you'll find numerous gift and souvenir shops.

1 The Shopping Scene

The heart of Seattle's shopping district is the corner of Pine Street and Westlake Avenue. Within one block of this intersection are two major department stores—Nordstrom and the Bon Marché—and a shopping mall. If you possess a very personal idea of style, head over to Broadway on Capitol Hill to do your shopping. Pioneer Square, Seattle's historic district, is filled with art galleries, antiques shops, and other unusual stores.

Hours　Shops in Seattle are generally open Monday through Saturday from 9 or 10am to 5 or 6pm, with shorter hours on Sunday. The major department stores usually stay open later on Friday evenings, and many shopping malls stay open until 9pm Monday through Saturday.

2 Shopping A to Z

ANTIQUES

For an absolutely astounding selection of antiques, head north of Seattle to the town of Snohomish (near Everett),where you'll find more than 150 antiques shops.

Honeychurch Antiques
1008 James St. ☎ **206/622-1225**.

For high-quality Asian antiques, including Japanese wood-block prints, textiles, furniture, and ivory and wood carvings, few Seattle antiques stores can approach Honeychurch Antiques. (The owners also have a shop in Hong Kong.) Regular special exhibits give this shop the feel of a tiny museum.

The Crane Gallery
1203-B Second Ave. ☎ **206/622-7185.**

Chinese, Japanese, and Korean antiquities are the focus of this shop, which prides itself on selling only the best pieces. Imperial Chinese porcelains, bronze statues of Buddhist deities, rosewood furniture, Japanese ceramics, netsukes, snuff bottles, and Chinese archaeological artifacts are just some of the quality antiques you will find here. Some Southeast Asian and Indian objects are also available.

Jean Williams Antiques
115 S. Jackson St. ☎ **206/622-1110.**

If your taste in antiques runs to 17th-, 18th-, and 19th-century French and English furniture, this Pioneer Square antique dealer may have something to add to your collection.

ANTIQUE MALLS AND FLEA MARKETS

Downtown Antique Market
2218 Western Ave., Suite 100. ☎ **206/448-6307.**

Housed in a turn-of-the-century warehouse three blocks north of Pike Place Market, this antiques mall houses dozens of dealers and a wide variety of antiques and collectibles.

Freemont Sunday Market
Freemont Ave. N. and N. 35th St. ☎ **206/282-5706.**

Crafts, imports, antiques, collectibles, fresh produce, and live music all combine to make this Seattle's second favorite public market (after Pike Place Market). The market is open from the end of April through Christmas.

Pioneer Square Mall
602 First Ave. ☎ **206/624-1164.**

This underground antiques mall is in the heart of Pioneer Square and contains 80 stalls selling all manner of antiques and collectibles.

ART GALLERIES

Pioneer Square area has Seattle's greatest concentration of art galleries. Wander around south of Yesler Way and you are likely to stumble upon a gallery showing the very latest contemporary art from the Northwest. There are also many antiques stores and galleries selling Native American art in the Pioneer Square area.

NATIVE AMERICAN ART

Flury & Company
322 First Ave. S. ☎ **206/587-0260.**

This Pioneer Square gallery specializes in prints by photographer Edward S. Curtis, who is known for his portraits of Native Americans. The gallery also has an excellent selection of antique Native American art.

✪ The Legacy
1003 First Ave. ☎ **206/624-6350.**

The Legacy is Seattle's oldest and finest gallery of contemporary and historic Northwest Coast Indian and Alaskan Eskimo art and artifacts. You'll find a large selection of masks, boxes, bowls, baskets, ivory artifacts, jewelry, prints, and books. For the serious collector.

Northwest Tribal Art
1417 First Ave. ☎ **206/467-9330.**

Located next to Pike Place Market, this is one of Seattle's most important galleries selling Northwest Coast Native American and U.S. Eskimo art. Traditional and contemporary wood carvings, masks, fossilized ivory carvings, soapstone carvings, scrimshaw, jewelry, drums, and even totem poles are available.

GLASS ART

Foster/White Gallery
311½ Occidental Ave. S. ☎ **206/622-2833.**

Seattle's largest fine-arts dealer represents the foremost contemporary artists of the Northwest, including artists from the Pilchuck School of Glass, renowned for its creative glass sculpture.

There is another Foster/White Gallery in Kirkland at 126 Central Way (☎ 206/822-2305).

The Glass Eye
1902 Post Alley, Pike Place Market. ☎ **206/441-3221.**

The Glass Eye is one of Seattle's oldest art-glass galleries, specializing in glass made from Mount St. Helens ash. These hand-blown pieces all contain ash from the volcano's 1980 eruption.

Glasshouse
311 Occidental Ave. S. ☎ **206/682-9939.**

Located in the Pioneer Square area, this gallery also houses a studio where you can observe art glass being created. Many of the area's top glass artists are represented.

BOOKS

Bowie & Company Booksellers
314 First Ave. ☎ **206/624-4100.**

Located in the Pioneer Square area, this bookstore specializes in old, rare, out-of-print, and hard-to-find books. Lots of signed editions in stock.

Elliott Bay Book Company
101 S. Main St. ☎ **206/624-6600.**

With heavy wooden fixtures, balconies, and an open staircase descending to the basement, this could very well be the most aesthetically pleasing bookstore in the Northwest. They have an excellent selection of books on Seattle and the Northwest, so if you want to learn more or are planning further excursions around the region, stop by. It's located just south of Pioneer Square.

Shorey's Book Store
1411 First Ave. ☎ **206/624-0221.**

In business since 1890, Shorey's will be happy to find you books from the year they opened (or any other year for that matter). Rare, antiquarian, and out-of-print books are their specialty. With more than a million items in stock, Shorey's is sure to have that obscure tome you've been seeking for years. If they don't have it, they'll search the world to find it for you. The store's motto is "The oldest, the biggest, the best!"

CLOTHING

Eddie Bauer
Fifth Ave. and Union St. ☎ **206/622-2766.**

Eddie Bauer got his start here in Seattle back in 1922 and today is one of the country's foremost purveyors of upscale outdoor fashions. A visit to this store is a must for anyone who dresses the Eddie Bauer look.

Northwest Pendleton
1313 Fourth Ave. ☎ **206/682-4430.**

For northwesterners, and many other people across the nation, Pendleton is and always will be *the* name in classic wool fashions. This store features tartan plaids and Indian-pattern separates, accessories, and blankets. Other Pendleton stores are at Southcenter Mall, Bellevue Square, and Tacoma Mall.

Weather or Not
Westlake Center, 400 Pine St. ☎ **206/682-3797.**

Seattle's inclement weather is legendary, and so it comes as no surprise that there is a store here devoted exclusively to weathering this climate. Weather or Not sells everything from umbrellas and raincoats to underwater paper, waterproof matches, and floating briefcases.

CHILDREN'S CLOTHING

Alfino Gallery
1908 Post Alley. ☎ **206/443-9504.**

If you're looking for a truly special ensemble for that special child in your life, try Alfino. The clothes here are costumey, with lots of embroidery and spangles. They also have similar fashions for women.

Boston St.
101 Stewart St. ☎ **206/728-1490.**

With sizes 0 through 14, this store stocks fun play clothes as well as more dressy fashions for kids. There's lots of 100 percent cotton clothing, and prices are moderate. A second store is at 1815 N. 45th Ave. (☎ 206/634-0580).

MEN'S CLOTHING

The Forum
95 Pine St. ☎ **206/624-4566.**

Located in the Pike Place Market neighborhood, The Forum features sophisticated fashions from the likes of Perry Ellis, Girbaud, and Robert Comstock.

Zebraclub
1901 First Ave. ☎ **206/448-7452.**

If you're young and hip and believe that clothes shopping should be an audiovisual experience, make the scene at Zebraclub, where rock videos playing on overhead monitors set the shopping tempo.

WOMEN'S CLOTHING

Ardour
1115 First Ave. ☎ **206/292-0660.**

The fashions here are romantic without being fussy and are something of a cross between the Seattle and the Paris looks. You can put together a very nice ensemble here, though it won't be cheap.

Baby & Co.
1936 First Ave. ☎ **206/448-4077.**

Claiming stores in Seattle and Mars, this trendy store stocks up-to-the-minute out-of-this-world fashions. Whether you're into earth tones or bright colors, you'll likely find something you can't live without.

Passport
123 Pine St. ☎ **206/628-9799.**

If your style is ethnic, be sure to drop in at this large store near Pike Place Market. Passport stocks everything from Indonesian batiks to Lithuanian linens.

Local Brilliance
1535 First Ave. ☎ **206/343-5864.**

If you want to return from your trip to Seattle wearing a dress you know no one else at the office will have ever seen before, visit Local Brilliance. The shop carries a wide selection of fashions by the northwest's best fashion designers.

✪ Ragazzi's Flying Shuttle
607 First Ave. ☎ **206/343-9762.**

Fashion becomes art and art becomes fashion at this chic boutique-cum-gallery on Pioneer Square. Hand-woven fabrics and hand-painted silks are the specialties here, but of course such sophisticated fashions require equally unique body decorations in the form of exquisite jewelry creations. Designers and artists from the Northwest and the rest of the nation find an outlet for their creativity at the Flying Shuttle.

CRAFTS

The Northwest is a leading center for craftspeople, and one of the places to see what they are creating is Pike Place Market. Although there are quite a few permanent shops within the market that sell local crafts, you can meet the artisans themselves on weekends when they set up tables on the main floor.

✪ Fireworks Fine Crafts Gallery
210 First Ave. S. ☎ **206/682-8707.**

Playful, outrageous, bizarre, beautiful—these are just some of the terms that can be used to describe the eclectic collection of Northwest crafts on sale at this Pioneer Square-area gallery. A table with place setting and food painted onto its top, cosmic clocks, and wildly creative jewelry are some of the fine and unusual items you'll find here. Other stores are at Westlake Center, 400 Pine St. (☎206/682-6462) and 2016 Bellevue Square (☎ 206/688-0933).

✪ Northwest Gallery of Fine Woodworking
202 First Ave. ☎ **206/625-0542.**

This store is a showcase for some of the most amazing woodworking you'll ever see. Be sure to stroll through here while in the Pioneer Square area. The warm hues of the exotic woods are soothing and the designs are beautiful. Furniture, boxes, sculptures, vases, bowls, and much more are created by more than 35 Northwest artisans. A second shop is at 122 Central Way, Kirkland, WA (☎ 206/889-1513).

DEPARTMENT STORES

✪ Nordstrom
1501 Fifth Ave. ☎ **206/628-2111.**

This is my pick for best department store in Seattle. Known for personal service, Nordstrom stores have gained a reputation as one of the premier department stores in the United States. The company originated here in Seattle, and its customers are devotedly loyal. Whether it's your first visit or your 50th, the knowledgeable staff will help you in any way they can. Prices are comparable to those at other department stores, but you also get the best service available. There are very popular sales in January (for men), June (for women and children), July (for men and women), and November (for women and children).

The Bon Marché
Third Ave. and Pine St. ☎ **206/344-2121.**

Seattle's only full-line department store, the Bon offers seven floors of merchandise. You'll find nearly anything you could possibly want at this store.

DISCOUNT STORES

J. Thompson
205 Pine St. ☎ **206/623-5780.**

This store sells designer women's clothing at 30 to 70 percent off retail. Styles are rather conservative.

✪ The Rack
1601 Second Ave. ☎ **206/448-8522.**

Discounts similar to those at J. Thompson are available at The Rack, which sells clearance items from Nordstrom.

FOOD
COFFEE
✪ Starbucks
Pike Place Market. ☎ 206/448-8762.

Seattle has developed a reputation as a city of coffeeholics, and Starbucks is one reason why. This company has coffeehouses all over town, but this is probably the most convenient if you are just visiting Seattle. With some 36 types of coffee available by the cup or by the pound, you can do a bit of taste testing before making a decision.

SEAFOOD
After tasting the bounty of seafood available in Seattle, it's almost impossible to do without. Any of the seafood vendors in Pike Place Market will pack your fresh salmon or Dungeness crab in an airline-approved container that will keep it fresh for up to 48 hours.

✪ Pike Place Fish
86 Pike Place, Pike Place Market. ☎ 206/682-7181.

Located just behind Rachel, the life-sized bronze pig, this fishmonger is famous for flying fish. Pick out a big silvery salmon, ask them to filet it, and watch the show. They'll also deliver your packaged order to your hotel, ready to carry onto your plane. Another Pike Place Fish is at Crossroads Mall in Bellevue (☎ 206/644-7402).

Port Chatham Smoked Seafood
1306 Fourth Ave., Rainier Square. ☎ 206/623-4645.

Northwest Coast Native Americans relied heavily on salmon for sustenance, and to preserve the fish they used alder-wood smoke. This tradition is still carried on today to produce one of the Northwest's most delicious food products. This store sells smoked sockeye, king salmon, rainbow trout, and oysters—all of which will keep without refrigeration until the package is opened.

Other stores are at 632 NW 46th Street (☎ 206/783-8200) and in Bellevue Square Mall (☎ 206/453-2441).

GIFTS/SOUVENIRS
Pike Place Market is the Grand Central Station of Seattle souvenirs, with stiff competition from Seattle Center and Pioneer Square.

Made In Washington
Pike Place Market (Post Alley at Pine St.). ☎ 206/467-0788.

Whether it's salmon, wine, or Northwest Native American masks, you'll find a selection of Washington State products in this shop, which is an excellent place to pick up gifts for all those who didn't get to come with you on your visit to Seattle. Other Made in Washington locations include Westlake Center (☎ 206/623-9753); Bellevue Square, Bellevue (☎ 206/454-6907); Gilman Village, Issaquah (☎ 206/392-4819); and Northgate Shopping Center (☎ 206/361-8252).

JEWELRY

Fox's Gem Shop
1341 Fifth Ave. ☎ 206/623-2528.

This is Seattle's premier jeweler. Among other elegant lines, they feature the Tiffany Collection. Displays here, including an 11,000-year-old mastodon skeleton, make shopping here a bit like visiting a museum.

MALLS/SHOPPING CENTERS

Bellevue Square
Bellevue Way and NE 8th Ave., Bellevue

Over in Bellevue, on the east side of Lake Washington, you'll find one of the area's largest shopping malls, with more than 200 stores. There's even an art museum—the Bellevue Art Museum—here in the mall.

Broadway Market
401 Broadway E.

A trendy mall located in the stylish Capitol Hill neighborhood, the Broadway Market houses numerous small shops and restaurants with reasonable prices.

Century Square
Fourth Ave. and Pike St.

There are many fine stores in this upscale mall a block from Westlake Center.

City Centre
Sixth Ave. and Union St.

This upscale downtown shopping center houses such stores as Barneys New York, Benetton, and Ann Taylor. Displays of art glass by Dale Chihuly and his contemporaries make City Centre worth a visit even if you're only window shopping.

Rainier Square
1326 Fifth Ave.

Rainier Square is filled with about 60 upscale shops and restaurants. Built on the bottom floors of several skyscrapers, Rainier Square mall is a veritable maze.

Southcenter
I-5 and I-405.

Located south of Seattle at the junction of I-5 and I-405, Southcenter is the largest indoor shopping mall in Washington.

Westlake Center
400 Pine St.

This downtown shopping mall is in the heart of Seattle's shopping district and includes more than 80 specialty shops. The monorail terminal is on the third floor of the mall.

MARKETS

✪ Pike Place Market
Pike St. and First Ave. ☎ 206/682-7453.

Pike Place Market is one of Seattle's most famous landmarks and tourist attractions. Not only are there produce vendors, fishmongers, and butchers, but also artists, craftspeople, and performers. A trip here can easily be an all-day affair. Hundreds of shops are tucked away in hidden nooks and crannies on the seemingly endless levels. Several of Seattle's best restaurants are located in or near this megamarket.

Uwajimaya
519 Sixth Ave. S. ☎ 206/624-6248.

Typically, your local neighborhood supermarket has a section of Chinese cooking ingredients; it's probably about 10 feet long, with half that space taken up by various brands of soy sauce. Now imagine your local supermarket with nothing *but* Asian foods, housewares, produce, and toys. That's Uwajimaya, Seattle's Asian supermarket in the heart of the International District.

RECREATIONAL GEAR

The North Face
1023 First Ave. ☎ 206/622-4111.

The North Face is one of the country's best-known names in the field of outdoor gear, and here in their downtown shop, you can choose from among their diverse selection.

Great Pacific/Patagonia
2100 First Ave. ☎ 206/622-9700.

Patagonia has built up a very loyal clientele based on the durability of its outdoor gear and clothing.

REI
1525 11th Ave. ☎ 206/323-8333.

Recreational Equipment, Incorporated (REI) was founded here in Seattle 1938 and today is the nation's largest co-op selling outdoor gear. There is an amazing selection of gear on the many floors of this store, which is located on Capitol Hill.

TOYS

Archie McPhee Toy Story
3510 Stoneway N. ☎ 206/545-8344.

You may already be familiar with this temple of the absurd through its mail-order catalog. Now imagine wandering through aisles and aisles full of goofy gags. Give yourself plenty of time and take a friend.

✪ Magic Mouse
603 First Ave. ☎ 206/682-8097.

Adults and children alike have a hard time pulling themselves away from this, the most fun toy store in Seattle. It is conveniently located on Pioneer Square and has a good selection of European toys.

Wood Shop Toys

320 First Ave. S. ☎ **206/624-1763.**

Just two blocks away from Magic Mouse is another Seattle favorite that sells wooden toys and puppets. This place is worth a look even if you're not in the market for toys.

WINE

The Northwest is rapidly becoming known as a producer of fine wine. The relatively dry summer with warm days and cool nights provides a perfect climate for growing grapes. After you have sampled Washington or Oregon vintages, you might want to take a few bottles home.

Pike & Western Wine Merchants

1934 Pike Place, Pike Place Market. ☎ **206/441-1307.**

Visit this shop for an excellent selection of Northwest Californian, Italian, and French wine. The extremely knowledgeable staff will be happy to send you home with the very best wine available in Seattle.

9

Seattle After Dark

Though Seattleites spend much of their free time enjoying the natural surroundings, they have not overlooked the more cultured evening pursuits. Theater, opera, and ballet flourish here, and music lovers will find a plethora of classical, jazz, and rock offerings. Much of the evening entertainment is clustered in the Seattle Center or Pioneer Square area, which makes a night out on the town surprisingly easy. To make things even easier, you can buy half-price tickets at **Ticket/ Ticket,** which has two sales booths. The Pike Place Market location, First Avenue and Pike Street (☎ 206/324-2744), is open Tuesday through Sunday from noon to 6pm. The other booth is on the second floor of the Broadway Market, 401 Broadway E. (☎ 206/324-2744). It's open Tuesday through Sunday from 10am to 7pm. The booths offer half-price day-of-show tickets only and levy a service charge of 50¢ to $3 depending on the ticket price. If you want to pay full price with your credit card, call **Ticketmaster Northwest** (☎ 206/ 292-ARTS or 206/628-0888), open Monday through Saturday from 8am to 10pm and on Sunday from 10am to 6pm.

To find out what's going on when you are in town, pick up a copy of **Seattle Weekly** (75¢), which is Seattle's weekly arts-and-entertainment newspaper. You'll find it in bookstores, convenience stores, grocery stores, and newsstands. The Friday **Seattle Times** also has a guide, "Tempo," to the week's arts and entertainment offerings.

1 The Performing Arts

The main venues for the performing arts in Seattle are clustered in the Seattle Center. Here, in the shadow of the Space Needle, you'll find the Opera House, Bagley Wright Theater, Intiman Playhouse, Seattle Children's Theatre, The Group, Seattle Center Coliseum, and Memorial Stadium.

MAJOR PERFORMING ARTS COMPANIES
OPERA & CLASSICAL MUSIC COMPANIES

Northwest Chamber Orchestra
1305 Fourth Ave., Suite 522. ☎ **206/343-0445.** Tickets $13–$19.50.

The Northwest Chamber Orchestra, active for more than 20 seasons now, is a showcase for Northwest performers. The annual Bach festival is the highlight of the season, which runs from September to April.

Performances are held primarily in Kane Hall on the University of Washington campus. There is also a series of concerts at the Seattle Art Museum.

Seattle Opera Association

Seattle Opera House, Third Ave. N. and Mercer St. ☎ **206/389-7699.** Tickets $28–$95.

The Seattle Opera is considered one of the finest opera companies in the country and is *the* Wagnerian opera company. The stagings of Wagner's four-opera *The Ring of the Nibelungen* are breathtaking spectacles that draw crowds from around the country. In addition to classical operas, the season usually includes a more contemporary musical (*Porgy and Bess* during the 1994–95 season).

Seattle Symphony Orchestra

Seattle Opera House, Fourth Ave. and Mercer St. ☎ **206/443-4747.** Tickets $8–$51.

Each year the Seattle Symphony Orchestra, under the baton of Gerard Schwarz, offers an amazingly diverse musical season that runs from September to May. There are evenings of classical, light classical, and pops, plus morning concerts, children's concerts, guest artists (the 1994–95 season included performances by Leontyne Price, the Labeque sisters, Pinchas Zukerman, and even Garrison Keillor), and much more.

THEATER COMPANIES

✪ A Contemporary Theater [ACT]

100 W. Roy St. ☎ **206/285-5110.** Tickets $13.50–$26.

This theater offers slightly more adventurous productions than the other major theater companies in Seattle, although it is still not as avant-garde as some of the smaller companies. The season runs from the end of April to mid-November.

Intiman Theatre Company

Intiman Playhouse, Seattle Center, 201 Mercer St. ☎ **206/626-0782.** Tickets $16–$34; $10 for standing room only.

With a season that starts in May and then picks up again in August, this company is a favorite of Seattle theatergoers. Past seasons have included the world premiere of the Pulitzer Prize winner *The Kentucky Cycle* and an acclaimed production of Tony Kushner's award-winning epic *Angels in America.*

Seattle Repertory Theater

Bagley Wright Theater, Seattle Center, 155 Mercer St. ☎ **206/443-2222.** Tickets $10.50–$34.

The Rep season picks up where the Intiman leaves off, giving Seattle excellent year-round professional theater. The season is October to May with six plays performed in the main theater and three more in the intimate PONCHO theater. The Rep has been around for more than 30 years and is consistently outstanding. Productions range from classics to world premieres to Broadway musicals.

SEATTLE ON THE FRINGES

In recent years, Seattle has become something of an arts mecca. The Seattle Opera is ranked one of the top operas in the country and its stagings of Wagner's *Ring* series have achieved near-legendary status. The Seattle Symphony also receives accolades, and the Seattle Repertory Theatre has received Tony awards for its productions. With such a burgeoning mainstream performing-arts community, it is not at all surprising that the city is now developing the sort of fringe theater life once only associated with such cities as New York, London, and Edinburgh. The city's more avant-garde performance companies have been grabbing their share of the limelight with daring, outrageous, and thought-provoking productions.

A perusal of a few local entertainment publications recently turned up the following fringe theater performances (all taking place in the same two-week period): *Star Drek: The Musical* (a parody of you-know-what); *Plays by Poets* (just what it sounds like); *Undesirable Elements* (on the meaning of being an immigrant in the United States); *Airsick* (a play about a sky-diving public defender); *Grandma, 82, Gives Birth to Devil Cult, and Other Tabloid Obsessions* (short plays drawn from everyone's favorite supermarket reading material); *All About Alice* (a gay and lesbian theater festival); *Jodie's Body* (about an artist's model and performed in the nude); *Tormenting Impulses, A Queer Girl's Retrospective* (a lesbian comedy); and *Insatiable Cabaret Devours the American Dream* (an out-of-this-world cabaret).

Seattle's newfound interest in fringe theater finds its greatest expression each spring, when the Seattle Fringe Theater Festival (☎ 206/325-5446), which provides venues for small, self-producing theater companies, is staged at various Capitol Hill venues. The 1995 festival included more than 300 performances by 75 theater groups from around the country.

Even if you don't happen to be in town for Seattle's annual fringe binge, check out the following venues for way-off Broadway productions, performance art, poetry jams, and spoken word performances:

Aha! Theater
2222 Second Ave. ☎ **206/728-1375**.

Outrageous reworkings of classics, satirical musicals, comedies.

Annex Theater
1916 Fourth Ave. ☎ **206/728-0933**.

Thought-provoking dramas and comedies, cabaret theater.

Book-It Repertory Theatre
1219 Westlake Ave., Suite 301. ☎ **206/216-0833**.

Works by local playwrights.

Brown Bag Theatre
Newmark Center, 1401 Second Ave. ☎ **206/343-7328**.

Brown-bag lunch theater, primarily one-act plays.

Empty Space Theatre
3509 Fremont Ave. N. ☎ **206/547-7500.**

Mostly comedy, popular with a young crowd.

The Group
Seattle Center, Center House, 305 Harrison St. ☎ **206/441-1299.**

Multicultural theater.

New City Theater
1634 11th Ave. ☎ **206/323-6800.**

Performance art, works by local playwrights.

Northwest Asian American Theatre
Theatre Off Jackson, 409 Seventh Ave. S. ☎ **206/340-1049.**

Works by Asian-American writers, actors, and musicians.

Re-Bar
1114 Howell St. ☎ **206/233-9873.**

Primarily gay and lesbian performance art and theater.

Velvet Elvis Arts Lounge Theatre
107 Occidental Ave. ☎ **206/624-8477.**

Performance art, poetry nights, alternative video productions.

The Weathered Wall
1921 Fifth Ave. ☎ **206/448-5688.**

Spoken word performances, poetry jams, live contemporary music.

DANCE COMPANIES

On the Boards
Washington Hall Performance Gallery, 153 14th Ave. ☎ **206/325-7901.** Tickets $5–$16.

This is Seattle's premier modern-dance company, satisfying the city's year-round craving for innovative dance. The Northwest New Works Festival, which is held every spring, is one of the season's highlights. In addition to performances by the company, there are special appearances by internationally known artists.

Pacific Northwest Ballet
Seattle Opera House, Third Ave. N. and Mercer St. ☎ **206/292-2787.** Tickets $11–$65

If you happen to be in Seattle in December, try to get a ticket to this company's performance of *Nutcracker*. In addition to outstanding dancing, you'll enjoy sets and costumes by children's book author Maurice Sendak. During the rest of the season, which runs from September to June, the company presents a wide range of classics, new works and pieces choreographed by George Balanchine.

PERFORMING ARTS SERIES

In addition to the series listed below, there is the Broadway at the Paramount series, and at The 5th Avenue Theatre, there is the 5th Avenue Music Theater Company.

Seattle International Music Festival
93 Pike St., Suite 313. ☎ **206/233-0993**. Tickets $20–$25.

This summer classical music series is primarily a chamber music festival with performances being held at various venues over a two week period each summer. Call for details.

UW World Series
Meany Theater, University of Washington campus. ☎ **206/543-4880**. Tickets $24–$33.

Under this umbrella series name, the university stages a chamber music series, classical piano series, world dance series, and a world music and theater series. Together these four series keep the Meany Theater's stage busy between October and April. Special events are also scheduled.

Seattle Fringe Theater Festival
☎ **206/325-5446**. Tickets $8, $5 senior citizens and students.

Seattle loves the theater and each spring, the city binges on the fringes with a festival that provides venues for small, self-producing theater companies. The 1995 festival included 75 theater groups from around the country giving more than 300 performances at seven venues in the Capitol Hill area.

MAJOR PERFORMANCE HALLS

The 5th Avenue Theatre
1308 Fifth Ave. ☎ **206/625-1418**. Tickets $19–$45.

First opened in 1926 as a vaudeville house, The 5th Avenue Theatre is a loose re-creation of the imperial throne room in Beijing's Forbidden City. In 1980, the theater underwent a complete renovation that restored this Seattle jewel to its original splendor. In addition to hosting performances by national touring shows and concerts, the theater has its own resident musical-theater company. Don't miss an opportunity to attend a performance here.

Paramount Theatre
Pine St. and Ninth Ave. ☎ **206/682-1414**. Tickets $20–$65.

The Paramount, one of Seattle's historic theaters, was restored to its original beauty in early 1995, and today shines with all the brilliance it did when it first opened. New lighting and sound systems have brought the theater up to contemporary standards. A Broadway series brings the best touring shows to town. The theater also stages contemporary and classical concerts and many other performances.

CHILDREN'S THEATER COMPANIES

Seattle Children's Theatre
Charlotte Martin Theatre at Seattle Center, Second Ave. N. and Thomas St. ☎ **206/441-3322**. Tickets $10–$16.

Housed in a striking new building containing two theaters, the Seattle Children's Theatre stages both entertaining classics such as *Winnie the Pooh* and thought-provoking dramas such as *The Yellow Boat* (about an eight-year-old hemophiliac with AIDS).

Northwest Puppet Center

9123 15th Ave. NE. ☎ **206/523-2579.** Tickets $6.50 adults, $4.50 children.

Drawing on international themes and traditional tales from around the world, this innovative puppet theater stages performances that will appeal to adults as well as children. Puppet companies from around the world perform throughout the year. There is also a puppet museum here.

2　The Club & Music Scene

If you have the urge to do a bit of nightclubbing and barhopping while in Seattle, there's no better place to start than in Pioneer Square. Good times are guaranteed whether you want to hear a live band, hang out in a good old-fashioned bar, or dance.

FOLK, COUNTRY & ROCK

For the past few years, Seattle bands have been making rock 'n' roll headlines with their distinctive "grunge" rock sound. If the Seattle sound is your thing, grab a copy of *Seattle Weekly* and check the club listings for where the hot new bands are appearing.

The Pioneer Square area is Seattle's main live music neighborhood (almost everything but classical) and the clubs have banded together to make things easy on music fans. The "Joint Cover" plan lets you pay one admission to get into 10 or so clubs. The charge is $5 on weeknights and $7 on weekends. Participating clubs currently include The Fenix, Fenix Underground, Doc Maynard's, Central Cafe, Colourbox, The Bohemian Cafe, and a few other night spots.

✪ Backstage

2208 NW Market St. ☎ **206/781-2805.** Cover $5–$20.

This is Seattle's top venue for contemporary music of all kinds and packs in the crowds most nights. The audience ranges from drinking age up to graying rock 'n' rollers. The music runs the gamut from Afro pop to zydeco.

Ballard Firehouse

5429 Russell St. ☎ **206/784-3516.** Cover $3–$20.

A similarly eclectic assortment of musical styles finds its way onto the bandstand of this converted firehouse in the old Scandinavian section of northwest Seattle. Now it's just the music that's hot, and that's the way they want to keep it. You might catch one of your jazz favorites here, or maybe someone who used to be famous but decided to make good music instead of selling out for big bucks. People having dinner here get the best tables.

Central Cafe

207 First Ave. ☎ **206/622-0209.** Cover $5–$7.

The crowd is young and the music is rock and R&B. You can catch both local and out-of-town bands here.

Crocodile

2200 Second Ave. ☎ **206/441-5611.** Cover $2–$7.

With its rambunctious and wild decor, this Belltown establishment is a combination nightclub, bar, and restaurant. There's live rock Tuesday through Saturday nights. Grunge dominates the schedule, but folk and jazz sometimes show up.

Doc Maynard's

610 First Ave. ☎ **206/682-4649.** Cover $6–$12.

By day it's the starting point of the family oriented Underground Tour, but by night it's one of Seattle's most popular clubs for live rock 'n' roll. This place attracts all types of rock-music lovers, and you'll be welcome as long as you like your music loud.

Fenix/Fenix Underground

315 and 323 Second Ave. ☎ **206/467-1111.** Cover $5–$18.

Located in the heart of the Pioneer Square area, these two clubs are among the best in the area and book an eclectic blend of rock, reggae, and world-beat music by primarily regional acts. Open Wednesday through Sunday.

✪ Kells

1916 Post Alley, Pike Place Market. ☎ **206/728-1916.** Cover Fri–Sat only, $3.

This friendly Irish pub has the look and feel of a casual Dublin pub. They pull a good Guinness stout and feature live traditional Irish music Wednesday through Saturday. This is also a restaurant serving traditional Irish meals.

JAZZ & BLUES

✪ Dimitriou's Jazz Alley

2033 Sixth Ave. ☎ **206/441-9729.** Cover $10.50–$18.50.

This is *the* place for great jazz music in Seattle. Cool and sophisticated, Dimitriou's books only the very best performers and is reminiscent of New York jazz clubs.

New Orleans Creole Restaurant

114 First Ave. S. ☎ **206/622-2563.** No cover weeknights; weekends $7.

If you like your food and your jazz hot, check out the New Orleans. Tuesday is Cajun night, but the rest of the week you can hear Dixieland, R&B, jazz, and blues.

DANCE CLUBS

Downunder

2407 First Ave. ☎ **206/728-4053.** Cover $5.

Located in the Belltown neighborhood north of Pike Place Market, the Downunder is another underground club. Wild decor, light shows, and a high-energy music attract a Generation X crowd. Techno to grunge. Open Friday and Saturday 9pm to 4am.

Iguana Cantina

2815 Alaskan Way. ☎ **206/728-7071.** Cover $3–$8.

Over on the waterfront is a cavernous place popular with Seattle's singles set. There's live Top 40 dance music most nights, and the restaurant has great views of Elliott Bay.

GAY & LESBIAN DANCE CLUBS

Neighbours

1509 Broadway. ☎ **206/324-5358.** Cover Sun–Thurs, $1; Fri–Sat, $3.

This has been the favorite dance club of Capitol Hill's gay community for years, and recently word has gotten out to straights. Still, the clientele is primarily gay. Friday and Saturday buffets are extremely popular.

RE-BAR

1114 Howell St. ☎ **206/233-9873.** Cover $3–$10

Each night there's a different theme, with the DJs spinning everything from world beat to funk and soul to theater performances. Popular with straights and visiting celebrities as well. Thursday and Saturday nights attract the gayest crowds.

3 The Bar Scene

BREW PUBS

Big Time Brewery and Alehouse

4133 University Way NE. ☎ **206/545-4509.**

Located in the University District and decorated to look like a turn-of-the-century tavern complete with 100-year-old back bar and wooden refrigerator, the Big Time serves up three to five of its own brews, which you can see being made on the premises.

Pacific NW Brewing Co.

322 Occidental Ave. S. ☎ **206/621-7021.**

The Pioneer Square area is filled with bars and nightclubs, but if what you really want is a selection of microbrews, check out this brewpub. They usually have six of their own brews on tap, plus plenty of other popular local micros.

The Pub at the Hart Brewery

1201 First Ave. S. ☎ **206/682-8322.**

This pub is located south of the Kingdome and serves Thomas Kemper lagers and Pyramid ales and offers brewery tours, good pub food, and other special events.

✪ **Trolleyman**

3400 Phinney Ave. N. ☎ **206/548-8000.**

This is the taproom of the Redhook Ale Brewery, one of the Northwest's most celebrated microbreweries. It's located in a restored trolley barn on the Lake Washington Ship Canal. You can sample the ales brewed here, have a bite to eat, and even tour the brewery if you are interested.

SPORTS BARS

FX McRory's Steak, Chop, and Oyster House
419 Occidental Ave. S. ☎ **206/623-4800.**

The clientele is upscale, and you're likely to see members of the Seahawks or the SuperSonics at the bar. The original Leroy Neiman paintings on the walls lend class to this sports bar. You'll also find Seattle's largest selection of bourbon and microbrew beers and ales.

Sneakers
567 Occidental Ave. S. ☎ **206/625-1340.**

Located almost directly across the street from the Kingdome, Sneakers is a favorite of Seattle sports fans. The walls are covered with celebrity signatures and old sports photos.

BANKERS' BARS

McCormick & Schmick's
1103 First Ave. ☎ **206/623-5500.**

If the mahogany paneling, sparkling cut glass, and waiters in bow ties don't convince you that you're drinking with money, a glance at the clientele will. Happy hour is very busy as brokers wind down with a few stiff drinks. If you long to rub shoulders with the movers and shakers of Seattle, this is the place for you.

McCormick's Fish House & Bar
722 Fourth Ave. ☎ **206/682-3900.**

This dining-and-drinking establishment provides the same atmosphere as McCormick and Schmick's. Elbow your way up to the bar during after-work hours and you just might overhear a hot tip on the market. Be sure to look your best when you stop in here for a drink.

GAY AND LESBIAN BARS

The Easy
916 E. Pike St. ☎ **206/323-8343.**

This Capitol Hill bar is popular with the lesbian singles crowd and doubles as a dance club.

The Seattle Eagle
314 E. Pike St. ☎ **206/621-7591.**

If you like to hang with the leather and Levi's set, drop by this bar in the Capitol Hill area.

Thumpers
1500 E. Madison St. ☎ **206/328-3800.**

Perched high on Capitol Hill with an excellent view of downtown Seattle, Thumpers is a classy bar done up with lots of oak. The seats by the fireplace are perfect on a cold and rainy night. Great snacks to go with the drinks.

Wildrose

1021 E. Pike St. ☎ **206/324-9210.**

This friendly restaurant/bar is another long-time favorite with the Capitol Hill lesbian community.

4 Cinemas & Movie Houses

Movies come close behind coffee and reading as a Seattle obsession. The city supports a surprising number of cinemas and movie houses showing foreign, independent, and nonmainstream films, as well as first-run movies. These include the **Varsity,** 4329 University Way NE (☎ 206/632-3131); **Grand Illusion,** NE 50th Ave. and University Way NE (☎ 206/523-3935); **Neptune,** NE 45th Ave. and Brooklyn St. NE (☎ 206/633-5545); **Harvard Exit**, 807 E. Roy St. (☎ 206/323-8986); and the **Egyptian,** 801 E. Pine St. (☎ 206/323-4978).

The **Seattle International Film Festival** is held each May, with around 150 films being shown at various theaters. Check the local papers for details.

10

Excursions from Seattle

After you have explored Seattle for a few days, consider heading out of town on a day trip. Within an hour to an hour and a half of the city you can find yourself in the mountains, inside the world's largest building, cruising up a fjordlike arm of Puget Sound, or strolling through a town you may recognize from a hit TV series. The four excursions listed below are all fairly easy day trips that will give you glimpses of the Northwest outside the Emerald City. One other possible excursion is to visit Mount St. Helens National Volcanic Monument. I list this excursion as a day trip from Portland simply because it takes about an hour less to reach the monument from Portland than it does from Seattle.

1 Mount Rainier

Weather forecasting for Seattleites is a simple matter: Either "the Mountain" is out and the weather is good, or it isn't (out or good). "The Mountain" is of course Mount Rainier, the 14,410-foot-tall dormant volcano that looms over Seattle on clear days. Mount Rainier may look as if it were on the edge of town, but it's actually 90 miles southeast of the city.

The mountain and some 235,400 acres surrounding it are part of Mount Rainier National Park, which was established in 1899 as the fifth U.S. national park. From downtown Seattle, the easiest route to the mountain is via I-5 south to exit 127. Then take Wash. 7 south, which in some 30 miles becomes Wash. 706. The route is well marked.

WHAT TO SEE & DO

You'd be well advised to leave as early as possible, especially if you are heading to the mountain on a summer weekend. Traffic along the route and crowds at the park can be daunting. Before leaving, you might contact the park for information. Write or call **Mount Rainier National Park,** Tahoma Woods, Star Route, Ashford, WA 98304 (☎ 206/569-2211). Keep in mind that during the winter the four visitor centers in the park are only open on weekends.

On the way to or from the park on Wash. 7, you might want to stop in the town of **Elbe** to ride on the **Mount Rainier Scenic Railroad** (☎ 206/569-2588). The old steam trains pull vintage cars through lush forests and over old bridges, then wind up at Mineral Lake. The trip covers 14 miles and takes an hour and a half. Fares are $6.95 for adults, $5.95 for senior citizens, $4.95 for ages 12 to 17, and $3.95 for children under age 12. The train operates daily from June 15 to Labor Day, with departures at 11am, 1:15pm, and 3:30pm. From Memorial Day to June 15 and from Labor Day to the end of September, the train operates on weekends only.

If you plan ahead, you can also ride the **Cascadian Dinner Train** from Morton (farther south on Wash. 7) to Elbe. This four-hour, 40-mile trip includes a prime rib dinner and costs $55 per person. The dinner train operates on summer Sundays only and prepaid reservations are required.

Mount Rainier National Park admission is $5 per motor vehicle or $2 per person for pedestrians and bicyclists. Just past the main southwest entrance (Nisqually), you'll come to Longmire, site of the National Park Inn, Longmire Museum (exhibits on the park's natural and human history), a hiker information center that issues backcountry permits, and a ski-touring center where you can rent cross-country skis in winter. The road then continues climbing to Paradise (elevation 5,400 feet), the aptly named mountainside acre that affords a breathtaking close-up view of the mountain. Paradise is the park's most popular destination, so expect crowds. During July and August the meadows here are ablaze with wildflowers. The circular Henry M. Jackson Memorial Visitor Center provides 360° panoramic views, and a short walk away is a spot from which you can look down on Nisqually Glacier. It's not unusual to find plenty of snow at Paradise as late as July. In 1972 the area set a world's record for snowfall in one year—93.5 feet!

In summer you can continue beyond Paradise to the Ohanapecosh Visitor Center, where you can walk through a forest of old-growth trees, some more than 1,000 years old. Continuing around the mountain, you'll reach the turnoff for Sunrise. At 6,400 feet, Sunrise is the highest spot accessible by car. A beautiful old log lodge serves as visitor center. From here you can see not only Mount Rainier, seemingly at arm's length, but also Mounts Baker and Adams.

If you want to avoid crowds and see a bit of dense forest or hike without crowds, head for the park's Carbon River entrance in the northwest corner. This is the least visited region of the park, because it only offers views to those willing to hike several miles uphill. Carbon River is formed by the lowest-elevation glacier in the contiguous 48 states.

Impressions

There is a great deal in the remark of the discontented traveller: "When you have seen a pine forest, a bluff, a river, and a lake, you have seen all the scenery of western America. Sometimes the pine is three hundred feet high, and sometimes the rock is, and sometimes the lake is a hundred miles long. But it's all the same don't you know. I'm getting sick of it."
— Rudyard Kipling

Seattle Excursions

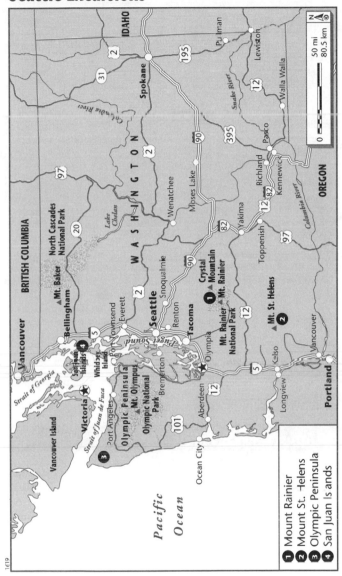

WHERE TO STAY

Besides the two accommodations listed below, there are several **campgrounds** in Mount Rainier National Park.

National Park Inn

P.O. Box 108, Ashford, WA 98304. ☎ **360/569-2275.** 25 rms (18 with private bath). Rates: $60 double without bath; $84 double with bath; $110 double, or triple in two-room unit with bath. AE, CB, DC, DISC, MC, V. Free parking.

Located in Longmire in the southwest corner of the park, this rustic lodge was opened in 1920 and fully renovated in 1990. With only 25 rooms and open all year, the National Park Inn makes a great little getaway or base for exploring Mount Rainier. The inn's front veranda has a view of the mountain, and inside, there's a lounge with a river-rock fireplace that's perfect for winter-night relaxing. Guest rooms vary in size, but come with rustic furniture, new carpeting, clock radios, and coffeemakers. No smoking permitted, anywhere in lodge.

Dining/Entertainment: The inn's restaurant has a limited menu that nevertheless manages to offer something for everyone. There's also a small bar.

Facilities: Gift shop, cross-country ski rental shop adjacent.

Paradise Inn

P.O. Box 108, Ashford, WA 98304. ☎ **360/569-2275**. 126 rms (95 with private bath), 2 suites. $64 double with shared bath; $90 double with bath; $116 double, or triple for a two-room unit with bath; $123 double, or triple suite. AE, CB, DC, DISC, MC, V. Free parking. Closed early Oct–mid May.

Built in 1917 high on the flanks of Mount Rainier in an area aptly known as Paradise, this rustic lodge offers breathtaking views of the mountain and nearby Nisqually Glacier. Cedar-shake siding, huge exposed beams, cathedral ceilings, and a gigantic stone fireplace all add up to a quintessential mountain retreat. A warm, cozy atmosphere prevails. Guest rooms vary in size and some have shared baths. Miles of trails and meadows spread out from the lodge making this the perfect spot for some relatively easy alpine exploring.

Dining/Entertainment: The inn's large dining room serves three meals a day. The Sunday brunch is legendary. A snack bar and lounge are dining options.

Facilities: Gift shop.

2 Across Puget Sound

Outlined here is a possible day trip that starts on one ferry and ends on another. The excursion takes in the quiet and picturesque bedroom community of Bainbridge Island, which is popular for its miles of waterfront, sound-and-mountain views, and rural feel. Continuing on, you can visit a Scandinavian town, a museum dedicated to undersea exploration, a mothballed destroyer, a Native American museum, and a town full of antiques malls. There's more here than you can easily do in one day, so you should pick and choose what interests you the most.

Start the trip by taking the Bainbridge Island ferry from the ferry terminal at Pier 52 on the Seattle waterfront. The fares are $5.90 to $7.10 for a vehicle and driver and $3.50 each for passengers. For a current sailing schedule, contact **Washington State Ferries** (☎ 206/464-6400 or 800/84-FERRY). From on board, you can get a view of the Seattle skyline, and on a clear day, Mount Rainier to the southeast and the Olympic Mountains to the west.

Just up the hill from the Bainbridge Island ferry terminal is the island's main shopping district where you'll find some interesting shops and restaurants. If you'd like to sample the local wine, drop in at the **Bainbridge Island Winery** (☎ 206/842-WINE), which is located a quarter mile up the hill from the ferry landing. Down at the south end of the island, you'll find Fort Ward State Park on the quiet shore of Rich Passage. The **Bainbridge Island Historical Museum** (☎ 206/842-2773) is located at Strawberry Hill Park one mile west of Wash. 305 on High School Road and is housed in a restored one-room schoolhouse built in 1908. The museum is open on Saturdays and Sundays from 11am to 3pm. Garden enthusiasts will want to call ahead and make a reservation to visit the **Bloedel Reserve,** 7571 NE Dolphin Drive (☎ 206/842-7631), which is six miles north of the ferry terminal off Wash. 305 (turn right on Agate Point Road). Expansive and elegant grounds are the ideal place for a quiet stroll amid plants from around the world. Nearby, at the northern tip of the island, you'll find **Fay Bainbridge State Park,** which offers camping and great views across the sound to the Seattle skyline.

After crossing the Agate Passage Bridge to the mainland of the Kitsap Peninsula, take your first right and as you approach the town of Suquamish, you will see signs for the grave of Chief Sealth, for whom Seattle was named. To visit the site of the Old Man House, which was a large Native American longhouse, return to Wash. 305, continue west, turn left at the Suquamish Hardware building, and watch for the sign. The Old Man House itself is long gone, but you'll find an informative sign and a small park with picnic tables. Continuing a little farther on Wash. 305, you'll see signs for the **Suquamish Museum,** 15838 Sandy Hook Road (☎ 360/598-3311), on the Port Madison Indian Reservation. The museum houses a compelling history of Puget Sound's native people. The museum is open May through September daily from 10am to 5pm and October through April Friday through Sunday from 11am to 4pm. Admission is $2.50 for adults, $2 for senior citizens, and $1 children.

Continuing north on Wash. 305, you next come to the small town of Poulsbo, which overlooks fjordlike Liberty Bay. Settled in the late 1880s by Scandinavians, Poulsbo was primarily a fishing, logging, and farming town until the town decided to play up its Scandinavian heritage. Shops in the Scandinavian-inspired downtown sell all manner of Viking and Scandinavian souvenirs. Between downtown and the waterfront, you'll find Liberty Bay Park, and at the south end of Front Street, you'll find the **Marine Science Center,** 17771 Fjord Drive NE (☎ 360/779-5549), which houses interpretive displays on the Puget Sound. The center is open Tuesday through Saturday from 10am to 4pm. Admission is $2 for adults, $1 for senior citizens and children ages 2 through 12, $5 for families (free admission on Tuesday). If you have a sweet tooth, don't miss **Sluys Poulsbo Bakery,** 18924 Front St. NE (☎ 360/697 BAKE), which bakes mounds of goodies, as well as stick-to-your-ribs breads. If you enjoy microbrewery ales, head north of Poulsbo 2 miles to the **Thomas Kemper Brewery,** 22381 Foss Road NE (☎ 360/697-1446), which is also a good spot for lunch. In May the annual Viking Fest celebrates traditional Scandinavian culture, as do the Midsommar Fest and Yule Log Festival.

If you have time and enjoy visiting historic towns, continue north from Poulsbo on Wash. 3 to Port Gamble. This community was established in 1853 as a company town for the Pope and Talbot lumber mill, which today is the oldest operating lumber mill on the West Coast. Along the town's shady streets are many Victorian homes that were restored by Pope and Talbot. Stop by the **Port Gamble Country Store** (☎ 360/297-2623), which now houses the Port Gamble Historical Museum as well as the Of Sea and Shore Museum. The former is a collection of local memorabilia, while the latter exhibits seashells from around the world.

From Port Gamble, head south on Wash. 3 toward Bremmerton to begin an exploration of the area's naval history. Between Poulsbo and Silverdale, you will be passing just east of the Bangor Navy Base, which is home port for a fleet of Trident nuclear submarines. The base is on Hood Canal, a long narrow arm of Puget Sound. Near the town of Keyport, you can visit the **Naval Undersea Museum,** (☎ 360/396-4148), which is located three miles east of Wash. 3 on Wash. 308. The museum explores all aspects of undersea exploration, with interactive exhibits, models, displays that include a deep-sea exploration and research craft, a Japanese kamikaze torpedo, and a deep-sea rescue vehicle. The museum is open daily from 10am to 4pm (closed on Tuesdays between October and May) and admission is free.

Continuing south, you come to Bremerton, which is home to the Puget Sound Naval Shipyard, where mothballed U.S. Navy ships have included the aircraft carriers USS *Nimitz* and USS *Midway* and the battleships USS *Missouri* and USS *New Jersey*. One mothballed destroyer, the **USS *Turner Joy,*** is now operated by the **Bremerton Historic Ships Association** (☎ 360/792-2457) and is open to the public as a memorial to those who have served in the U.S. Navy and who have helped build the navy's ships. The *Turner Joy* is docked about 150 yards east of the Washington State Ferries terminal and is open Thursday through Monday from 10am to 4pm. Admission is $5 for adults, $4 for senior citizens and the military, and $3 for children ages 5 to 12. Nearby is the **Bremerton Naval Museum,** 130 Washington Avenue (☎ 360/479-7447), which showcases naval history and the historic contributions of the Puget Sound Naval Shipyard. The museum is open Monday through Saturday from 10am to 5pm and Sunday from 1 to 5pm (closed Monday Labor Day through Memorial Day). Admission is free.

At one time dozens of small ferries, known as the mosquito fleet, operated around the Puget Sound. One of the last remaining private mosquito fleet ferries still operates between Bremmerton and Port Orchard. If you park your car on the waterfront in Bremmerton, you can step aboard the little passenger-only ferry and cross the bay to Port Orchard. In this little waterfront town, you'll find several antique malls that can provide hours of interesting browsing.

To return to Seattle, take the foot ferry back to Bremmerton, pick up your car and drive on to the car ferry to Seattle. Fares back to Seattle are charged for vehicles and drivers only, not for passengers.

An alternative excursion for anyone who would like to spend more time on the water and less time driving is also possible. Start out by taking the Bremerton ferry from Seattle. In Bremerton, you can then take the **Kitsap Harbor Tours** (☎ 360/377-8924) fast ferry that goes to the Naval Undersea Museum and Poulsbo. This ferry operates four times a day during the summer months. After returning to Bremerton, if you still have time, you can visit Port Orchard.

3 North of the City

This driving excursion takes in the world's largest building, a town full of antiques stores, wineries and a picturesque lakeshore community.

Roughly 30 miles north of Seattle on I-5 on the shore of Puget Sound is the city of **Everett**. Though for the most part it has become a bedroom community for Seattle commuters, it is also home to the region's single largest employer: Boeing. It is here in Everett that the aircraft manufacturer has its main assembly plant. This is the single largest building, by volume, in the world and easily holds several 747s. Free guided tours of the facility are held Monday through Friday between 9am and 1pm, and sometimes again later in the day. Children under four feet tall are not allowed, and the tours are first-come, first-served. For more information, contact the **Boeing Tour Center,** Wash. 526, Everett (☎ 206/342-4801).

A few miles east of Everett off U.S. 2, you can jump from the jet age to horse-and-buggy-days in the historic town of **Snohomish.** Established in 1859 on the banks of the Snohomish River, this historic town was, until 1897 the county seat. However, when the county seat was moved to Everett, Snohomish lost its regional importance and development slowed considerably. Today, an abundance of turn-of-the-century buildings are the legacy of the town's early economic growth. By the 1960s these old homes began attracting people interested in restoring them to their original condition, and soon antique shops began proliferating in historic downtown Snohomish. Today the town has more than 300 antique dealers and is without a doubt the antique capital of the northwest. Surrounding the town's commercial core of antique stores are neighborhoods full of restored Victorian homes. Each year in September, you can get a peek inside some of the town's most elegant homes on the annual **Historical Society Home Tour.** You can pick up a copy of a guide to the town's antiques stores and its historic homes by stopping by or contacting the **Snohomish Chamber of Commerce,** Waltz Building, Avenue B (P.O. Box 135), Snohomish, WA 98290 (☎ 360/568-2526).

Right next door to the chamber of commerce building is the **Blackman Museum** (☎ 360/568-5235) at 118 Avenue B. This 1879 Queen Anne Victorian has been restored and filled with period furnishings. The museum is open daily from noon to 4pm in summer (Wednesday through Sunday from noon to 4pm other months), and admission is $1 for adults and 50¢ for senior citizens and children. For another glimpse into the town's past, head over to Pioneer Village, a collection of restored cabins and other old buildings on Second Street. Each of the buildings is furnished with period antiques.

Heading south from Snohomish to Woodinville brings you into the Puget Sound's small winery region. Largest and most famous of the wineries in the area is **Château St. Michelle,** One Stimson Lane, Woodinville (☎ 206/488-4633), which is located in a grand château on a historic estate that was established in 1912. An amphitheater on the grounds stages music performances throughout the summer. To reach the winery, head south from Woodinville on Wash. 202 and watch for signs. Right across the road from Château St. Michelle, you'll find **Columbia Winery,** 14030 NE 145th St. (☎ 206/488-2776). Other wineries in the area include **French Creek Cellars,** 17721 132nd Avenue NE (☎ 206/486-1900), which is just north of Woodinville, and **Facelli Winery,** 12335 134th Court NE, Redmond (☎ 206/823-9466), which is south of Château St. Michelle off of NE 14th Street.

Finish your day with a walk around downtown Kirkland, which is along the Moss Bay waterfront. You can stroll along the waterfront and stop in at interesting shops and any of more than a dozen art galleries. There are also several decent restaurants in the area. I like the **Cafe Juanita,** 9702 NE 120th Place (☎ 206/823-1505), an excellent Italian restaurant. To get back to Seattle, take I-405 south to I-90.

4　East of the City

If you were a fan of *Northern Exposure* or of the David Lynch TV program *Twin Peaks,* you can visit some spots you'll likely recognize by heading east from Seattle to see where these shows were filmed. Even if you aren't a fan of either TV show, you'll likely enjoy a trip out this way for its mountain scenery and a chance to visit the most spectacular waterfall in the Seattle area.

Snoqualmie Falls, located 35 to 45 minutes east of downtown Seattle on I-90, plummet 270 feet into a pool of deep blue water. The falls are surrounded by a park owned by Puget Power, which operates a hydroelectric plant inside the rock wall behind the falls. The plant, built in 1898 was the world's first underground electric-generating facility. Within the park you'll find two overlooks near the lip of the falls and a half-mile-long trail leading down to the base of the falls.

Anyone interested in seeing other *Twin Peaks* filming sites should stop by the Salish Lodge before heading into the town of North Bend to the **Mar-T Cafe** (☎ 206/888-1221), where you can still get "damn good pie."

One of the best ways to see this area is from a rail car on the **Puget Sound and Snoqualmie Railroad** (☎ 206/746-4025), which has historic depots in Snoqualmie and North Bend. The excursion trains operate on weekends between April and October, but be sure to call ahead for a current schedule. The fares are $6 for adults, $5 for senior citizens, and $4 for children ages 3 to 12.

Continuing east on I-90 another 50 miles or so will bring you to the remote town of **Roslyn,** which was just a quietly decaying old coal-mining town until television turned it into Cicely, Alaska, for the hit TV show *Northern Exposure*. Now the little town has become a major tourist attraction and popular day trip from Seattle. Crowds of visitors wander up and down the town's two-block-long main street hoping to catch a glimpse of someone they recognize from the TV show. Aside from dining at the **Roslyn Cafe,** Pennsylvania and Second streets (☎ 509/649-2763), you can pay a visit to the Roslyn Museum next door to the cafe. About the only other activity in town is wandering through the town's 25 cemeteries, which are up the hill from the Roslyn Cafe. These cemeteries each contain the graves of different nationalities of miners who lived and died in Roslyn.

On your way back to Seattle, you may want to stop in Issaquah, at Gilman Village, an interesting collection of old homes that have been restored and turned into shops and restaurants. Take exit 17.

WHERE TO STAY

Salish Lodge

37807 SE Fall City-Snoqualmie Rd. (P.O. Box 1109), Snoqualmie, WA 98065. ☎ **206/888-2556** or 800/826-6124. 91 rms, 4 suites. A/C TV TEL. Rates: $165–$295 double; $500–$575 suite. AE, CB, DC, DISC, MC, V. Free parking.

Set at the top of 270-foot Snoqualmie Falls and only 35 minutes east of Seattle on I-90, Salish Lodge is a popular weekend getaway spot for folks from Seattle. With its country lodge atmosphere, the Salish aims for casual comfort and hits the mark. Guest room are furnished with wicker and Shaker furnishings and have down comforters on the beds. With fireplaces and whirlpool baths in every room, this lodge is made for romantic weekend getaways. Anyone who was a fan of *Twin Peaks* should immediately recognize the hotel.

Dining/Entertainment: The lodge's country breakfast is a legendary feast that will likely keep you full right through to dinner when you can dine on creative Northwest cuisine in the Salish Dining Room. The dining room also has one of the most extensive wine lists in the state. In the Attic Lounge, you can catch a glimpse of the falls through the window.

Services: Room service, valet/laundry service.

Facilities: Exercise room, hot tub, general store, volleyball/badminton court.

11

Introducing Portland

1 Frommer's Favorite Portland Experiences

- **Hiking and Skiing on Mount Hood.** Less than hour from Portland, Mount Hood offers year-round skiing and hiking. Timberline Lodge, high on the extinct volcano's slopes, was built by the Works Project Administration during the Great Depression and is a showcase of craftsmanship.

- **People Watching at Pioneer Courthouse Square.** This is the heart and soul of downtown Portland and no matter what time of year or what the weather, people gather here. Grab a latte at the Starbucks and sit by the waterfall fountain. In summer, there are concerts here, both at lunch and in the evenings, and any time of year you might catch a rally, performance, or installation of some kind. Don't miss the weather machine show at noon.

- **Hanging Out at Powell's.** They don't call Powell's the City of Books for nothing. This bookstore, selling both new and used books, is huge (you have to get a map at the front door). No matter how long I spend here, it's never long enough. A large cafe makes it all that much easier to while away hours reading something you found on the shelves but aren't sure you want to buy.

- **Beer Sampling at Brewpubs.** They may not have invented beer here in Portland, but they certainly have turned it into an art form. Whether you're looking for a cozy corner pub or an upscale tap room, you'll find a brewpub where you can feel comfortable sampling what local brewmeisters are concocting. Try a raspberry hefeweizen for a true Northwest beer experience.

- **An Afternoon at the Portland Saturday Market.** This large arts-and-crafts market is an outdoor showcase for hundreds of the Northwest's creative artisans. You'll find fascinating one-of-a-kind clothes, jewelry, kitchen wares, musical instruments, and much, much more. The food stalls serve up some great fast food, too.

- **Strolling the Grounds at the Japanese Gardens.** These are the best Japanese Gardens in the United States, perhaps the best anywhere outside of Japan. My favorite time to visit is in June when the Japanese irises are in bloom. There's no better stress-reducer in the city.

- **Summer Music Festivals at Waterfront Park.** Each summer, Tom McCall Waterfront Park, which stretches along the Willamette River in downtown Portland, becomes the staging ground for everything from Rose Festival events to the Oregon Brewers Festival. Some festivals are free and some have small cover charges, but all are lots of fun.

- **Concerts at the Schnitz.** The Arlene Schnitzer Concert Hall is a restored 1920s movie palace and is the city's most impressive place to attend a performance. Even if the show is bad, you can enjoy the classic architectural details. This theater is home to the Oregon Symphony.

- **Free Rides on the Vintage Trolleys.** Tri-Met buses and Max light-rail trolleys are all free within a large downtown area known as the fareless square. That alone should be enough to get you on some form of public transit while you're in town, but if you're really lucky, you might catch one of the vintage trolley cars. There aren't any San Francisco–style hills, but these old trolley cars are still fun to ride.

- **Summertime Concerts at the Washington Park Zoo.** Summertime in Portland means partying with the pachyderms. Two evenings a week throughout the summer, you can catch live music at the zoo's amphitheater. Musical styles include blues, bluegrass, folk, ethnic, and jazz. For the price of zoo admission, you can catch the concert and tour the zoo (if you arrive early enough). Picnics are encouraged, but no alcohol is allowed into the zoo (however, beer and wine are on sale during concerts).

- **First Thursday Art Walk.** On the first Thursday of every month, Portland goes on an art binge. People get dressed up and go gallery hopping from art opening to art opening. There are usually hors d'oeuvres and wine available, and sometimes there's even live music. The galleries stay open until 9pm and there are usually free shuttles to get you from one gallery district to another.

- **Mountain-Biking the Leif Ericson Road.** Forest Park is the largest forested city park in the country, and running its length is the unpaved Leif Ericson Road. The road is closed to cars and extends for 12 miles. Along the way, there are occasional views of the Columbia River and the city's industrial neighborhoods. This is a pretty easy ride, without any strenuous climbs.

- **Kayaking around Ross Island.** Seattle may be the sea kayaking capital of the Northwest, but Portland's not a bad spot for pursuing this sport either. You can paddle on the Columbia or Willamette River, but my favorite easy paddle is around Ross Island in the Willamette River. You can even paddle past the submarine at the Oregon Museum of Science and Industry and pull out at Tom McCall Waterfront Park.

- **Driving and Hiking in the Gorge.** No matter what time of year it is, the drive up the Columbia Gorge is spectacular. If you've got time to spare, take the scenic highway; if not, take I 84. However, no matter which road you take, be sure to pull off at Multnomah Falls. There are dozens of easily accessible hiking trails throughout the length of the gorge. For an alternative point-of view, drive through on the Washington side of the river and stop to climb to the top of Beacon Rock.

2 The City Today

While Seattle has zoomed into the national consciousness, Portland has, until recently, managed to dodge the limelight and the problems that come with skyrocketing popularity. For many years now Portland has looked upon itself as a small, accessible city, vaguely European in character. "Clean" and "friendly" are the two terms that crop up most often in descriptions of the city. However, as word has spread about overcrowding in Seattle, people looking for the good life and affordable housing have turned to Portland. Today the city is beginning to experience the same rapid growth that Seattle went through six or eight years back.

Today, the Portland metropolitan area is facing a battle over how best to develop while still maintaining its distinctive character. To anyone who lives in Portland, the city's greatest attributes are its ease of accessibility to the mountains and the coast and the close proximity of idyllic rural settings.

Within 30 minutes' drive from downtown, you can be out in the country, and within an hour and a half, you can be walking on the beach, skiing on Mount Hood, fishing in the Sandy River, hiking the Barlow Trail, or sampling a Pinot Noir at a winery. The city's distinct boundary between urban and rural is no accident. Portland's Urban Growth Boundary (UGB) was a demarcation line drawn in the 1970s to prevent the city from experiencing the sort of suburban sprawl characteristic of Californian cities. The UGB has worked well for the past 20 years but has recently come under attack from land developers.

At the same time, Portland has been expanding its light rail system into its western suburbs of Beaverton and Hillsboro, which are the heart of the region's high-tech industries and home to such companies as Intel, Epson, Fujitsu, and NEC. It is also here that athletic-wear giant Nike is headquartered.

With growth has come the renovation and gentrification of long neglected neighborhoods throughout Portland. Northwest Portland's Nob Hill area, once filled with funky boutiques, has gone progressively upscale over the past few years. Today fans of funky shops and eateries must venture farther from downtown to areas such as the Hawthorne District, Irvington, Sellwood, Southeast Belmont Street, and Multnomah Village. However, the very fact that these neighborhoods are alive and well is a sign that Portland is taking its growth in stride.

Old Town, one neighborhood that should be the busiest in the city, has never managed to slough off its negative image. Home to both the city's finest restored historic buildings and several missions and soup kitchens for the homeless, the area attracts street people and drug dealers, which together keep most people from venturing into this area except on weekends when the Portland Saturday Market is in full swing. This market is a point of pride to Portlanders who like to show off the creativity of the region's many craftspeople.

Another positive aspect of Portland's current growth is the restaurant renaissance the city is currently experiencing. New restaurants are opening all over the city. Where once good restaurants were confined to a few neighborhoods, today you are as likely to find a great French restaurant in an obscure residential neighborhood as you are to find a fine Northwest-style restaurant downtown.

Other signs of Portland's changing character include the construction of a huge new stadium for the city's NBA basketball team the Portland Trailblazers. A sudden explosion of nightclubs featuring live rock music has many people wondering whether Portland will succeed Seattle as the rock-music capital of America. As yet no Portland band has had the sort of success experienced by Seattle grunge bands Pearl Jam, Nirvana, Alice in Chains, or Soundgarden, but can such stardom be far away?

Two Portlanders who have made a national name for themselves are independent filmmaker Gus van Sant and Claymation animation wizard Will Vinton. Though van Sant's cinematic rendering of Tom Robbins's 1970s cult classic *Even Cowgirls Get the Blues* bombed at the box office, earlier features *Drugstore Cowboy* and *My Own Private Idaho* received very favorable reviews for their portrayals of the seamier side of life in Portland. Will Vinton made his fortune with his animated television commercials featuring the California Raisins. He also applied his own unique animation styling to videos for Michael Jackson.

Portland today is growing quickly, though so far with a deliberation that has not compromised the city's values and unique characteristics. Whether this controlled and intelligent growth can continue remains to be seen. However, for now Portland remains a city both cosmopolitan and accessible.

Portland likes to think of itself as a big little city. It long ago gave up trying to compete with Seattle for the title of the Northwest's Pacific Rim trade capital, and by giving up this goal, it has been able to concentrate on being a very livable city. Compared to the rapid growth in the Seattle area, Portland's progress is moving slowly. However, this hasn't prevented the city from building a new sports arena, extending its light-rail system and opening some very appealing hotels and restaurants that are as good as any you'll find elsewhere.

3 A Look at the Past

Portland was once a very inexpensive piece of property. In 1844 it sold for $50, double the original price of Manhattan Island. Before that, it had been purchased for just 25¢, although the original purchaser had to borrow the quarter. Remember that there was nothing here at the

Dateline
- 1804 Lewis and Clark expedition passes down

continues

the Columbia River on its journey to the Pacific Ocean.

- **1834** Methodist missionaries settle at the confluence of the Columbia and Willamette rivers.

- **1843** Asa Lovejoy and William Overton file a claim for 640 acres on the site of present-day Portland. Filing fee: 25¢.

- **1844** Francis Pettygrove enters into partnership with Lovejoy, buying Overton's share for $50.

- **1845** The name Portland wins over Boston in a coin toss between Pettygrove and Lovejoy.

- **1851** Portland is incorporated.

- **1872** Fire levels most of city.

- **1873** A second fire devastates Portland.

- **1888** First Portland rose show.

continues

time. This was a wilderness, and anyone who thought it would ever be anything more was either foolish or extremely farsighted.

Asa Lovejoy and William Overton, the two men who staked the original claim to Portland, were the latter: farsighted. From this spot on the Willamette River they could see snow-capped Mount Hood 50 miles away; they liked the view and figured other people might also. These two were as disparate as a pair of founding fathers could be. Overton was a penniless drifter. No one is sure where he came from, or where he went when he left less than a year later. Lovejoy had attended Harvard College and graduated from Amherst. He was one of the earliest settlers to venture by wagon train to the Oregon country.

These two men were traveling by canoe from Fort Vancouver, the Hudson's Bay Company fur-trading center on the Columbia River, to the town of Oregon City on the Willamette River. Midway through their journey they stopped to rest at a clearing on the west bank of the Willamette. Overton suggested they stake a claim to the spot. It was commonly believed that Oregon would soon become a U.S. territory and that the federal government would pass out free 640-acre land claims. Overton wanted to be sure that he got his due. Unfortunately, he didn't have the 25¢ required to file a claim. In exchange for half the claim, Lovejoy loaned him the money. Not a bad return on a 25¢ investment!

Wanderlust struck Overton before he could do anything with his claim, and he bartered his half to one Francis Pettygrove for $50 worth of supplies and headed off for parts unknown. Overton must have thought he had turned a pretty deal— from a borrowed quarter to $50 in under a year is a respectable return. Pettygrove, a steadfast Yankee like Lovejoy, was a merchant with ideas on how to make a fortune. Alas, all poor Overton got in the end was a single street named after him.

Pettygrove lost no time in setting up a store on the waterfront, and now with a single building on the site, it was time to name the town. Pettygrove was from Maine and wanted to name the new town for his beloved Portland; Lovejoy was from Boston and wanted that name for the new settlement. A coin was flipped, Pettygrove called it correctly, and a new Portland was born.

Portland was a relative latecomer to the region. Oregon City, Fort Vancouver, Milwaukie, and St. Helens were all doing business in the area when Portland was still just a glimmer in the eyes of Lovejoy and Overton. But in 1846 things changed quickly. Another New Englander, Capt. John Couch, sailed up the Willamette, dropped anchor in Portland, and decided to make this the headquarters for his shipping company.

Another enterprising gentleman, this one a southerner named Daniel Lownsdale, opened a tannery outside town and helped build a road through the West Hills to the wheat farms of the Tualatin Valley. With a road from the farm country and a small port to ship the wheat to market, Portland rapidly became the most important town in the region.

With the 1848 discovery of gold in California (by a former Oregonian), and the subsequent demand for such Oregon products as grain and timber, Portland became a booming little town of 800.

By the late 1880s Portland was connected to the rest of the country by several railroad lines, and by 1900 the population had grown to 90,000. In 1905 the city hosted the Lewis and Clark Exposition, that year's World's Fair, which celebrated the centennial of the explorers' journey to the Northwest. The fairgrounds, landscaped by John Olmsted, successor to Central Park (New York City) designer Frederick Law Olmsted, were a great hit. The city of Portland also proved popular with visitors; by 1910 its population had exploded to 250,000.

By this time, however, there were even more roses than there were people. Since 1888 Portland had been holding an annual rose show, but in 1907 it had blossomed into a full-fledged Rose Festival. Today the annual festival, held each June, is still Portland's favorite celebration. More than 400 varieties bloom in the International Rose Test Gardens in Washington Park, lending Portland the sobriquet City of Roses.

The 1900s have been a roller-coaster ride of boom and bust for Portland. The phenomenal growth of the city's first 50 years has slowed. Timber and agriculture have been the mainstays of the Oregon economy, but the lumber-industry recession of recent years has nearly crippled the Oregon economy. Luckily, the Portland

- **1905** Centenary celebration of the Lewis and Clark expedition.
- **1907** Annual rose show becomes Portland Rose Festival.
- **1927** Downtown wharves are demolished and a seawall is built.
- **1974** Expressway removed from the west bank of Willamette River to create Waterfront Park.
- **1980** Design for Pioneer Courthouse Square, which has become the city's heart and focal point of downtown activities, is chosen.
- **1988** Portland is named "Most Livable U.S. City" by the U.S. Conference of Mayors.
- **1990** The striking Oregon Convention Center is completed.

area has developed a high-tech industrial base that has allowed it to weather the storm and continue to prosper.

Portlanders tend to have a different idea of prosperity than residents of most other cities. Since its beginnings, nature and the city's relationship to it have been an integral part of life here. As far back as 100 years ago the Willamette River was a favored recreation site, with canoe clubs racing on its clean waters. But the industries of the 20th century brought the pollution that killed the river. Downtown Portland lost its preeminence as a shipping port, and eventually the wharves were torn down and replaced by a freeway. This was akin to cutting out Portland's very heart and soul. But the freeway did not last long.

With the heightened environmental awareness of the 1960s and 1970s, Portland's basic character and love of nature began to resurface. A massive cleanup of the Willamette was undertaken—and was eventually so successful that today salmon once again can be seen from downtown Portland. The freeway was torn up and replaced with Tom McCall Waterfront Park (or just Waterfront Park), a large expanse of lawns, trees, fountains, and promenades. But this is only one in a grand network of parks. The city is ringed with them, including Forest Park, the largest wooded city park in the United States, and Washington Park, which is home to the International Rose Test Garden, Japanese Gardens, Metro Washington Park Zoo, and Hoyt Arboretum. Mount Hood, only 90 minutes from downtown, and the hundreds of thousands of acres of national forest surrounding it are well used by the outdoors-conscious citizens of this green city.

Being a "big little city," Portland isn't interested in growth quite so much as Seattle, its main competitor in the Northwest. Economic progress is less important to the city than quality of life. Portland is a clean city, a polite city. Littering is almost unheard of, and in case a bit of trash does make it to the streets and sidewalks, there's a special cleaning crew that works overtime to keep the downtown area sparkling. The city's Percent for Art program also ensures a beautiful downtown. Every new public building must spend slightly more than 1 percent of building costs on public art.

Portland could be considered a bit eccentric. Many Portlanders claim that the hippies of the 1960s are alive and well and selling their crafts at the Portland Saturday Market. You won't find any Styrofoam containers at fast-food restaurants in Portland; they've been banned because of the difficulty of disposing of them after use. Likewise, damaging aerosols have also been banned. And although I haven't been able to verify this statistic, a reliable local source tells me that Portland has the country's highest per capita consumption of Grape Nuts.

Impressions

Oregon is seldom heard of. Its people believe in the Bible, and hold that all radicals should be lynched. It has no poets and no statesmen.
—H. L. Mencken, *Americana*, 1925

12

Planning a Trip to Portland

Planning before you leave can make all the difference between enjoying your trip and wishing you had stayed home. For many people, in fact, planning a trip is half the fun of going. You can write to the addresses below for interesting packets of information that are created to get you excited about your upcoming trip. One of your first considerations should be when you want to visit. Summer is the peak season in the Northwest. That's when the sun shines and outdoor festivals and events take place. During the summer, hotel and car reservations are almost essential; the rest of the year, they are highly advisable. You usually get better rates by reserving at least one or two weeks in advance.

1 Information

For information on Portland and the rest of Oregon, contact the **Portland/Oregon Visitors Association,** Three World Trade Center, 26 SW Salmon St., Portland, OR 97204-3299 (☎ 503/222-2223, or 800/345-3214). There is also an information booth by the baggage-claim area at Portland Airport.

2 When to Go

CLIMATE

This is the section you've all been looking for. You've all heard about the horrible weather in the Northwest. It rains all year, right? Wrong! The Portland area has some of the most beautiful summer weather in the country—warm, sunny days with clear blue skies and cool nights perfect for sleeping. During the months of July, August, and September, it almost never rains. And the rest of the year? Well, yes, it rains in those months and it rains regularly. However, the rain is generally a fine mist and not the torrential downpour most people associate with the word *rain*. In fact, it often rains less in Portland than it does in New York, Boston, Washington, D.C., and Atlanta.

There, now I've let the secret out. Let the stampede begin! Winters here aren't too bad, either. They're warmer than in the Northeast, but there is snow in nearby mountains. In fact, there's so much snow on Mount Hood, only 90 minutes from downtown Portland, that you can ski right through the summer. A raincoat, an umbrella, and a sweater or jacket are all absolutely way of life in this part of the country.

Of course you're skeptical about the amazing information I just presented, so here are the statistics.

Average Temperature & Days of Rain

	Jan	Feb	Mar	Apr	May	June	July	Aug	Sept	Oct	Nov	Dec
Temp. (°F)	40	43	46	50	57	63	68	67	63	54	46	41
Temp. (°C)	4	6	8	10	14	17	20	19	17	12	8	5
Rain (Days)	18	16	17	14	12	10	4	5	8	13	18	19

A CITY OF FESTIVALS

There is nothing Portland enjoys more than a big get-together. Because of the winter weather conditions, these festivals, free concerts, and fairs tend to take place in summer. Not a week goes by then without some sort of event. For a calendar of special events in and around Portland, contact the **Portland Oregon Visitors Association,** Three World

What Things Cost In Portland	U.S. $
Taxi from the airport to the city center	23.00
Bus or tram ride between downtown points	Free
Local telephone call	.25
Double at The Heathman Hotel (very expensive)	160.00–185.00
Double at Riverside Inn (moderate)	89.00
Double at Cypress Inn-Portland Downtown (inexpensive)	63.00
Lunch for one at B. Moloch (moderate)	10.00
Lunch for one at Macheezmo Mouse (inexpensive)	6.00
Dinner for one, without wine, at The Heathman Restaurant (expensive)	29.00
Dinner for one, without wine, at Ristorante Pazzo (moderate)	21.00
Dinner for one, without wine, at Mayas Tacquerie (inexpensive)	7.00
Pint of beer	3.25
Coca-Cola	1.00
Cup of espresso	1.50
Roll of ASA 100 Kodacolor film, 36 exposures	6.00
Admission to the Portland Art Museum	5.00
Movie ticket	6.00–6.50
Oregon Symphony ticket at Arlene Schnitzer Concert Hall	8.00–50.00

Trade Center, 26 SW Salmon St., Portland, OR 97204-3299 (☎ 503/222-2223, or 800/345-3214). To find out what's going on during your visit, pick up a copy of **Willamette Week, Portland Guide** (available in hotels), or the Friday and Sunday **Oregonian.** Some of the larger and more popular special and free events are listed there.

Portland Parks and Recreation also sponsors concerts in more than half a dozen parks throughout the city every summer. Write to them (and include a self addressed, stamped envelope) at 1120 SW Fifth Ave., Portland, OR 97204, for a free schedule of concerts.

PORTLAND CALENDAR OF EVENTS

February
- **Portland International Film Festival,** various theaters around the city. Third weekend in February until March (☎ 503/221-1156).

April
- **Hood River Blossom Festival**, Hood River. Celebration of the blossoming of the orchards outside the town of Hood River. Late April (☎ 800/366-3530).

May
- **Cinco de Mayo Festival,** downtown Portland. Hispanic celebration with food and entertainment (☎ 503/823-4572).
- **Mother's Day Rhododendron Show,** Crystal Springs Rhododendron Gardens. Mother's Day (☎ 503/771-8386).

June
- **Rhythm and Zoo,** Metro Washington Park Zoo. Rhythm and blues concerts are held on Thursday nights from June to August. ☎ 503/226-1561.
- **Your Zoo and All That Jazz,** Metro Washington Park Zoo. Jazz concerts are held on Wednesday nights from June to August (☎ 503/226-1561).
- ✪ **Portland Rose Festival.** From its beginnings back in 1888, when the first rose show was held, the Rose Festival has blossomed into Portland's biggest celebration. The festivities now span 3½ weeks and include a rose show, parade, rose queen contest, music festival, car races, footrace, boat races, and even an air show later on in July. Most of the events take place in the first two weeks of June, and hotel rooms can be hard to come by. Plan ahead.

  Where: All over the city and surrounding communities. **When:** First three weeks of June. **How:** Contact the Portland Rose Festival Association, 220 NW Second Ave., Portland, OR 97209 (☎ 503/227-2681), for information on tickets to specific events.

- **Peanut Butter & Jam Sessions,** Pioneer Courthouse Square, free lunchtime music concerts. They're held every Tuesday and Thursday, mid-June to mid-August (☎ 503/223-1613).

July

- **Fourth of July Fireworks,** Vancouver, WA. Since Vancouver's fireworks display is the biggest west of the Mississippi, Portland wisely decided not to try and compete. Vancouver is just across the river, though, so you can see the fireworks from plenty of spots in Portland. For a close-up view, head up to Jantzen Beach. For an elevated perspective, climb up in the West Hills.
- **Oregon Brewers Festival,** Waterfront Park. American's largest festival of independent brewers features lots of local microbrew and music. Last weekend in July (☎ 503/281-2437).
- **Multnomah County Fair,** Portland Exposition Center. Last week in July (☎ 503/248-5144).
- **Waterfront Blues Festival,** Waterfront Park. Late July (☎ 503/282-0555).
- **Cathedral Park Jazz Festival,** under St. John's Bridge in Cathedral Park. Free performances by nationally known jazz artists. End of July.

August

- **Mount Hood Festival of Jazz,** Mount Hood Community College, Gresham (less than 30 minutes from Portland). For the serious jazz fan, this is the festival of the summer. It features the greatest names in jazz first weekend in August (☎ 503/666-3810).
- **The Bite,** Waterfront Park. Portland's finest restaurants serve up sample portions of their specialties at this food and music festival. A true gustatory extravaganza second weekend in August (☎ 503/248-0600).

September

- **Artquake,** radiating out from Pioneer Courthouse Square along Broadway, Portland's grandest festival of the arts. Visual arts, music, theater, dance, festival foods, and a crafts market are all part of this celebration. Labor Day weekend (☎ 503/227-2787).

October

- **Hood River Harvest Festival,** Hood River. Celebration of the harvest season with crafts and food booths, pie-eating contests, and lots of entertainment. Third weekend in October (☎ 800/366-3530).

December

- **Festival of Trees,** Oregon Convention Center. Extravagantly decorated Christmas trees are displayed among gingerbread houses and trains. Early December (☎ 503/235-7575).
- **Winter Solstice Festival,** Oregon Museum of Science and Industry. In a 4,000-year-old tradition, the lengthening of the days is

celebrated with entertainment, arts and crafts, and special events.
Dec. 20 or 21 (☎ 503/797-4000).

3 Tips for Special Travelers

FOR THOSE WITH DISABILTIES

Many hotels listed in this book feature special rooms for the disabled,
but when making a hotel reservation, be sure to ask.

All MAX light-rail (trolley) system stations have wheelchair lifts, and
there are two wheelchair spaces available on each train. Be sure to wait
on the platform lift. Many of the Tri-Met buses also are equipped with
wheelchair lifts and wheelchair spaces. Look for the wheelchair symbol
on buses, schedules, and bus stops. There is also a special door-to-door
service provided for people who are not able to use the regular Tri-Met
service, but they must have an eligibility card from another public
bus system. Phone 503/238-4952 for information. **Broadway Cab**
(☎ 503/227-1234) and **Radio Cab** (☎ 503/227-1212) both have
vehicles for transporting the disabled.

FOR SENIORS

Many hotels, museums, theaters, gardens, and tour companies offer
special discounts for senior citizens. I have noted this in listings. See
"For Seniors" in the Seattle section for additional information.

There's no doubt about it, single travelers are discriminated against
by hotels and motels. A lone traveler often has to pay the same room
rate as two people, and if you want to spend time at an expensive
hotel, this can make a vacation a very costly experience. Unless you are
dead set on staying at a particular hotel, you might be able to save some
money by finding a comparable hostelry that offers separate rates for
single and double rooms.

FOR FAMILIES

At many hotels in Portland, kids stay free in their parents' room. Be
sure to check the listing or ask when you contact a hotel. As many as
three children under age six can ride free with an adult on Tri-Met
buses and MAX.

FOR STUDENTS

Student discounts are available at many museums, theaters, and
concert halls. Be sure to carry a current student ID and ask about
discounts.

4 Getting There

BY PLANE

Portland International Airport (PDX) (☎ 503/335-1234) Oregon's
main airport is located ten miles northeast of downtown Portland,
adjacent to the Columbia River. The airport is relatively small but offers some amenities you wouldn't expect at a facility this size. Tops on
this list is the PDX Conference Center which offers businesspeople a
secluded and quiet working space.

The Major Airlines   About 15 carriers service Portland Airport to and from some 100 cities worldwide. The major airlines include **Alaska Airlines** (☎ 503/224-2547, or 800/426-0333), **America West** (☎ 800/235-9292), **American Airlines** (☎ 800/433-7300), **Delta** (☎ 800/221-1212), **Horizon** (☎ 800/547-9308), **Southwest** (☎ 800/466-7747, or 800/435-9792), **Northwest** (☎ 800/225-2525), **TWA** (☎ 503/282-1111, or 800/221-2000), **United Airlines** (☎ 800/241-6522), and **USAir** (☎ 800/428-4322).

BY TRAIN

Amtrak passenger trains connect Portland with Seattle, San Francisco, Salt Lake City, Chicago, and the rest of the country and stop at Union Station, 800 NW Sixth Ave. (☎ 503/273-4866), about 10 blocks from the heart of downtown Portland. For Amtrak schedule information and reservations, call 800/872-7245.

BY BUS

Greyhound Bus Lines connects Portland with the rest of the country. The bus station is at 550 NW Sixth Ave. (☎ 503/243-2316, or 800/231-2222).

BY CAR

Portland is linked to the rest of the United States by a number of interstate highways and smaller roads. I-5 runs north to Seattle and south as far as San Diego. I-84 runs east as far as Salt Lake City. I-405 arcs around the west and south of downtown Portland. I-205 bypasses the city to the east. U.S. 26 runs west to the coast.

Here are some driving distances from selected cities (in miles):

Los Angeles	1,015
San Francisco	640
Seattle	175
Spokane	350
Vancouver, B.C.	285

13

Getting to Know Portland

Portland's compactness makes it a wonderfully easy city to explore. Although the airport is in the northeastern part of the city, most important sights and hotels are in the southwestern part. The Willamette River forms a natural dividing line between the eastern and western portions of the city, while the Columbia River forms a boundary with the state of Washington to the north. The West Hills, Portland's prime residential district, are a beautiful backdrop for this attractive city. Covered in evergreens, the hills rise to a height of 1,000 feet at the edge of downtown. Within these hills are Metro Washington Park Zoo, the International Rose Test Garden, the Japanese Gardens, and several other attractions. When you're ready to leave Portland and explore the beautiful Oregon countryside, it's easy to drive away on an Interstate and be far from the city in 30 minutes.

1 Orientation

ARRIVING

By Plane   Portland International Airport (PDX) (☎ 503/335-1234) is located ten miles northeast of downtown Portland. The trip into town is entirely on interstates and takes about 20 minutes. The airport is small enough to be convenient but large enough to offer amenities you wouldn't expect. Tops on this list is the **PDX Conference Center,** which offers businesspeople a secluded and quiet working space. There are meeting rooms, fax machines, computer workstations, secretarial help, and more. Also at the airport is the **Oregon Market,** a shopping mall featuring Oregon-based retail stores and food and beverage vendors. You can pick up a pair of Nikes as you run to make your flight or hook into a fresh salmon packed to go.

There's an information booth by the baggage-claim area where you can pick up maps and brochures and find out about transportation into the city.

Many hotels near the airport provide courtesy shuttle service to and from the airport. Be sure to check at your hotel when you make a reservation.

If you haven't rented a car at the airport, the best way to get into town is to take the **Raz Transportation Downtown Shuttle** (☎ 503/246-3301), located outside the baggage claim area. They'll take you

Portland Orientation

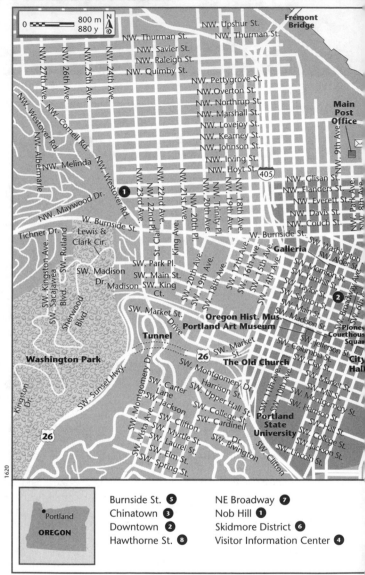

Burnside St. **5**	NE Broadway **7**
Chinatown **3**	Nob Hill **1**
Downtown **2**	Skidmore District **6**
Hawthorne St. **8**	Visitor Information Center **4**

OREGON

• Portland

directly to your hotel for $8.50. They operate every 30 minutes from 5am to midnight daily.

Tri-Met public bus no. 12 leaves the airport approximately every 15 minutes from 5:30am to 11:50pm for the trip to downtown Portland. The trip takes about 40 minutes and costs $1. The bus between downtown and the airport operates between 5am and 12:30am and leaves from SW Sixth Avenue and Main Street.

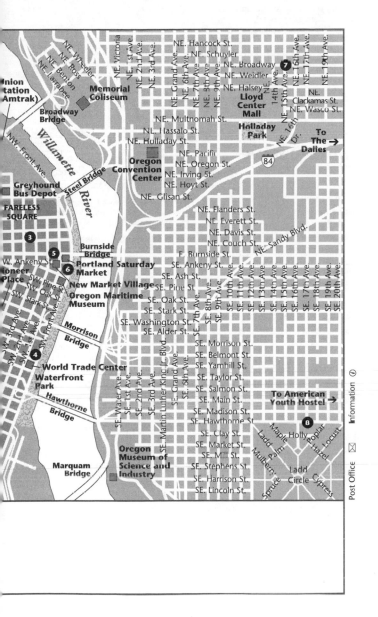

A **taxi** into town costs around $23.

By Train   Amtrak trains use historic **Union Station,** 800 NW Sixth Ave. (☎ 503/273-4866). For Amtrak schedule and fare information and reservations, call 800/872-7245.

By Bus   The **Greyhound bus station** is located at 550 NW Sixth Ave. (☎ 503/243-2316 or 800/231-2222).

By Car   Portland's major interstates and smaller highways are **I-5** (north and south), **I-84** (east), **I-405** (circles around the west and south of downtown Portland), **I-205** (bypasses the city to the east), and **U.S. 26** (west).

If you have rented a car at the airport and want to reach central Portland, follow signs for downtown. These signs will take you first to I-205, then I-84, which brings you to the Willamette River. Take the Morrison Bridge exit to cross the river.

VISITOR INFORMATION

The **Portland Oregon Visitors Association Information Center** is at Two World Trade Center, 25 SW Salmon St. (☎ 503/222-2223, or 800/345-3214). There is also an information booth by the baggage-claim area at Portland Airport. If you happen to see two people walking down a Portland street wearing matching kelly-green hats and jackets, they are probably members of the **Portland Guide** service run by the Association for Portland Progress (☎ 503/224-8684). They'll be happy to answer any question you have about the city.

CITY LAYOUT

Portland is located in northwestern Oregon at the confluence of the Columbia and Willamette rivers. To the west are the West Hills, which rise to more than 1,000 feet. Some 90 miles west of the West Hills are the spectacular Oregon coast and the Pacific Ocean. To the east are rolling hills that extend to the Cascade Range, about 50 miles away. The most prominent peak in this section of the Cascades is Mount Hood (11,235 feet), a dormant volcanic peak that looms over the city on clear days. From many parts of Portland it's also possible to see Mount St. Helens, another volcano, which erupted spectacularly in 1980.

With about 1.6 million people in the entire metropolitan area, Portland is a relatively small city. This is especially evident when one begins to explore the compact downtown area. Nearly everything is accessible on foot, and the city authorities do everything they can to encourage this.

Main Arteries & Streets   **I-84 (Banfield Freeway** or **Expressway)** enters Portland from the east. East of the city is **I-205,** which bypasses downtown Portland and runs past the airport. **I-5 (East Bank Freeway)** runs through on a north-south axis, passing along the east bank of the Willamette River directly across from downtown. **I-405 (Stadium Freeway** and **Foothills Freeway)** circles around the west and south sides of downtown. **U.S. 26 (Sunset Highway)** leaves downtown heading west toward Beaverton and the coast. **Oregon Hwy. 217 (Beaverton-Tigard Highway)** runs south from U.S. 26 in Beaverton.

The most important artery within Portland is **Burnside Street.** This is the dividing line between north and south Portland. Dividing the city from east to west is the **Willamette River,** which is crossed by eight bridges in the downtown area. All these bridges are named; from north to south they are Fremont, Broadway, Steel, Burnside, Morrison, Hawthorne, Marquam, and Ross Island. There are additional bridges beyond the downtown area.

For convenience sake I'll define downtown Portland as the 300-block area within **Fareless Square.** This is the area in which you can ride for free on the city's public buses and the MAX light-rail system. Fareless Square is bounded by I-405 on the west and south, by Hoyt Street on the north, and by the Willamette River on the east.

Finding an Address Finding an address in Portland can be easy if you keep a number of things in mind. Almost all addresses in Portland, and even extending for miles beyond the city, include a map quadrant—NE (Northeast), SW (Southwest), and so forth. The dividing line between east and west is the Willamette River; between north and south it's Burnside Street. Any downtown address will be labeled either SW (Southwest) or NW (northwest). An exception to this rule is the area known as North Portland. Streets here have a plain "North" designation. This is the area across the Willamette River from downtown going toward Jantzen Beach.

Avenues run north-south and streets run east-west. Street names are the same on both sides of the Willamette River. Consequently, there is a Southwest Yamhill Street and a Southeast Yamhill Street. In northwest Portland street names are alphabetical going north from Burnside to Wilson. Front Avenue is the road nearest the Willamette River on the west side, and Water Avenue is the nearest on the east side. Beyond these are numbered avenues. On the west side you'll also find Broadway and Park Avenue between Sixth Avenue and Ninth Avenue. With each block, the addresses increase by 100, beginning at the Willamette River for avenues and at Burnside Street for streets. Odd numbers are generally on the west and north sides of the street, and even numbers on the east and south sides.

Here's an example. You want to go to 1327 SW Ninth Avenue. Because it's in the 1300 block, you'll find it 13 blocks south of Burnside and, because it's an odd number, on the west side of the street.

Street Maps Stop by the **Portland Oregon Visitors Association** Information Center, Two World Trade Center, 25 SW Salmon St. (☎ 503/222-2223, or 800/345-3214), for a free map of the city. **Powell's "City of Books,"** 1005 W. Burnside St. (☎ 503/228-4651, or 800/878-7323), has an excellent free map of downtown that also includes a walking-tour route and information on many of the sights you'll pass along the way. Members of the **American Automobile Association** can obtain a free map of the city at the AAA offices at 600 SW Market St. (☎ 503/222-6734) and 8555 SW Apple Way in Beaverton (☎ 503/243-6444).

2 Neighborhoods in Brief

Downtown This term usually refers to the business and shopping district south of Burnside and north of Jackson Street between the Willamette River and 13th Avenue. You'll find the major department stores, dozens of restaurants, most of the city's performing arts venues, and almost all of the best hotels in this area.

Pearl District This neighborhood of galleries, artist's lofts, cafes, breweries, and shops is bounded by the Park blocks, Lovejoy Street, I-405, and Burnside Street. Crowds of people come out here on First Thursday when the galleries and other businesses are open late.

Chinatown Portland has had a Chinatown almost since the earliest days. It is entered through the colorful Chinatown Gate at West Burnside Street and Fourth Avenue.

Skidmore District Also known as Old Town, this is Portland's original commercial core and overlaps with Chinatown for a few streets. The center of this district is the Skidmore Fountain at SW Ankeny Street and SW Front Avenue. Many of the restored buildings in this neighborhood have become retail stores, which, along with the presence of the Portland Saturday Market here, has made this one of Portland's popular shopping districts. There are also half a dozen or so nightclubs.

Nob Hill Centered along NW 23rd Avenue at the foot of the West Hills, Nob Hill is an old residential neighborhood that now includes interesting shops and restaurants. This is by far the most stylish neighborhood in town. It's named for Nob Hill in San Francisco.

Irvington Though not as attractive as Nob Hill, Irvington, centered around Broadway in northeast Portland, is equally trendy. For several blocks along Broadway you'll find unusual boutiques, stores selling imports, and lots of excellent but inexpensive restaurants.

Hollywood District One of the latest neighborhoods to attract attention in Portland is the Hollywood District of northeast Portland. This area, which centers around the busy commercial activities of Sandy Boulevard near 42nd Avenue, came into being in the early years of this century. The name is taken from the Hollywood Theater, an Art Deco–style area landmark. Throughout this neighborhood are craftsman-style houses and vernacular architecture of the period.

Sellwood Situated in the southeast, this is Portland's antique store district and contains many restored Victorian houses. There are also excellent restaurants.

Hawthorne District This enclave of southeast Portland is full of eclectic boutiques, moderately priced restaurants, and hip college students from nearby Reed College.

3 Getting Around

BY PUBLIC TRANSPORTATION

Free Rides Portland is committed to keeping its downtown uncongested, and to this end it has invested heavily in its public-transportation system. The single greatest innovation and best reason to ride the Tri-Met public buses and the MAX light-rail system is that they're free within an area known as the **Fareless Square.** That's right, free! There are 300 blocks of downtown included in the Fareless Square, and as long as you stay within the boundaries, you don't pay a cent. The

Fareless Square covers the area between I-405 on the south and west, Hoyt Street on the north, and the Willamette River on the east.

Bus   Tri-Met buses operate daily over an extensive network. You can pick up the *Tri-Met Guide,* which lists all the bus routes with times, or individual route maps and time schedules at the **Tri-Met Customer Assistance Office,** behind and beneath the waterfall fountain at Pioneer Courthouse Square (☎ 503/238-7433). The office is open Monday through Friday from 9am to 5pm.

Outside Fareless Square, fares on both Tri-Met buses and MAX are $1 or $1.30, depending on how far you travel.

Seniors 65 years and older pay 50¢ with valid proof of age.

You can also make free transfers between the bus and the MAX light-rail system. A **day ticket** costing $3.25 is good for travel to all zones and is valid on both buses and MAX. Day tickets can be purchased from any bus driver. Nearly all Tri-Met buses pass through the Transit Mall on SW Fifth Avenue and SW Sixth Avenue.

MAX   The **Metropolitan Area Express (MAX)** is Portland's above-ground light-rail system that now connects downtown Portland with the eastern suburb of Gresham. MAX is basically a modern trolley; reproductions of vintage trolley cars operate during certain times on weekends. You can ride MAX for free if you stay within Fareless Square, which includes all the downtown area. However, be sure to buy your ticket before you board MAX if you're traveling out of Fareless Square. Fares are the same as on buses. There are ticket-vending machines at all MAX stops that tell you how much to pay for your destination; these machines also give change. The MAX driver cannot sell tickets. There are ticket inspectors who randomly check tickets. If you don't have one, you can be fined up to $300.

The MAX light-rail system crosses the Transit Mall on SW Morrison Street and SW Yamhill Street. Transfers to the bus are free.

BY TAXI

Because most everything in Portland is fairly close, getting around by taxi can be economical. Although there are almost always taxis waiting in line at major hotels, you won't find them cruising the streets—you'll have to phone for one. **Broadway Cab** (☎ 503/227-1234) and **Radio Cab** (☎ 503/227-1212) both offer 24-hour radio-dispatched service and accept American Express, Discover, MasterCard, and VISA credit cards. Fares are $2 for the first mile and $1.50 for each additional mile.

BY CAR

Car Rentals   For the best deal on a rental car, I highly recommend making a reservation at least one week before you arrive in Portland. It also pays to call several times over a period of a few weeks just to ask prices; the last time I rented a car, the same company quoted me different prices every time I called to ask about rates. Remember the old Wall Street adage: Buy low! If you didn't have time to plan ahead, ask about special weekend rates or discounts you might be eligible for. And don't forget to mention that you are a frequent flyer. You might be able to get miles for your car rental. Also, be sure to find out whether your credit card pays the collision-damage waiver, which can add a bundle to the cost of a rental. Currently, daily rates for a subcompact are around $25 to $35 and weekly rates are around $130 to $150.

The major car-rental companies are represented in Portland, and there are also many independent and smaller car-rental agencies listed in the Portland Yellow Pages. At Portland International Airport, across the street from the baggage-claim area in the short-term parking garage you'll find the following companies:

Avis (☎ 503/249-4950 or 800/831-2847), which also has an office downtown at 330 SW Washington St. (☎ 503/227-0220) and in Beaverton at 11135 SW Canyon Rd. (☎ 503/526-0614). **Budget** (☎ 503/249-6500 or 800/527-0700), which also has offices downtown at 2033 SW Fourth Ave., on the east side at 2323 NE Columbia Blvd., and in Beaverton at 10835 SW Canyon Rd. **Dollar** (☎ 503/249-4792 or 800/800-4000), which also has an office downtown at NW Broadway and NW Davis St. (☎ 503/228-3540). **Hertz** (☎ 503/249-8216 or 800/654-3131), which also has an office downtown at 1009 SW Sixth Ave. (☎☎ 503/249-5727). **National** (☎ 503/249-4900 or 800/227-7368). Outside the airport is **Thrifty,** at 10800 NE Holman St. (☎ 503/254-6563 or 800/367-2277), which also has an office downtown at 632 SW Pine St. (☎ 503/227-6587).

Parking   Parking downtown can be a problem, especially if you show up weekdays after workers have gotten to their offices. There are a couple of very important things to remember when parking downtown.

When parking on the street, be sure to notice the meter's time limit. These vary from as little as 15 minutes (these are always right in front of the restaurant or museum where you plan to spend two hours) to long term (read long walk). Most common are 30- and 60-minute meters. You don't have to feed the meters after 6pm or on Sunday.

The best parking deal in town is at the **Smart Park** garages, where the cost is 75¢ per hour or $3 all day on the weekends. Look for the red, white, and black signs. You'll find Smart Park garages at First Avenue and Jefferson Street; Fourth Avenue and Yamhill Street; Tenth Avenue and Yamhill Street; Third Avenue and Alder Street; O'Bryant Square; and Front Avenue and Davis Street.

If you're going shopping, look for a red and green sign that says 2 HR FREE PARK DOWNTOWN at pay parking lots and garages. Spend $15 or more at any participating merchant and you get two hours of free parking at these garages or at Smart Park, above. Don't forget to have the merchant validate your parking stub.

Rates in other public lots range from about $1 up to about $2.75 per hour.

Driving Rules   You may turn right on a red light after a full stop, and if you are in the far left lane of a one-way street, you may turn left into the adjacent left lane at a red light after a full stop.

BY BICYCLE

Bicycles are a very popular way of getting around Portland. For leisurely cycling, try the promenade in Waterfront Park. The east side of the river between the Hawthorne and Burnside bridges. The Terwilliger Path runs for 10 miles from Portland State University to Tryon Creek State Park in the West Hills. You can pick up a copy of a bike map of the city of Portland at most bike shops. At **Agape Cycle and Sport,** 2314 SE Division St. (☎ 503/230-0317), you can rent a road or mountain bike for $15 a day or $75 a week. They're open Tuesday to Saturday from 10:30am to 6pm.

ON FOOT

City blocks in Portland are about half the size of most city blocks else-where, and the entire downtown area covers only about 13 blocks by 26 blocks. These two facts make Portland a very easy place to explore on foot. The city has been very active in encouraging people to get out of their cars and onto the sidewalks downtown. The sidewalks are wide, and there are many small parks with benches for resting, fountains for cooling off, and works of art for soothing the soul.

If you happen to spot a couple of people wearing kelly-green base-ball caps and jackets and navy-blue pants, they're probably a pair of Portland Guides. These informative souls are there to answer any ques-tions you might have about Portland—"Where am I?" for instance. Their job is simply to walk the streets and answer questions.

FAST FACTS: Portland

Airport   **Portland International Airport (PDX)** is located ten miles northeast of downtown Portland; for information call 503/335-1234.

American Express   The **American Express Travel Service Office** (☎ 503/226-2961) is located at 1100 SW Sixth Ave.—corner of Sixth and Main. The office is open Monday through Friday from 9am to 5pm. You can cash American Express traveler's checks and exchange the major foreign currencies here.

Area Code   The area code for Portland and the entire state of Oregon is **503.**

Babysitters   Call Wee-Ba-Bee Child Care (☎ 503/786-3837) if your hotel doesn't offer baby-sitting services.

Car Rentals   See Section 3 of this Chapter.

Climate   See "Climate" in Section 2 of Chapter 12.

Dentist   If you need a dentist while you are in Portland, contact the **Multnomah Dental Society** for a referral (☎ 503/223-4738).

Doctor   If you need a physician while in Portland, contact the **Multnomah County Doctor Referral Service** for a referral (☎ 503/222-0156).

Drugstore   Convenient to most downtown hotels, **Central Drug,** 538 SW Fourth Ave. (☎ 503/226-2222), is open Monday to Friday from 9am to 6pm, on Saturday from 10am to 4pm.

Emergencies   For police, fire, or medical emergencies, phone 911.

Hospitals   Three area hospitals are **Legacy Good Samaritan,** 1015 NW 22nd Ave. (☎ 503/229-7711); **St. Vincent Hospital,** 9205 SW Barnes Rd. (☎ 503/291-2115), off U.S. 26 (Sunset Highway) before Oregon Hwy. 217; and the **Oregon Health Sciences University Hospital,** 3181 SW Sam Jackson Park Rd. (☎ 503/494-8311), just southwest of the city center.

Information   For tourist information, stop by the **Portland Oregon Visitors Association** Information Center at Two World Trade Center, 25 SW Salmon St. (☎ 503/222-2223, or 800/345-3214). While you're in Portland, if you spot members of the **Portland Guide Service**—dressed in kelly-green hats and jackets—they'll be happy to answer any question you have about the city.

Liquor Laws   The legal minimum drinking age in Oregon is 21.

Lost Property   If you lose something on a bus or the MAX, call 503/238-4855 Monday through Friday from 9am to 5pm. If you lose something at the airport, call 503/335-1277.

Luggage Storage/Lockers   You'll find coin-operated luggage-storage lockers at the **Greyhound Bus Station,** 550 NW Sixth Ave. (☎ 503/243-2316).

Newspapers/Magazines   Portland's morning daily newspaper is *The Oregonian.* For arts and entertainment information and listings, consult the *Arts and Entertainment* section of the Friday *Oregonian* or pick up a free copy of *Willamette Week* at Powell's Books and other bookstores or cafes.

   The *Portland Guide* is a weekly tourism guide to Portland and is available at hotels.

Photographic Needs   **Flashback Foto,** 900 SW Fourth Ave. (☎ 503/224-6776), and 730 SW Alder (☎ 503/224-6775), offers 1-hour film processing. It's open Monday through Friday from 7am to 7pm, on Saturday from 10am to 6pm, and on Sunday from noon to 5pm. **Camera World,** 400 SW Sixth Ave. (☎ 503/222-0008), is the largest camera and video store in the city; open Monday through Thursday from 9am to 6pm, Friday from 9am to 8pm, Saturday from 10am to 6pm, and Sunday from 11am to 5pm.

Police   To reach the police, call 911.

Post Offices   The **main post office,** 715 NW Hoyt St. (☎ 503/294-2300), is open Monday through Friday from 7:30am to 6:30pm, Saturday from 8:30am to 5pm. There are also convenient post offices at 204 SW Fifth Ave. (☎ 503/221-0202), open Monday through Friday from 8:30am to 5pm, and 1505 SW Sixth Ave. (☎ 503/221-0199), open Monday through Friday from 7am to 6pm, Saturday from 10am to 3pm.

Radio   KOPB-FM (91.5) is the local National Public Radio station.

Impressions

We invite you to visit our State of Excitement often. Come again and again. But for heaven's sake, don't move here to live. Or if you do have to move in to live, don't tell any of your neighbors where you are going.

—Gov. Tom McCall, 1971

Restrooms   There are public restrooms underneath Starbucks coffee shop in Pioneer Courthouse Square and in downtown shopping malls.

Safety   Because of its small size and emphasis on keeping the downtown alive and growing, Portland is still a relatively safe city; in fact, strolling the downtown streets at night is a popular pastime. Take extra precautions, however, if you venture into the entertainment district along West Burnside Street or Chinatown at night. Parts of northeast Portland are controlled by street gangs, so before visiting any place in this area, be sure to get very detailed directions so that you don't get lost. If you plan to go hiking in Forest Park, don't leave anything valuable in your car. This holds true in the Old Town district as well.

Taxes   Portland is a shopper's paradise—there's no sales tax. However, there is a 9 percent tax on hotel rooms within the city of Portland. Outside the city, the room tax varies.

Taxis   To get a cab, call **Broadway Cab** at 503/227-1234, or **Radio Cab** at 503/227-1212. See also Section 3 of this chapter.

Television   Channels in Portland are 2 (ABC), 6 (CBS), 8 (NBC), 10 (PBS), 12, 24 (religious), and 49 (Fox). All major cable networks are also available.

Time   Portland is on **Pacific Time,** making it three hours behind the East Coast.

Transit Information   For bus information, call the **Tri-Met Customer Assistance Office** at 503/238-7433. They're open Monday through Friday from 7:30am to 5:30pm. You can pick up a *Tri-Met Guide* from their office located beneath the waterfall fountain at Pioneer Courthouse Square. For **Amtrak** schedule and fare information, call 800/872-7245. To reach **Union Station** (for train arrival times only), call 503/273-4865. For the **Greyhound bus station,** call 503/243-2316.

Useful Telephone Numbers   You may find the following telephone numbers useful during your stay in Portland: **Alcoholics Anonymous** (☎ 503/223-8569); **Portland Center for the Performing Arts Information Hotline** (☎ 503/796-9293); **rape hotline** (☎ 503/235-5333); **suicide prevention** (☎ 503/223-6161).

Weather   If it's summer, it's sunny; otherwise, there's a chance of rain. This is almost always a sufficient weather forecast in Portland, but for specifics, call weather information (☎ 503/236-7575).

4   Networks & Resources

FOR STUDENTS

There are no huge universities in Portland, but there are a number of smaller ones. **Portland State University,** 724 SW Harrison St. (☎ 503/725-3000), in downtown Portland, is a state-run commuter college. The **University of Portland,** 5000 N. Willamette Blvd. (☎ 503/283-7911), in North Portland, is operated by the Holy Cross Fathers of Notre Dame. The parklike campus is situated on a scenic bluff high over the Willamette River. **Reed College,** 3203 SE Woodstock St. (☎ 503/771-1112), a small private college of the liberal arts in southeastern Portland, was an anachronism when it opened in 1911. It shunned fraternities, sororities, athletics, and other aspects of college life in favor of academic excellence. Today it ranks highest in the number of Rhodes Scholars produced for a college of its size.

FOR GAY MEN & LESBIANS

Gay men and lesbians visiting Portland should be sure to pick up a free copy of *Just Out,* a monthly newspaper for the gay community. You can usually find copies at **Powell's Books,** 1005 W. Burnside St., or phone 503/236-1252 to find out where you can obtain a copy. The newspaper covers local news of interest to gays. They also publish a resource guide for lesbians and gays called *The Just Out Pocket Book.* Call the above number to find out where you can get a copy. The guide is a free directory of Portland businesses that welcome gay customers.

FOR WOMEN

Old Wives' Tales, 1300 E. Burnside St. (☎ 503/238-0470), is a restaurant that, although not strictly for women, has for years been popular with feminists and single mothers. It's open daily for breakfast, lunch, and dinner. They have newspapers to read and a children's playroom. The women's **crisis hotline** number is 503/235-5333.

FOR SENIORS

Be sure to carry some form of photo ID with you when visiting Portland. Many hotels, museums, theaters, gardens and tour companies offer special discounts for senior citizens, which I have noted in listings.

Portland Accommodations

1 Best Bets

Best Grand Old Hotel (or Best Lobby for Railroad Baron Wannabes): With its walnut paneling, Italian marble, and crystal chandeliers, the Hotel Benson is the pinnacle of 19th-century elegance. Order a snifter of brandy, sink into one of the leather chairs by the fireplace, and you too can conjure up your past life as a railroad baron (☎ 503/228-2000).

Best for Business Travelers: For all-around convenience, location, and amenities, it's hard to beat the RiverPlace Hotel. The hotel is right on the Willamette River, within walking distance of downtown businesses, and has several good restaurants within a block or two. Complimentary shoe shines and morning papers start your day off right, and when it's time to do some work in the room, there are in-room modem and fax hook-ups and voice mail. Plus, you get to use the adjacent full-scale athletic club (☎ 503/228-3233).

Best for a Romantic Getaway: If you're looking for the most romantic room in town, book a starlight room at the Hotel Vintage Plaza. Located on one of the hotel's upper floors, these rooms are basically solariums with curving walls of glass that let you lie in bed and gaze up at the stars. Just be sure to come in the summer when there aren't as many clouds in the sky (☎ 503/228-1212).

Best for Families: With both a shopping mall and a park across the street, the Red Lion-Lloyd Center is a great choice if you're traveling with kids. The Rose Garden sports arena is also nearby as are quite a few good, casual restaurants (☎ 503/281-6111).

Best Moderately Priced Hotel: It's hard to find a moderately priced downtown hotel in any city, and Portland is no exception. However, if you don't mind a bit of faded glory, the Mallory Hotel is the best choice in town. The rooms are far from luxurious, but they suffice, and at less than half the price of hotels only four blocks away it's a great deal (☎ 503/223-6311).

Best B&B: With views, a swimming pool, attractive gardens, a secluded feel, and the shops, restaurants, and cafes for Northwest 23rd Avenue only blocks away, the Heron Haus gets my bet for best B&B in Portland (☎ 503/274-1846).

Best Location: Though it's only a few blocks from downtown businesses, the RiverPlace Hotel, wedged between the Willamette River and Tom McCall Riverfront Park, feels a world away from the city. In the summer, the park is used for countless festivals (☎ 503/228-3233).

Best Exercise Facilities: If you stay at the Governor Hotel, you need only head down to the basement for a total workout at the Princeton Athletic Club. You'll find a lap pool, running track, exercise room, whirlpool spas, saunas, and steam rooms. Sure, it costs an extra $10 a day, but you can bill it to your company (☎ 503/224-3400).

Best Atmosphere: The west is full of Victorian bed-and-breakfast inns, but few have gone all out the way the John Palmer House has. The folks who own this stately old painted lady went to great lengths when it came to restoration. The rooms are crammed with Victoriana, and the inn even does high tea and horse-drawn carriage rides (☎ 503/284-5893).

Best Views: So, you've seen that photo of the Portland skyline with Mount Hood in the distance and you want that view while you're in town. Sorry, you'll have to sleep in Washington Park for that one. But, the next best bet would be an east-side room on an upper floor of the Portland Marriott Hotel (☎ 503/226-7600).

Best Hotel Restaurant: With the feel of a casual cafe, superb Northwest cuisine, and the service of a four-star restaurant, the dining room at the Heathman Hotel offers the best hotel dining in the city (☎ 503/241-4100).

Best Hotel Art Collection: Stay at the Heathman Hotel and you can almost skip visiting the Portland Art Museum while you're in town. Almost everywhere you look—lobby, restaurant, halls—there are works of art on display. My personal favorites are the "Endangered Species" series of prints by Andy Warhol (☎ 503/241-4100).

Best Room Decor: Whether you're here for a romantic vacation or just in town on business, you'll enjoy every minute you're in your room at the Hotel Vintage Plaza. Italianate styling and rich color schemes give these rooms a classy and classic feel that most deluxe hotels fall far short of accomplishing (☎ 503/228-1212).

Best Room Service: The dining room at the Heathman Hotel is one of Portland's best restaurants, and just about anything you can order in the restaurant, you can have sent up to your room. The past decade has seen a downtown hotel renaissance in Portland. Several old hotels have been renovated and other historic buildings have been converted and renovated to serve as hotels. Such hotels include The Benson Hotel, the Governor Hotel, The Heathman Hotel, and the Hotel Vintage Plaza. Today these hotels offer some of Portland's most comfortable and memorable accommodations.

The city's largest concentrations of hotels are in downtown and near the airport. If you don't mind the high prices, the downtown hotels are the most convenient for most visitors. However, if your budget won't allow for a first-class business hotel, try near the airport or elsewhere on the outskirts of the city where you are more likely to find inexpensive to moderately priced motels. You'll find the greatest concentration of bed-and-breakfast inns in northeast Portland. This area is close to downtown and is generally quite convenient even if you are here on business.

In the following listings, **very expensive** hotels are those charging **more than $125 per night** for a double room; **expensive** hotels, **$90 to $125 per night** for a double; **moderate** hotels, **$60 to $90 per night** for a double; and **inexpensive** hotels, **less than $60 per night** for a double. These rates do not include the hotel-room tax of 9 percent. **Parking** rates are per day.

If you are planning to visit during the busy summer months, make reservations as far in advance as possible and be sure to ask if special rates are available. Almost all large hotels offer weekend discounts of as much as 50 percent. Also keep in mind that room rates are almost always considerably lower from October through April.

Most all hotels in the Portland area now offer no-smoking rooms, and, in fact, most bed-and-breakfast inns are exclusively no-smoking establishments. Most hotels also offer wheelchair-accessible rooms.

If you enjoy staying in bed-and-breakfast homes and inns, you may wish to call **Northwest Bed and Breakfast Travel Unlimited,** 610 SW Broadway, Portland, OR 97205 (☎ 503/243-7616, fax 503/243-7672). This service represents more than 75 B&Bs in the Portland and Seattle areas. It also lists about 300 homes throughout Oregon, Washington, and British Columbia and in parts of California. Included are some unhosted city apartments, mountain cabins, and beach houses. All homes have been inspected and are clean and comfortable. Some offer airport pick-up. Rates average between $35 and $60 for singles and between $45 and $85 for doubles; special amenities or locations can be more expensive.

For information on other B&Bs in the Portland area, call the **Portland Oregon Visitors Association,** (☎ 503/222-2223, or 800/345-3214) for a brochure put out by **Metro Innkeepers.** For information on B&Bs in both Portland and Oregon, send a stamped, self-addressed envelope to the **Oregon Bed and Breakfast Guild,** P.O. Box 3187, Ashland, OR 97520 (☎ 800/944-6196) or send $2 to **Oregon B&B Directory,** P.O. Box 1283, Grants Pass, OR 97526 (☎ 800/841-5448).

2 Downtown

VERY EXPENSIVE

The Benson Hotel

309 SW Broadway, Portland, OR 97205. ☎ **503/228-2000** or 800/426-0670. Fax 503/226-4603. 287 rms, 46 junior suites, 7 suites. A/C TV TEL. $170–$210 double; $185–$210 junior suite, $275–$600 suite. AE, CB, DC, DISC, ER, JCB, MC, V. Valet parking $12.

With its mansard roof and French baroque lobby, the Benson, built in 1912, exudes old-world sophistication and elegance. Circassian walnut from Russia covers the lobby walls, framing a marble fireplace. A

Portland Accommodations

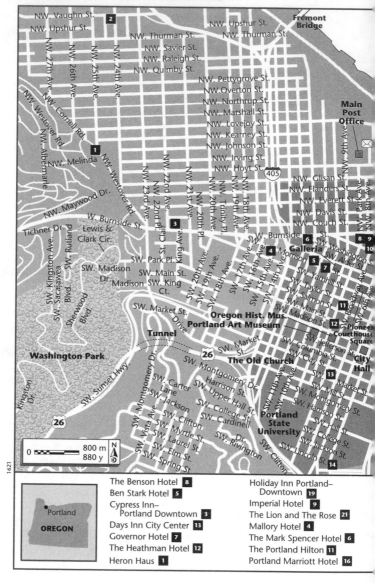

marble staircase with wrought-iron railing leads from the grand lobby to the mezzanine, and Austrian crystal chandeliers hang from the ornate plaster work ceiling. It's easy to imagine movie stars or royalty rushing in surrounded by popping flashbulbs.

The guest rooms, housed in two towers above the lobby, have all been redone in shades of pale gray, with elegant classic French Second Empire furnishings that include large desks and armoires that hide the

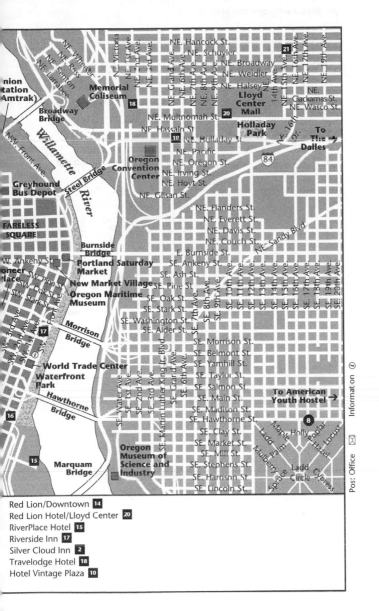

TVs. The deluxe kings are particularly roomy and come with seven pillows per bed. Baths, unfortunately, include little shelf space for spreading out your toiletries.

Dining/Entertainment: In the vaults below the lobby is the London Grill (see next chapter), one of Portland's best dining establishments. Open for breakfast, lunch, and dinner, it features fresh seafood specialties. Trader Vic's serves up all the expected meals and colossal cocktails. The Lobby Court has a bar and also serves a buffet lunch Monday through Friday.

Services: 24-hour room service, concierge, valet parking, in-room movies, in-room voice mail and computer modems, valet/laundry service.

Facilities: Weight room, gift shop.

Governor Hotel

SW 10th Ave. and Alder St., Portland, OR 97205. ☎ **503/224-3400** or 800/554-3456. Fax 503/241-2122. 100 rms, 28 suites. A/C TV TEL MINIBAR. $175–$195 double; $195–$500 suite. Weekend and special packages available. AE, CB, DC, JCB, MC, V. Valet parking $10.

Listed on the National Register of Historic Places, this hotel is an homage to the Lewis and Clark Expedition. Throughout the hotel, you'll spot references to the famous explorers, but it is the wall mural in the lobby that most captures the attention. A fireplace and heavy overstuffed chairs add to the ranch atmosphere of the lobby.

Guest rooms, on the other hand, are anything but rustic, and instead feature an Asian influence, such as painted porcelain lamps and black and gold lacquered tables. Because this is an old building and most rooms did not originally have bathrooms, rooms vary considerably in size. The least expensive are rather small but are nevertheless very comfortable. Unfortunately, bathrooms are in general quite small and lack counter space. Suites on the other hand are spacious, and some even have huge patios overlooking the city.

Dining/Entertainment: Jake's Grill is a grand, old-fashioned hall with burnished wood columns and slowly turning overhead fans (see next chapter). The menu features American grill cuisine. Between the lobby and the restaurant, you'll find the Dome Room, notable for its stunning stained-glass dome skylight.

Services: 24-hour room service; concierge; personal computers, fax machines available; complimentary morning newspaper and coffee; overnight shoeshine; valet/laundry service.

Facilities: Business center; hearing-impaired accommodations; Princeton Athletic Club, in basement, with lap pool, running track, whirlpool spa, steam rooms, sauna, exercise room.

✪ The Heathman Hotel

SW Broadway at Salmon St., Portland, OR 97205. ☎ **503/241-4100** or 800/551-0011. Fax 503/790-7110. 151 rms, 40 suites. A/C TV TEL. $175–$200 double; $190–$325 suite. Weekend and other packages available. AE, CB, DC, MC, V. Parking $12.

Understated luxury, style, and sophistication have made the Heathman the finest hotel in Portland. Opened in 1927, it is listed on the National Register of Historic Places. Original art, from 18th-century oil paintings to Andy Warhol prints, give the place a museum atmosphere. A marble and teak lobby opens onto the Tea Court, where a fireplace, sweeping staircase, grand piano, and the original eucalyptus paneling create a warm atmosphere.

Every guest room is decorated with original works of art and photographs, matching bedspreads, and unusual Roman shades in English chintzes, torchère lamps, rattan bedsteads, and glass-topped tables. An elegant wood armoire hides the remote-control TV. Live plants impart a homey feel. In the bath you'll find European soaps and shampoos, plush terry-cloth robes, and large towels.

Dining/Entertainment: The Heathman Restaurant and Bar is one of the finest restaurants in Portland, and has been receiving rave reviews since it opened. The menu, which changes seasonally, emphasizes fresh local produce, seafood, and game, all combined in imaginative and delectable creations with a French accent. B. Moloch/Heathman Bakery and Pub, the hotel's informal, but equally popular, second restaurant is located two blocks away at 901 SW Salmon St. The emphasis is similar, but prices are much lower. The two restaurants have cozy bars. (See next chapter for details on both.) At the hotel's Mezzanine Bar, there is live jazz music several nights a week for most of the year. Afternoon tea is served daily in the Lobby Lounge.

Services: 24-hour room service, concierge, valet parking, 400 film videotape library, valet/laundry service, complimentary newspaper, international business services, waterproof running map.

Facilities: Privileges at nearby athletic club, on site fitness suite, gift shop.

⑤ Hotel Vintage Plaza

422 SW Broadway, Portland, OR 97205. ☎ **503/228-1212** or 800/243-0555. Fax 503/228-3598. 107 rms. 31 suites. A/C MINIBAR TV TEL. $160 double (including continental breakfast); $165–$205 suite. Children under 16 stay free in parents' room. AE, CB, DC, DISC, MC, V. Valet parking $12.

This recently renovated deluxe hotel sports Italianate decor and a wine theme that plays up the Oregon wine industry. The intimate lobby is divided into two seating areas with low lighting and comfortable easy chairs. In the main seating area, there is a fireplace flanked by bookshelves that hold old volumes. Soaring up from the lobby is a 10-story atrium that gives this old building a very modern feel.

All accommodations are different, and though the starlight rooms and two-level suites are real scene-stealers, the standard rooms also have much to recommend them. Roman window shades and old Italian architectural prints are elements of the Italianate decor. Long pink granite counters, gold-tone designer faucets, and green taffeta shower curtains and walls make the bathrooms here the classiest in town. However, it is the starlight rooms that are truly extraordinary. Though small, they have greenhouse-style wall-into-ceiling windows that provide very romantic views at night and let in lots of light during the day. The two-level suites, some with Japanese soaking tubs and one with a spiral staircase, are equally stunning.

Dining/Entertainment: Ristorante Pazzo is a dark and intimate trattoria just off the lobby (see next chapter). Prominently displayed wine racks remind you of the hotel's theme once again.

Services: Complimentary evening wine, shoeshine service, morning newspaper and complimentary coffee, valet/laundry service, turn-down service, foreign currency exchange.

Facilities: Executive gym, business center.

The Portland Hilton Hotel

921 SW Sixth Ave., Portland, OR 97204-1296. ☎ **503/226-1611** or 800/HILTONS. Fax 503/220-2565. 455 rms, 16 suites. A/C TV TEL. $150–$200 double; $300–$900 suite. Weekend and other packages available. AE, CB, DC, DISC, JCB, MC, V. Valet parking $16.

Centrally located near businesses, the performing arts center, and several museums, this modern high-rise attracts many tour groups and conventions and is usually bustling with activity.

Other than the Hilton name, you don't really get much for your money here. Most rooms are rather small, as are bathrooms, which lack much counter space. However, for the overworked business traveler, there are comfortable chairs and two phones in the rooms.

Be sure to request a floor as high as possible to take advantage of the views. The corner rooms with king-size beds are my favorites.

Dining/Entertainment: From its 23rd-floor aerie, Alexander's offers a striking panorama of Portland, the Willamette River, and snow-covered Mount Hood (see next chapter). Back down at lobby level is the informal Bistro 921 restaurant, with regional cuisine. There is a casual bar just off the lobby.

Services: Room service, concierge, in-room movies, laundry/valet service, overnight shoeshine service.

Facilities: Fitness center, indoor swimming pool, gift shop, beauty salon/barber, business center.

Portland Marriott Hotel

1401 SW Front Ave., Portland, OR 97201. ☎ **503/226-7600** or 800/228-9290. Fax 503/221-1789. 503 rms, 28 suites. A/C TV TEL. $109–$160 double; $300–$350 suite. Weekend and other packages available. AE, CB, DC, DISC, ER, JCB, MC, V. Valet parking $12.

Just across Front Avenue from the Willamette River, the Portland Marriott is the flashiest of the city's hotels. A massive portico complete with lava-rock waterfall and bamboo deer scarer ushers you into a high-ceilinged lobby filled with bright lights.

Many of the accommodations have small balconies, and if you ask for a room overlooking the river, you can throw back the glass door to the balcony, and consider that the view used to be of a noisy freeway. On a clear day Mount Hood looms in the distance. The decor in the rooms is simple but attractive.

Dining/Entertainment: Fazzio's is a family restaurant serving breakfast, lunch, and dinner. Champions is a very popular sports bar with all the requisite sports memorabilia on the walls; on weekends there's dancing to recorded music. The lobby bar attracts a much more sedate crowd.

Services: Room service, concierge floor, in-room movies, valet/laundry service, shoeshine stand, babysitting service, valet parking, video checkout and message viewing, massage.

Facilities: Exercise room, indoor pool, whirlpool, saunas, games room, weight room, sundeck, hair salon and barber shop, gift shop, newsstand.

✪ RiverPlace Hotel

1510 SW Harbor Way, Portland, OR 97201. ☎ **503/228-3233** or outside Oregon 800/227-1333. Fax 503/295-6161. 84 rms. 47 suites. A/C TV TEL. $175–$195 double (including continental breakfast); $185–$215 junior suite, $205–$600 suite. AE, CB, DC, JCB, MC, V. Valet parking $10.

With the sloping lawns of Waterfront Park to one side and the Willamette River at its back doorstep, the RiverPlace occupies an enviable location in downtown Portland. If you prefer the quiet atmosphere of a European-style small resort over the crowds of a convention hotel, try the RiverPlace.

Spacious rooms are decorated with wingback chairs, teak tables, writing desks, and lacquered armoires. More than half the rooms here are suites, and some come with wood-burning fireplaces and whirlpool baths.

All rooms come with wet bars and large windows you can open to let in cool breezes that waft down the Willamette. In the bath you'll find a delightful assortment of luxurious soaps, shampoos, lotions, and gels, and in the closet terry-cloth robes.

Guests here have privileges at the nearby RiverPlace Athletic Club, one of the best in town. Planning a long stay in Portland? The hotel can arrange for you to stay in one of their adjacent condominiums.

Dining/Entertainment: The Esplanade Restaurant overlooks the river. Northwest and Continental cuisines are the specialty here (see next chapter). For al fresco dining there's the Patio, featuring sandwiches, burgers, and steaks. Just off the lobby is a very comfortable bar where light meals are served to the accompaniment of live piano music and a crackling fire in cool weather.

Services: 24-hour room service, concierge, turn-down service, complimentary shoeshine, valet/laundry service, complimentary morning paper, running map.

Facilities: Whirlpool, sauna, privileges at nearby athletic club, in-room computer and fax connections, voice mail.

EXPENSIVE

Red Lion Hotel/Downtown

310 SW Lincoln St., Portland, OR 97201. ☎ **503/221-0450** or 800/547-8010. Fax 503/226-6260. 235 rms. 3 suites. A/C TV TEL. $114–$120 double; $225–$325 suite. Weekend and other packages available. AE, CB, DC, DISC, ER, JCB, MC, V. Free parking.

Situated on a shady tree-lined street on the southern edge of downtown Portland, this low-rise hotel offers convenience and comfort. The design and landscaping reflect the Northwest, and in the courtyard surrounding the swimming pool are lush plantings of evergreens and other shrubs.

Red Lion Inns are noted for the spaciousness of their guest rooms, and this one is no exception. Large windows let in lots of precious Northwest light when the sun shines. All rooms come with king- or queen-size beds, and courtyard rooms are slightly more expensive.

Dining/Entertainment: The Cityside Restaurant offers a wide variety of well-prepared meals, with the focus on fresh local seafood. Club Max is the hotel's disco, with live music Thursday through Saturday.

Services: Room service, complimentary airport shuttle, valet/laundry service.

Facilities: Outdoor pool, gift shop, coin laundry.

MODERATE

Ⓢ Imperial Hotel

400 SW Broadway, Portland, OR 97205. ☎ **503/228-7221** or 800/452-2323. 136 rms. A/C TV TEL. $70–$85 double. AE, CB, DC, DISC, MC, V. Free parking.

Although it doesn't quite live up to its regal name, this older hotel—catercorner to the Benson Hotel—is a fine choice if you're on a budget. It has been undergoing a complete renovation. Rooms here are clean and comfortable, with new furniture (pseudo-Louis XIV) and lavender color schemes. Bathrooms are older (they even have porcelain shower knobs) but in good shape. The corner king rooms, with large windows, or the newly renovated rooms are the best choices here. All rooms come with clock radios; the new rooms have in-room safes, minirefrigerators, and hairdryers. Local phone calls are free.

Dining/Entertainment: The hotel's restaurant/lounge is a popular meeting place with downtown businesspeople.

Services: Morning newspaper, valet/laundry service, room service.

Ⓢ Mallory Hotel

729 SW 15th Ave., at Yamhill St., Portland, OR 97205-1994. ☎ **503/223-6311** or 800/228-8657. Fax 503/223-0522. 140 rms, 13 suites. A/C TV TEL. $60–$100 double; $90–$100 suite. AE, CB, DC, MC, V. Free parking (a real plus this close to downtown).

The Mallory has long been a favorite of Portland visitors who want the convenience of a downtown lodging but aren't on a bottomless expense account. It's also a local favorite for when your parents come to town and neither you nor they have loads of dough. This is an older hotel, and though the lobby, which is done in deep forest green with ornate gilt plaster work trim and crystal chandeliers, has a certain classic grandeur, it also has that faded feel you might expect from a hotel in a Humphrey Bogart movie.

The rooms are not as luxurious as the lobby might suggest, but they are comfortable and clean. With rates this low, you might want to go for one of the king-size suites. These rooms are about as big as they come, with walk-in closets, minirefrigerators, and sofa beds. All rooms have new carpets, drapes, and furniture.

Dining/Entertainment: The dining room at the Mallory continues the grand design of the lobby. Heavy drapes hang from the windows, and faux-marble pillars lend just the right air of imperial grandeur.

Services: Free local calls, 2pm checkout, in-room movies, valet/laundry service.

The Mark Spencer Hotel

409 SW 11th Ave., Portland, OR 97205. ☎ **503/224-3293** or 800/548-3934. Fax 503/223-7848. 101 rms. A/C TV TEL. $65 studio, single or double; $99

one-bedroom. Lower weekly and monthly rates are also available. Children 12 and under stay free in parents' room. AE, CB, DC, MC, V. Free parking.

If you're planning an extended stay in Portland and need to be within walking distance of downtown, this is the place for you. Although the hotel is not in the best neighborhood in the city, it's just around the corner from Jake's Famous Crawfish, one of Portland's oldest and most popular restaurants. The building itself has been attractively restored, with flower baskets hanging from old-fashioned street lamps out front.

Both studios and one-bedrooms feature kitchenettes and attractive modern furnishings, including plush-velvet wingback chairs and couches in some rooms. Walk-in closets are a definite plus for those planning a long stay in town.

Services: Free housekeeping, coin-operated laundry and valet service, private mailboxes, personal phone lines.

Facilities: Privileges at nearby athletic club.

Days Inn City Center

1414 SW Sixth Ave., Portland, OR 97201. ☎ **503/221-1611** or 800/648-6440. 173 rms. A/C TV TEL. $71–$76 double. AE, CB, DC, MC, V. Free parking.

Located in the heart of downtown, this hotel is an excellent choice for budget-minded business travelers and family vacationers. From the moment you walk into the royal blue and beige lobby and see the humongous railway clock behind the tiny check-in desk, you'll know you've stumbled onto something unusual. You'll be surprised to discover a small library of old hardbound books in every room. In addition, there are brass beds and framed old photos of Portland and famous people. Each room has a large picture window to let in lots of sunlight.

Dining/Entertainment: With its brass rails and wood trim, the Portland Bar and Grill is popular with the business set for lunch and happy-hour hors d'oeuvres.

Services: Valet/laundry service, room service, complimentary newspaper.

Facilities: Outdoor swimming pool.

Riverside Inn

50 SW Morrison Ave., Portland, OR 97204. ☎ **503/221-0711** or 800/648-6440. Fax 503/274-0312. 139 rms. A/C TV TEL. $95 double. AE, CB, DC, DISC, MC, V. Free parking.

Overlooking Waterfront Park and located on the MAX light-rail transit system line, Riverside has many unexpected features. As the name implies, you are only steps from the Willamette River, but you are also close to businesses, fine restaurants, and shopping. Colorful fine-art posters enliven the walls of the small lobby, giving the seating area a homey feel. Rooms, many with excellent views of the river and Morrison Bridge, feature a small library of hardbound books and modern furnishings.

Dining/Entertainment: The Riverside Café and Bar is a bright and airy restaurant with large windows looking out over the Waterfront Park and the river. Seafood steaks, pastas, and sandwiches are the specialty here.

Services: Room service, valet/laundry service, complimentary newspaper, use of fitness club.

INEXPENSIVE

Cypress Inn-Portland Downtown

809 SW King St., Portland, OR 97205. ☎ **503/226-6288** or 800/225-4205. Fax 503/274-0038. 82 rms. A/C TV TEL. $63–$89 double (including continental breakfast). AE, DC, DISC, MC, V. Free parking.

Though the standard rooms here are rather cramped, for just a few dollars more you can get a much larger room, which may even have a kitchenette. Because the motel sits a little bit up into the hills west of downtown, it has some nice views over the city. You'd expect to spend quite a bit more for such views, which makes these rooms a good value. Another plus here is that you are within walking distance of both the Nob Hill shopping and restaurant district and Washington Park, which is home to the Japanese Gardens and the International Rose Test Garden. Be sure to avail yourself of the free local phone calls and the courtesy airport shuttle.

Ben Stark Hotel

1022 SW Stark St., Portland, OR 97205. ☎ **503/274-1223.** Fax 503/274-1033. 96 rms (40 with private bath). TV TEL. Hostel $13.76; single or double without bath $36; single or double with bath $40. AE, DISC, MC, V.

If you're a hardened hosteler or budget traveler used to Spartan accommodations that provide a place to crash and little more in the way of comforts, the Ben Stark should meet with your approval. Rooms are quite basic, but as you would expect, you'll meet some interesting folks hanging around the common areas. Actually the building, erected in 1912, is one of Portland's few remaining historic hotels, and the owners are working hard to restore some of its lost grandeur. Mahogany doors and claw-foot tubs are just two of the classic touches here. Facilities include a laundry, bike storage area, luggage storage room, safe deposit boxes, and free parking.

3 Northwest Portland

✪ Heron Haus

2545 NW Westover Rd., Portland, OR 97210. ☎ **503/274-1846.** Fax 503/243-1075. 5 rms. TV TEL. $125–$250 double (including continental breakfast). Corporate rate available. MC, V. Free parking.

A short walk from the bustling Nob Hill shopping and dining district of northwest Portland, Heron Haus offers outstanding accommodations, spectacular views, and tranquil surroundings. There is even a small swimming pool with sundeck.

Surprisingly, the house still features some of the original plumbing. In most places this would be a liability but not here, since the plumbing was done by the same man who plumbed Portland's famous Pittock Mansion. Many of that building's unusual bath features are to be found at the Heron Haus as well. One shower has seven shower

👥 Family-Friendly Hotels

Embassy Suites Hotel *(see pg. 181)* An indoor pool and large atrium make this a safe bet for kids any time of year, and the huge Washington Square Mall is just down the street.

Red Lion Hotel/Lloyd Center *(see pg. 176)* Let the kids loose in the huge Lloyd Center Shopping Mall across the street and they'll stay entertained for hours. There is even an ice-skating rink in the mall.

Portland Marriott Hotel *(see pg. 170)* The game room and indoor pool are popular with kids, and just across the street is 2-mile-long Tom McCall Waterfront Park, which runs along the Willamette River.

heads; another has two. In another room there's a modern whirlpool spa that affords excellent views of the city.

🟢 Silver Cloud Inn

2426 NW Vaughn St., Portland, OR 97210-2540. ☎ **503/242-2400** or 800/ 551-7207 no. 8. Fax 503/242-1770. 81 rms. A/C TV TEL. $60–$93 double (including continental breakfast). AE, DC, DISC, MC, V.

This newer hotel is located just north of Portland's trendy Nob Hill neighborhood, and though it faces the beginning of the city's industrial area, it is still a very attractive and comfortable place. Reasonable rates are the main draw here, but the hotel is also within a five-minute drive of half a dozen of the city's best restaurants. The standard rooms have small refrigerators, while the minisuites come with refrigerators, wet bars, microwave ovens, and a separate seating area. The most expensive rooms are the king rooms with whirlpool tubs. Local phone calls are free, and facilities include a fitness room and a whirlpool spa. Try to get a room away from Vaughn Street. To find the hotel, take I-405 to Ore. 30 west and get off at the Vaughn street exit.

4 Northeast & North Portland

Located in North Portland, on Hayden Island in the Columbia River, is the shopping and resort area of Jantzen Beach, named for the famous swimwear manufacturer that originated in Portland. Although you'll find Red Lion Inns throughout the West, including three others in Portland, the pair listed here are two of the nicest and most impressive. *One warning:* Both hotels are in the flight path for the airport, and although the rooms themselves are adequately insulated against noise, the swimming pools and sundecks are not.

VERY EXPENSIVE

Red Lion Hotel/Columbia River

1401 N. Hayden Island Dr., Portland, OR 97217. ☎ **503/283-2111** or 800/ 547-8010. Fax 503/283-4718. 351 rms, 10 suites. A/C TV TEL. $120–$130 double;

$195–$300 suite. Weekend and other packages available. Children under 18 stay free in parents' room. AE, CB, DC, DISC, ER, JCB, MC, V. Free parking.

An attractive low-rise design that's slightly reminiscent of a Northwest Native American longhouse has kept this hotel popular for many years. The lobby, on the other hand, features cherry wood and faux green-marble accents for that Ivy League look.

As with all Red Lions, the rooms are spacious and comfortable, and are done in shades of sea-foam green and mauve. Floral-print bed-spreads with a beige background, as well as framed watercolors, give the rooms a country appeal.

Dining/Entertainment: The Coffee Garden, just off the lobby, offers coffee shop meals from early morning to evening. Great views of the Columbia River are to be had at Brickstones Restaurant, which features an international menu emphasizing fresh local seafoods and produce. For late-night entertainment, there's the Brickstones Bar, where nightly there is a DJ. For a quieter atmosphere, try the aptly named Quiet Bar, a small glass-walled octagonal building just off the lobby and overlooking the pool.

Services: Room service, complimentary airport shuttle, valet/laundry service.

Facilities: Heated outdoor swimming pool, whirlpool spa, putting green, gift shop, barbershop, beauty salon.

Red Lion Hotel/Jantzen Beach

909 N. Hayden Island Dr., Portland, OR 97217. ☎ **503/283-4466** or 800/547-8010. Fax 503/283-4743. 320 rms. 24 suites. A/C TV TEL. $125–$145 double; $160–$450 suite. AE, CB, DC, DISC, ER, JCB, MC, V. Free parking.

Everything about this resort hotel is spacious. An imposing portico that reflects Northwest tribal designs leads to the massive lobby, which is fronted by a long wall of glass. Thick carpets muffle every sound. Dark woods impart a warmth and Northwest feel.

Arranged in wings around a central garden courtyard and swimming pool, the rooms are as large as you're likely to find in any hotel. Most have balconies and excellent views of the river and sometimes Mount St. Helens. The baths, each with an assortment of soaps, shampoos, and lotions, are equally spacious.

Dining/Entertainment: Elegant dining in plush surroundings with great river views can be found in Maxi's Restaurant, which specializes in Continental-style seafood and steaks. For much more casual dining there's the Coffee Garden in the lobby. Tuesday through Saturday nights come alive to the sound of live rock 'n' roll bands at Maxi's Lounge, which has art nouveau decor.

Services: Room service, complimentary airport shuttle, valet/laundry service.

Facilities: Heated outdoor pool, whirlpool, tennis courts, gift shop, helicopter port, privileges at nearby athletic club ($7).

EXPENSIVE

Red Lion Hotel/Lloyd Center

1000 NE Multnomah St., Portland, OR 97232. ☎ **503/281-6111** or 800/547-8010. Fax 503/284-8553. 476 rooms, 10 suites. A/C TV TEL. $139–$164 double; $435–$535 suite (lower rates off-season). AE, CB, DC, DISC, ER, JCB, MC, V. Parking $6.

In the busy lobby of this modern high-rise, glass elevators shuttle up and down through the skylighted ceiling. Overstuffed chairs and plants create a warm greenhouse atmosphere. Spreading out in different directions are hallways leading to the restaurants, gift shops, a swimming pool, and an elegant lounge. Large leaf patterns in bas-relief decorate the walls, and tubular glass chandeliers sparkle overhead.

As you've come to expect, the Red Lion's rooms are spacious beyond compare, and some have balconies. The views from the higher floors are stunning. On a clear day you can see Mount Hood, Mount St. Helens, and even Mount Rainier.

Dining/Entertainment: Maxi's Restaurant, with its etched glass walls, chandeliers, and baffled ceiling, is just off the lobby. Local seafood and steaks are the well-prepared specialties here. If you're more in the mood for Mexican, cross the lobby to Eduardo's Cantina, with stucco walls, tile floors, rough-hewn wood beams, and rattan chairs. Family dining is possible in the Coffee Garden, which opens directly onto the lobby. For those seeking a quiet place for conversation and a drink, there's the Quiet Bar, which sometimes has live piano music.

Services: Room service, concierge, complimentary airport shuttle, in-room movies, valet/laundry service.

Facilities: Heated outdoor swimming pool, exercise room, gift shop.

MODERATE

⑤ Holiday Inn Portland-Downtown

1021 NE Grand Ave., Portland, OR 97232. ☎ **503/235-2100** or 800/HOLIDAY. Fax 503/238-0132. 166 rms, 6 suites. A/C TV TEL. $65–$95 double; $125–$250 suite. Special packages for senior citizens. AE, CB, DC, DISC, MC, V. Free parking.

This reasonably priced hotel, located across the street from the architecturally striking Oregon Convention Center, is a popular choice with conventioneers who don't want to spend an arm and a leg. Because Portland's MAX light-rail system stops one block from the hotel, this is also a convenient location if you want to go downtown.

You'll find all the rooms attractively furnished in muted colors and modern decor with an Asian touch. Large tables, writing desks, two phones, and comfortable armchairs allow guests to spread out. Upper floors have good views either west to the city skyline or east to the Cascades and Mount Hood, and the twin peaks of the Convention Center loom just across the street.

Dining/Entertainment: Windows, the hotel's aptly named top-floor restaurant, provides the hotel's best views and is a popular dining spot. You can dine on fresh Northwest cuisine or just have a drink in the lounge or outdoor terrace.

Services: Room service, valet/laundry service.

Facilities: Sauna, fitness center.

Travelodge Hotel

1441 NE Second Ave., Portland, OR 97232. ☎ **503/233-2401** or 800/255-3050. Fax 503/238-7016. 237 rms, 1 suite. A/C TV TEL. $65–$89 double; $5 each additional person; $200–$250 suite. AE, CB, DC, DISC, MC, V. Free parking.

Convenient to both the city center and the Convention Center, the Travelodge offers excellent views from its modern 10-story building. Soothing pastels are used in the small lobby and in the guest rooms, all of which have large windows to let in as much of that rare Northwest sunshine as possible. In the baths you'll find marble countertops and tile floors, and a coffeemaker in every room. There is also an executive club floor offering additional security, hairdryers, and free local phone calls.

Dining/Entertainment: Traders, just off the lobby, is the hotel's restaurant, and fresh seafood and steaks are the specialty. For cocktails and conversation, there's the adjacent Encore Lounge.

Services: Room service, in-room movies, complimentary airport shuttle, valet/laundry service, free jogging maps.

Facilities: Heated outdoor swimming pool, exercise facility.

INEXPENSIVE

⑤ Ho-Jo Inn

3939 NE Hancock St., Portland, OR 97212. ☎ **503/288-6891.** Fax 503/288-1995. 48 rms. A/C TV TEL. $52–$56 double. AE, CB, DC, DISC, MC, V. Free parking.

Located in the Hollywood District of northeast Portland about halfway between the airport and downtown, Ho-Jo Inn is an excellent choice in the budget range. Some rooms are exceptionally large and were renovated a few years ago. Attractive modern furniture and comfortable beds will make your stay here enjoyable. Take a stroll around the neighborhood and you'll see why they call this the Hollywood District—the same style of Southern California Hollywood architecture prevails. There is free coffee and a coin laundry within walking distance.

BED & BREAKFASTS

✪ John Palmer House

4314 N. Mississippi Ave., Portland, OR 97217. ☎ **503/284-5893.** 6 rms (1 with private bath), 3 suites (all with private bath). $45–$85 double (including continental breakfast); $85–$125 double suite. AE, DISC, MC, V.

Even before you set foot inside the door of this restored Queen Anne Victorian home in an unassuming neighborhood in North Portland, you know that you've stumbled onto something special. Cross the Italianate veranda, step through the double stained-glass doors, and you are enveloped in the Victorian era. The interior has been done with all the flair for which that period was known. Dozens of different wallpapers turn the walls into a coordinated riot of colors and patterns.

Guest accommodations are actually in two houses: the main Palmer House and Grandma's Cottage. Each room in the main house is decorated with massive Victorian furnishings, and stained-glass windows throughout the house filter the sunlight into magical hues. In one bedroom there's a stuffed moose head that seems to take up almost the entire room. Decor in Grandma's Cottage is much simpler. In the morning you will be served a delicious gourmet breakfast. There is also a whirlpool in a gazebo, plus a croquet court.

Sunday, high tea is served from 1 to 3pm; before tea, a tour is given. The price of tea and tour is $17.50. The Palmer House also offers fine dining by reservation.

The Lion and the Rose

1810 NE 15th Ave., Portland, OR 97212. ☎ **503/287-9245** or 800/955-1647. Fax 503/287-9247. 7 rms (5 with private bath). TEL. $80–$120 double with shared bath (including full breakfast); $105–$120 double with private bath. AE, MC, V.

This imposing Queen Anne Victorian bed-and-breakfast inn is one block off Northeast Broadway and is one of the best-located B&Bs in Portland. Within four blocks are half a dozen excellent restaurants, numerous cafes, eclectic boutiques, and a huge shopping mall. Yet, the Lion and Rose itself is in a fairly quiet residential neighborhood. Even if this inn were not so splendidly located, it would still be a gem. Set up a flight of stairs from the street, it looms over its corner like a castle. The living room and dining room are surprisingly spacious for a Victorian home and are beautifully decorated with period antiques, including an ornate pump organ and an upright piano. Breakfasts are sumptuous affairs that are meant to be lingered over.

Guest rooms each have a distinctively different decor and feel ranging from the bright colors and turret sitting area of the Lavonna room to the deep greens of the Starina room, which features an imposing Edwardian bed and armoire. The Garden room and the shared bathroom have claw-foot tubs, but some rooms have cramped, though attractive, bathrooms. If you have problems climbing stairs, ask for the Rose room, which has a modern whirlpool tub in the bathroom.

Portland's White House

1914 NE 22nd Ave., Portland, OR 97212. ☎ **503/287-7131**. 6 rms (all with private bath). $96–$112 double (including full breakfast). MC, V.

This imposing Greek-revival mansion bears a more than passing resemblance to its namesake in Washington, D.C. Massive columns frame the entrance and a patio area where, on sunny days, you can sit at a table and enjoy a picnic lunch. A long semicircular driveway sweeps up to the entrance, and a fountain bubbles in the garden.

Behind the mahogany doors is a huge entrance hall with original hand-painted wall murals. To your right is the parlor, with its French windows and piano. To your left is the formal dining room, where the large breakfast is served amid sparkling crystal chandeliers. A double staircase leads past a large stained-glass window to the second-floor accommodations.

Canopy and brass queen beds, antique furnishings, and bathrooms with claw-foot tubs await you at the end of a weary day. Request the balcony room and you can gaze out past the Greek columns and imagine you're the president. This is a no-smoking inn, and hosts Larry and Mary Hough prefer guests who are more than 12 years old. There is free airport pick-up and afternoon tea.

5 Southeast & Southwest Portland

Portland AYH Hostel

3031 SE Hawthorne Blvd., Portland, OR 97214. ☎ **503/236-3380.** $36–$50 beds. $12 member, $15 nonmember. MC, V. Bus: 14 from downtown or 12 then 14 from airport.

The Hawthorne District is a shopping and dining area popular with students, artists, and musicians, so it makes an ideal location for a youth hostel. Housed in an old house on a busy street, this hostel is small and has primarily dormitory beds. The common room is also small, but a large wraparound porch makes up for the lack of space inside. There is a large kitchen where guests can prepare their own meals, with a grocery store a short walk away. However, an all-you-can-eat pancake breakfast for $1 shouldn't be missed. Located just down the street is an American Youth Hostel (AYH) Travel Center, where hostel members can get student IDs and buy books, travel packs, and Eurailpasses. Membership is $10 per year for youths under 17, $25 for adults, and $15 for senior citizens over 55. Between May and September, the hostel offers van tours to Mount St. Helens, Mt. Hood, the Columbia River Gorge, the Oregon coast and even microbrewery and wine tours.

6 Near the Airport

EXPENSIVE

Shilo Inn Suites Hotel

11707 NE Airport Way, Portland, OR 97220-1075. ☎ **503/252-7500** or 800/222-2244. Fax 503/254-0794. 200 suites. A/C TV TEL. $112–$139 double (including continental breakfast). AE, DC, DISC, MC, V.

If you want to stay near the airport and want space and the facilities of a deluxe hotel, this is one of your best bets. All the rooms here are called suites, and although they don't actually have separate seating and sleeping rooms, they do have plenty of room and lots of other amenities. There are large closets with mirrored doors, lots of bathroom counter space, and three TVs in the rooms (including ones in the bathrooms). Other amenities include hairdryers, VCRs, and double sinks. The main drawback here is that this is a convention hotel and is often very crowded. To find this hotel, head straight out of the airport, drive under the I-205 overpass and watch for the hotel ahead on the left.

Dining/Entertainment: The hotel's dining room is in the convention center wing and serves surprisingly creative dishes amid casual surroundings. There's a piano lounge adjacent to the restaurant. The complimentary breakfast is served in a large TV lounge just off the lobby.

Services: Room service, complimentary airport shuttle, valet service.

Facilities: Indoor swimming pool, whirlpool spa, exercise room.

MODERATE

In addition to the two moderately priced hotels listed below, you'll also find a **Super 8 Motel** at 11011 NE Homan Street (tel. 503/253-1427) just off of Airport Way after you go under the I-205 overpass. This motel charges a surprisingly high $57 a night for a double.

Courtyard by Marriott

11550 NE Airport Way, Portland, OR 97220. ☎ **503/252-3200** or 800/321-2211. Fax 503/252-8921. 150 rms, 10 suites. A/C TV TEL. $54–$83 double; $100–$110 suite. AE, DC, DISC, MC, V.

Despite the name, this modern six-story hotel has no courtyard. What it does have is an elegant little lobby featuring lots of marble and modest but comfortable guest rooms. If you need some extra room, opt for one of the suites, which come with microwave ovens, wet bars, and small refrigerators. Ask for a room away from the road if you're a light sleeper. This is one of the most convenient hotels to the airport; to find it, just head straight out of the airport, go under the I-205 overpass and you'll see the hotel ahead on the right.

Dining/Entertainment: There's a comfortable lounge off the lobby as well as a moderately priced dining room.

Services: Room service, complimentary airport shuttle.

Facilities: Tiny outdoor swimming pool, whirlpool spa, fitness room.

Quality Inn/Portland Airport

8247 NE Sandy Blvd., Portland, OR 97220. ☎ **503/256-4111** or 800/246-4649. Fax 503/254-1507. 120 rms, 4 suites. A/C TV TEL. $65–$75 double; $100 suite. AE, CB, DC, DISC, ER, JCB, MC, V. Free parking.

Although the rooms here are a bit small and dark, they are very comfortable and clean, and the attractively landscaped surroundings more than make up for any inadequacies in the accommodations. If you are willing to spend a bit more, there are suites and rooms with whirlpool baths.

Dining/Entertainment: Steamers Restaurant and Lounge specializes in fresh seafood. If you're a fan of the steam era, you'll love this place. There are plenty of old photos on the walls, and bits and pieces rescued from paddle wheelers and steam locomotives.

Services: Complimentary airport shuttle, same-day valet service, complimentary morning newspaper, free local phone calls.

Facilities: Heated outdoor pool, laundry facilities.

7 Beaverton/Tigard Area

VERY EXPENSIVE

✪ Embassy Suites Hotel

9000 SW Washington Square Rd., Tigard, OR 97223. ☎ **503/644-4000** or 800/ EMBASSY. Fax 503/641-4654. 354 suites. A/C TV TEL. $109–$142 double (including full breakfast). AE, DC, DISC, MC, V. Free parking.

Beaverton and Tigard are at the heart of Oregon's rapidly growing high-tech industries, and whether you are traveling on business or for pleasure, this outstanding nine-story hotel should be your first choice in the area. It is built around a soaring atrium, with colorful kites suspended high above the gardenlike lobby and courtyard dining area. Tropical plants are everywhere, and waterfalls add their pleasant music. A glass elevator whisks guests to their floors.

As the name implies, every room is a suite—each beautifully decorated in greens and pastels, with plush carpets. In the sitting room you'll find a huge stereo console TV, a relaxing couch, a telephone, and a large table. There are also a microwave, minirefrigerator, wet bar, and irons and ironing boards in each suite. In the bedroom you'll find another TV, a clock radio, and a second phone. The large bath is equally appealing with its hairdryers, and soaps, shampoos, and lotions on the large counter.

Dining/Entertainment: At the Crossroads Restaurant, Continental cuisine is served. For more casual dining, seat yourself amid the lush foliage of the Atrium. There's also the Crossroads Lounge, with live entertainment.

Services: Room service, valet/laundry service, nightly manager's reception with complimentary drinks, courtesy transportation to Washington Square Mall, complimentary newspapers.

Facilities: 24-hour indoor pool, whirlpool, sauna, fitness room and privileges at nearby health club.

MODERATE

Greenwood Inn

10700 SW Allen Blvd., Beaverton, OR 97005. ☎ **503/643-7444** or 800/289-1300. Fax 503/626-4553. 250 rms. A/C TV TEL. $96–$109 double. AE, CB, DC, DISC, MC, V. Free parking.

Two-story buildings set amid attractively landscaped grounds give the Greenwood the feel of a small resort. Only 10 minutes from downtown Portland. If you are in the area to do business in the "Silicon Forest," the Greenwood is well located. Guest rooms are large and comfortable and most are done in earth tones with exposed brick accents. There's plenty of counter space for toiletries. Executive rooms, which cost about $15 extra, are exceptional, with original artwork on the walls, a desk/work area, cherry wood furnishings, and a warm coppery color scheme.

Dining/Entertainment: The Pavilion Bar and Grill serves moderate to high priced meals in a plant-filled atrium dining room. On weekends there is live Top 40 dance music in the hotel's Wanigan Lounge, while the Pavilion Bar provides a quiet spot for a drink.

Services: Access to nearby athletic club, morning newspaper, shopping shuttle.

Facilities: Exercise room, sauna, outdoor swimming pool, hot tub.

15

Portland Dining

1 Best Bets

Best Spot for a Romantic Dinner: See **Best Italian,** below.

Best Spot for a Business Lunch: The London Grill at the Benson Hotel is *the* place to network with local business people (☎ 503/228-2000).

Best Spot for a Celebration: With a decor that harkens back to the days of fin de siècle Paris, Brasserie Montmartre has live jazz and a performing magician nearly nightly. Plus, your entire party can color all over the (paper) tablecloths with crayons (☎ 503/224-5552).

Best Decor: Wildwood, a new restaurant in the trendy Northwest neighborhood, fairly glows with urban chic (☎ 503/248-WOOD).

Best View: On the 30th floor of the U.S. Bancorp Tower, Atwaters offers elegant opulence, spectacular views of Portland and Mount Hood, and delectable Northwest cuisine. It's open for dinner only (☎ 503/275-3600).

Best Wine List: You can sit at the wine bar at Westmoreland Bistro and Wines, and sample some of the best wines around. The food here is award-winning Northwest cuisine (☎ 503/236-6457).

Best Value: Quaff microbrews and consume a wood oven baked pizza with creative trimmings such as smoked salmon, rock shrimp, or olive paste at B. Moloch/Heathman Bakery and Pub (☎ 503/227-5700).

Best for Kids: Old Wives Tales (☎ 503/238-0470) has a children's playroom, as does Aztec Willie, Joey Rose Taqueria at 1501 NE Broadway (☎ 503/280-8900).

Best Italian: You can get a four- or seven-course fixed-price dinner at Genoa, which has only 10 tables. Everything is made in the kitchen here, and service is personal. This is also a good spot for a special, romantic dinner (☎ 503/238-1464).

Best Northwest: The Heathman Restaurant at the elegant Heathman Hotel features the very best Northwest meat, seafoods, wild game, and produce, with a French accent (☎ 503/241-4100).

Best Mediterranean: Daring in both decor and menu, Zefiro's is usually busy serving its loyal clientele imaginative Mediterranean dishes highly influenced by French, Italian, Moroccan, Greek, and Spanish cuisine (☎ 503/226-3394).

Best Mexican: You'll find wild decor and all the usual Mexican dishes done very well at Esparza's Tex-Mex Café, plus buffalo and smoked salmon enchiladas, tacos, and tamales, and nopalitos (fried cactus) too (☎ 503/234-7909).

Best Desserts: Papa Haydn offers a symphony that includes lemon chiffon torte, raspberry gâteau, and Georgian peanut butter mousse, to name but a few. There's usually a waiting line at the door, but don't let that deter you (☎ 503/228-7317).

Best Afternoon Tea: In the lounge at the Heathman Hotel, tea hostesses in lace aprons will serve you tea and finger sandwiches on bone china (☎ 503/241-4100).

Best Brunch: The most lavish brunch in Portland is served at the Benson Hotel's London Grill, located downstairs from the marble-floored lobby (☎ 503/228-2000).

Best Pre-theater Dinner: Conveniently located in Portland's theater district, a dinner at Higgins sets the stage for a special evening out (☎ 503/222-9070).

Best Fast Food: You'll find good home-cooked Mexican food, fast, at Mayas Tacqueria, which has three different locations (☎ 503/226-1946).

Best Espresso: Best Espresso, "No Backtalk." Coffee People is at 806 NW 23rd Ave. (☎ 503/221-0235) and other locations. One of their outlets is an "Immediate Care Center," also on NW 23rd Ave.

Best Burger: The best that I've found in Portland is at Dots, 2521 SE Clinton St. (☎ 503/235-0203), a neighborhood place that serves two-fisted juicy burgers and french fries that come with a jalapeño sauce.

Best Lunch Spot with a View: Mingle with the business set at Rene's while you enjoy a view of the West Hills and more, all for the very reasonable price of lunch (☎ 503/241-0712).

Best Crayfish: Get'em while they're hot at Jake's Famous Crayfish—they've been serving up these miniature lobsters for years (☎ 503/226-1419).

Best Seafood: Couch Street Fish House serves a wide variety of seafood dishes from a traditional lobster thermidor to oysters with Asiago cheese and roasted pepper relish (☎ 503/223-6173).

Best Steaks: Most people in Portland would send you to the RingSide West. I will, too (☎ 503/223-1513).

Best Vegetarian: Santé serves highly imaginative northwestern and international dishes, but it is not exclusively vegetarian, so people with meat or fish preferences will want to dine here, too (☎ 503/233-4340).

Best Traditional Spot: Huber's is the oldest restaurant in Portland, and specializes in anything made with turkey (☎ 503/228-5686).

Portland may not be garnering as much praise for its restaurants as Seattle, but there certainly are restaurants here that are every bit the equal of Seattle's. Young and innovative chefs are cooking up a quiet storm in Portland these days, and prices are very reasonable. For these listings, I considered a restaurant **expensive** if a meal with wine or beer would average **$25 or more** per person. **Moderate** restaurants offer complete dinners in the **$15 to $30** range, and **inexpensive** eateries are those where you can enjoy a complete meal for **less than $15.**

Be sure to accompany your dinner with one of Oregon's fine wines. Quite a few have won taste-test competitions with California and French wines in recent years.

2 Restaurants by Cuisine

AMERICAN

Kitchen Table Cafe (Southeast Portland, IE)

Zell's, An American Cafe (Southeast Portland, IE)

BURGERS

Hamburger Mary's (Downtown & Old Town, IE)

BREAKFAST/BRUNCH

Bijou Cafe (Southwest Portland, IE)

Bread & Ink Cafe (Southeast Portland, M)

Cafe du Berry (Downtown & Old Town, M)

The London Grill—Benson Hotel (Downtown & Old Town, E)

Salty's (Noreast Portland, E)

Santé (Southeast Portland, M)

Wildwood (Northwest Portland, E)

Zell's, An American Cafe (Southeast Portland, IE)

CAJUN

Montage (Southeast Portland, M)

CHINESE

Fong Chong (Downtown & Old Town, IE)

Hunan (Downtown & Old Town, M)

Noodlehead (Northeast Portland, IE)

CONTINENTAL

Alexander's (Downtown & Old Town, E)

The Heathman Restaurant and Bar (Downtown & Old Town, M)

Huber's (Downtown & Old Town, M)

Western Culinary Institute International Dining Room (Downtown & Old Town, M)

DELICATESSENS

Kornblatts (Northwest Portland, IE)

FRENCH

Brasserie Montmartre (Downtown & Old Town, M)

Cafe du Berry (Downtown & Old Town, M)

L'Auberge (Northwest Portland, E)

L'Etoile (Northeast Portland, E)

Le Canelet (Southeast Portland, M)

GREEK

Alexis Restaurant (Downtown & Old Town, M)

INDIAN

Indigine (Southeast Portland, M)
Plainfield's Mayur Restaurant
& Art Gallery (Downtown
& Old Town, M)

INTERNATIONAL

Indigine (Southeast Portland,
M)
Old Wives' Tales (Southeast
Portland, IE)
Santé (Southeast Portland, M)

ITALIAN

Delphina's Ristorante Italiano
(Northwest Portland, M)
Genoa (Southeast Portland, E)
Il Piatto (Southeast
Portland, M)
Merchant of Venice
(Northeast Portland, IE)
Ristorante Pazzo (Downtown
& Old Town, M)

JAPANESE

Bush Garden (Downtown &
Old Town, M)

LATE NIGHT DINING

Montage (Southeast Portland, M)

MEDITERRANEAN

Higgins (Downtown & Old
Town, E)
Wildwood (Northwest
Portland, E)
Zefiro Restaurant & Bar
(Northwest Portland, M)

MEXICAN

Aztec Willie, Joey Rose
Taqueria (Northeast
Portland, IE)
Casa-U-Betcha (Northwest
Portland, M)
Mayas Tacqueria (Downtown
& Old Town, IE)

MEXICAN/SALVADORAN

El Palenque (Downtown &
Old Town, IE)

NATURAL FOODS

Bijou Cafe (Downtown &
Old Town, IE)

NORTHWEST

Atwater's (Downtown &
Old Town, E)
B. Moloch/Heathman Bakery
& Pub (Downtown &
Old Town, M)
Brasserie Montmartre (Down-
town & Old Town, M)
Bread & Ink Cafe (Southeast
Portland, M)
Esplanade Restaurant (Down-
town & Old Town, M)
The Heathman Restaurant
and Bar (Downtown &
Old Town, M)
Higgins (Downtown &
Old Town, E)
L'Auberge (Northwest
Portland, E)
Ron Paul Charcuterie
(Northeast Portland, IE)
Santé (Southeast Portland, M)
Westmoreland Bistro and Wines
(Southeast Portland, M)

SEAFOOD

Couch Street Fish House
(Downtown & Old Town, E)
Dan & Louis Oyster Bar
(Downtown & Old Town, M)
Harborside Restaurant (Down-
town & Old Town, E)
Jake's Famous Crawfish
(Downtown & Old Town, E)
Jake's Grill (Downtown & Old
Town, M)
McCormick & Schmick's
(Downtown & Old Town, E)
Newport Bay Restaurant
(Downtown & Old Town, M)

Opus Too Restaurant & Jazz
   de Opus Bar (Downtown &
   Old Town, E)
Rafati's on the
   Waterfront (Downtown &
   Old Town, M)
Salty's on the Columbia
   (Northeast Portland, E)

STEAK

Jake's Grill (Downtown &
   Old Town, M)
Opus Too Restaurant
   & Jazz de Opus Bar
   (Downtown &
   Old Town, E)

Rafati's on the Waterfront
   (Downtown & Old
   Town, M)
Ringside West (Downtown &
   Old Town, E)

TEX/MEX

Esparza's Tex-Mex Cafe
   (Southeast Portland, IE)

VEGETARIAN

Old Wives' Tales (Southeast
   Portland, IE)

VIETNAMESE/THAI

Saigon Kitchen (Southeast
   Portland, IE)

3 Downtown & Old Town

EXPENSIVE

Alexander's

Portland Hilton Hotel, 921 SW Sixth Ave. ☎ **503/226-1611.** Reservations recommended. Main dishes $15–$21. AE, CB, DC, MC, V. Dinner only, Mon–Sat 5:30–10pm. CONTINENTAL.

Way up on the 23rd floor of the Hilton is this excellent restaurant. Be sure to have a drink in the lounge, which looks out over the densely wooded West Hills. Move on to the dining room and you are treated to a view encompassing Mount Hood, the Willamette River, and downtown Portland. The entrance to the restaurant is past a wall of rough stones, which creates a rustic mountain resort atmosphere. However, lavender tones and flowers on the tables leave no doubt as to the sophisticated ambience at Alexander's. Fresh seafood is the star on the menu, and you can choose from about six fresh fish dishes, prepared in a variety of ways. There are also duck and pheasant dishes.

Atwater's Restaurant and Lounge

U.S. Bancorp Tower, 111 SW Fifth Ave. ☎ **503/275-3600.** Reservations highly recommended. Main dishes $18–$25; fixed-price meals—$35 five courses ($7–$50 with wine). AE, CB, DC, MC, V. Dinner Mon–Thurs 5:30–9:30pm; Fri–Sat 5:30–10pm, Sun 5–9pm. NORTHWEST.

Atwater's whispers elegance from the moment you step off the elevator on the 30th floor. A rosy light suffuses the hall at sunset, and blond-wood trim fairly glows in the warm light. Richly colored carpets on a blond hardwood floor and large, dramatic flower arrangements add splashes of color throughout the restaurant. In the middle of the dining room is a glass-enclosed wine room that would put many wineshops to shame. Far below you are the Willamette River and Portland, and off in the distance stands Mount Hood. Pacific Northwest

Portland Dining

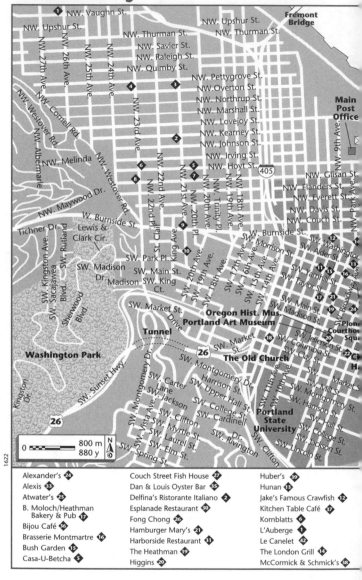

Alexander's ㉔	Couch Street Fish House ㉗	Huber's ㊴
Alexis ㉝	Dan & Louis Oyster Bar ㉟	Hunan ⑬
Atwater's ㉕	Delfina's Ristorante Italiano ②	Jake's Famous Crawfish ⑫
B. Moloch/Heathman Bakery & Pub ⑰	Esplanade Restaurant ㉚	Kitchen Table Café ㊲
Bijou Café ㊱	Fong Chong ㉘	Kornblatts ⑥
Brasserie Montmartre ⑯	Hamburger Mary's ㉑	L'Auberge ①
Bush Garden ⑮	Harborside Restaurant ㉛	Le Canelet ㊷
Casa-U-Betcha ⑤	The Heathman ⑲	The London Grill ⑭
	Higgins ⑳	McCormick & Schmick's ㊳

cuisine is the specialty here, and it's done to perfection. The combinations of ingredients are unexpected and delectable.

Couch Street Fish House

105 NW Third Ave., at Couch St. ☎ **503/223-6173.** Reservations highly recommended. Main dishes $14–$24; four-course sunset dinners $12.95. AE, CB, DC, DISC, MC, V. Dinner only, Mon–Thurs 5–10pm, Fri–Sat 5–11pm. SEAFOOD.

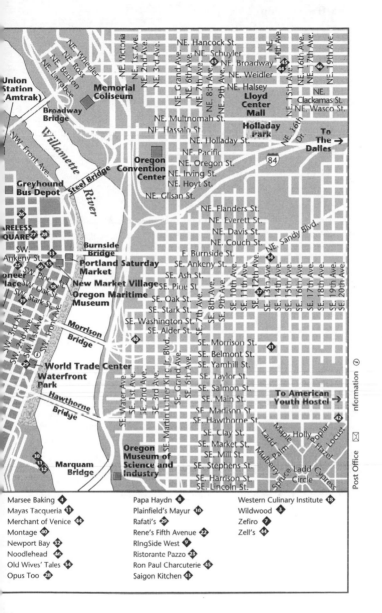

Marsee Baking 4
Mayas Tacqueria 11
Merchant of Venice 14
Montage 40
Newport Bay 32
Noodlehead 46
Old Wives' Tales 34
Opus Too 28

Papa Haydn 8
Plainfield's Mayur 10
Rafati's 29
Rene's Fifth Avenue 22
RingSide West 5
Ristorante Pazzo 23
Ron Paul Charcuterie 15
Saigon Kitchen 13

Western Culinary Institute 18
Wildwood 3
Zefiro 7
Zell's 44

Located in the heart of Old Town, this award-winning restaurant specializes in the Northwest's freshest seafood. The restaurant occupies two historic structures, one of which is merely the facade of an Italianate Victorian hotel built in 1883; this, in fact, must be the only historic parking lot in the country. The other historic building has been completely remodeled into a dark and intimate restaurant. Antiques and exposed brick abound.

The succulent seafood main dishes run the gamut from oysters with Asiago cheese and roasted pepper relish to salmon with mustard hollandaise to such classics as lobster thermidor and shrimp scampi. Red meat eaters are also served with the likes of rack of lamb and filet tenderloin with shiitake mushroom glaze. Even though there are fresh flowers and linen on the tables, casual dress is acceptable here. The sunset dinner, served between 5 and 6pm, is a good deal, offering lighter fare and a chance to sample several tastes for $12.95.

Harborside Restaurant

0309 SW Montgomery St. ☎ **503/220-1865.** Reservations recommended. Main dishes $6.50–$22.50; lunches $5–$11. AE, CB, DC, DISC, MC, V. Lunch Mon–Sat 11:30am–2pm; dinner Sun–Thurs 5–10pm, Fri–Sat 5–11pm. SEAFOOD.

Anchoring the opposite end of RiverPlace from the RiverPlace Hotel is this large and very popular restaurant. The clientele is mostly upscale, especially at lunch and in the après-work hours.

Four dining levels assure everyone a view of the river and marina below. Because it's so popular, the place tends to be noisy and the help seems a bit harried; however, don't let this detract from the fine food. Nearly any time of year, if the weather is good, you'll find folks dining al fresco along the promenade in front of the restaurant.

Although seafood (such as crab-stuffed salmon, razor clams with rémoulade sauce, and grilled sea scallop fettuccine) is the main attraction here, the menu is quite extensive. The long list of hot and cold salads is very tempting.

⑤ Higgins

1239 SW Broadway. ☎ **503/222-9070.** Reservations highly recommended. Main courses $13.25–$18.50. AE, DC, MC, V. Lunch Mon–Fri 11:30am–2pm. dinner daily 5–10:30pm. NORTHWEST/MEDITERRANEAN.

Higgins, located just up Broadway from the Heathman Hotel, where chef Greg Higgins first made a name for himself in Portland, strikes a balance between contemporary and classic in both its decor and its cuisine. The trilevel dining room is divided into two distinctly different seating areas, with the wood-paneled lower area being the more popular section. Waiters wear long white aprons and copper pots hang on the wall of the open kitchen. It is these details that give the restaurant its classic ambiance, but the menu, which changes every Thursday, explores more contemporary culinary horizons.

The duck liver flan with green peppercorns and walnut crackers is a light and creamy twist on a classic pâté, while oysters on the half shell are served with a spicy smoked-chile mignonette. Entrées usually include a range of the rustic and the cultured. For example, a recent menu included grilled sausage made from chicken, sun-dried tomatoes, and rosemary and served with fettucine, greens, and a mustard-Romano cream sauce, but the menu also included Dungeness crab purses with seared scallops and braised leeks.

✪ Jake's Famous Crawfish

401 SW 12th Ave. ☎ **503/226-1419.** Reservations recommended. Main dishes $11–$27. AE, DC, DISC, MC, V. Lunch Mon–Fri 11:30am–5pm; dinner Mon–Thurs 5–11pm. Fri–Sat 5pm–midnight, Sun 5–10pm. SEAFOOD.

Jake's has been serving up crawfish (crayfish)—like miniature lobsters—since 1909 at an address that has housed a restaurant or bar since 1892. The back bar came all the way around Cape Horn in 1880, and much of the rest of the restaurant's decor looks just as old and well worn. The noise level after work, when local businesspeople pack the bar, can be loud, and the wait for a table can be long if you don't make a reservation. However, don't let these obstacles dissuade you from visiting this Portland institution.

A large selection of seafood and an extensive wine list make this one of the city's most popular restaurants. There's a daily menu sheet listing 12 to 15 specials, all of which are fresh from the market. However, there is really no question about what to eat at Jake's—crawfish are always on the menu and may be prepared several different ways. If you really want something else, their other seafoods and steaks are equally delectable.

The London Grill

The Benson Hotel, 309 SW Broadway. ☎ **503/228-2000.** Reservations highly recommended. Main dishes $18.75–$23; Sun brunch $19.50. AE, CB, DC, DISC, ER, JCB, MC, V. Sunday champagne brunch 9:30am–1pm; breakfast Mon–Sat 6:30–11am; lunch daily 11:30am–2pm; dinner daily 5–10pm. CONTINENTAL.

Down in the basement of the luxurious Benson Hotel is one of Portland's top restaurants. Modeled after the original London Grill, which was a favorite with Queen Elizabeth I, it has a vaulted ceiling that enhances the wine-cellar feel of the room and mahogany paneling that reflects the glowing chandeliers. Service by casually attired waiters is impeccable. Both breakfast and lunch are popular with business executives. The chef emphasizes uncompromising gourmet meals. The ingredients are always fresh and of the highest quality, including many of the finest local fruits and vegetables. If you have a craving for some imaginative Northwest cuisine, this restaurant should set your tastebuds singing.

McCormick & Schmick's

235 SW First Ave. ☎ **503/224-7522.** Reservations highly recommended. Main dishes $9–$20; bar meals $1.95; lunches $6–$12. AE, DC, MC, V. Lunch Mon–Fri 11:30am–3pm; dinner Sun–Thurs 5–10pm. Fri–Sat 5–11pm; bar meals Mon–Sat 1:30–6:30pm and 9:30pm–close. SEAFOOD.

Although it opened in 1979, McCormick and Schmick's appears as if it has been around as long as Jake's. The owners wanted to open a restaurant/bar that was based on traditional seafood establishments. What they succeeded in creating was a very popular place noted for the freshness of its ingredients. Both the up-and-coming and the already-there keep this place bustling.

Whether it's king salmon or Dungeness crab, seafood is king here. The oysters in the oyster bar go by name, including Olympia, Royal Miyagi, and Quilcene. The daily fresh menu sheet begins with a listing of what's available that day and might list 25 different types of seafood; it even lists the home port of each offering. If you aren't interested in live oysters as an appetizer, there are plenty of cooked seafoods to start you out. Some outstanding main dishes on a recent visit included grilled rainbow trout with apple bacon and current chutney, Cajun catfish with black beans and corn relish, and alder-smoked sturgeon with braised greens. The extensive wine list features excellent Oregon wines, and while you're waiting for a table, you might want to try one of the more than 30 single-malt scotches available. There's an $8.25 dinner menu daily from 5 to 6:15pm and 9:30pm until closing.

Opus Too Restaurant & Jazz De Opus Bar

33 NW Second Ave. ☎ **503/222-6077.** Reservations recommended. Main dishes $10–25. AE, CB, DC, MC, V. Lunch Mon–Sat 11:30am–3pm; dinner Tues–Sat 5pm–midnight, Sun–Mon 5–11pm. Bar open until 2am. SEAFOOD/STEAK.

Anyone who has outgrown sushi but still enjoys the camaraderie and floor show of a sushi bar should stop by this popular restaurant in the heart of Portland's Old Town. Solo diners can sit at the grill bar and watch the cooks mesquite-broil thick seafood steak, beefsteak, and chops. The flames leap and dance; the steaks sizzle. What a show! You'll know you've found the right place when you see the window full of artfully arranged fresh seafood steak. In the bar, you can listen to excellent jazz recordings and share an intimate moment with someone special. Though the menu is short compared with those of other nearby seafood restaurants, Opus Too makes up for this by grilling your order to perfection. If the chefs aren't too busy, they will also prepare a traditional sauce upon your request.

RingSide West

2165 W. Burnside St. ☎ **503/223-1513.** Reservations recommended. Steaks $12–$21; seafood main dishes $15.75–$36.75. AE, DC, DISC, MC, V. Dinner only, Mon–Sat 5pm–midnight, Sun 4–11:30pm. STEAK.

Stop a Portlander on the street and ask where to get the best steak in town and you will invariably be pointed in the direction of RingSide. Though boxing is the main theme of the restaurant, the name delivers a two-fisted pun as well, referring to the incomparable onion rings that should be an integral part of any meal here. Have your rings with a side order of one of their perfectly cooked steaks for a real knockout meal.

There is also a **RingSide East** at 14021 Northeast Glisan Street (☎ 503/255-0750), on Portland's east side, with the same menu. It's open for lunch Monday through Friday from 11:30am to 2:30pm.

MODERATE

Alexis Restaurant

215 W. Burnside St. ☎ **503/224-8577.** Reservations recommended. Main dishes $9–$14. AE, CB, DC, DISC, MC, V. Lunch Mon–Fri 11:30am–2pm; dinner Mon–Thurs 5–10pm, Fri and Sat 5–11pm. Sun 4:30–9pm. GREEK.

Alexis is a classic Greek taverna, and the crowds keep it packed as much for the great food as for the fun atmosphere. On weekends there's belly dancing, and if you happen to be in town on March 25, you can help Alexis celebrate Greek Independence Day with a rousing big party.

The menu has all your Greek favorites. The main dishes are good, but the appetizers are out of this world. The not-to-be-missed list includes saganaki (panfried cheese flamed with ouzo), kalamarakia (perfectly fried squid), octopus, and the tart and creamy avgolemono soup. Accompany these with Alexis's own fresh bread, and wash it all down with a bottle of Demestica wine for a meal beyond compare.

B. Moloch/Heathman Bakery & Pub

901 SW Salmon St. ☎ **503/227-5700.** Reservations not accepted. Main dishes $8–$13.25. AE, DC, DISC, MC, V. Mon–Thurs 7am–10:30pm, Fri 7am–11:30pm, Sat 8am–11:30pm, Sun 8am–10:30pm. NORTHWEST.

At B. Moloch, corporate climbers and bicycle messengers rub shoulders, quaff microbrews, and chow down on creative pizzas baked in a wood-burning oven. Get here before the downtown offices let out or you won't get a seat. The atmosphere is bright and noisy amid an industrial decor softened by colorful images of salmon.

Ostensibly, this is the bakery for the Heathman Hotel dining room a block away, and to that end a cavernous wood-burning brick oven was installed. Luckily, someone had the idea to bake a few pizzas in that amazing oven, and today those very nouvelle pizzas are the mainstay of the menu here. If you're in the mood for pizza like you'll never get from Mario's back home, try the pie with smoked salmon, rock shrimp, roasted peppers, onions, feta cheese, capers, and olive paste. In addition to pizza, there are sandwiches, pasta dishes, great salads, and daily specials. My personal favorites are the small plates such as grilled goat cheese, smoked tomatoes, and roasted garlic. You have to place your order at the counter here, but a waitperson will bring the food to your table.

The restaurant also houses a microbrewery. You can sit in the bar here and watch the brewers at work while sipping one of their beers.

Brasserie Montmartre

626 SW Park Ave. ☎ **503/224-5552.** Reservations highly recommended. Main dishes $9–$17.50. AE, CB, DC, MC, V. Mon–Thurs 11:30am–2am, Fri 11:30am–3am, Sat 10am–3am, Sun 10am–2am; bistro menu available daily from 2pm–closing. NORTHWEST/FRENCH.

Though the menu lacks the creativity of other Northwest and French restaurants in Portland, The Bra (as it's known) is hardly the stodgy and expensive place its full name implies. There is nightly jazz music from 8pm on Monday to Thursday and Sunday and from 8:30pm on Friday and Saturday, and on every table you'll find a paper tablecloth and a container of crayons. Let your artistic ambitions run wild while you wait for dinner or linger over drinks. Tuesday through Saturday nights, a magician performs amazing feats of digital dexterity.

This playfulness is balanced out by spacious and dark formal dining rooms. Massive white pillars, black and white tile floors, velvet banquettes, and silk lamp shades lend an air of fin de siècle Paris.

You might start your meal with a ménage à trois of pâtés, then have a cup of onion soup with three cheeses, move on to salmon with lingonberry-and-ginger butter, and finish off with one of the divinely decadent pastries. The wine list is neither extensive nor expensive. And if you've grown attached to your tabletop art, they'll be happy to let you take it with you.

Bush Garden

900 SW Morrison St. ☎ **503/226-7181.** Reservations recommended. Main dishes $10.50–$25; lunches $6.50–$11. AE, DC, DISC, JCB, MC, V. Lunch Mon–Fri 11:30am–1:45pm; dinner Mon–Sat 5–9:45pm, Sun 5–8:45pm. JAPANESE.

Japanese businessmen are delighted when their companies send them on assignment to Portland. Why? Because here they can get Japanese food that's as good as back home, and it costs far less. Groups, and anyone seeking privacy and a special experience, should have their meal in one of the traditional tatami rooms with the shoji rice-paper-screen walls. If you can't sit cross-legged through dinner, don't worry, beneath the low tables are wells that allow you to sit as you are accustomed.

The moment you step through the door here, enticing aromas greet you—the outstanding salmon teriyaki, perhaps, or the delicate tempura. If there are two or more of you, you should definitely opt for one of the special dinners. Shabu-shabu is my favorite; you get to do the cooking yourself. For the ultimate Japanese banquet, order the kaiseki dinner, which includes two appetizers, sushi or sashimi, tempura, fish, beef, and dessert.

⑤ Dan & Louis Oyster Bar

208 SW Ankeny St. ☎ **503/227-5906.** Reservations recommended. Main dishes $6–$13. AE, CB, DC, MC, V. Sun–Thurs 11am–10pm, Fri–Sat 11am–11pm. SEAFOOD.

Dan and Louis has been serving up succulent oysters since 1907. The oysters come from Dan and Louis's own oyster farm on Yaquina Bay—they don't come much fresher than this. Half the fun of eating here is enjoying the old-fashioned surroundings. The front counter is stacked high with candies and cigars much as it would have been in the 1920s. The walls are covered with founder Louis Wachsmuth's own collection of old and unusual plates. Beer steins line the shelves, and nautical odds and ends are everywhere.

Louis began his restaurant business serving only two items—oyster stew and oyster cocktails. These two are still on the menu, and as good today as they were 85 years ago. Main courses are simple, no-nonsense seafood dishes, mostly fried, but the prices are great.

Esplanade Restaurant

RiverPlace Hotel, 1510 SW Harbor Way. ☎ **503/295-6166.** Reservations recommended. Main dishes $12.50–$24. AE, CB, DC, JCB, MC, V. Breakfast Mon–Sat 6:30–11am; Sun 6:30–10am; lunch Mon–Fri 11:30am–2pm; dinner Mon–Sat 5:30–9pm; brunch Sun 11am–2pm. NORTHWEST.

The Esplanade, surrounded by the quietly sophisticated European-resort atmosphere of the RiverPlace Hotel, is one of the city's few waterfront restaurants. Understated elegance and expansive views of the marina and the city's bridges combine for a stunning setting, and even on the grayest day of Portland's long winter, the warm adobe-colored walls and colorful contemporary art will cheer you up. However, it's the superb cuisine that is truly calculated to brighten your day. Imaginative combinations of fresh seasonal ingredients capture the spirit of the Northwest.

✪ The Heathman Restaurant and Bar

The Heathman Hotel, SW Broadway at Salmon St. ☎ **503/241-4100**. Reservations highly recommended. Main dishes $9.50–$25. AE, CB, DC, MC, V. Breakfast Mon–Fri 6:30–11am, Sat 6:30am–2pm, Sun 6:30am–3pm; lunch Mon–Fri 11am–2pm; dinner daily 5–11pm. NORTHWEST/CONTINENTAL.

The menu in this elegant hotel dining room changes seasonally, but one thing remains constant: ingredients used are the very freshest of Oregon and Northwest seafoods, meat, wild game, and produce with a French accent. Small and bright, the restaurant exudes a bistro atmosphere. On the walls are Andy Warhol's Endangered Species—a rhino, zebra, lion, panda, and others—part of the Heathman's extensive collection of classic and contemporary art. A recent autumn menu offered red snapper with a potato and parsley crust, wild mushroom fettucine, and venison wrapped in applewood-smoked bacon. Local fruit appears in many of the rich desserts. In the bar, there are Northwest microbrewery beers on tap, while an extensive wine list spotlights Oregon.

Huber's

411 SW Third Ave. ☎ **503/228-5686**. Reservations recommended, but not accepted Friday evenings. Main dishes $6.50–$15. AE, DC, DISC, MC, V. Lunch Mon–Fri 11am–4pm; dinner Mon–Thurs 4–10pm, Fri–Sat 4–11pm. CONTINENTAL.

Portland's oldest restaurant first opened its doors to the public in 1879, though it didn't move to its present location until 1911. You'll find this very traditional establishment tucked inside the Oregon Pioneer Building. Down a quiet hallway you'll come to a surprising little room with vaulted stained-glass ceiling, Philippine mahogany paneling, and the original brass cash register. The house specialty has been turkey since the day the first Huber's opened, so there really isn't any question of what to order. You can gobble turkey sandwiches, turkey Delmonico, turkey nouvelle, or turkey mushroom pie. The menu even has wine recommendations to accompany your different turkey dishes. Lunch prices are much lower, with the turkey sandwich the star of the hour.

Hunan

515 SW Broadway, at Morgan's Alley. ☎ **503/224-8063**. Reservations recommended for five or more. Main dishes $6.50–$24; lunch main dishes $4.50–$6. MC, V. Mon–Fri 11am–9pm, Sat noon–10pm, Sun 5–9pm. Parking: SW 10th Ave. and Washington St., with refund after 6pm. CHINESE.

Located at the end of Morgan's Alley, which is lined with interesting little shops and boutiques, is one of Portland's most reliable Chinese restaurants. Hunan exudes a quiet sophistication. Although the menu lists such appetizing main dishes as champagne chicken and Peking duck, there are two items that should absolutely not be missed. General Tso's chicken is both crispy and chewy at the same time, and the succulent sauce has just the right touch of fire. Lover's eggplant is "dedicated to those of our guests with romantic inclinations as well as to all genuine lovers of eggplant," states the menu. With an introduction like that, how can you pass it by? Beautifully presented and prepared chunks of creamy eggplant are truly an eggplant lover's dream come true.

Jake's Grill

Governor Hotel, SW 10th Ave. and Alder St. ☎ **503/220-1850.** Reservations recommended. Main dishes $9–$30; lunch main dishes $5–$15. AE, CB, DC, MC, V. Breakfast Mon–Fri 6:30–10:30am, Sat–Sun 7:30am–3pm; lunch daily 11:30am–2pm (continues to 5pm at bar area); dinner Sun–Thurs 5–10pm, Fri–Sat 5–11pm. STEAK/SEAFOOD.

Jake's Grill is a member of the McCormick and Schmick's chain, and as such offers fairly consistent food. This incarnation harkens back to the early 1900s when Americans flocked to eat their chops at the corner grill. Those who like large porterhouse steaks will find them here, grilled on a high-temperature steak appliance that cooks both sides at once. Another standout is the pork chop with applesauce, and seafood preparation is reliable. In keeping with the Americana theme, meatloaf with gravy and chicken pot pie (with hazelnut shortbread) are also on the menu.

Newport Bay Restaurant

0425 SW Montgomery St. ☎ **503/227-3474.** Reservations recommended. Main dishes $10–$19; lunches and light main dishes $5.25–$10. AE, CB, DC, DISC, MC, V. Winter hours Sun–Thurs 11am–10pm, Fri–Sat 11am–11pm, Sun brunch 11am–3pm (one hour earlier in summer). Open one hour later in summer. SEAFOOD.

Though there are Newport Bay restaurants all over Portland, this one has the best location. It's in the middle of the Willamette River. Well, not actually in the middle, kind of to one side. If you feel this building rocking while you dine, it's no surprise—it's floating. Located in the marina at the RiverPlace shopping and dining complex, Newport Bay provides excellent views of the river and the city skyline, especially from the deck. Inside, the atmosphere is cheery and the service is efficient.

Nearly everything on the menu has some sort of seafood in it—even the quiche, salads, and pastas. Main dishes are mostly straightforward and well prepared, nothing too fancy. The wine list focuses on West Coast wines at reasonable prices.

✪ Plainfield's Mayur Restaurant & Art Gallery

852 SW 21st Ave. ☎ **503/223-2995.** Reservations recommended. Main dishes $8.50–$18. AE, DISC, MC, V. Dinner only, daily 5:30–10pm. INDIAN.

In the words of a friend, "With an Indian restaurant like Mayur's, who needs anything else?" Located in an elegant old Portland home, this is in fact the city's premier Indian restaurant (and includes an art gallery). You can watch the cooks bake bread and succulent tandoori chicken in a tandoor show kitchen. The atmosphere is refined, with bone china and European crystal, and the service is informative and gracious. In addition to the three floors of dining rooms inside, there is a patio out back.

Every dish on the menu is perfectly spiced so that the complex flavors and aromas of Indian cuisine shine through. Be sure to ask them to go easy on the chile peppers if you can't handle spicy food. A tray of condiments accompanies each meal. The dessert list is also an unexpected and pleasant surprise. Save room! The wine list here is one of the finest in the city.

(i) Family-Friendly Restaurants

Aztec Willie, Joey Rose Taqueria *(see Mayas Tacqueria, pg. 199)* at 1501 NE Broadway (☎ 503/280-8900) has a glass-enclosed play area overseen by a huge Mayan-like head. They serve Mexican food from a walk-up counter.

Brasserie Montmartre *(see pg. 193)* Though this is more of an adult restaurant, there are paper tablecloths and crayons to keep kids entertained and even a strolling magician most evenings.

Dan & Louis Oyster Bar *(see pg. 194)* You'll think you're eating in the hold of an old sailing ship, and all the fascinating stuff on the walls will keep kids entertained.

Old Wives' Tales *(see pg. 205)* This is just about the best place in Portland to eat if you've got small children. There are children's menus at all meals and in the back of the restaurant, there's a play-room that will keep the kid entertained while you enjoy your meal.

Rafati's on the Waterfront

25 SW Salmon St. ☎ **503/248-9305.** Reservations highly recommended. Main dishes $13.75–$19.75. AE, JCB, MC, V. Lunch Mon–Fri 11:30am–2pm; dinner Tues–Thurs 5:30–9pm, Fri–Sat 5:30–10pm. SEAFOOD/STEAK.

Popular with executives and other business types, this small restaurant overlooking Tom McCall Waterfront Park prides itself on the award-winning wine list, excellent service, and well-prepared steak and seafood. The steak is only the finest corn-fed, dry-aged beef, and the seafood, lamb, and veal are of equal quality and freshness.

The specialty of the house is flame-broiling over mesquite charcoal. With this in mind, you might try Ahi tuna in tangerine sauce; filet mignon glazed with cream, cognac, whisky, and green peppercorns; raspberry teriyaki chicken; or any of the other mouth-watering offerings. And Rafati's seafood paella, though not mesquite broiled, is an outstanding mélange of fresh flavors from the sea.

Among my favorites are the crab cakes, which come prepared different ways, such as with basil mayonnaise or Indonesian style with curry dipping sauce. For dessert, there are outstanding seasonal fruit tarts. Be sure to peruse the extensive wine list, which features local, California, and imported wine.

○ Ristorante Pazzo

Hotel Vintage Plaza, 627 SW Washington St. (at Broadway). ☎ **503/228-1515.** Reservations highly recommended. Main dishes: $8–$17; lunch main dishes $8–$14. AE, CB, DC, DISC, MC, V. Breakfast Mon–Fri 7am–10:30am, Sat–Sun 8am–10:30am; lunch Mon–Sat 11:30am–2:30pm; dinner Mon–Thurs 5pm–10pm, Fri–Sat 5pm–11pm, Sun noon–10pm. ITALIAN.

The Italianate elegance of Hotel Vintage Plaza demands an Italian res-taurant, and as luck would have it, Italian food has of late been enjoy-ing a renaissance under the title of Mediterranean cuisine. Whatever you want to call the style of meals served at Pazzo, I call it great. The atmosphere is not nearly as rarefied as in the adjacent hotel lobby and, in fact, if you take a seat at Pazzo's bar, you'll practically be ducking hanging hams, sausages, and garlic braids. Rustic decor and the stereotypical red-and-white-checked tableclothes speak of an Italian country ristorante, though the city passes by just outside. As you step through the restaurant's front door, you'll find yourself looking into a glass case full of roasted garlic bulbs.

⑤ Western Culinary Institute International Dining Room

1316 SW 13th Ave. ☎ **503/223-2245** or 800/666-0312. Reservations required. Five-course lunch $7.95; six-course dinner $14–$18; Thursday buffet $14.95. MC, V. Lunch Tues–Fri 11:30am–1pm; dinner Tues–Fri 6–8pm. CONTINENTAL.

If you happen to be a frugal gourmet whose palate is more sophisticated than your wallet can afford, you'll want to schedule a meal here. The dining room serves four- to six-course gourmet meals prepared by advanced students at prices even a budget traveler can afford.

Meals are served in a quiet dining room done in pleasing pastels. The decor is modern and unassuming, and the students who wait on you are eager to please. For each course you have a choice among two to five offerings. A sample dinner menu might begin with velouté Andalouse followed by pâté of rabbit, a pear sorbet, grilled chicken breast mahi with blackberry-balsamic sauce, Chinese salad with smoked salmon, and divine chocolate-mousse cake. Remember, that's all for less than $20 on this treat. The four-course lunch for only $7.95 is an even better deal.

INEXPENSIVE

⑤ Fong Chong

301 NW Fourth Ave. ☎ **503/220-0235.** Reservations not accepted. Appetizers $3–$5.50; main dishes $4–$10; dim sum meals, under $10. MC, V. Mon–Thurs 10:30am–9pm, Fri–Sun 10:30am–10pm; dim sum 11am–3pm daily. CHINESE.

This popular Chinese restaurant is in a grocery store. Don't worry, you won't be eating between the aisles; the restaurant occupies its own room. Although most of the food here is above average, the dim sum is the best in the city. Flag down a passing cart and point to the most appetizing looking little dishes. Be careful or you might end up with a plate of chicken feet. At the end of the meal, your bill is calculated by the number of plates on your table.

Hamburger Mary's

840 SW Park Ave. ☎ **503/223-0900.** Reservations not accepted. $4.90–$10.25. AE, CB, DC, MC, V. Daily 7am–2am. BURGERS.

As the name implies, this is a place to eat a hamburger—one of the best hamburgers in Portland. It's thick and juicy, piled high with crisp lettuce and ripe tomatoes, and served on a whole-wheat bun. You can't miss this little place—a tiny building surrounded by skyscrapers. Step inside and you enter a crowded room where the walls and ceiling are covered with everything from a rusting sousaphone to an upside-down floor lamp. Stop by in the morning (or whenever you're ready for breakfast) and create your own omelet from the list of more than 20 possible ingredients.

Mayas Tacqueria

1000 SW Morrison St. ☎ **503/226-1946.** Prices $2.25–$7.95. AE, MC, V. Daily 11am–10pm. MEXICAN.

Nothing fancy here, just good home-cooked Mexican food—fast—and you can watch the cooks prepare your meal just as in any tacqueria in Mexico. The menu above the counter lists the different meals available, and on a separate list you'll find the choice of meats, which include mole chicken, chile verde pork or chicken, chile Colorado beef or chicken, and carne asada. Watch for the Maya-style murals on the walls out front. Sante Fe Tacqueria at 831 NW 23rd Ave. (☎ 503/220-0406) and Aztec Willie, Joey Rose Taqueria at 1501 NE Broadway (☎ 503/280-8900) are run by the same folks and serve equally delicious food.

Rene's Fifth Avenue

1300 SW Fifth Ave. ☎ **503/241-0712.** Reservations recommended. Lunches $6–$9. MC, V. Mon–Fri 11:30am–2:30pm. CONTINENTAL.

Comfortable and elegant, this 21st-floor lunch spot in the First Interstate Tower is always crowded. Local businesspeople flock here as much for the great view as for the food. The menu, though short, is varied and includes daily specials and plenty of seafood. When I last visited, I had blackened salmon with a lemon sauce, pasta salad, soup, and a splendid view of the Northwest hills, for $7.95. You won't find a view this good at better prices anywhere else in the city.

4 Northwest Portland

EXPENSIVE

⑤ L'Auberge

2601 NW Vaughn St. ☎ **503/223-3302.** Reservations highly recommended. Main dishes $8.50–$19.75; four-course, fixed-price dinner $34.50–$36. AE, CB, DC, DISC, MC, V. Dinner only, Mon–Thurs 5pm–midnight, Fri–Sat 5pm–1am, Sun 5pm–midnight. NORTHWEST/FRENCH.

Located at the edge of the industrial district, this little country cottage offers some of the best French and Northwest cuisine in Portland and has done so for many years. The restaurant is divided into the main dining room and the lounge and deck area. An à la carte international bistro menu is available and there is an extensive wine list. On Sunday nights the French flavor is forsaken in favor of succulent ribs, and a movie is shown in the bar. A more formal atmosphere reigns in the main dining room, even on Sunday nights. A fireplace and a few antiques create a homey feel, and etched glass between booths lends an air of sophistication. A few works of contemporary art add drama to the setting.

The fixed-price dinners feature meals with a French origin but translated with a Northwest accent. If you happen to be dining downstairs, be sure to stop by the bar first to have a look at the delectable morsels on the dessert tray. Dinners start. There are a couple of choices of main dishes, such as rack of lamb with port garlic sauce and duck breast with green peppercorns in lime demi-glace. This is all topped off with a choice from that dessert tray.

✪ Wildwood

1221 NW 21st Ave. ☎ **503/248-WOOD.** Reservations highly recommended. Main courses $13.50–$22. AE, MC, V. Lunch Mon–Sat 11:30am–2:30pm; dinner Mon–Thurs 5:30–10pm, Fri–Sat 5:30–10:30pm, Sun 5–8:30pm; Sun brunch 10am–2pm. MEDITERRANEAN.

In the past few years, Northwest 21st Avenue has become Portland's hottest restaurant row, and Wildwood, way up at the north end, is one of the hottest spots on the street. With an elegant and spare interior decor straight out of *Architectural Digest* and a menu that changes daily, it isn't surprising that Wildwood is a hit with urban sophisticates. With booths, a meal counter, a bar area, and a patio, the restaurant appeals to celebratory groups, businesspeople, couples, and solo diners. The short menu relies primarily on the subtle flavors of the Mediterranean, which often seem both exotic and familiar at the same time. Recently, the appetizers list included fennel-cured salmon with a cucumber-and-red-onion salad as well as a couple of pizzas, one of which had a cornmeal-and-sage crust and was topped with cheddar cheese, walnuts, and bacon. Entrées included grilled salmon with tangerine, blood orange, and grilled red onion; roast lamb with a white bean purée, red chard, and grilled mushrooms; and grilled swordfish with saffron-braised leeks, Manila clams, and olive tapenade.

MODERATE

ⓢ Casa-U-Betcha

612 NW 21st Ave. ☎ **503/222-4833.** Reservations recommended. Main dishes $8.50–$12.25. AE, MC, V. Daily 5–10pm. MEXICAN.

If you like your restaurant to be a work of art, slide into one of the colorful booths at this trendy nouvelle Mexican restaurant. Garishly painted tables, strings of chile pepper lights, and neoindustrial cacti create a real "scene" at Casa-U-Betcha. Located on an up-and-coming street with art galleries, a repertory movie theater, and retro clothing stores, this is Portland's hippest Mexican restaurant. Big baskets of corn chips with bowls of red and green salsa wait on every table. I find the appetizers menu so fascinating that I usually just make a meal of a couple of these and skip the combo dinners and other Mexican main dishes. My favorite appetizer is the Mexican sushi made with tortillas, smoked salmon, black beans, guacamole, and wasabi. The ginger-jalapeño dipping sauce that comes with it is a real knockout.

The bar, which serves about 20 different kinds of tequilas, is very popular with the locals and when it's crowded, the restaurant can get a bit noisy.

Another Casa-U-Betcha with equally distinctive decor is located at 1700 NE Broadway (☎ 503/282-4554).

Delfina's Ristorante Italiano

2112 NW Kearney St. ☎ **503/221-1195.** Reservations highly recommended; required for Back Kitchen Dinner. Pastas $12–$15; main dishes $15–$17. AE, DC, DISC, MC, V. Lunch Mon–Fri 11:30am–2:30pm; dinner daily 5–11pm. ITALIAN.

Long a Nob Hill mainstay, Delfina's offers excellent Italian food in a casual neighborhood-bistro atmosphere. The tile floors, exposed brick walls, and cafe curtains on the windows all contribute to the comfortable feeling, while smiling, friendly service makes you feel right at home. Be sure to notice the colander lamps hung from the ceiling.

Northern Italian fare predominates here, but southern Italian and even Pacific Northwest manage to sneak onto the menu. You might want to try the roasted New Zealand rack of lamb with red wine, garlic, and rosemary or Dungeness crab with dill, spinach, a lemon cream sauce and homemade fettuccine.

Delfina's most unusual meal is the Back Kitchen Dinner for parties of eight or more people, for $40 to $50 per person with wine. You get to dine in the bustling kitchen, where the chef surprises you with a multicourse menu that your Italian mother-in-law would envy.

✪ Zefiro Restaurant & Bar

500 NW 21st Ave. ☎ **503/226-3394.** Reservations highly recommended. Main dishes $14–$17.50. AE, MC, V. Lunch Mon–Fri 11:30am–2:30pm; dinner Mon–Sat 5:30–10pm. MEDITERRANEAN.

The Northwest restaurant graveyard is crowded with ghosts of daring restaurants that served imaginative cuisine, garnered rave reviews, and disappeared as quickly as a luscious crème brûlée. Luckily for the adventurous palates of Portland, Zefiro has not suffered this ignoble fate. Unpainted fiberboard walls and tiny black-matte halogen lamps hanging from the ceiling lend this restaurant a minimalist urban chic that allows the outstanding creativity of the kitchen to take to the fore.

The menu can only be categorized as Mediterranean, with old-style French and Italian predominating. However, Moroccan, Greek, Spanish, and even Asian influences creep in. Don't be surprised if you find yourself asking your waiter to define unfamiliar menu terms. For a starter, be sure to try the fragrant bowl of warm polenta with marjoram and mascarpone if it happens to be on the menu. Salads, with diverse ingredients like fennel, blood orange, and radishes with mint-citrus vinaigrette, are always menu highlights. Roasted mahimahi with an herb salsa verde made from tarragon, parsley, thyme, oregano, capers, garlic, lemon, and olive oil was a recent entrée that captured all the fragrance of a Mediterranean herb garden in one dish. For dessert a lemon tartlet will round out the meal with its tangy citrus flavor.

INEXPENSIVE

Kornblatts

628 NW 23rd Ave. ☎ **503/242-0055.** Reservations not accepted. Sandwiches $4.50–$8.25; dinner $8.50–$11. MC, V. Sun–Wed 7am–9pm, Thurs–Sat 7am–10pm. DELICATESSEN.

In the heart of NW 23rd, a dozen tables and a take-out corner are the setting for some really satisfying Jewish soul food. The corned beef and pastrami come directly from Brooklyn and there are pickles on the tables to nosh. If you're unfamiliar with the likes of Nova lox, smoked sturgeon, sable, knishes, potato latkes, or blintzes, there's a glossary on the menu for explanation. If the above choices don't tempt you, how about a selection of five different kinds of cheesecake?

5 Southeast Portland

EXPENSIVE

✪ Genoa

2832 SE Belmont St. ☎ **503/238-1464.** Reservations required. Fixed-price four-course dinner $40; seven-course dinner $48. AE, CB, DC, DISC, MC, V. Dinner only. Mon-Sat 5:30–9:30pm (four-course from 5:30–6pm only). ITALIAN.

Without a doubt, this is the best Italian restaurant in Portland, and with only 10 tables, it's also one of the smallest. Everything is made fresh in the kitchen, from the breads to the luscious desserts that are temptingly displayed on a maple burl table just inside the front door. This is an ideal setting for a romantic dinner, and service is personal, as only a restaurant of this size can provide.

The fixed-price menu changes every couple of weeks, but a typical dinner might start with bruschetta and a shellfish stew followed by a creamy wild mushroom soup. The pasta course could be fresh wide noodles in a spicy tomato sauce. This might then be followed by a salad of Belgian endive, roasted walnuts, and gorgonzola. There is always a choice of main courses such as duck breast sautéed with shallots and Bosc pear poached in wine and black peppercorns and then glazed with wine sauce or pork tenderloin marinated with gin, juniper berries, coriander, and rosemary and then skewered and grilled with pancetta bacon, chicken livers, and fresh sage, all served over polenta with a veal demi-glaze and flamed Marsala.

MODERATE

Bread & Ink Cafe

3610 SE Hawthorne St. ☎ **503/239-4756.** Reservations recommended. Main dishes $5.25–$14.50; Sun brunch $11.50. AE, DISC, MC, V. Breakfast Mon–Fri 7-11:30am. Sat 8am–noon; lunch Mon–Fri 11:30am–5pm, Sat noon–5pm; dinner Mon–Thurs 5–10pm, Fri–Sat 5–11pm, Sun 5–9pm, Sun brunch 9am–2pm. NORTHWEST.

This is a casual neighborhood cafe, bright and airy, with pen-and-ink artwork on the walls. Every meal here is carefully and imaginatively prepared using fresh Northwest ingredients. The last time I visited, I had an unusual appetizer—chicken liver paté, seasoned with apples, sage, juniper berries, and dry vermouth.

This dish was influenced by traditional Northwest Native American cooking. Desserts are a mainstay of Bread & Ink's loyal patrons, so don't pass them by. The Yiddish Sunday brunch is one of the most filling in the city.

⑤ Il Piato

2348 SE Ankeny St. ☎ **503/236-4997.** Reservations strongly recommended Thurs–Sat. Lunch courses $6.25–$8.50, pastas $7–$12.50, entrées $10.25–$13. MC, V. Lunch Tues–Fri 11:30am–2:30pm; dinner Sun–Thurs 5:30pm–10pm, Fri–Sat 5:30pm–11pm; Sun brunch 9:30am–2:30pm. Coffee house Tues–Thurs 9:30am–10pm, Fri 9:30–11pm. ITALIAN.

At the corner of Ankeny and 24th Avenue there's a popular neighborhood restaurant with a relaxed atmosphere. Antiqued walls, dried
flowers, and overstuffed chairs in the lounge area provide a comfort
able place for sipping coffee or waiting for your table. Eugen Bingham,
the accomplished chef, is from another well known downtown Italian
eatery, and his wife, Lenore, is the convivial hostess. Start your meal
with oven-dried tomato pesto that you spread on crusty bread. The
pastas are wonderful. I chose risotto de Gamberi, arborio rice with
sautéed prawns, mussels, and leeks, with a low-key taste of saffron that
was intriguing. The marinated rabbit has also gotten rave reviews.
Italian desserts such as tiramisu made with cornmeal cake are all made
here in the kitchen by the pastry chef. For coffee and pastries, Il Piatto
is open during the day.

✪ Indigine

3725 SE Division St. ☎ **503/238-1470.** Reservations required. Main dishes
$10–$14; three-course dinners $16–$20; Sat—night Indian feast $26. MC, V. Dinner
only, Tues–Sat 5:30–10pm. INDIAN/INTERNATIONAL.

At Indigine you can take your tastebuds dancing through tantalizing
flavors the likes of which you may never have encountered before. Step
through the door of this nondescript brown house with a red roof, red
trim, and a riotous little flower and herb garden and you are halfway
into the kitchen, which gives you the feel of dining at a friend's house.

The menu at Indigine is eclectic, with Indian, Mexican, French, and
American offerings during the week and an extravagant Indian feast on
Saturday evenings. In what must be the greatest understatement on any
Portland menu, the regular meals are called "Simple Suppers." These
begin with freshly baked rolls and a salad basket of definitively fresh
vegetables, usually accompanied by a vegetable dip such as herbed
guacamole. When the irresistibly tempting appetizer tray comes
around, keep in mind that dinner portions here are large enough for
two people. During the week you can sample some of Indigine's
flavorful Indian cuisine by ordering the vegetarian sampler. On the
other hand, the creamy seafood enchilada perfectly mixes cheeses with
shrimp and scallops so fresh you can almost smell the salt air. Before
it's too late, stop and save room for one of the luscious desserts, such
as ginger cheesecake. If you have never had Indian chai (tea), don't miss
this opportunity—it's flavored with cardamom.

❸ Le Canelet

1925 SE Hawthorne Blvd. ☎ **503/232-0667.** Reservations recommended. Main courses
$12.25–$15; fixed-price dinner $16. JCB, MC, V. Mon–Sat 5:30–10pm. FRENCH.

French bistros are popping up around Portland like daffodils on the
Champs Elysée, but there is none more French than Le Canelet. On
an otherwise forgettable block, this hole-in-the-wall has made a big
impression with its atmosphere, very reasonable prices, and complexly
flavored dishes. The menu changes regularly, but you might encounter duck liver pâté in port jelly or a salad with smoked chicken, pear
confit, and chevre. Main courses might include the likes of duck confit
with raspberries or grilled swordfish with a black pepper-cognac sauce.
Currently they allow you to bring your own wine, but charge a $12
corkage fee.

✪ Santé

3000 SE Division St. ☎ **503/233-4340.** Reservations recommended. Main courses $11–$15. MC, V. Dinner, Sun–Thurs 5–9pm; Fri–Sat 5–10pm; breakfast/lunch, Sat–Sun 9am–3pm. NORTHWEST/INTERNATIONAL.

Though cafes and casual eateries frequently show up in Portland grocery stores, this is the first upscale restaurant in a supermarket. Located in the Nature's Northwest natural foods grocery, Santé serves highly imaginative northwestern and international dishes that are delicious, healthful, and sustainably (and often organically) grown. Although there are plenty of vegetarian dishes on the menu, this is not specifically a vegetarian restaurant. The menu changes daily and on a recent evening included such appetizers as lentil cakes with *mole* sauce and pear salsa and a tartlet filled with goat cheese, arugula, and crimini mushrooms. How about a stew of heirloom beans with roasted garlic, sun-dried tomatoes, capers, and olive oil; pan-roasted chicken with a maple-pecan sauce; or lamb chops topped with chestnuts, bing cherries, and a red-wine demi-glaze? On weekends, Santé does a brisk breakfast and lunch business serving the likes of teriyaki fish and eggs, organic buckwheat pancakes, and even Jamaican jerk burgers.

Westmoreland Bistro and Wines

7015 SE Milwaukie Ave. ☎ **503/236-6457.** Reservations highly recommended. Main dishes $14–$16. MC, V. Lunch Tues–sat 11am–4pm; dinner Tues–Sat 5–8:30pm. NORTHWEST.

Westmoreland Bistro and Wines is easy to miss. It's small, it's nondescript, and it's located in a neighborhood that, though attractive, is not one of the city's busiest. Caprial Pence, who helped put the Northwest on the national restaurant map, is the chef here. The menu changes monthly and is limited to four or five main dishes and as many appetizers. About half the restaurant is given over to a superb selection of wine, and if you simply crave a glass of great local wine, you can sit at the wine bar. Even though this is a strong contender for best restaurant in Portland, it is a very casual place with only about 12 tables. There's no need to dress up, but you do need to make reservations well in advance (at least a week ahead for Friday or Saturday night). I'm a sucker for roasted goat cheese, and here you can slather it, along with hazelnuts, on crunchy, chewy crostini bread. Salads are simple and delicious and made with only the finest greens and vegetables. Main dishes combine perfectly cooked meat and fish, such as roast pork loin or lightly breaded oysters, with vibrant sauces like cranberry-shallot compote or sweet red pepper pesto. Desserts, such as chocolate-almond-ricotta cake, are rich without being overly sweet. You'll get a large piece of whatever you order, so save room.

INEXPENSIVE

El Palenque

8324 SE 17th Ave. ☎ **503/231-5140.** Main courses $5.15–$12.40. MC, V. Daily 11am–9:30pm. MEXICAN/SALVADORAN.

Though El Palenque bills itself as a Mexican restaurant, the Salvadoran dishes are the real reason for a visit. If you've never had a *pupusa*, this is your opportunity. A pupusa is basically an extrathick corn tortilla with a meat or cheese filling inside. Instead of adding the filling after the tortilla is cooked, the filling goes in beforehand. What you end up with is a sort of griddle-cooked turnover. Accompany your pupusa with some fried plantains and a glass of *horchata* (sweet and spicy rice drink) for a typically Salvadoran meal.

✪ Esparza's Tex-Mex Cafe

2725 SE Ankeny St. ☎ **503/234-7909.** Reservations not accepted. Main courses $5.25–$10. MC, V. Tues–Sat 11:30am–10pm (in summer, Fri–Sat until 10:30pm). TEX-MEX.

With red-eyed cow skulls on the walls and marionettes, model planes, and stuffed animals (iguanas, armadillos, white-tailed deer's rump) hanging from the ceiling, the decor here can only be described as Tex-eclectic, an epithet that is equally appropriate when applied to the menu. Sure there are enchiladas and tamales and tacos, but they might be filled with buffalo, smoked salmon, or even calf brains (for the adventurous). Main courses come with some of the best rice and beans I've ever had, and if you want your meal hotter, they'll toss you a couple of jalapeño peppers. You should also give the *nopalitos* (fried cactus) a try. The margaritas just might be the best in Portland. While you're waiting for a seat (there's almost always a wait), check out the vintage tunes on the jukebox.

Kitchen Table Café

400 SE 12th St. ☎ **503/230-6977.** Reservations not accepted. Pastries $1.25–$2.25; soup $3.25. No credit cards. Mon–Fri 7am–9pm, Sat 9am–3pm. AMERICAN.

You can't miss this yellow and purple building on the corner of SE Oak and SE 12th streets. Inside, more bright colors, kitchen tablecloths, and cavorting aprons on the walls (a kitschy trademark of Anne Hughes, who runs this place, and also the café at Powell's Books) makes this place feel like your own kitchen—only you don't have to cook. The menu is limited to soups and bread, salad, pastries such as coffee cake and pie. Try the berry pie if it's available.

Old Wives' Tales

1300 E Burnside St. ☎ **503/238-0470.** Reservations recommended for dinner. Breakfasts $2.50–$6.50; lunch and dinner main dishes $4.25–$9.50. AE, MC, V. Mon–Thurs 7am–10pm, Fri 7am–11pm, Sat 8am–11pm, Sun 8am–10pm. INTERNATIONAL/VEGETARIAN.

Old Wives' Tales is a sort of Portland countercultural institution. The menu is mostly vegetarian, with such tried-and-true dishes as spana-kopita, burritos, and tempeh burgers. But you can also get a hot pastrami sandwich, rosemary chicken, or a BLT. Breakfast is the restaurant's most popular meal and is served until 2pm daily. Old Wives' Tales's other claim to fame these days is as the city's best place to eat out with kids if you aren't into the fast food scene. There are children's menus and a play area.

6 Northeast Portland

EXPENSIVE

L'Etoile

4627 NE Fremont St. ☎ **503/281-4869.** Reservations highly recommended. Main courses $17–$24.75. MC, V. Tues–Sat 5–9:30pm. FRENCH.

In the past few years, Portland has seen a flowering of neighborhood restaurants, and few of these are as noteworthy as L'Etoile. With its *fin de siècle* decor, intimate Parisian bar, and Edith Piaf on the stereo, L'Etoile is quintessentially French, elegant without being pretentious. The dishes here revel in the richness of classic French cuisine. From the crusty French bread to the escargots (here simmered with garlic, tomatoes, walnuts, and bacon) to the roast quail with rosemary stuffing, the flavors will be refreshing yet familiar to aficionados of the Gallic kitchen. Here duck liver terrine is flavored with a dash of Armagnac, and seared scallops are served with a beet glaze. And these are just appetizers. Main courses might include venison with a chestnut, fennel, walnut, and onion compote or duck breast with tangerines and cranberries. The dessert list is more extensive than even the entrée menu but always includes plenty of rich chocolate desserts. However, I am always tempted by the more unusual, such as a pumpkin tart with praline ice cream or a Bosc pear poached in port with pear sorbet and raspberry-port coulis. There is, of course, a good selection of domestic and French wines to accompany meals, including plenty of dessert wines for rounding out your meal.

Salty's on the Columbia

3839 NE Marine Dr. ☎ **503/288-4444.** Reservations highly recommended. Main dishes $13–$22. AE, CB, DC, DISC, MC, V. Lunch Mon–Sat 11am–3pm; dinner Mon–Thurs 5pm–9:30pm, Fri–Sat 5pm–10pm, Sun 5–9pm; Sun brunch 9:30am–2pm.

Despite Portland's two rivers, there aren't many waterfront restaurants, and Salty's is by far the best. Located out on the Columbia River near the airport, this sprawling restaurant offers views that take in rivers, mountains, and forests. A huge anchor out front and a miniature lighthouse on the roof let you know you've found the place. Preparations here are creative, especially on the daily specials menu, and portions are large. Salmon is particularly popular. Try it smoked over alder wood, which is a traditional Northwest preparation. A few choice offerings of steak and chicken dishes offer options to those who don't care for seafood. A warning: Though the decks look appealing, the noise from the airport can be distracting.

INEXPENSIVE

Merchant of Venice

1432 NE Broadway. ☎ **503/284-4558.** Reservations not accepted. Sandwiches $2.25–$4.25; main dishes $5.25–$9.50. AE, MC, V. Mon–Thurs 11am–9pm; Fri–Sat 11am–10pm. ITALIAN.

If you're over on the east side and want a quick, inexpensive lunch or dinner, duck in at Merchant of Venice, a tiny cafe and deli specializing in pizza, pasta, and sandwiches. The prices are great and the food is hard to beat. The pizza here is what has locals raving. Try the Merchant of Venice, which is topped with homemade chicken sausage, mushrooms, and artichokes. If you'd rather go for a sandwich, try the Shylock, which is stuffed with chicken salad made with celery, olives, sun-dried tomatoes, capers, and herb mayonnaise; you can also order Italian wine by the bottle or glass to accompany your sandwich. Although the restaurant looks small, there's a room off to the side with additional seating.

Noodlehead

1708 NE Broadway. ☎ **503/282-8424.** Reservations recommended. Main dishes $6–$8.25. AE, MC, V. Mon–Fri 11:30am–10pm; Sat–Sun 5–11pm. CHINESE/THAI.

Maybe you already guessed from the name that this is not your ordinary Chinese restaurant, and when you see Noodlehead, you'll know for sure that this isn't your local Lucky Dragon. Though the dishes on the menu are, for the most part, familiar, the decor is Memphis contemporary (and I don't mean Memphis, Tennessee). A purple velvet bench winds sinuously through the narrow dining room. The back wall is covered with gold leaf, and a side wall is a high-gloss black. Throw in a few green-velvet upholstered walls, red-dyed wood, and funnel-shaped overhead lamps that sprout fiber-optic noodles and you have the setting for an ultrahip postcontemporary eatery. Noodlehead does for Chinese what the adjacent Casa-U-Betcha does for Mexican, so it's not surprising to learn that they are under the same ownership. Looks aside, the food is great and if you keep your eyes open you'll find some unusual combinations of flavorings

Ron Paul Charcuterie

1441 NE Broadway. ☎ **503/284-5347.** Also at 6141 SW Macadam Ave. (☎ 503/977-0313). Reservations not accepted. Lighter fare $2.75–$8; sandwiches $5.25–$7.75; main dishes $5.75–$14.25. AE, MC, V. Mon–Thurs 8am–10:30pm, Fri 8am–midnight, Sat 9am–midnight, Sun 9am–4pm. PACIFIC NORTHWEST.

Chef Ron Paul has become a Portland institution over the years. He started out with a catering business that became so popular that clients demanded he open a restaurant. This is a casual deli-style place in an upwardly mobile neighborhood in northeast Portland. Light streams in the walls of glass illuminating long cases full of tempting pasta and vegetable salads, cheeses, quiches, pizzas, sandwich fixings, and, most tempting of all, shelves covered with decadent desserts. After 5pm, there are specials such as lamb in filo with goat cheese and mint or spring vegetable ravioli with asparagus, snow peas, and a red pepper coulis. Both locations serve brunch on Saturday and Sunday, and have an extensive selection of Northwest wines.

Saigon Kitchen

835 NE Broadway. ☎ **503/281-3669.** Reservations suggested. Main dishes $5.25–$15. AE, MC, V. Daily 11am–10pm. VIETNAMESE/THAI.

Vietnamese restaurants have been opening around Portland's east side. They are generally quite inexpensive, offer amazing variety, and provide some of the most interesting flavor combinations this side of Thailand. Saigon Kitchen is among the best of these restaurants. Don't expect a fancy atmosphere inside this pink stucco building, just good home cooking, Vietnamese style. If the menu proves too bewildering, try a combination dinner and let the kitchen make the decisions. The spring rolls (chazio rolls on the menu) shouldn't be missed, however, nor should the curried chicken. The salads, such as shrimp and barbecued pork, are tangy and spicy. There is even a menu of Thai dishes for those who prefer this similar cuisine. Another Saigon Kitchen is at 3954 SE Division St. (☎ 503/236-2312).

7 Cafés, Coffee Bars & Tea Rooms

If you'd like to sample some cafes around Portland that serve not only the full gamut of coffee drinks, but also have a lot of atmosphere, I recommend the following:

The Pied Cow, 3244 SE Belmont St. (☎503/230-4866) is in a Victorian house decorated in Bohemian chic, where there are couches on which to lounge and an outdoor garden. Sandwiches and soups are served, too.

Torrefazione Italia, 838 NW 23rd Ave. (☎ 503/228-2528) serves its classic brew in hand-painted Italian crockery, and has a good selection of pastries to go with your drink.

The Brazen Bean, 2075 NW Glisan St. (☎503/294-0636) is open in the mornings, and evenings until late—which suits its opulent Victorian theme. There are board games to play, and a smoking room.

Café Lena, 2239 SE Hawthorne Blvd. (☎503/238-7087) located in the funky SE Hawthorne neighborhood, has live music and tasty food but is best known for their poetry nights.

TeleCafé, 1022 SW Clay St. (☎ 503/227-7211) is a tiny café with a 1950's garage sale ambiance near Portland State University.

BAKERIES/DESSERT PLACES

Marsee Baking
1323 NW 23rd Ave. ☎ **503/295-4000.** Reservations not accepted. Sweets $1–$5; sandwiches $1–$5.50. Mon–Thurs 6am–9pm, Fri 6am–10pm, Sat 7:30am–10pm, Sun 7:30am–8pm. BAKERY.

When you've just got to have something gooey and rich, there's no better place to get it than at this little bakery on trendy 23rd Avenue. The cases are crammed to overflowing with cakes, pies, and tarts as well as less ostentatious pastries, bagels, focaccia, baguettes, and other breads. There are also panini (Italian sandwiches) and bagels with various fillings.

Papa Haydn
701 NW 23rd Ave. ☎ **503/228-7317.** Reservations not accepted. Main dishes $15–$24; desserts $4–$5. AE, MC, V. Tues–Thurs 11:30am–11pm, Fri–Sat 11:30am–midnight, Sun brunch 10am–3pm. ITALIAN.

Say the words Papa Haydn to a Portlander and you'll see eyes glaze over. A wispy, blissful smile will light up that Portlander's face, and then praises will spill forth. What is it about this little bistro that sends locals into accolades of superlatives? Just desserts. That's right, though Papa Haydn is a respectable Italian restaurant, it is legendary for dessert. At last count the menu included 25 decadent delicacies. Specials add to this list. Lemon chiffon torte, raspberry gâteau, black velvet, Georgian peanut butter mousse torte, tiramisu, boccone dolce. These are just some of the names that stimulate a Pavlovian response in locals. But don't take my word for it, go see for yourself, go *taste* for yourself. Expect a line at the door (that's the real price you pay for a Papa Haydn symphony). Another Papa Haydn is at 5829 SE Milwaukee Ave. (☎ 503/232-9440).

AFTERNOON TEA

British Tea Garden

725 SW Tenth Ave. ☎ **503/221-7817.** Reservations not necessary. Tea $1.50–$3; set teas and lunches $4–$7. AE, DISC, MC, V. Mon and Sat 10am–5pm, Tues–Thurs 10am–6pm. TEA/BRITISH.

Though Portland is a city of java junkies, tea is making a strong showing these days as well. You can get all manner of exotic teas at coffeehouses, but for the genuine, British tea experience, you need to take time out at the British Tea Garden. Not only can you get clotted Devonshire cream and crumpets here, but you can also get Cornish pasties, bangers, shepherd's pie, and finger sandwiches. Don't worry if you're not dressed for tea, it's a casual place.

The Heathman Hotel

1001 SW Broadway at Salmon St. ☎ **503/241-4100.** Reservations recommended. $6–$14. AE, CB, DC, DISC, MC, V. Daily 2–4:30pm. TEA.

Once again I must send you back to The Heathman Hotel. (See "Downtown Hotels," in chapter 14, for a description of the hotel.) In the hotel's lobby lounge, tea hostesses in lace aprons serve finger sandwiches, scones, pastries, and of course excellent tea (blended especially for the hotel). The service is on Royal Doulton's "Twilight Rose" bone china at marble-topped tables, and on chilly afternoons a fire crackles in the fireplace. An elegant affair, tea at the Heathman is a welcome respite from shopping or business meetings.

8 Early Morning & Late-Night Bites

BREAKFAST/BRUNCH

Portland's most sumptuous Sunday brunch is held in the **Benson Hotel's** London Grill. You'll want to dress up for this one. A different sort of brunch is offered at **Bread and Ink Cafe,** which serves a three-course Yiddish repast that your mother would be proud of. Don't feel guilty if you can't finish your meal. Other popular spots for brunch include **Wildwood** (1994's hottest Portland restaurant), **Santé** (gourmet natural foods breakfasts and lunches on weekends only), and **Salty's on the Columbia** (brunch with a view of the Columbia River) See above for details on these three restaurants.

Bijou Café

132 SW Third Ave. ☎ **503/222-3187.** Reservations not accepted. $2.75–$6.25. No credit cards. Daily 7am–3pm. NATURAL FOODS.

Although open only for breakfast and lunch, the Bijou is still one of the most popular restaurants in Portland, and the lines can be long, especially on weekends. The folks here take both food and health seriously. They'll let you know that the eggs are from Chris's Egg Farm in Hubbard, Oregon, and they'll serve you a bowl of steamed brown rice for breakfast. However, the real hits here are the hash browns and the muffins. Don't leave without trying these two. At lunch, there are salads made with organic produce whenever possible. Even the meats are natural. If you're concerned about how you eat, drop by the Bijou. Your body will be happy that you did.

Café du Berry

6439 SW Macadam Ave. ☎ **503/244-5551.** Reservations not accepted. Breakfasts $4–$11; dinner main courses $12–$20. AE, DISC, MC, V. Breakfast daily 7am–3pm; dinner Wed–Sat 6–9pm. BREAKFAST/FRENCH.

Café du Berry bills itself as a country French restaurant. However, the busiest meal here is breakfast and the most popular dishes are the French toast and omelets. These two breakfast standards are treated with Gallic reverence at Café du Berry, which is why it has become known as one of the most memorable breakfasts in town. The daily breakfast special goes for a whopping $11, but might be a shiitake mushroom omelet or some other such gourmet creation.

Zell's, An American Cafe

1300 SE Morrison St. ☎ **503/239-0196.** Reservations not accepted. Breakfast $4–$7.50; lunch $5.25–$7.50. AE, MC, V. Breakfast Mon–Fri 7–11:30am, Sat 7am–3pm, Sun 8am–3pm; lunch Mon–Fri 11:30am–2pm, Sat–Sun noon–3pm. AMERICAN.

Zell's used to be a pharmacy, and now it's a place famed for delicious breakfasts such as oyster omelets, German apple pancakes, and real corned beef hash. Come early if you want to try the cinnamon rolls, but if those are gone you can content yourself with other bakery treats such as dark gingery bread or light and airy scones. The service is great, children are welcomed—and if the restaurant isn't crowded, you can sit as long as you like and the waiter will keep refilling your coffee cup.

LATE NIGHT

Garbanzo's

NW 21st Ave. and NW Lovejoy St. ☎ **503/227-4196.** Reservations not accepted. Salads $2–$4.50; sandwiches $3.50–$4.50; dinners $6.50–$7.50. AE, DISC, MC, V. Sun–Thurs 11:30am–1:30am, Fri–Sat 11:30am–3am (close one hour earlier in winter). MIDDLE EASTERN.

Calling itself a falafel bar, this casual little place has become very popular, especially late at night. The menu includes all the usual Middle Eastern offerings, most of which also happen to be American Heart Association approved. You can eat at one of the tiny cafe tables or get your order to go. They even serve beer and wine. Another Garbanzo's is at 3433 SE Hawthorne Blvd. (☎ 503/239-6087).

Montage

301 SE Morrison St. ☎ **503/234-1324.** Reservations not accepted. Main courses $6–$15. No credit cards. Daily 6pm–4am. CAJUN.

The latest in-spot in town is located here under the Morrison bridge. Walk in to a cacophony of voices and throbbing bass music, punctuated by waiters bellowing out an order for oyster shooters. They have the right idea—Cajun dishes like blackened catfish, rabbit sausage with linguini, jambalaya, frog legs, and alligator pâté at low prices. A lengthy wine menu promises you will find something to your liking. The high energy staff provide efficient service. If you don't like noisy places, you should steer clear of this one—otherwise, it's great fun.

16

What to See & Do in Portland

Portland does not have very many museums, and those that it does have are rather small. This isn't to say that there isn't much for the visitor to see or do. Portlanders are active folks and they prefer snow skiing on Mount Hood to museum-going. They prefer gardening over old-homes tours, and consequently there are numerous world-class public gardens and parks within the city. You can easily see all of Portland's tourist attractions in one or two days. No visit to Portland would be complete, however, without venturing out into the Oregon countryside. This is the city's real attraction. Within an hour and a half you can be skiing on Mount Hood or swimming in the chilly waters of the Pacific Ocean. However, for those who prefer more urban and urbane activities, the museums and parks listed below should satisfy.

SUGGESTED ITINERARIES

If You Have 1 Day

Day 1 Start your day at Skidmore Fountain and walk around Old Town. If it's a Saturday or Sunday, you can visit Portland Saturday Market underneath Burnside Bridge. While in this area, you can also stroll through Chinatown. Walk south through downtown after lunch and visit the Oregon Historical Center and the Portland Art Museum. Finish your day at the Japanese and International Rose Test gardens in Washington Park.

If You Have 2 Days

Day 1 Spend your first day as outlined above, except for visiting the Japanese and International Rose Test gardens.
Day 2 After visiting the Japanese and International Rose Test gardens in the morning, take the miniature train over to Metro Washington Park Zoo. In the afternoon, visit the World Forestry Center across the street from the zoo, and finish the day at the Oregon Museum of Science and Industry, on the east bank of the Willamette River.

If You Have 3 Days

Days 1–2   Follow the two-day strategy as outlined above.
Day 3   On your third day, do the Mount Hood Loop, as described in Chapter 20.

If You Have 5 Days or More

Days 1–3   Follow the three-day strategy as outlined above.
Day 4   In the morning, visit Pittock Mansion and perhaps stroll through Hoyt Arboretum or Forest Park. In the afternoon, visit Fort Vancouver across the Columbia River in Washington State.
Day 5   Drive to the coast or tour through the wine country.

1   The Top Attractions

American Advertising Museum

524 NE Grand Ave. ☎ **503/226-0000.** Admission $3 adults, $1.50 children under 12. Wed–Sun 11am–5pm. Call for hours. Bus: 6.

I long ago gave up watching television and listening to commercial radio because I have no tolerance for advertising. That this is my favorite Portland museum should tell you something about the exhibits. You'll learn (and perhaps reminisce) about historic advertisements, celebrities, and jingles from the 1700s to now. The museum is in the process of moving to its new location on Grand Avenue, and should have its permanent collection in place sometime in 1996. Until then, traveling exhibits will be showcased and hours of operation may be irregular.

Portland Art Museum

1219 SW Park Ave. Tel. **503/226-2811.** Admission $5 adults, $3.50 seniors, $2.50 students ages 6–18, under age 5 free, senior citizens free every Thurs. Free 4–9pm on first Thurs of each month. Tues–Sat 11am–5pm, Sun 1–5pm; first Thurs of each month 11am–9pm. Any downtown bus. MAX: Library Station.

Although this small museum has a respectable collection of European, Asian, and American art, it is the Northwest Coast Native American exhibit that requires a special visit. Particularly fascinating are the transformation masks. Worn during ritual dances, the masks are transformed from one face into a completely different visage by pulling several strings. A totem pole and many other wood carvings show the amazing creative imagination of Northwest Indians. There are also exhibits of regional contemporary art, Asian antiquities, African art from Cameroon, and a large hall for temporary exhibits. If you happen to be in town on the first Thursday of any month, you can save the admission by coming between 4 and 9pm; this free admission is part of the First Thursday program of art gallery openings throughout Portland. On Wednesday nights from 5:30 to 7:30pm (except in summer), the Museum After Hours program presents live music.

Oregon History Center

1200 SW Park Ave. ☎ **503/222-1741.** Admission $4.50 adults and senior citizens, $1.50 students and children ages 5–18, free to members and children under age 5, and on Thursdays, free to seniors. Mon–Sat 10am–5pm, Sun noon–5pm. Any downtown bus. MAX: Library station.

Portland Attractions

NW. Vaughn St.
NW. Upshur St.
NW. Upshur St.
Fremont Bridge
NW. Thurman St.
NW. Thurman St.
NW. Savier St.
NW. Raleigh St.
NW. Quimby St.
NW. 27th Ave.
NW. 26th Ave.
NW. 25th Ave.
NW. 24th Ave.
NW. Westover Rd.
NW. Cornell Rd.
NW. Pettygrove St.
NW. Overton St.
NW. Northrup St.
Main Post Office
NW. Marshall St.
NW. Lovejoy St.
NW. Kearney St.
NW. Johnson St.
NW. Melinda
NW. Albermarle
NW. Irving St.
NW. Hoyt St.
405
NW. Glisan St.
NW. Flanders St.
NW. Everett St.
NW. Davis St.
NW. Couch St.
NW. Maywood Dr.
NW. Westover Rd.
NW. 22nd Ave.
NW. 23rd Ave.
NW. 22nd Ave.
NW. 21st Ave.
NW. 20th Ave.
NW. Trinity Pl.
NW. 19th Ave.
NW. 18th Ave.
SW. Burnside
Galleria
SW. Washington
Tichner Dr.
W. Burnside St.
Lewis & Clark Cir.
Morrison
SW. Alder
SW. Park Pl.
NW. Clair St.
SW. 20th Ave.
SW. 19th Ave.
SW. 17th Ave.
SW. 16th Ave.
SW. 15th Ave.
SW. 14th Ave.
SW. Yamhill St.
Broadway Ave.
SW. Kingston Ave.
SW. Rutland
SW. Madison Dr.
SW. Madison
SW. Main St.
King Ave.
SW. Taylor St.
SW. Salmon St.
SW. Main St.
SW. Sacajavea Blvd.
SW. Madison Dr.
SW. King Ct.
SW. Madison St.
1
SW. Market St.
Drive
SW. Jefferson St.
5
6
2
Shenwood Blvd.
Tunnel
26
SW. Market St.
SW. Columbia St.
SW. Clay St.
4
3
Washington Park
Kingston Dr.
SW. Sunset Hwy.
SW. Montgomery Dr.
SW. Carter Lane
SW. Jackson
SW. Upper Hall St.
SW. Harrison St.
Harrison St.
SW. Market St.
SW. Mill St.
SW. Montgomery St.
SW. Harrison St.
26
SW. Vista Ave.
SW. Clifton
SW. Myrtle St.
SW. Laurel St.
SW. Elm St.
SW. Spring St.
SW. College St.
SW. Cardinel
SW. Rivington Dr.
SW. Clifton
Portland State University
SW. College St.
SW. Hall St.
SW. Jackson St.
SW. Lincoln St.

0   800 m
0   880 y
N

1623

American Advertising Museum ⑭
Church of Elvis ⑨
International Rose Test Garden ❶
Japanese Gardens ❷
Mill Ends Park ⑫
The Old Church ❹

OREGON
• Portland

Oregon Territory was a land of promise and plenty. Thousands of hardy individuals set out along the Oregon Trail, crossing a vast and rugged country to reach the fertile valleys of Oregon's rivers. Others came by ship around the Horn. Today the state of Oregon is still luring immigrants with its bountiful natural resources, and those who wish to learn about the people who discovered Oregon before them should visit this well-designed museum. Oregon history from before the arrival

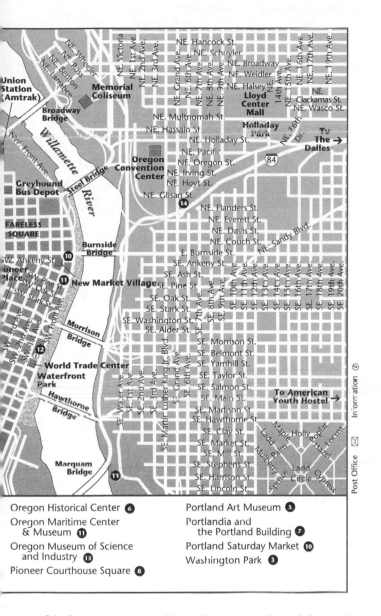

Union Station (Amtrak)

Broadway Bridge

NE. Wheeler
NE. Ross
NE. Benton
NE. Larrabee

NE. Victoria
NE. 1st. Ave.
NE. 2nd. Ave.
NE. 3rd. Ave.

NE. Hancock St.
NE. Schuyler
NE. Broadway
NE. Weidler
NE. Halsey

Memorial Coliseum

NE. Grand Ave.
NE. 6th. Ave.
NE. 7th. Ave.
NE. 8th. Ave.
NE. 9th. Ave.

NE. 14th Ave.
NE. 15th Ave.
NE. 16th Ave.
NE. 17th Ave.
NE. 19th Ave.

NE.
Clackamas St.
NE. Wasco St.

Lloyd Center Mall

Willamette River

Steel Bridge

NE. Multnomah St.
NE. Hassalo St.
NE. Holladay St.

Holladay Park

NE. 16th Dr.

To The Dalles →

Greyhound Bus Depot

Oregon Convention Center

NE. Pacific
NE. Oregon St.
NE. Irving St.
NE. Hoyt St.
NE. Glisan St.

84

FARELESS SQUARE

Burnside Bridge

14

NE. Flanders St.
NE. Everett St.
NE. Davis St.
NE. Couch St.

NE. Sandy Blvd.

SW. Ankeny St.
10
Pioneer Place
SW. Pine St.
SW. Oak St.
SW. Stark St.

11
New Market Village

E. Burnside St.
SE. Ankeny St.
SE. Ash St.
SE. Pine St.
SE. Oak St.
SE. Stark St.
SE. Washington St.
SE. Alder St.

SE. 7th Ave.
SE. 8th Ave.
SE. 9th Ave.
SE. 10th Ave.
SE. 11th Ave.
SE. 12th Ave.
SE. 13th Ave.
SE. 14th Ave.
SE. 15th Ave.
SE. 16th Ave.
SE. 17th Ave.
SE. 18th Ave.
SE. 19th Ave.
SE. 20th Ave.

SW. 3rd. Ave.
SW. 2nd. Ave.
SW. 1st. Ave.
SW. Front Ave.

Morrison Bridge

12
World Trade Center
Waterfront Park

Hawthorne Bridge

SE. Water Ave.
SE. 1st. Ave.
SE. 2nd. Ave.
SE. 3rd. Ave.
SE. Martin Luther King Jr. Blvd.
SE. Grand Ave.
SE. 6th. Ave.

SE. Morrison St.
SE. Belmont St.
SE. Yamhill St.
SE. Taylor St.
SE. Salmon St.
SE. Main St.
SE. Madison St.
SE. Hawthorne St.
SE. Clay St.
SE. Market St.
SE. Mill St.
SE. Stephens St.
SE. Harrison St.
SE. Lincoln St.

To American Youth Hostel →

Marquam Bridge

13

Maple
Holly
Poplar
Locust
Hazel
Ladd
Palm
Mulberry
Spruce
Cypress
Ladd Circle

Information ⓘ

Post Office ✉

Oregon Historical Center **6**

Oregon Maritime Center & Museum **11**

Oregon Museum of Science and Industry **13**

Pioneer Courthouse Square **8**

Portland Art Museum **5**

Portlandia and the Portland Building **7**

Portland Saturday Market **10**

Washington Park **3**

of the first Europeans to well into this century is chronicled in an educational and fascinating exhibit. The displays incorporate parts of old buildings; objects such as snow skis, dolls, and bicycles; fashions; Native American artifacts; nautical and surveying instruments; even a covered wagon. Museum docents, with roots stretching back to the days of the Oregon Trail, are often on hand to answer questions. There is also a research library that includes many journals from early pioneers.

Kitsch'n Around Portland

Either you love it or you hate it, but there's no denying that kitsch is in, and Portland is thriving on it. Retro furniture stores sell 1950s chairs and tables at 1990s prices, vintage clothing stores sell platform shoes and bell bottoms, and Elvis worship is raised to an art form. If this is your schtick, then let's go "kitsch'n" around Portland.

The **Church of Elvis,** 720 SW Ankeny St. (☎ 503/226-3671) is Portland's longtime temple of kitsch. Coin-operated art, a video psychic, Elvis-officiated weddings, and other absurd assemblages and interactive displays cram this second-floor oddity. If you've seen Elvis anytime in the past decade, you owe it to yourself to stop in. Guided tours are available on weekends between noon and 5pm.

Close on the heels of the Church of Elvis is the **UFO Museum,** 1637 SW Alder St. (☎ 503/227-2975), based on a similar aesthetic of more is better, this hole-in-the-wall art gallery is a barrage of bizarre. The main focus is on aliens and UFOs à la supermarket tabloids, but all things weird are fair game here. Be sure to pick up a copy of the museum's *Offbeat Tourist Guide to the Wild and Wacky Side of Portland, Oregon.*

In the same neighborhood as the UFO Museum are several vintage clothing and furniture stores. The biggest and best of these is **Habromania,** 203 SW Ninth Ave. (☎ 503/223-0767), which has two floors of vintage collectibles from the 1930s through the 1960s. Need a chrome and Formica kitchen table? They've got the best selection in town. Right next door is the smaller, but no less eclectic, **Palookaville,** 211 SW Ninth Ave. (☎ 503/241-4751). Across the street, there are **Avalon,** 318 SW Ninth Ave. (☎ 503/224-7156),

Oregon Museum of Science and Industry [OMSI]

1945 SE Water Ave. ☎ **503/797-4000** or 800/955-6674. Museum, $7 adults, $6 senior citizens, $4.50 children ages 3–17; OMNIMAX, $7 adults, $6 senior citizens, $4.50 children ages 3–17; Sky Theater, $4.50 adults, $4 senior citizens, $3.50 children ages 3–17; Light Show—Evening, $6.50 adults, senior citizens, and children. Combination tickets also available at considerable discount. Sat–Wed 9:30am–5:30pm (until 7pm in summer). Thurs–Fri 9:30am–9pm. Closed Dec 25. Bus: 63.

Formerly located in Washington Park, the Oregon Museum of Science and Industry moved to a large and impressive new building on the east bank of the Willamette River in late 1992. Six huge halls have given the museum lots of space to play with, and kids and adults are finding the new exhibits both fun and fascinating. Two of the most exciting exhibits allow visitors to touch a tornado or ride an earthquake. This is a hands-on museum and everyone is urged to get involved with displays. There's plenty of pure entertainment as well with Oregon's first OMNIMAX theater and the Murdock Sky Theater, which features laser light shows and astronomy presentations.

and **Magpie,** 324 SW Ninth Ave. (☎ 503/220-0920), which are *the* places in Portland to outfit yourself for disco nights at local dance clubs.

If you're doubtful about the collectibility of some of the goods at Habromania, stop in at the **Vacuum Cleaner Museum** at Stark's Vacuum Cleaner Sales and Service, 107 NE Grand Ave. (☎ 503/232-4101). A while back, there was talk of a toaster museum moving to Portland to Seattle, but as of this writing, I've been unable to track it down. Maybe you can find it.

If after all this you're ready for some refreshment, head over to the **Telecafe,** 1022 SW Clay St. (☎ 503/227-7211), where you can sip a cup of java with Generation X'ers who can't get enough of that sixties stuff. If you're in need of a more substantial meal, head over to **Dots Cafe,** 2521 SE Clinton St. (☎ 503/235-0203) where you can nosh on the best burgers in Portland while oohing and ahhing over the vintage decor. Once again, this is a Generation X hangout. For a genuine retro experience, try **Fuller's Restaurant,** 136 NW Ninth Ave. (☎ 503/222-5608), a classic diner straight out of an Edward Hopper painting. This one is in the same neighborhood as the above-mentioned shops and museums.

While you wander the streets of Portland tracking down kitsch of all kinds, keep your eyes out for Our Lady of Eternal Combustion, one of the city's most famous art cars. This old station wagon is completely covered with glued-on trinkets. A real head-turner. If you pay attention, you're likely to see many other art cars as well. One of my favorites has a miniature La Brea tar pits on the roof.

Pittock Mansion

3229 NW Pittock Dr. ☎ **503/823-3624.** Admission $4 adults, $3.50 senior citizens, $1.50 ages 6–18. Daily noon–4pm. Closed three days in late November, most major holidays, and the first three weeks in January. Bus: 20 to Burnside and Barnes. Half-mile walk.

At nearly the highest point in the West Hills, 1,000 feet above sea level, stands the most impressive mansion in Portland. Once slated to be torn down to make way for new housing, this grand château built by the founder of Portland's *Oregonian* newspaper has been fully restored and is open to the public. Built in 1914 in a French Renaissance style, the mansion featured many innovations, including a built-in vacuum system and amazing multiple showerheads in the baths. Today it is furnished with 18th and 19th-century antiques, much as it might have been at the time the Pittocks occupied the building. Lunch and afternoon tea are available in the Gate Lodge, the former caretaker's cottage. Reservations are recommended (☎ 503/823-3627).

✪ Portland Saturday Market

Underneath Burnside Bridge between SW First Ave. and SW Ankeny St. ☎ **503/222-6072.** Free admission. Mar–Christmas Eve, Sat 10am–5pm and Sun 11am–4:30pm. Any downtown bus. MAX: Skidmore Fountain Station.

Portland Saturday Market (held on both Saturday and Sunday) is arguably the city's single most important and best-loved event. For years the Northwest has attracted artists and craftspeople, and every Saturday and Sunday nearly 300 of them can be found selling their exquisite creations here. In addition to the dozens of crafts stalls, you'll find flowers, fresh produce, ethnic and unusual foods, and lots of free entertainment. This is the single best place in Portland to shop for one-of-a-kind gifts. The atmosphere is always cheerful and the crowds colorful. At the heart of the Skidmore District, Portland Saturday Market makes an excellent starting or finishing point for a walk around Portland's most historic neighborhood. Don't miss this unique market. On Sunday, on-street parking is free.

World Forestry Center

4033 SW Canyon Rd. ☎ **503/228-1367.** Admission $3 adults, $2 senior citizens and ages 6–18, under age 6 free. The second Sunday of the month is free. Daily 9am–5pm and 10am–5pm in winter. Closed Christmas Day. Bus: 63.

Although with each passing year Oregon depends less and less on the timber industry, the World Forestry Center is still busy educating visitors about the importance of our forest resources. Step inside the huge wooden main hall and you come face to bark with a very large and very lifelike tree. Press a button at its base and it will tell you the story of how trees live and grow. In other rooms you can see exhibits on forests of the world, old-growth trees, and a rain forest exhibit from the Smithsonian.

In summer, a vintage carousel is on the grounds.

2 More Attractions

A LANDMARK

The Old Church

1422 SW 11th Ave. ☎ **503/222-2031.** Free admission. Mon–Fri 11am–3pm. Any downtown bus. MAX: Library Station.

Built in 1883, this wooden Carpenter Gothic church is a Portland landmark. It incorporates a grand traditional design, but is constructed with spare ornamentation. An active church until 1967, the deteriorating building was to be torn down; however, preservationists stepped in to save it. Today it's a community facility, and every Wednesday there's a free lunchtime classical music concert.

A MUSEUM

Oregon Maritime Center & Museum

113 SW Front Ave. ☎ **503/224-7724.** Admission $4 adults $3 senior citizens, $2 students, free for children under age 8. Summer, Wed–Sun 11am–4pm; winter, Fri–Sun 11am–4pm. Any downtown bus. MAX: Skidmore Fountain Station.

Inside the museum, you'll find models of ships that once plied the Columbia and Willamette. Also on display are early navigation instruments, artifacts from the battleship *Oregon,* old ship hardware, and other maritime memorabilia. The stern-wheeler *Portland,* moored across Waterfront Park from the museum, is also open to the public. Inside this old vessel, you'll hear explanations of how steam-driven machinery operates and more displays on maritime history.

OUTDOOR ART/PLAZAS/ARCHITECTURAL HIGHLIGHTS

Church of Elvis

720 SW Ankeny St. ☎ **503/226-3671.** Donation. Irregular hours; call. Any downtown bus.

This is Portland's most bizarre attraction: the first 24-hour video psychic and church of Elvis. This upstairs "museum" is full of kitschy contraptions bearing the visage of the King and other pop culture characters. What is it? Well, for a quarter, you can find out. Care to have Elvis hear your confession? No problem. The King will absolve you of sin, unless, of course, you have committed the unforgivable sin of believing that Elvis is dead. Great fun if you are a fan of Elvis, tabloids, or the unusual.

Oregon Convention Center

777 NE Martin Luther King Jr. Blvd. ☎ **503/235-7575.** Free admission for self-guided tours. Mon–Fri 8am–5pm. Bus: 63. MAX: Convention Center Station.

As you approach downtown Portland from the direction of the airport, it is impossible to miss this unusual architectural bauble on the city skyline. Christened "Twin Peaks" even before it opened in the summer of 1990, the center is worth a visit even if you don't happen to be in town for a convention. Its "twin peaks" are two tapering glass towers that channel light into the center of this huge complex. Outside the main entrance are two Asian temple bells. Inside are paintings on a scale to match the building, a dragon boat hanging from the ceiling, and a brass pendulum swinging slowly through the hours. Small plaques on the outside wall of the main lobby spotlight telling quotes about life in Oregon.

☢ Pioneer Courthouse Square

Bounded by Broadway, Sixth Avenue, Yamhill Street, and Morrison Street. MAX: Pioneer Courthouse Square Station. Any downtown bus.

Today it is the heart of downtown Portland and acts as an outdoor stage for everything from flower displays to concerts to protest rallies, but not too many years ago this beautiful brick-paved square was nothing but a parking lot. The parking lot itself had been created by the controversial razing in 1951 of the Portland Hotel, an architectural gem of a Queen Anne-style château. Today the square, with its tumbling waterfall fountain and free-standing columns, is Portland's favorite gathering spot, especially at noon, when the *Weather Machine,* a mechanical sculpture, forecasts the upcoming 24 hours. Amid a fanfare of music and flashing lights, the *Weather Machine* sends up clouds of mist and then raises either a sun (clear weather), a dragon (stormy weather), or a blue heron (clouds and drizzle). Keep your eyes on the square's brick pavement. Every brick contains a name (or names) or statement, and some are rather curious.

✪ Portlandia and the Portland Building
1120 SW Fifth Ave.

Portlandia is the symbol of the city, and this hammered bronze statue of her is the second-largest such statue in the country. The largest, of course, is New York City's Statue of Liberty. The massive kneeling figure holds a trident in one hand and with the other reaches toward the street. Strangely enough, this classically designed figure reminiscent of a Greek goddess perches above the entrance to Portland's most controversial building: The Portland Building, considered the first postmodern structure in the country. Today anyone familiar with the bizarre constructions of Los Angeles architect Frank Gearhy would find it difficult to understand how such an innocuous and attractive building could have ever raised such a fuss, but it did.

PARKS & GARDENS

Crystal Springs Rhododendron Garden
SE 28th Ave. ☎ **503/777-1734.** Admission $2. Mar 1–Labor Day, Thurs–Mon from 10am–6pm, Daily dawn to dusk. Bus: 19

Eight months out of the year this is a tranquil garden, with a waterfall and ducks to feed. But when the rhododendrons and azaleas bloom from March to June, it becomes a spectacular mass of blazing color. The Rhododendron Show and Plant Sale is held here on Mother's Day weekend.

Forest Park
Bounded by W. Burnside Street, Newberry Road, St. Helens Road, and Skyline Rd. ☎ **503/823-4492.** Free admission. Daily dawn to dusk. Bus: 15, 17, 20, or 63.

With 4,800 acres of wilderness, this is the largest forested city park in the United States. There are 50 miles of trails and old fire roads for hiking and jogging. More than 100 species of birds call these forests home, making this park a birdwatcher's paradise.

✪ International Rose Test Garden
400 SW Kingston Ave., Washington Park. ☎ **503/823-3636.** Free admission. Daily, dawn to dusk. Bus: 63.

Covering 4¹/₂ acres of hillside in the West Hills above downtown Portland, these are the largest and oldest rose test gardens in the United States. They were established in 1917 by the American Rose Society, itself founded in Portland. Though you will likely see some familiar roses in the Gold Medal Garden, most of the 400 varieties on display here are new hybrids being tested before marketing. Among the roses in bloom from late spring to early winter, you'll find a separate garden of miniature roses. There is also a Shakespearean Garden that includes flowers mentioned in the works of William Shakespeare. After seeing these acres of roses, you will certainly understand why Portland is known as the City of Roses and why the Rose Festival in June is the city's biggest annual celebration.

✪ Japanese Garden Society of Oregon

Off Kingston Avenue in Washington Park. ☎ **503/223-1321**. Admission $5 adults, $2.50 students and senior citizens, under age 6 free. Apr 1–May 31 and Sept 1–Sept 30, daily 10am–6pm; June 1–Aug 31, daily 9am–8pm; Oct 1–Mar 31, daily 10am–4pm. Closed Thanksgiving, Christmas, and New Year's Day. Bus: 63.

I have always loved Japanese gardens and have visited them all over the world. Outside of those in Japan, this is still my favorite. What makes it so special is not only the design, plantings, and tranquillity, but the view. From the Japanese-style wooden house in the center of the garden, you have a view over Portland to Mount Hood on a clear day. This perfectly shaped volcanic peak is so reminiscent of Mount Fuji that it seems almost as if it were placed there just for the sake of this garden.

✪ Mill Ends Park

SW Taylor Street and SW Front Avenue.

Pay attention as you cross the median strip on Front Avenue or you might walk right past this famous Portland park. The smallest public park in the world, it contains a whopping 452.16 square inches of land. It was the whimsical creation of Dick Fagen, a local journalist who used to gaze down from his office at a hole left after a telephone pole was removed from the middle of Front Avenue. He dubbed the park Mill Ends (the name of his column) and peopled it with leprechauns. On St. Patrick's Day 1976, it was officially designated a Portland city park. Despite the diminutive size of the park, it has been the site of several weddings.

A ZOO

✪ Metro Washington Park Zoo

4001 SW Canyon Rd., Washington Park. ☎ **503/226-1561**. Admission $5.50 adults, $4 senior citizens, $3.50 ages 3–11, under age 2 free; free second Tues of each month from 3pm to closing. Memorial Day–Labor Day, daily 9:30am–6pm; Labor Day–Memorial Day, daily 9:30am–4pm. Bus: 63.

This zoo has been successfully breeding elephants for many years and has the largest breeding herd of elephants in captivity. The Africa exhibit, which includes a very lifelike rain forest, displays zebras, rhinos, giraffes, hippos and other animals, is the most lifelike habitat I have ever seen in a zoo—and it's giving the elephants a lot of competition. Equally impressive is the Alaskan tundra exhibit, with grizzly bears, wolves, and musk oxen. The Cascade Exhibit includes otters and beavers, and other Northwest natives. For the younger set, there's a children's petting zoo filled with farm animals.

The Washington Park and Zoo Railway travels between the zoo and the International Rose Test and Japanese gardens. Tickets for the miniature railway are $2.75 for adults, $2 for senior citizens and children 3 to 11. In the summer, there are jazz concerts on Wednesday nights and rhythm and blues type concerts on Thursday nights from 7 to 9pm. Concerts are free with zoo admission.

3 Especially for Kids

The **Oregon Museum of Science and Industry** is primarily for kids, with lots of hands-on exhibits, including a NASA training room, a full computer lab, a chicken hatchery, and laser shows in its planetarium. At the **World Forestry Center,** there is a carousel operating during the summer months.

The **Metro Washington Park Zoo** is one of the best in the country, and is particularly well known for its elephant-breeding program. From inside the zoo, it's possible to take a small train through Washington Park to the International Rose Test Garden. In addition to these attractions, described earlier in this chapter, there are two other attractions in Portland of particular interest to kids:

Portland Children's Museum

3037 SW Second Ave. ☎ **503/823-2227.** Admission $3.50 adults and children, under 1 year free. Daily 9am–5pm. Closed some national holidays. Bus: 1, 12, 40, 41, 43, or 45.

Although this museum is small, it's loads of fun. Visitors can shop in a kid-size grocery store, play waiter or diner in a restaurant, or pretend to be a doctor in a medical center. Clayshop is usually open for families who want to build with clay. In H2 Oh! kids can blow giant bubbles and pump water. The Children's Cultural Center presents a child's view of such environments as an African or Native American village complete with artifacts and hands-on activities.

Listening to seashells, sculpting clay, blowing bubbles—there's plenty to entertain kids at this big little museum.

Oaks Park

East end of the Sellwood Bridge. ☎ **503/233-5777.** Free admission (all activities are on individual tickets). Mar–June 18, Sat–Sun 12–5pm; June 18–Labor Day, Tues–Thurs noon–9pm, Fri–Sat noon–10pm, Sun noon–7pm. Bus: 40.

What would summer be without the screams of happy thrill-seekers risking their lives on a roller coaster? Pretty boring, right? Just ask the kids. They'll tell you that the real Portland excitement is at Oaks Park. Covering more than 44 acres, this amusement park first opened in 1905 to coincide with the Lewis and Clark Exposition. Beneath the shady oaks for which the park is named, you'll find waterfront picnic sites, miniature golf, music, and plenty of thrilling rides. The largest roller-skating rink in the Northwest is also here.

4 Organized Tours

BUS TOURS

Gray Line

☎ **503/285-9834.** Adults $18–$38, $9–$19 children.

Gray line offers several half-day and full-day tours. One tour visits the International Rose Test Garden and the grounds of Pittock Mansion, another stops at the Japanese Gardens and the World Forestry Center. The trip I most recommend is the full-day Mt. Hood loop—if you aren't doing the driving, you can enjoy the scenery more. Other tours offered are an excursion to the Columbia Gorge that includes a ride on a sternwheeler, and a northern Oregon coast tour.

BOAT TOURS

Columbia Gorge Stern-Wheeler

☎ **503/223-3928.** 2-hour cruise, adults $11.95, children $5.95. Other tours, prices vary.

This stern-wheeler cruises the Columbia River between mid-June and mid-October and the Willamette River between October and mid-June. A trip up the Columbia River, with its towering cliffs, is a spectacular and memorable excursion. It includes stops at the Cascade Locks and Bonneville Dam. Call for information on lunch, dinner, and dance cruises.

Rose City Riverboat Cruises

☎ **503/234-6665.** Adults $9–$27; lower fares for children and seniors.

A modern catamaran power yacht cruises the Willamette River on a regular basis from mid-April through October. Dinner, moonlight, Sunday brunch, Portland Harbor, and historical river tours are offered.

CARRIAGE TOURS

John Palmer House Tours

☎ **503/284-5893.** $65 for a carriage of 4 people.

The John Palmer House offers horse-drawn carriage tours and is also a restored Victorian bed-and-breakfast. June through August and December, carriage rides are given daily from 6 to 10pm. In September through November and January through May, they are given on Friday and Saturday from 6 to 10pm and on Sunday from noon to 6pm.

OTHER TOURS

Apple Tours

☎ **503/638-4076,** or 800/939-6326. Adults $15, children $5, seniors $13.

If you'd like to learn more about downtown Portland and the city's history, contact Apple Tours for a foot tour of the area.

Ecotours of Oregon

1906 SW Iowa St., Portland, OR 97201. ☎ **503/245-1428.** Tours $45–$60.

Ecotours offers many tours and hikes for small groups on short notice. They travel to the Columbia River Gorge, Mt. Hood, Mt. St. Helens, the Oregon coast, ancient forests, and places to whale-watch or experience Native American culture. Visits to wineries, microbreweries, and custom tours can all be arranged.

Grape Escape

☎ **503/282-4262.** Tour $60.

Escape from Portland for a day for an in-depth winery tour of the Willamette Valley. An all-day tour includes three wineries, an elegant picnic lunch, and pick-up and drop-off at your hotel.

Spirit of Oregon Dinner Train
☎ **503/324-1919.** Dinner $75, brunch $60.

This train ride begins in the Oregon countryside and takes passengers up into the coastal mountain range to the summit, and then back down, passing over trestles and a tunnel that were built in 1911. Two separate 4¹/₂-hour rides are available, one for dinner and one for Sunday brunch.

The Wild Side
P.O. Box 973, Hood River, OR 97031. ☎ **503/354-3112.** Trip $45–$125.

If you'd like to explore this part of the Northwest's great outdoors, this company offers mountain-biking trips, as well as fishing, hiking, and cross-country skiing trips.

5   Outdoor Activities

BEACHES

The nearest ocean beach to Portland is **Cannon Beach,** about 90 miles to the west. See Section 2 of Chapter 20 for more information.

There are a couple of freshwater beaches on the Columbia River within 45 minutes of Portland. **Rooster Rock State Park,** just off I-84 east of Portland, includes several miles of sandy beach as does **Sauvie Island,** off Oregon Hwy. 30 northwest of Portland. You'll need to obtain a parking permit for Sauvie Island; it's available at the convenience store located just after you cross the bridge onto the island. Both beaches include sections that are clothing optional.

BICYCLING

You'll notice many bicyclists on Portland streets. If you want to get rolling with everyone else, head over to **Fat Tire Farm,** 2714 NW Thurman St. (☎ 503/222-3276) to rent a mountain bike for $30 a day. In nearby Forest Park, the **Leif Erikson Trail** is a car-less stretch of road that goes on for miles and is popular with bicyclists and runners. Or try **Agape Cycle and Fitness** 2314 SE Division St. (☎ 503/230-0317), where you can rent mountain bikes for about $20 per day. Once you have your bike, you can head for **Waterfront Park,** where there's a two-mile bike path. The **Terwilliger Path** starts at the south end of Portland State University and travels for 10 miles up into the hills to Tryon Creek State Park. The views from the top are breathtaking. Stop by a bike shop to pick up a copy of the "Getting There by Bike" map.

FISHING

The Portland area is salmon, steelhead, sturgeon, and trout country. You can find out about licenses and seasons from the **Oregon Department of Fish and Wildlife,** P.O. Box 59, Portland, OR 97207 (☎ 503/229-5403). If you prefer to have a guide take you where the big ones are always biting, contact **Oregon Guides and Packers Association,** P.O. Box 10841, Eugene, OR 97440 (☎ 503/

683-9552), for a copy of their annual directory. A day of fishing will cost you around $100.

GOLF

If you're a golfer, don't forget to bring your clubs along on a trip to Portland. There are plenty of public courses around the area, and greens fees for nonresidents are only $19 for 18 holes on a weekday and $21 on weekends and holidays. Public golf courses operated by the Portland Bureau of Parks and Recreation include **Eastmorcland Golf Course,** 2425 SE Bybee Blvd. (☎ 503/775-2900); **Heron Lakes Golf Course,** 3500 N. Victory Blvd. (☎ 503/289-1818); **Rose City Golf Course,** 2200 NE 71st Ave. (☎ 503/253-4744); and **Double Eagle Golf Center Progress Downs Golf Course,** 8200 SW Scholls Ferry Rd., Beaverton (☎ 503/646-5166).

HIKING

Hiking opportunities in the Portland area are almost unlimited. In fact, if you head over to Mount Hood National Forest, you can get on the **Pacific Crest Trail** and hike all the way to Mexico. Of course, there are also plenty of other shorter hikes in this region. For details, contact the **U.S. Forest Service,** 70220 E. Hwy. 26, Zig Zag, OR 97049 (☎ 503/666-0704 or 503/622-3191).

If you are interested in a more strenuous mountain experience, Mount Hood offers plenty of mountain- and rock-climbing opportunities. **Timberline Mountain Guides,** P.O. Box 23214, Portland, OR 97281 (☎ 503/636-7704), leads summit climbs from December to July, with ski descents during these same months. They also offer climbing courses between November and December. You can buy or rent camping and climbing equipment from **REI Co-op,** 1798 Jantzen Beach Center (☎ 503/283-1300) or at 7410 SW Bridgeport Rd., Tualatin (☎ 503/624-8600). This huge outdoor recreation supply store also sells books on hiking in the area.

For shorter hikes, you need not leave the city. Bordered by West Burnside Street on the south, Newberry Road on the north, St. Helens Road on the east, and Skyline Road on the west, **Forest Park** is the largest forested city park in the country. You'll find more than 50 miles of trails through this urban wilderness.

If you have been keeping up with the controversy over saving the remaining old-growth forests of the Northwest, you might want to go see an ancient forest for yourself. Though there isn't much publicly accessible ancient forest right in Portland, you can find plenty within

Impressions

While the people of Portland are not mercurial or excitable—and by Californians or people "east of the mountains" are even accused of being lymphatic, if not somnolent—they are much given . . . to recreation and public amusements. —Harvey Scott, editor of the *Oregonian,* 1890

an hour-and-a-half's drive. Along the coast, Ecola State Park, Oswald West State Park, Cape Meares State Park, and Cape Lookout State Park all have trails through stands of old-growth trees. If you are heading to Mount Hood, you can detour to Oxbow Park in Sandy to see a small grove of old-growth trees.

IN-LINE SKATING

Waterfront Park is a popular and fairly level place for skating. In-line skates can be rented at the nearby **Sports Works,** 421 SW Second Ave. (☎ 503/227-5323) for $20 a day, which includes all safety gear.

SAILBOARDING

Serious enthusiasts already know about the sailboarding mecca at the town of **Hood River** on the Columbia River. The winds come howling down the gorge with enough force to send sailboards airborne.

SKIING

Portland has several ski resorts, all within about an hour's drive, on the slopes of Mount Hood. One of them even boasts skiing all summer.

Timberline Ski Area (☎ 503/231-7979 in Portland, or 503/272-3311 outside Portland; 503/222-2211 for snow report) is the highest ski area on Mount Hood and has one slope that is open all the way through summer. This is the site of the historic Timberline Lodge, which was built during the Depression by the WPA. Adult lift ticket prices range from $10 for night skiing to $28 for a weekend all-day pass. Call for hours of operation.

Mount Hood Meadows (☎ 503/337-2222; 503/227-7669 for snow report) is the largest ski resort on Mount Hood, with more than 2,000 skiable acres, 2,777 vertical feet, and a wide variety of terrain. Lift ticket prices range from $14 for night skiing to $37 for a weekend all-day pass. Call for hours of operation.

Mt. Hood SkiBowl (☎ 503/272-3206; 503/222-2695 for snow report) is the closest ski area to Portland and with 1,500 vertical feet, has more expert slopes than any other ski area on the mountain. SkiBowl also claims to be the largest lighted ski area in the United States. Adult lift ticket prices range from $13 for midweek night skiing to $28 for a weekend all-day pass. Call for hours of operation.

TENNIS

Portland Parks and Recreation operates more than 120 tennis courts, both indoor and out, all over the city. Outdoor courts are generally free and available on a first-come, first-served basis. My personal favorites are those in Washington Park just behind the International Rose Test Garden. Some of these courts can be reserved by contacting the **Portland Tennis Center,** 324 NE 12th Ave. (☎ 503/823-3189). Rates are $2 per hour. If the weather isn't cooperating, head for the Portland Tennis Center itself. They have indoor courts and charge $11–$12.50 per hour for singles matches and $15–$17 per hour for doubles. The hours here are 6:30am to 10pm.

WHITE-WATER RAFTING

The Cascade Range produces some of the best white-water rafting in the country and Deschutes River, White Salmon River, and Clackamas River offer plenty of opportunities to shoot the rapids from early spring to early fall. **River Drifters,** 13570 NW Lakeview Dr., Portland, OR 97229 (☎ 503/645-6264 or 800/972-0430), leads trips on these rivers for $65 (with lunch included). **Carrol White-Water Rafting,** P.O. Box 130, Maupin, OR 97037 (☎ 503/395-2404), and **Ewings' Whitewater,** P.O. Box 265, Maupin, OR 97037 (☎ 800/538-7238), offer similar trips on the Deschutes and other rivers. A four-hour trip costs $75, and includes a barbecue lunch. Longer trips are also possible.

6 Spectator Sports

AUTO RACING

Portland International Raceway, 1940 N. Victory Blvd. (☎ 503/285-6635), operated by the Portland Bureau of Parks and Recreation, is home to road races, drag races, motocross and other motorcycle races, go-kart races, and even vintage-car races. February to October are the busiest months here. Admission is $5.50 to $75.

BASEBALL

The **Portland Rockies Baseball Club** plays class A minor-league ball at Civic Stadium, SW 20th Avenue and Morrison Street (☎ 503/223-2837). The box office is open Monday through Friday from 9am to 5pm and from 9am the day of the game. Admission is $5 to $6 for adults, $4 for ages 14 and under.

BASKETBALL

The **Portland Trail Blazers,** one of the hottest NBA teams in recent years, pound the boards at the Rose Garden (☎ 503/231-8000), between fall and spring. Call for current schedule and ticket information. Tickets are $15 to $68.70. To get there, take the Broadway exit off I-5.

GREYHOUND RACING

The race season at the **Multnomah Greyhound Track,** NE 223rd Avenue, Wood Village (☎ 503/667-7700), runs from April to September. Post time is 7:30pm Wednesday through Saturday, with Saturday and Sunday matinees at 1pm. In July and August, there are also Tuesday night races. You must be 18 to bet on the greyhounds, and if you've never bet on dog races before, they'll gladly give you a quick course. To reach the track, take I-84 east to the 181st Street exit south and then turn left on Glisan Street. It's also easy to reach the park by public transit. Take the MAX light-rail system to the Gresham City Hall or Central Station and transfer to bus no. 82, which goes directly to the racetrack. Admission is $1 to $3.50.

HORSE RACING

Portland Meadows, 1001 N. Schmeer Rd. (☎ 503/285-9144), is the place to go if you want a little horse-racing action. The race season runs from October to April, with post time at 6pm on Friday and 12:30pm on Saturday and Sunday. By car, take I-5 north to the Delta Park exit. Admission is $2 to $3.

ICE HOCKEY

The **Portland Winter Hawks,** a junior-league hockey team, carve up the ice at Memorial Coliseum, 1401 N. Wheeler St. (☎ 503/238-6366), from October to March. Call for schedule and ticket information. Admission is $8.75 to $12.75.

MARATHON

The **Portland Marathon** is held sometime in late September to early October. For further information, call 226-1111.

17

Strolling Around Portland

Portland's compactness makes it an ideal city to explore on foot. In fact, the local government is doing all it can to convince Portland's citizens to leave their cars behind when they come downtown. There's no better way to gain a feel for Portland than to stroll through the Skidmore Historic District, down along Tom McCall Waterfront Park and through Pioneer Courthouse Square. If it happens to be a weekend, you'll also be able to visit the Portland Saturday Market. No matter where you walk in Portland, you're never far from a public work of art. Keep your eyes peeled. (For additional information on several stops, see Chapter 16.)

WALKING TOUR
OLD TOWN & DOWNTOWN

Start: Skidmore Fountain.
Finish: Pioneer Courthouse Square.
Time: Allow approximately 2 to 2¹/₂ hours, not including breaks and shopping stops.
Best Times: Saturday and Sunday, when the Portland Saturday Market is open (except January and February).
Worst Times: After dark, when the Skidmore neighborhood is not as safe as in daylight.

Although Portland was founded in 1843, most of the buildings in Old Town date only from the 1880s. A fire in 1872 razed much of the town, which afterward was rebuilt with new vigor. Ornate pilasters, pediments, and cornices grace these brick buildings, one of the largest collections of such structures in the country. However, their most notable features are their cast-iron facades.

Begin your exploration of this 20-block historic neighborhood at the corner of SW First Avenue and Ankeny Street at:

1. **Skidmore Fountain,** the heart of Old Town. Erected in 1888, the fountain was intended to provide refreshment for "horses, men, and dogs," and it did that for many years. Today, however, the bronze and granite fountain is purely decorative. Across SW First Avenue is the:

2. **New Market Block,** constructed in 1872 to house the unlikely combination of a produce market and a theater. The New Market Block now contains popular shops and restaurants, as do many of

the restored historic buildings in this area. The freestanding wall of archways extending out from the New Market Building was salvaged from another Old Town structure that didn't survive the urban renewal craze of the 1960s. Two blocks south is the:

3. **Failing Building,** 235 SW First Ave. Built in 1886, this attractive structure integrates French and Italian influences. Turn left on SW Oak Street and left again on SW Front Avenue and you'll pass by:

4. **Smith's Block,** containing some of the most beautifully restored buildings in Old Town. At one time this whole district was filled with elegant structures such as these. The cast-iron filigree appears both solid and airy at the same time. This building houses the:

5. **Oregon Maritime Center & Museum,** 113 SW Front Ave., which is dedicated to Oregon's shipping history.

Continue along Front Avenue to SW Ankeny, where you will see the:

6. **Jeff Morris Memorial Fire Museum,** housing Portland's historic horse-drawn steamers from the early part of this century.

If it's a Saturday or Sunday from March through December, you will no doubt have noticed the crowds under the Burnside bridge ahead of you. This is the:

7. **Portland Saturday Market,** where you'll find the best of Northwest crafts being sold by their makers. There typically are more than 250 booths plus entertainers and food vendors.

☕ **TAKE A BREAK**   Portland Saturday Market makes an excellent refueling stop in this neighborhood. In the market's food court you can get all manner of delicious, healthful, and fun foods. Stalls sell everything from "dragon toast" to over-stuffed fajitas to pad thai to barbecued ribs.

After you've visited the market, cross Front Ave. and in Waterfront Park, just north of the Burnside Bridge, you'll find the:

8. **Japanese American Historical Plaza/Bill of Rights Memorial.** Walk north on Front Avenue and take a left on NW Couch (pronounced "Kooch") Street, where at the corner of First Avenue you will come to the:

9. **Blagen Block,** another excellent example of the ornate cast-iron facades that appeared on nearly all the buildings in this area at one time. Note the cast-iron figures of women wearing spiked crowns. They are reminiscent of the Statue of Liberty, which had been erected two years before this building opened in 1888. Across First Avenue you will see the covered sidewalk of the:

10. **Norton House.** Though this is not the original covered sidewalk, it is characteristic of Portland buildings 100 years ago.

11. **Erickson's Saloon Building,** 9 NW Second Ave. Back in the late 1800s this building housed the very popular Erickson's Saloon, with a 684-foot-long bar, card rooms, and a brothel. If you return to NW Couch Street and continue to the corner of NW Third Avenue, you will see on the northwest corner:

Walking Tour—Old Town & Downtown

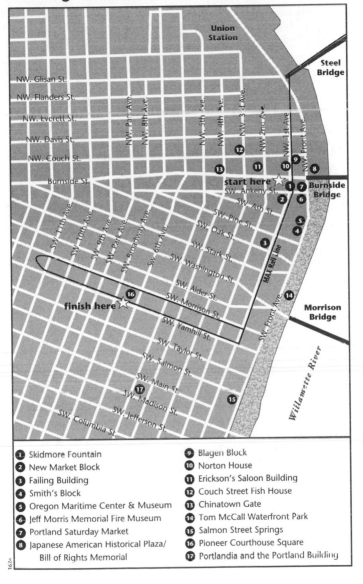

1. Skidmore Fountain
2. New Market Block
3. Failing Building
4. Smith's Block
5. Oregon Maritime Center & Museum
6. Jeff Morris Memorial Fire Museum
7. Portland Saturday Market
8. Japanese American Historical Plaza/ Bill of Rights Memorial
9. Blagen Block
10. Norton House
11. Erickson's Saloon Building
12. Couch Street Fish House
13. Chinatown Gate
14. Tom McCall Waterfront Park
15. Salmon Street Springs
16. Pioneer Courthouse Square
17. Portlandia and the Portland Building

12. Couch Street Fish House, an excellent example of using innovative methods to renovate Old Town. This excellent and highly recommended restaurant incorporates two historic structures into its design. One houses the restaurant itself, the inside of which is very modern. The other is merely an ornate brick facade behind which you'll find the restaurant's parking lot. Continue up NW Couch Street to Fourth Avenue and turn left. Directly ahead of you is:

13. Chinatown Gate. Since you are already in Chinatown, you will have to cross to the opposite side of the brightly painted three-tiered gateway to appreciate its ornateness, including two huge flanking bronze Chinese lions.

Here you have two choices. If you don't want to walk a lot, take the westbound MAX rail (the stop is just north of the Skidmore Fountain) and ride to **Pioneer Courthouse Square** (see no. 16 below). If you want to walk about two dozen blocks, cross Burnside Street, walk south on Fourth Avenue, and then east on Pine Street to:

14. Tom McCall Waterfront Park, where many of Portland's outdoor festivals are held and where you'll find Portlanders biking, skating, or simply enjoying the outdoors. Walk south and soon you'll come to the:

15. Salmon Street Springs fountain, where it's fun to watch kids play in the water on a hot day. Walk west on Salmon Street, north on Fourth Avenue, and east on Yamhill until you reach:

16. Pioneer Courthouse Square, which is bordered by Yamhill, Morrison, Sixth Avenue, and Broadway. Works of art here include *Allow Me,* a bronze sculpture of a man carrying an umbrella, and the fabulous *Weather Machine,* which displays one of three creatures that represent the current weather—a sun (sunny), a dragon (stormy), or a blue heron (drizzle). The block east of the square contains the courthouse, and around this block are sculptures of bronze animals playing in their own pools of water. Continue walking south on SW Fifth Avenue to:

17. Portlandia and the **Portland Building,** located between SW Main Street and SW Madison Street. This building, designed by Michael Graves, is considered the first postmodern building in the world. Out front is Raymond Kaskey's hammered-copper statue of **Portlandia,** the second-tallest beaten-copper statue in the world, second only to the Statue of Liberty. Stroll back to Pioneer Courthouse Square where you can take an espresso break at the ubiquitous Starbucks.

18

Portland Shopping

Perhaps the single most important fact about shopping in Portland, and all of Oregon for that matter, is that there is no sales tax. The price on the tag is the price you pay. If you come from a state with a high sales tax, you might want to save your shopping for your visit to Portland.

1 The Shopping Scene

Over the past few years Portland has managed to preserve and restore a good deal of its historic architecture, and many of these late 19th-century and early 20th-century buildings have been turned into unusual and very attractive shopping centers. New Market Village (50 SW Second Ave.), Morgan's Alley (515 SW Broadway), and Skidmore Fountain Square (28 SW First Ave.) are all outstanding examples of how Portland has preserved its historic buildings and kept its downtown area filled with happy shoppers.

Portland's most "happening" area for shopping is the Nob Hill district of northwestern Portland. Northwest 23rd Avenue beginning at West Burnside Street is the heart of Nob Hill. Along this stretch of road, and on adjoining streets, you'll find antique stores, boutiques, card shops, design studios, ethnic restaurants, florists, galleries, home furnishings stores, interior decorators, pubs, and all the other necessities of a bohemian neighborhood gone upscale.

Hours Most small stores in Portland are open Monday through Saturday from 9 or 10am to 5 or 6pm. Shopping malls are usually open Monday through Friday from 9 or 10am to 9pm, on Saturday from 9 or 10am to 6pm, and on Sunday from noon until 5pm. Most art galleries and antiques stores are closed on Monday. Department stores stay open on Friday night until 9pm.

2 Shopping A to Z

ANTIQUES
Old Sellwood Antique Row, at east end of Sellwood Bridge on SE 13th Street. With its old Victorian homes and turn-of-the-century architecture, Sellwood is Portland's main antique district. You'll find 13 blocks with more than 30 antique dealers and restaurants.

ART GALLERIES

If you're in the market for art, try to arrange your visit to coincide with the first Thursday of a month. On these days galleries in downtown Portland schedule coordinated openings in the evening. Stroll from one gallery to the next, meeting artists and perhaps buying an original work of art. As an added bonus, the **Portland Art Museum,** 1219 SW Park Ave. (☎ 503/226-2811), offers free admission from 4 to 9pm on these nights.

An art gallery guide listing more than 50 Portland galleries is available at the **Portland Oregon Visitors Association Information Center,** Two World Trade Center, 25 SW Salmon St. (☎ 503/222-2223 or 800/345-3214).

Gango Gallery

205 SW First Ave. ☎ **503/222-3850.**

Gango offers a juried selection from more than fifty contemporary regional and national artists, both established and emerging, in a variety of media.

The Laura Russo Gallery

805 NW 21st Ave. ☎ **503/226-2754.**

The focus here is on Northwest contemporary artists. Young emerging artists as well as the estates of well-know artists are showcased.

Quartersaw Gallery

528 NW 12th Ave. ☎ **503/223-2264.**

With an emphasis on figurative and expressionistic landscape, Quartersaw is a showcase for progressive Northwest art.

✪ Quintana Galleries—Old Town

139 NW Second Ave. ☎ **503/223-1729.**

Virtually a small museum of Native American art, this Old Town store sells everything from masks to contemporary painting and sculpture by various Indian artists. The jewelry selection is outstanding. Prices, however, are not cheap.

Quintana grew so big that it had to split off its Northwest Coastal Indian and Inuit art offerings, as well as Edward S. Curtis photogravures. These can now be found at the North American Indian gallery, 818 SW First Ave. (☎ 503/223-4202). Masks, rugs, and prints fill this latter gallery.

BOOKS

A Children's Place

1631 NE Broadway. ☎ **503/284-8294.**

If you have a special child in mind, you'll find something for him or her at this small store, which has a wide selection of books, tapes, and CDs.

✪ Powell's City of Books

1005 W. Burnside St. ☎ **503/228-4651** or 800/878-7323.

This is one of the largest bookstores in the United States selling new and used books, and no visit to Portland would be complete without a stop here. You'll find nearly a million volumes in this massive store. To help you locate subjects, there's a handy map of the store available at the front door. Just so you don't starve while wandering the aisles, they also have a coffee shop. You should actually try to make this one of your first stops in town so you can pick up a copy of their excellent free map of downtown Portland. Open Monday through Saturday 9am to 11pm, Sunday 9am to 9pm.

If you are looking for a technical book, try **Powell's Technical Books,** 33 NW Park St. (☎ 503/228-3906), a block away.

Powell's Travel Store

701 SW Sixth Ave. ☎ **503/228-1108.**

Located beneath Pioneer Courthouse Square at the corner of SW Sixth Avenue and Yamhill Street, this travel bookstore has plenty of books and maps on Portland, the Northwest, and every other part of the world. The map collection is one of the region's largest, and if you ask at the front counter, you can pick up a free Portland walking tour map. Open Monday to Saturday 9am to 7pm, Sunday 10am to 5pm.

CLOTHING & MORE

✪ Nike Town

930 SW Sixth Ave. ☎ **503/221-6453.**

This superglitzy, ultracontempo showcase for Nike products blasted onto the Portland shopping scene with all the subtlety of a Super Bowl celebration. Matte black decor, George Segal–style plaster statues of athletes, and videos everywhere give Nike Town the feel of a sports museum or disco. A true shopping experience.

Norm Thompson

327 SW Morrison St. ☎ **503/243-2680.**

Known throughout the rest of the country from its mail-order catalogs, Norm Thompson is a mainstay of the well-to-do in Portland. Classic styling for men and women is the name of the game here. A second store is at Portland International Airport (☎ 503/249-0170).

The Portland Pendleton Shop

900 SW Fifth Ave. (between Salmon and Taylor). ☎ **503/242-0037.**

Pendleton wool is as much a part of life in the Northwest as forests and salmon. This company's fine wool fashions for men and women define the country-club look in the Northwest and in many other parts of the country. Pleated skirts and tweed jackets are de rigueur here, as are the colorful blankets that have helped keep generations of northwesterners warm through long chilly winters.

MEN'S CLOTHING

Mario's

921 SW Morrison St. ☎ **503/227-3477.**

Located inside the Galleria, Mario's sells self-consciously stylish European men's fashions straight off the pages of *GQ* and *M.* Prices are as high as you would expect. If you long to be European, but your birth certificate says otherwise, here you can at least adopt the look.

The City of Books

Though Seattle claims the largest library system in the country, Portland has **Powell's City of Books,** 1005 W. Burnside St. (☎ 503/228-4651), the bookstore to end all bookstores. Covering an entire city block three floors deep, Powell's sells more than three million volumes each year. Though there are arguments over whether the City of Books is the biggest bookstore in the country, most people agree that Powell's has more titles on its shelves than any other bookstore in the United States. In any case, there's no denying Powell's is a contender for the claim to biggest bookstore in the country.

Powell's has its origins in two used bookstores, one in Chicago and one in Portland, both of which opened in the early 1970s. The Chicago store was opened by current store owner Michael Powell, while the Portland store was opened by Walter Powell, Michael's father. In 1979, Michael joined his father in Portland, and together they began building the store into what it is today.

The City of Books is different from many other bookstores in that it shelves all its books, new and used, hardback or paperback, together, and with roughly three-quarters of a million new and used books on the shelves at any given time, the store had to give up trying to keep a computer inventory of what's in stock. This can be extremely frustrating if you're looking for an old or out-of-print title, but employees are good about searching the shelves for you, and if they don't have what you're looking for, they can try tracking a copy down. The up side of not being able to go straight to the book you're looking for is that you end up browsing.

Browsing is what Powell's is really all about. Before you even get through the front door, you can browse the display of bizarre book titles in the front window. Titles such as *What Sign Is Your Pet, Euclid's Outline of Sex, Moby Dick: A Hindu Avatar, The Mysterious You,* and *It's a Gas: A Study of Flatulence* reflect the store's literary sense of humor. Once inside you can pick up a store map that will direct you

WOMEN'S CLOTHING
Byrkit
2006 NE Broadway. ☎ **503/282-3773.**

Byrkit specializes in natural fabric clothing of cotton, silk, rayon, and linen for women. The contemporary designs, including dresses, jumpers, and separates, are built for comfort but include a lot of style.

Changes
927 SW Yamhill St. ☎ **503/223-3737.**

Located next door to The Real Mother Goose gallery, this shop specializes in handmade clothing, including hand-woven scarves, jackets, and shawls, hand-painted silks, and other wearable art.

to color-coded rooms containing different collections of books. In the Gold Room, you'll find science fiction and children's books; in the Rose Room, you'll find books on ornithology, civil aviation, Christian theology, and metaphysics among other subjects; in the Orange Room, there are books on art history, antiques, film, drama, and music. Serious book collectors won't want to miss a visit to the Rare Book Room, where you could if you wished buy a copy of a copy of the writing's of Cicero published by the Aldine Press in 1570. Of course, you'd need to read Latin. The most expensive book ever sold here was a Fourth Folio Shakespeare with archival repairs for $6,000.

It's so easy to forget the time while browsing at Powell's, that many customers miss meals and end up in the store's in-house cafe. The Anne Hughes Coffee Room serves espresso and pastries and is always packed with folks perusing books they've pulled from the shelves. This is also where Powell's keeps its extensive magazine rack. So, don't fret if you forgot to pack a lunch for your Powell's outing.

But wait, I forgot to mention that the City of Books outgrew this space and had to open a few satellite stores. There's **Powell's Technical Bookstore,** 33 NW Park St. (☎ 503/228-3906); **Powell's Books for Cooks,** 3739 SE Hawthorne Blvd. (☎ 503/235-3802); **Powell's Travel Store,** Pioneer Courthouse Square, SW Sixth Avenue and Yamhill Street (☎ 503/228-1108); **Powell's Books for Kids,** Cascade Plaza, 8775 SW Cascade Ave., Beaverton (☎ 503/671-0671); **Powell's Books For Health,** Emanuel Hospital, 501 N Graham St. (☎ 503/280-3988); **Powell's** at PDX, Portland International Airport (☎ 503/249-1950); and a couple of others.

One warning: Before stepping through Powell's door, check your watch. If you haven't got at least an hour of free time, you enter at your own risk. Getting lost in the miles of aisles at Powell's has caused many a bibliophile to miss an appointment. Be prepared.

The Eye of Ra

5331 SW Macadam Ave. ☎ **503/224-4292.**

Women with sophisticated tastes in ethnic fashions will want to visit this pricey shop in The Water Tower at John's Landing shopping center. Silk and rayon predominate, and there is plenty of ethnic jewelry by creative designers to accompany any ensemble you might put together here. Ethnic furniture and home decor are also for sale.

Marlo's for Women

811 SW Morrison St. ☎ **503/241-8111.**

Flip through the pages of a European edition of *Vogue* magazine and you'll get an idea of the fashions you can find at the women's version of fashionable Mario's. Up-to-the-minute and back-to-the-future European fashions fill the racks.

CRAFTS

For the largest selection of local crafts, visit Portland Saturday Market (see page 240). This entertaining outdoor market is a showcase for the high-quality crafts that are created in this part of the country.

Contemporary Crafts Gallery

3934 SW Corbett Ave. ☎ 503/223-2654.

In business since 1937, this is the nation's oldest nonprofit art gallery showing exclusively artwork in clay, glass, fiber, metal, and wood. It's located in a residential neighborhood between downtown and the John's Landing neighborhood, and has a spectacular tree-shaded porch overlooking the Willamette River. The bulk of the gallery is taken up by glass and ceramic pieces, with several cabinets of designer jewelry. Open Tuesday through Saturday 10am to 5pm, Sunday 1 to 5pm.

Hoffman Gallery

8245 SW Barnes Rd. ☎ 503/297-5544.

Hoffman Gallery is located on the campus of Oregon School of Arts and Crafts, which has been one of the nation's foremost crafts education centers since 1906. The gallery offers installations and group shows by local, national, and international artists. The adjacent gift shop has an outstanding selection of hand-crafted items.

✪ The Real Mother Goose

901 SW Yamhill St. ☎ 503/223-9510.

This is Portland's premier crafts shop. They showcase only the very finest contemporary American crafts, including imaginative ceramics, colorful art glass, intricate jewelry, exquisite wooden furniture, and sculptural works. Hundreds of craftspeople and artists from all over the United States are represented here, and even if you're not buying, you should stop by to see the best of American craftsmanship.

Other locations include Washington Square; Tigard (☎ 503/620-2243); and Portland International Airport, Main Terminal (☎ 503/284-9929).

DEPARTMENT STORES

Meier & Frank

621 SW Fifth Ave. ☎ 503/223-0512.

Meier and Frank is a Portland institution. They have been doing business here for more than 100 years. Their flagship store on Pioneer Courthouse Square was built in 1898 and, with 10 stories, was at one time the tallest store in the Northwest. Today those 10 stories of consumer goods still attract crowds of shoppers. The store is open daily, with Friday usually the late night. Other locations include 1100 Lloyd Center (☎ 503/281-4797) and 9300 SW Washington Square Rd. in Tigard (☎ 503/620-3311).

Nordstrom

701 SW Broadway. ☎ **503/224-6666.**

Directly across the street from Pioneer Courthouse Square and a block away from Meier and Frank, Nordstrom is a top-of-the-line department store that originated in the Northwest and takes great pride in its personal service and friendliness. This pride is well founded—the store has devoutly loyal customers who would never dream of shopping anywhere else.

FOOD

The Made in Oregon shops offer the best selection of local food products such as hazelnuts, marionberry and raspberry jam, and smoked salmon. See "Gifts/Souvenirs," below, for details.

GIFTS/SOUVENIRS

For unique locally made souvenirs, your best bet is Portland Saturday Market (see "Market," below, for details).

Made in Oregon

921 SW Morrison St. (in the Galleria). ☎ **503/241-3630** or 800/828-9673.

This is your one-stop shop for all manner of made-in-Oregon gifts, food products, and clothing. Every product they sell is either grown, caught, or made in Oregon. This is the place to visit for salmon, filberts, jams and jellies, Pendleton woolens, and Oregon wines.

Other Portland area branches can be found in Portland International Airport's Main Terminal (☎ 503/282-7827); in Lloyd Center, SE Multnomah St. and SE Broadway (☎ 503/282-7636); in Old Town at 10 NW First Ave. (☎ 503/273-8354). All branches are open daily, but hours vary from store to store.

JEWELRY

✪ Twist

30 NW 23rd Place, ☎ **503/224-0334.**

Twist showcases handmade jewelry from artists around the United States, from Thomas Mann techno-romantic jewelry to imaginative charm bracelets to hand-sculpted earrings. Surely you will find a piece you will want to wear every day. They also carry furniture, housewares, and pottery. Another store is located in Pioneer Place mall (☎ 503/222-3137).

MALLS/SHOPPING CENTERS

✪ The Galleria

921 SW Morrison St. ☎ **503/228-2748.**

Located in the heart of downtown Portland, The Galleria is a three-story atrium shopping mall with more than 50 specialty shops and restaurants, including a Made in Oregon store. Before being restored and turned into its present incarnation, this building was one of Portland's earliest department stores. Parking validation available at adjacent parking garage.

Jantzen Beach Center
1405 Jantzen Beach Center. ☎ **503/289-5555.**

This large shopping mall is located on the site of a former amusement park, and the old carousel still operates. There are four major department stores and more than 80 other shops. You'll also find the R.E.I. co-op recreational-equipment store here. This mall has long been popular with residents of Washington State, who come to shop where there is no sales tax.

Lloyd Center
Bounded by SE Multnomah Street, NE Broadway, NE 16th Avenue, and NE Ninth Avenue. ☎ **503/282-2511.**

Lloyd Center was the largest shopping mall on the West Coast when it opened in 1960. In 1991 an extensive renovation was completed to bring it up to current standards. There are now more than 165 shops here, including a Nordstrom and a Meier and Frank. A food court, ice-skating rink, and eight-screen cinema complete the mall's facilities.

✪ New Market Village
50 SW Second Ave. ☎ **503/228-2392.**

Housed in a brick building built in 1872, this small shopping center is listed in the National Register of Historic Places. You'll find it directly across the street from the Skidmore Fountain and the Portland Saturday Market. A long row of freestanding archways salvaged from a demolished building creates a courtyard on one side of the New Market Village building.

✪ Pioneer Place
700 SW Fifth Ave. ☎ **503/228-5800.**

Located only a block from Pioneer Courthouse Square, Portland's newest downtown shopping center is also its most upscale. Anchored by a Saks Fifth Avenue, Pioneer Place is where the elite shop when looking for high fashions and expensive gifts. You'll also find Portland's branch of the Nature Company and the city's only Godiva chocolatier here.

The Water Tower at Johns Landing
5331 SW Macadam Ave. ☎ **503/228-9431.**

As you're driving south from downtown Portland on Macadam Avenue, you can't miss the old wooden water tower for which this unusual shopping mall is named. Standing high above the roof of the mall, it was once used as a storage tank for fire-fighting water. Hardwood floors, huge overhead beams, and a tree-shaded courtyard paved with Belgian cobblestones from Portland's first paved streets give this place plenty of character. There are about 40 specialty shops and restaurants here.

A MARKET

✪ Portland Saturday Market
Underneath Burnside Bridge (between SW First Avenue and SW Ankeny Street). ☎ **503/222-6072.**

Portland Saturday Market (held on both Saturday and Sunday) is arguably the city's single most important and best-loved event. For years the Northwest has attracted artists and craftspeople, and every Saturday and Sunday nearly 300 of them can be found selling their exquisite creations here. In addition to the dozens of crafts stalls, you'll find flowers, fresh produce, ethnic and unusual foods, and lots of free entertainment. This is the single best place to shop for one-of-a-kind gifts in Portland. The atmosphere is always cheerful and the crowds are always colorful. At the heart of the Skidmore District, Portland Saturday Market makes an excellent starting or finishing point for a walk around Portland's most historic neighborhood. Don't miss this unique market. On Sunday, on-street parking is free. Open March through Christmas Eve, Saturday 10am to 5pm, Sunday 11am to 4:30pm; closed January and February. MAX: Skidmore Fountain station.

TOYS

✪ Finnegan's Toys & Gifts
922 SW Yamhill St. ☎ **503/221-0306.**

We all harbor a bit of child within ourselves, and this is the sort of place that has that inner child kicking and screaming in the aisles if you don't buy that silly little toy you never got when you were young. Kids love this place too. It's the largest toy store in downtown Portland.

WINE

Great Wine Buys
1515 NE Broadway. ☎ **503/287-2897.**

Oenophiles who have developed a taste for Oregon wines will want to stock up here before heading home. This is one of the best wine shops in Portland. The staff is helpful and many of them make wine. Wine tastings are on Friday from 4:30 to 7pm and Saturday from 2 to 6pm. Open Monday through Saturday 10:30am to 6:30pm, Sunday noon to 5pm.

Harris Wine Cellars Ltd.
2300 NW Thurman St. ☎ **503/223-2222.**

Located at the northern and less fashionable end of NW 23rd Avenue, Harris Wine Cellars caters to serious wine connoisseurs, and has been doing so for many years. It isn't glamorous, but the folks here know their wine. Hearty lunches are also available. Open Monday through Saturday from 10am to 6pm.

19

Portland After Dark

Portland has become the Northwest's second cultural center. Its symphony orchestra, ballet, and opera are all well regarded, and the many theater companies offer classic and contemporary plays. If you are a jazz fan, you'll feel right at home—there's always a lot of live jazz being played around town. In summer, festivals move the city's cultural activities outdoors.

To find out what's going on during your visit, pick up a copy of *Willamette Week*, Portland's weekly arts-and-entertainment newspaper. You can also check the Friday and Sunday editions of *The Oregonian*, the city's daily newspaper.

Many theaters and performance halls in Portland offer discounts to students and senior citizens. You can often save money by buying your ticket on the day of a performance or within a half hour of curtain time.

1 The Performing Arts

MAJOR PERFORMING ARTS COMPANIES
OPERA & CLASSICAL MUSIC

The Oregon Symphony

Arlene Schnitzer Concert Hall, 1111 SW Broadway, at SW Main St. ☎ **503/ 228-1353** or 800/228-7343. Tickets $10.50–$48. Sun matinees are the least expensive. Senior citizens and students may purchase half-price tickets one hour before a classical concert.

Founded in 1896, this is the oldest symphony orchestra on the West Coast, and under the expert baton of conductor James de Preist, it has achieved national recognition and status. Four series, including classical, pops, Sunday matinees, and children's concerts, are held during the September-to-June season.

Portland Opera

Portland Civic Auditorium, SW Third Ave., at SW Clay Street. ☎ **503/241-1802.** Prices: $20–$90. Students may attend dress rehearsals for a nominal charge.

The Portland Opera offers five different productions of grand opera and musical theater. The season runs from September to May.

THEATER

Portland Center Stage

Portland Center for the Performing Arts, 1111 SW Broadway. ☎ **503/274-6588.** Tickets $9–$33.

Formerly called the Oregon Shakespeare Festival Portland, this is Portland's largest professional theater company. They stage five classic and contemporary plays during their November-to-April season. The season generally includes one Shakespeare play.

✪ Portland Repertory Theater

World Trade Center, 25 SW Salmon St. ☎ **503/224-4491.** Tickets $25–$28; $20 preview tickets.

Portland's oldest Equity theater offers consistently excellent productions, and is acclaimed for its presentations ranging from off-Broadway hit comedies to world-premiere dramas by contemporary American and British playwrights.

Tygres Heart Shakespeare Co.

Dolores Winningstad Theatre, 1111 SW Broadway, at SW Main Street. ☎ **503/222-9220.** Tickets $7.50–$25.

The play's the thing at Tygres Heart and old Will would be proud. Tygres Heart remains true to its name and stages only works by the bard himself.

DANCE

Oregon Ballet Theatre

Portland Civic Auditorium, SW Third Ave., at SW Clay St. ☎ **503/222-5538.** Tickets $10–$60.

Though this company's sold-out performances each December of *The Nutcracker* are the highlight of the season, the company also stages an American Choreographers Showcase each year. This latter performance often features world premieres. Rounding out the season are performances of classic and contemporary ballets.

MAJOR CONCERT HALLS & ALL-PURPOSE AUDITORIUMS

The **Portland Center for the Performing Arts** has helped spur a renaissance along SW Broadway, once the heart of Portland's dining and entertainment district. The center includes four units.

✪ Arlene Schnitzer Concert Hall

1111 SW Broadway, at SW Main St. ☎ **503/248-4335.** Tours Wed 11am and Sat 11am, noon, and 1pm; free. Tickets $7–$50.

Formerly a 1920s movie palace, the Schnitz, as it is known locally, still displays the original Portland theater sign and marquee out front. Inside, you'll be thrilled by the immaculate restoration of this stately old theater. It is home to the Oregon Symphony, and also hosts popular music bands, lecturers, a travel-film series, and many other special performances.

New Theatre Building

1111 SW Broadway, at SW Main St. ☎ **503/248-4335.** Tours Wed 11am and Sat 11am, noon, and 1pm; free. Tickets $3.25–$55. Student and senior-citizen discounts sometimes available.

Across the street from the Schnitz is the beautiful New Theatre Building, which houses two smaller theaters: the **Intermediate** and the **Winningstad.** A brilliant contrast to the Art Deco Schnitz, this building is a sparkling glass jewel box. The Intermediate Theatre is home to Portland Center Stage Company, while the two theaters together host stage productions by local and visiting companies.

Portland Civic Auditorium

SW Third Ave., at SW Clay St. ☎ **503/248-4335.** Tickets $10–$90.

The Civic Auditorium is a few blocks from the three theaters mentioned above. It was constructed shortly after World War I and completely remodeled in the 1960s. Touring Broadway musicals perform in this 3,000-seat hall. This is also the home of both Oregon Ballet Theatre and the Portland Opera.

2 The Club & Music Scene

FOLK & ROCK

Aladdin Theater

3017 SE Milwaukee Ave. ☎ **503/233-1994.** Cover $10–$20.

This former movie theater now serves as one of Portland's main venues for touring performers from a very diverse musical spectrum that includes blues, rock, ethnic, country, folk, and jazz.

Key Largo

31 NW First Ave. ☎ **503/223-9919.** Cover $3–$8 (higher for national acts).

One of Portland's most popular nightclubs, Key Largo has been packing in music fans for more than a decade. A tropical atmosphere prevails at this spacious club and basic American food is served. Rock, reggae, blues, and jazz performers all find their way to the stage here, with local R&B bands a mainstay. A nationally known act occasionally shows up here. Open nightly.

La Luna

215 SE Ninth Ave. ☎ **503/241-5862.** Cover $6.50–$18.

The stage at La Luna is in a cavernous room with a ceiling so high that the cigarette smoke isn't too bad. Here you can catch a wide range of lesser known national acts for a reasonable price. The club also includes a small cafe where you can get a burrito between the acts, and a lounge with a pool table upstairs.

✪ Roseland Theater

8 NW Sixth Ave. ☎ **503/224-7469.** Cover $5–$15.

Roseland Theater is only a couple of blocks from Key Largo, and the same diversity of popular musical styles prevails. A couple of heavy-metal nights each week attract a rougher crowd than you're likely to find at Key Largo, but other nights you might encounter the likes of John Mayall or the latest Seattle grunge band. Open nightly.

Satyricon

125 NW Sixth Ave. ☎ **503/243-2380.** Cover $1–$5 (higher for national acts). No cover charge until 11pm on weeknights.

A block away from Roseland Theater, Satyricon leans heavily toward heavy metal, grunge rock, and neopsychedelia. Though most bands playing here are local, the occasional national act also appears. Crowds are young and rowdy. Open nightly.

JAZZ & BLUES

Brasserie Montmartre

626 SW Park Ave. ☎ **503/224-5552.** No cover.

There's live jazz nightly from 8:30pm at this French restaurant. Both food and music are popular with a primarily middle-aged clientele that likes to dress up when it goes out on the town. Open Sun–Thurs until 2am; Fri–Sat until 3am.

Jazz De Opus

33 NW Second Ave. ☎ **503/222-6077.** No cover; 50¢ surcharge on drinks.

This restaurant/bar has long been one of Portland's bastions of jazz, with a cozy fireplace room and smooth jazz on the stereo. Tuesday through Sunday nights, you can also catch live performances by local jazz musicians.

Parchman Farm

1204 SE Clay St. ☎ **503/235-7831.** Cover $2 after 9pm.

If you're into jazz, Parchman Farm is where you hang out in Portland. This club features a music library of more than 1,000 jazz albums, and there's live music nightly starting between 8 and 9:30pm.

DANCE CLUBS/DISCOS

Embers Avenue

110 NW Broadway. ☎ **503/222-3082.** Cover Thurs–Sat $3, Sun–Wed free.

Though this is still primarily a gay disco, straights have discovered its great dance music and have started making the scene as well. Lots of flashing lights and sweaty bodies until the early morning. There are drag shows seven nights a week.

Panorama

341 SW Tenth Ave. ☎ **503/221-7262.** Cover $3 Friday and Saturday.

Open Friday, Saturday, and Sunday, Panorama is a large dance club playing currently popular dance music. It's connected to The Brig, a smaller dance club, and Boxes, a video club. The admission allows you into all three. The scene here is primarily gay, but a lot of straight people come here too.

✪ Rock 'n' Rodeo

220 SE Spokane St. ☎ **503/235-2417.** No cover before 8:30pm. After 8:30pm, $5.

If you're a fan of western line dancing, West Coast swing, or the two-step (or you just want to learn), join the fun at Rock 'n' Rodeo where a one-hour lesson will cost only a buck. Lessons start at 7pm Mon–Thurs and at 6pm Fri–Sun. Afterward, this place becomes a swirl of cowboy boots, skirts, and tight jeans, attesting to the enthusiasm for the western dancing sport here.

3 The Bar Scene

PUBS

If you are a beer connoisseur, you'll probably find yourself with little time out from your brew tasting to see any other of Portland's sights. This is the heart of the Northwest microbrewery explosion and has more microbreweries than any other city in the United States. They're brewing beers up here the likes of which you won't taste anywhere else this side of the Atlantic. Although many of these beers—as well as ales, stouts, and bitters—are available in restaurants, you owe it to yourself to go directly to the source. At any of these pubs, you can pick up a guide and map to Portland's microbreweries and brew pubs.

Bridgeport Brewery & Brew Pub

1313 NW Marshall St. ☎ **503/241-7179.**

Portland's oldest microbrewery was founded in 1984, and is housed in the city's oldest industrial building. Windows behind the bar let you watch the brewers. It has four to seven of its brews on tap on any given night, and live music on the first Thursday of the month. They make great pizza here, too.

Dublin Pub

6821 Beaverton-Hillsdale Hwy. ☎ **503/297-2889.**

Located west of downtown toward the suburb of Beaverton, this pub plays up the Irish decor a bit too much and otherwise is a bit short on atmosphere. However, the pub's claim to fame is its 102 beer taps, the largest selection in the Northwest, and we're not talking Bud, Bud Lite, Bud Dry, Bud Ice, Bud Dry Ice, or the like; we're talking microbrews and imports.

✪ Hillsdale Brewery & Public House

1505 SW Sunset Blvd. ☎ **503/246-3938.**

This was the cornerstone of the McMenamin brothers' microbrewery empire, which now includes more than 20 pubs in the greater Portland metropolitan area. The McMenamins pride themselves in crafting flavorful and unusual ales with bizarre names like Terminator stout and Purple Haze.

Some of their other pubs include **Cornelius Pass Roadhouse,** Sunset Highway and Cornelius Pass Road, Hillsboro (☎ 503/640-6174), in an old farmhouse; **Blue Moon Tavern,** 432 NW 21st St.

(☎ 503/223-3184), on a fashionable street in northwest Portland; and **The Ram's Head,** 2282 NW Hoyt St. (☎ 503/221-0098), between 21st and 22nd avenues.

Kells
112 SW Second Ave. ☎ **503/227-4057.**

Located in Old Town, Kells is a traditional Irish pub and restaurant. In addition to pulling a good pint of Guinness, the pub has the most extensive Scotch whiskey list on the West Coast. Five nights a week, you can hear live music here.

Nor'wester Public House
66 SE Morrison St. ☎ **503/232-9771.**

Situated in the industrial neighborhood just across the river from downtown, this brewpub has the feel of a working-class tavern from the outside. However, inside the theme is the Northwest outdoors. Consequently, the clientele tends to be young and athletic. Always a good selection of reliably well-made brews.

SPECIALTY BARS

A BAR WITH A VIEW

Atwater's Restaurant and Lounge
111 SW Fifth Ave. ☎ **503/275-3600.**

Up on the 30th floor of the pale-pink U.S. Bancorp Tower is one of Portland's most expensive restaurants and certainly the one with the best view. However, if you'd just like to sit back and sip a martini while gazing out at the city lights below, they have a splendid bar. Perfect for a romantic nightcap. Thursday through Saturday there is live jazz from 9pm to 1am. The lounge menu here is the most creative in Portland.

A SPORTS BAR

Champions
Portland Marriott Hotel, 1401 SW Front Ave. ☎ **503/274-2470.**

Portland's premier sports bar boasts "good food, good times, and good sports." If sports are your forte, this is the bar for you. There is also a small dance floor here, with dancing Thursday through Saturday to Top 40 tunes.

GAY BARS

The area around the intersection of SW Stark Street and West Burnside Street has the largest concentration of gay bars in Portland. These include C. C. Slaughter's, 1014 SW Stark St. (☎ 503/248-9135), Eagle Tavern, 1300 W. Burnside St. (☎ 503/241-0105), Scandal's Tavern, 1038 SW Stark St. (☎ 503/227-5887), and Silverado, 1217 SW Stark St. (☎ 503/244-4493). Also in this same area, at the corner of Stark Street and 10th Avenue is Panorama (☎ 503/221-RAMA), a dance club popular with both gays and straights.

Portland's Brewing Up a Microstorm

Though espresso is the drink that drives Portland, it is to the city's dozens of brewpubs that educated beer drinkers head when they want to relax over a flavorful pint of ale. No other city in America has as great a concentration of brewpubs, and it was here that the microbrewery business got its start in the mid-1980s. Today, brewpubs continue to proliferate with cozy neighborhood pubs vying for business with big, polished establishments.

There are four basic ingredients in beer: malt, hops, yeast, and water. The first of these, malt, is made from grains, primarily barley and wheat, which are roasted to convert their carbohydrates into the sugar needed to grow yeast. The amount of roasting the grains receive during the malting process will determine the color and flavor of the final product. The darker the malt, the darker and more flavorful the beer or ale. There is a wide variety of malts, each providing its own characteristic flavor. Yeast in turn converts the malt's sugar into alcohol. There are many different strains of yeast that all lend different characters to beers. The hops are added to give beer its characteristic bitterness. The more "hoppy" the beer or ale, the more bitter it becomes. The Northwest happens to be the nation's only commercial hop-growing region with 75 percent being grown in Washington and 25 percent being grown in Oregon and Idaho.

Pilsners are the most common beers in America and are made from pale malt with a lot of hops added to give them their characteristic bitter flavor. Lagers are made in much the same way as pilsners but are cold-fermented, which gives them a distinctive flavor. Ales, which are the most common brews served at microbreweries, are made using a warm fermentation process and usually more and darker malt than is used in lagers and pilsners. Porters (also known as stouts) get their characteristic dark coloring and flavor from the use of dark, even charred, malt.

A bit out from the city, but close to I-84 in nearby Troutdale, there's McMenamin brother's sprawling **Edgefield** brewery complex, 2126 SW Halsey St. (☎ 800/669-8610), which includes a brewery and brewpub, a restaurant and bar, a winery, a bed-and-breakfast inn, and a hostel, all housed on the grounds of the completely renovated former Multnomah County poor farm. Another McMenamin brewpub, the **Cornelius Pass Roadhouse** east of Portland off Ore. 26 (Sunset Highway) in the town of Hillsboro is housed in yet another historic building, this time an old two-story farmhouse. Also on the grounds is a hexagonal barn that is one of the only such structures in the state.

If you prefer a more urban, though no less historic, setting in which to down a pint, try the **Bridgeport Brewery and Brew Pub,** 1313 NW Marshall St. (☎ 503/241-7179), which is housed in the oldest commercial building in the city and was the first brewpub to open in Portland. This is one of the few brewpubs in Portland that serves cask-conditioned "real" ales.

If you're an outdoors type interested in kayaking, mountain biking, skiing, and similar sports, you may want to pay a visit to the **Nor'wester Public House,** 66 SE Morrison St. (☎ 503/232-9771), where you'll likely be drinking with like-minded individuals who enjoy ales and beers with flavor and body.

If you prefer a lighter flavor in your beer, try *weizen* (wheat) beer, which is also served unfiltered as *hefeweizen.* The Widmer Brewing Company is Portland's undisputed king of hefeweizen. You can sample their suds at almost any pub in town, but you owe it to yourself to check out either their **Gasthaus,** 929 N. Russel St. (☎ 503/281-3333), which is located adjacent to their main brewery, or their smaller microbrewery at the **B. Moloch/Heathman Bakery and Pub,** 901 SW Salmon St. (☎ 503/227-5700), which is one of the most popular pubs in Portland due in large part to its excellent, inexpensive meals and lively, contemporary setting.

Microbrews are becoming big business (so big in fact that "microbrewery" is beginning to lose its meaning) and just as wineries in the Napa Valley have become more and more glitzy, so too have brewpubs. With huge copper fermenting vats proudly displayed in the window and polished to a high sheen, the **Portland Brewing Company's Brewhouse Tap Room and Grill,** 2730 NW 31st Ave. (☎ 503/228-5269), is by far the city's most ostentatious, though certainly not largest, brewpub. Running a close second is the new **Rock Bottom Brewery,** 206 SW Morrison St. (☎ 503/796-2739), in downtown Portland. This is an outpost of a small brewing empire that started out in Boulder, the west's other brewing capital. This place is a bit corporate, but is popular with the after-work crowd from downtown offices.

So, what it comes down to in the end is that no matter what vision you have of the ideal brewpub, you're likely to find your dream come true here in Portland. Whether your wearing bike shorts or a three-piece suit, there's a pub in Portland where you can get a hand-crafted beer, maybe a light meal, and enjoy the convivial atmosphere that only a pub can provide. And, if you're like me, half the fun will be finding your personal favorite.

4   Cinemas & Movie Houses

MOVIES

✪ Bagdad Theater & Pub

3702 SE Hawthorne Blvd. ☎ **503/230-0895.** Tickets $1.

In a reversal of recent cinematic trends, the ever-inspired McMenamin brothers restored a classic Arabian Nights movie palace to its original size after it had been split up into a multiplex theater. They now show second-run films and pull more than 20 microbrew drafts at the bar. There's good pizza by the slice to go with your brew and a separate nontheater pub.

Cinema 21

616 NW 21st Ave. ☎ **503/223-4515.** Tickets $5.

Located on the edge of Nob Hill, one of Portland's most fashionable neighborhoods, Cinema 21 is a reliable art-film house. This is also where you can catch animation festivals and the occasional revival of an obscure classic.

Koin Center

Third Ave. and Clay St. ☎ **503/243-3516.** Tickets $3 before 6pm, $6 after 6pm.

Located in the heart of downtown, this complex of six theaters is where Portland goes for first-run, foreign, and not-so-mainstream movies.

✪ Mission Theater & Pub

1624 NW Glisan St. ☎ **503/223-4031.** Tickets $1.

This was the McMenamin brothers' first theater pub. Movies are recent releases that have played the main theaters already but not yet made it onto video.

Northwest Film Center

1219 SW Park Ave. ☎ **503/221-1156.** Tickets $5–$6.

Affiliated with the Portland Art Museum, this repertory cinema schedules an eclectic blend of classics, foreign films, daring avant-garde films, documentaries, visiting artist programs, and thematic series. There's no telling what might turn up on a given night.

20

Excursions from Portland

Portland likes to boast about how close it is to both mountains and ocean, and no visit would be complete without a trip or two into the countryside. In an hour and a half you can be walking on Pacific Ocean beach or skiing in the Cascade Range. In fact, you'll even have this latter choice in the middle of summer, when there is still snow skiing on Mount Hood. A drive through the Columbia River Gorge, a National Scenic Area is an absolute must. If wine is your interest, you can spend a day visiting wineries and driving through the rolling farmland that enticed pioneers to travel the Oregon Trail beginning in the 1840s.

1 Mount Hood Loop

If you have time for only one excursion from Portland, I strongly urge you to do the Mount Hood Loop. This is a long trip, so start your day as early as possible.

To begin your trip, take I-84 east out of Portland. Sixteen miles from downtown, take the second Troutdale exit onto the **Columbia River Scenic Highway** (U.S. 30), which was opened in 1915. The highway is an engineering marvel, but it is dwarfed by the spectacular vistas that present themselves whenever the scenic road emerges from the dark forest. To learn more about the road and how it was built, stop at **Vista House,** 733 feet above the river on **Crown Point.** There are informative displays with old photos and a spectacular view of the gorge, including **Beacon Rock,** an 800-foot-tall monolith on the far side of the river.

Between Troutdale and Ainsworth State Park, 22 miles east, the road passes nine **waterfalls** and six state parks. Latourelle Shepperds Dell, Bridal Veil, Wahkeena, Horsetail, Oneonta, Multnomah—the names of the falls evoke the Native American and pioneer heritage of this region. Of all the falls, **Multnomah** is the most famous. At 620 feet from the lip to the pool, it's the tallest waterfall in Oregon.

The next stop on your tour should be the **Bonneville Lock and Dam.** Some of the dam's most important features, and the attractions drawing thousands of visitors each year, are the fish ladders. These ladders allow salmon and other anadromous fish (fish that are spawned in freshwater, mature in saltwater, and return to freshwater to spawn) to migrate upstream. Underwater windows permit visitors to see fish as they pass through the ladders. Visit the adjacent fish hatchery to see how trout, salmon, and sturgeon are raised before they are released into the river.

This is the first of many dams on the Columbia River and, along with the other dams, is currently the focus of a heated environmental debate over saving the region's dwindling native wild salmon populations. Despite fish ladders and fish hatcheries, salmon have been fighting a losing upstream battle for survival. Adult salmon heading upstream to spawn have to contend with fish ladders, fishermen (both commercial and sport), and spawning beds that are sometimes destroyed or silted up, often by the common practice of clear-cutting timber from steep mountainsides. Among the perils faced by young salmon heading downstream are slow, warm waters that delay the journey to the Pacific Ocean, electrical turbines in dams that kill countless numbers of fish, and irrigation culverts that often lead salmon out into farm fields. With many populations now listed as threatened species (a step below endangered species), a plan for salmon survival is being hammered out. It is hoped that the dams that once brought prosperity and cheap electricity to the Northwest won't bring about the demise of the salmon.

Not far past the dam is **Bridge of the Gods,** which connects Oregon to Washington at the site where an old Indian legend says a natural bridge once stood. Because of the unusual formation of rocks in the river at this site, as well as the frequent volcanic activity here in the past, geologists tend to believe the legend.

Just beyond Bridge of the Gods are the **Cascade Locks.** These navigational locks were built to enable river traffic to avoid the treacherous passage through the cascades here. In earlier years many boats were portaged around the cascades instead of attempting the dangerous trip. When the locks were opened in 1896, they made traveling between the Dalles and Portland much easier. But the completion of the Columbia River Scenic Highway in 1915 made the trip even easier by land. With the construction of the Bonneville Dam, the cascades were flooded and the locks became superfluous. There are two small museums here at the locks, one of which also holds the ticket office for the stern-wheeler *Columbia Gorge* (☎ 503/223-3928), which makes regular trips on the river all summer.

Anyone who sailboards has heard of the town of **Hood River.** This section of the Columbia River is one of the most popular sailboarding spots in the world because of the strong winds that come rushing down the gorge. Almost every other car in this once-sleepy little town has a sailboard on the roof. If you want to try this thrilling sport yourself, stop by one of the many sailboard shops downtown for rental information.

If you are staying overnight on the loop, you might want to consider getting out of your car and riding the rails. The **Mount Hood Railroad,** 110 Railroad Ave. (☎ 541/386-3556), operates its Fruit Blossom Special from mid-April to early December. The cars that carry you up the Hood River are vintage Pullman coaches, and the Mount Hood Railroad Depot is a National Historic Site. Departures are at

Portland Excursions

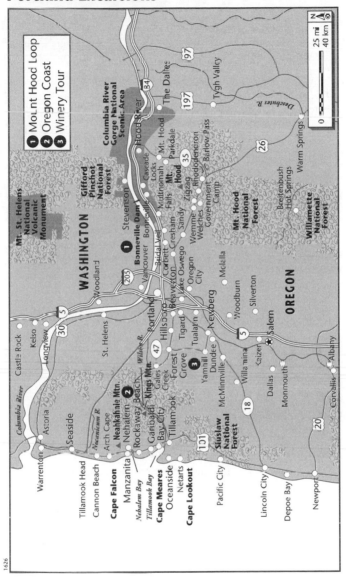

10am and 3pm. The trip lasts four hours and costs $19.95 for adults, $16.95 for senior citizens, and $11.95 for children 2 to 11. In summer the train runs daily except Monday, and in late spring and early fall it runs Wednesday through Sunday, changing to weekends only in the colder months.

From Hood River, turn south on Oregon Hwy. 35, passing through thousands of acres of apple and pear **orchards.** Every fall, roadside stands in this area sell fresh fruit, butter, and juice. The orchards are especially beautiful in the spring, when the trees are in bloom. No matter what time of year, you will have the snow-covered peak of Mount Hood in view as you drive through the orchards, making them all the more spectacular.

About 10 miles off Oregon Hwy. 35, just south of Parkdale, is the **Cooper Spur Ski Area,** a day-use area. (In summer, there is camping hereabouts at Cloud Cap Saddle Campground and Tilly Jane Campground.) **Mount Hood Meadows** (☎ 503/337-2222), the largest ski area on Mount Hood, is the next landmark you'll pass.

Just after Hwy. 35 merges into U.S. 26, turn right onto the road to Timberline Lodge. As the name implies this is the timberline, and a walk on one of the trails in the vicinity will lead you through wildflower-filled meadows in summer. Surprisingly you can also ski here all summer on a glacier above Timberline Lodge.

Back down on U.S. 26 heading west toward Portland, there is another popular ski area, **Mt. Hood SkiBowl** (☎ 503/222-2695). It's also open in summer, with an Alpine Slide and go-kart racing. SkiBowl, the closest ski area to Portland, is located near the town of Government Camp, which has many small lodges and restaurants that cater primarily to winter skiers.

Between Government Camp and the Resort at the Mountain, watch for the marker beside the road showing where the end of the **Barlow Trail toll road** (a section of the Oregon Trail) around Mount Hood was located. There is a reproduction of the gate that once stood on this spot, and you can still see the trail itself.

To return to Portland just stay on Oregon Hwy. 26 all the way back to town or follow the signs for I-84.

WHERE TO STAY

Columbia Gorge Hotel

4000 Westcliff Dr., Hood River, OR 97031. ☎ **541/386-5566** or 800/345-1921. Fax 503/386-3359. 42 rms. TV ☎ $190 double (including five-course breakfast); $145 special weekday rate. AE, DC, DISC, MC, V. Free parking.

Located just west of the town of Hood River off I-84, and opened shortly after the Columbia River Scenic Highway was completed in 1915, this little oasis of luxury in the wilderness was completely restored in 1989 and today offers the same genteel atmosphere that was once enjoyed by the likes of Rudolph Valentino and Clara Bow. With its yellow stucco walls and red-tile roofs, this hotel would be right at home in Beverly Hills; the hotel gardens could hold their own in Victoria, British Columbia. Despite the attractive furnishings and gardens, it is almost impossible to notice anything but the view out the windows. The hotel is perched more than 200 feet above the river on a steep cliff, and the stream that meanders through the gardens suddenly cascades over the precipice.

Guest rooms are all a little different, with a mixture of antique and classic furnishings. There are canopy beds, brass beds, and even some hand-carved wooden beds. Unfortunately, many of the rooms are rather cramped, as are the bathrooms, most of which have older fixtures and some exposed pipes. Also unfortunate is the fact that the original architect didn't design larger windows in the guest rooms.

Dining/Entertainment: The Columbia River Court Dining Room is one of the best restaurants in the Northwest, well known for a four-course farm breakfast. The breakfast nearly requires you to fast beforehand and diet after. Evening meals are rather pricey but feature Northwest cuisine with an emphasis on salmon, lamb, and venison.

Services: Limited room service, complimentary shuttle to Hood River.

Timberline Lodge

Timberline, OR 97028. ☎ **503/231-7979** or 800/547-1406. Fax 503/272-3710. 59 rms (49 with private bath). $62 double without bath: $92–$162 double with bath. AE, DISC, MC, V. Free parking. (sno-park permit required in winter).

Constructed during the Great Depression of the 1930s as a WPA project, this classic Alpine ski lodge overflows with craftsmanship. The grand stone fireplace, huge exposed beams, and wide plank floors of the lobby impress every first-time visitor. Details are not overlooked either. Wood carvings, imaginative wrought-iron fixtures, hand-hooked rugs, and handmade furniture complete the rustic picture.

Rooms vary in size considerably, with the smallest rooms lacking private bathrooms. However, no matter which room you stay in, you'll be surrounded by the same rustic furnishings. Unfortunately room windows are not very large, but you can always retire to the Ram's Head lounge for a better view of Mount Hood.

Dining/Entertainment: The Cascade Dining Room enjoys a nearly legendary reputation. Some people come to stay at the lodge just to have dinner here. The tables are rustic and the windows are small (which limits views), but the Northwest-style food is superb, if a bit pricey. There is also a casual snack bar in the Wy'East Day Lodge across the parking lot. The Blue Ox Bar is a dark dungeon of a place and the Ram's Head Bar is a more open and airy spot.

Services: Fire starters for rooms with fireplaces, guided hotel tours.

Facilities: Ski lifts, ski school and rentals, outdoor swimming pool, hiking trails, gift shop, coin laundry.

2 The Oregon Coast

The quickest route from Portland to the Oregon coast is via U.S. 26, also called Sunset Highway. From downtown to the beach takes less than two hours. Just before reaching the junction with U.S. 101, watch for a sign marking the **world's largest Sitka spruce tree.** This giant is located in a small park just off the highway. Trees of this size were once common throughout the Coast Range, but almost all have now been cut down. The fight to preserve the remaining big trees is a bitter one that has divided the citizens of Oregon.

At the junction with U.S. 101, turn south and watch for the turn-off to **Ecola Beach State Park.** Located just north of the town of Cannon Beach, this park provides some of the most spectacular views on the coast. Just offshore is **Haystack Rock,** a massive rock island 235 feet tall that is the most photographed rock on the coast.

And stretching out to the south is Cannon Beach. There are stands of old-growth spruce, hemlock, and Douglas fir in the park, and a number of trails offer a chance to walk through this lush forest. The trail down to the beach is steep, but you can still get a good view of sea lions basking in the sun even if you don't go all the way down.

Cannon Beach, known as the Provincetown or Carmel of the Northwest, depending on which coast you hail from, is named for the cannon of the USS *Shark,* which washed ashore here after the ship sank in 1849. Haystack Rock, only a few feet out from the beach, is popular with beachcombers and tide-pool explorers. In town, there are many art galleries and interesting shops, even a popular little theater (the Coaster Theater), that stages performances year-round. Every summer the **Cannon Beach Sandcastle Contest** attracts sand sculptors and thousands of appreciative viewers. Any time of year, you'll find the winds here ideal for kite flying.

Heading south out of Cannon Beach will bring you to the rugged and remote **Oswald West State Park,** named for the governor who promoted legislation to preserve all beaches as public property. The beach is in a cove that can only be reached by walking a few hundred yards through dense rain forest; once you are there, all you will hear is the crashing of the surf. The beach is strewn with huge driftwood logs that give it a wild look. High bluffs rise up at both ends of the cove and it is possible to hike to the top of them. There are plenty of picnic tables and a campground for tent campers only.

U.S. 101 continues south from Oswald West State Park and climbs up over **Neahkahnie Mountain.** Legend has it that at the base of this oceanside mountain, the survivors of a wrecked Spanish galleon buried a fortune in gold. Keep your eyes open for elk, which frequently graze on the meadows here.

Just below this windswept mountain is the quiet resort village of **Manzanita.** Tucked under the fir, spruce, and hemlock trees are the summer homes of some of Portland's wealthier residents. There is also a long stretch of sandy beach at the foot of the village.

Tillamook Bay is one of the largest bays on the Oregon coast and at its north end is the small town of Garibaldi, which is a popular sportfishing spot. If you aren't an angler, you can still go for a cruise either around the bay or to look for whales.

Just before reaching the busy town of **Tillamook,** you will come to the **Tillamook Cheese Factory.** This region is one of Oregon's main dairy-farming areas, and much of the milk is turned into cheddar cheese and butter. The first cheese factory opened here in 1894. Today you can watch the sophisticated cheese-making process through large windows. The cheese-factory store is a busy place, but the lines move quickly and you can be on your way to the next picnic area with an assortment of tasty cheeses or some ice cream cones.

From Tillamook the **Three Capes Scenic Route** leads to Cape Meares, Cape Lookout, and Cape Kiwanda, all of which provide stunning vistas of rocky cliffs, misty mountains, and booming surf. As the name implies, this is a very scenic stretch of road, and there are plenty of places to stop and enjoy the views and the beaches.

Cape Meares State Park perches high atop the cape, with the Cape Meares lighthouse just a short walk from the parking lot. This lighthouse, 200 feet above the water, was built in 1890. Today it has been replaced by an automated light a few feet away. Be sure to visit the **octopus tree** here in the park. This Sitka spruce has been twisted and sculpted by harsh weather.

As you come down from the cape, you will come to the village of Oceanside, which clings to the steep mountainsides of a small cove. One tavern and one restaurant are the only commercial establishments, and that's the way folks here like it. After seeing the overdevelopment in other coastal towns, you'll understand why.

South of Oceanside the road runs along a flat stretch of beach before reaching **Cape Lookout State Park.** Cape Lookout, a steep forested ridge jutting out into the Pacific, is an excellent place for whale watching in the spring. A trail leads from either the main (lower) parking area or the parking area at the top of the ridge out to the end of the point. From the upper parking lot it is a five-mile round trip to the point.

At Sandlake Junction, about 14 miles south of Oceanside, turn left and you will return to U.S. 101. Head north to Tillamook, where Ore. 6 heads east toward Portland. This road is subject to landslides and is sometimes closed so be sure to ask in Tillamook before heading east. Ore. 6 joins U.S. 26 about 25 miles west of Portland. Allow about 2 1/2 hours to get back from Tillamook.

3 A Winery Tour

In recent years Oregon wine has been winning many awards for outstanding quality. This isn't surprising when you realize that Oregon is on the same latitude as France's wine growing regions. The climate is also very similar—cool, wet winters and springs and long, dry summers with warm days and cool nights. These are ideal conditions for growing wine grapes, and local vineyards are making the most of a good situation.

A "Discover Oregon Wineries" brochure describing more than 50 Oregon wineries is available from the **Oregon Winegrowers' Association,** 1200 NW Front Ave., Suite 400, Portland, OR 97209 (☎ 503/228-8403). Almost all wineries are within an hour or two of Portland, and consequently a day of driving from one winery to another makes for a pleasant outing. I suggest picking four or five that sound interesting and then mapping out the best routes among them. A trip through wine country is a chance to see the fertile valleys that lured pioneers across the Oregon Trail. For more information about the Oregon wine scene, including a calendar of winery events, pick up a copy of *Oregon Wine,* a monthly newspaper, in any local wine shop, or contact the **Oregon Wine Press,** 644 SE 20th Ave., Portland, OR 97214 (☎ 503/232-7607). With summer festivals a big part of the Oregon winery scene, you can enjoy picnics while listening to live music at many vineyards.

The trip outlined below takes in some of the region's best wineries and most beautiful countryside. Allow yourself at least half a day for a winery tour. I recommend taking along a picnic lunch, which you can supplement with a wine purchase. Most wineries have picnic tables.

To begin your winery tour, head west out of Portland on U.S. 26 (Sunset Highway) and then take Ore. 6 toward Tillamook. After a few miles on this two-lane highway, watch for signs indicating a left turn onto Ore. 8 toward Forest Grove. Heading back east on this road, watch for a sign to **Laurel Ridge Winery,** 255 David Hill Rd. (☎ 503/359-5436). This is one of the oldest wineries in Oregon. The first grapes were planted here in the late 1800s, but Prohibition interrupted wine production and the vineyard was slow to return to wine making. However, today, Laurel Hill produces excellent Pinot Noir, Gewürztraminer, Semillon, Sylvaner, and Riesling. Laurel Ridge also produces excellent sparkling wine by the *méthode champagnoise.* The winery is open daily from noon to 5pm.

Continue into Forest Grove on Ore. 8 and then turn right onto Ore. 47 toward Yamhill. Just south of town, you'll see signs for **Montinore Vineyards,** 3663 SW Dilley Rd. (☎ 503/359-5012). This is the largest wine producer in the state and enjoys an enviable location with sweeping views across the Tualatin Valley to the Cascade Range. A tree-lined drive leads up to a Victorian mansion. With 14 wines and a large tasting room and gift shop, Montinore is popular with tour groups. Landscaped grounds invite a stroll or picnic after tasting a few wines. Pinot Noir, Pinot Gris, Chardonnay, and white Riesling are among the more popular wines produced here. The winery is open daily from noon to 5pm from May to October; the rest of the year it is open weekends only.

Back on Ore. 47, continue south to the small town of Yamhill where you turn east on Ore. 240. After a few miles watch for signs to **Knudsen Erath Winery,** Worden Hill Road (☎ 503/538-3318). Situated on 45 acres above the town of Dundee, this winery has one of the most spectacular settings in the region. The cedar-shingled buildings of the winery are set between forest and vineyard, and the views are stunning. Wines produced here include Pinot Noir, Riesling, Gewürztraminer, Chardonnay, Cabernet Sauvignon, and a brut. The winery is open daily from noon to 5pm.

At the bottom of the Knudsen Erath driveway, you'll find a shady little park that makes a good picnic spot if you haven't already eaten at one of the wineries.

Head downhill into the valley from Knudsen Erath and you will soon see a sign for **Lange Winery,** 18380 NE Buena Vista Rd. (☎ 503/538-6476). This is a tiny winery with only a few acres of its own grapes, and the tasting room is the basement of the owners' home. However, the wines produced here are some of the best in the state. Pinot Noir, Chardonnay, and Pinot Gris are specialties. The winery is open weekends from noon to 5pm.

Continuing down into the valley again, you will come to the town of Dundee and U.S. Hwy. 99W. Turn right on the highway and a few miles out of town you will see the sign for **Sokol Blosser Winery,** 5000 NE Sokol Blosser Lane (☎ 503/864-2282), which sits high on a hill overlooking the valley. This is one of the larger wineries in Oregon and maintains a spacious tasting room and gift shop. On any given day, three wines will be available for tasting. These might include Pinot Noir, Chardonnay, Gewürztraminer, Riesling, or Muller-Thurgau. The winery is open daily from 11am to 5pm.

Directly across the street from Sokol Blosser's driveway, you'll see **Laube Orchards.** This former roadside fruit stand is now a full-fledged specialty foods shop featuring Oregon products. Stop in and stock up on boysenberry jam or roasted hazelnuts. If it is late in the day, you might want to stop for dinner in Dundee, which has a couple of excellent restaurants. **Tina's,** 760 Hwy. 99W (☎ 503/538-8880), is a tiny place with a menu that is limited to about half a dozen well-prepared dishes. **Red Hills Provincial Dining,** 276 Hwy. 99W (☎ 503/538-8224), in an old house beside the highway, serves a combination of Northwest and Mediterranean cuisine. The dinner menu here changes every two weeks, and reservations are highly recommended.

Should you wish to spend the night, there are also quite a few bed-and-breakfast inns nearby. I suggest contacting **Yamhill County Bed and Breakfast Association,** P.O. Box 656, McMinnville, OR 97128. There are also motels in McMinnville and Newberg. To return to Portland, just head east on U.S. Hwy. 99W.

4 Vancouver, Washington

Because Vancouver, Washington, is part of the Portland metropolitan area and because it bears the same name as both a large island and a city in Canada, it is often overlooked by visitors to the Northwest. However, the city has several historic sites and other attractions that make if a good day-long excursion from Portland. The first three attractions listed here are all in the one-square-mile Central Park, which is located just east of I-5 (take the East Mill Plain Boulevard exit just after you cross the bridge into Washington).

It was here in the U.S. Vancouver that much of the Northwest's important early pioneer history unfolded at the Hudson's Bay Company's (HBC) Fort Vancouver. The HBC, a British company, came to the Northwest in search of furs and for most of the first half of the 19th century was the only authority in this remote region. Fur trappers, mountain men, missionaries, explorers, and settlers all made Fort Vancouver their first stop in Oregon. Today the **Fort Vancouver National Historic Site,** 1501 E. Evergreen Blvd. (☎ 360/696-7655), houses several reconstructed buildings that are furnished as they might have been in the middle of the 19th century. The fort is open daily from 9am to 5pm (4pm in the winter), and admission is $1.

After the British gave up Fort Vancouver, it became the site of the Vancouver Barracks U.S. military post, and stately homes were built for the officers of the post. These buildings are now preserved as the Officers' Row National Historic District. You can stroll along admiring the well-kept homes, and then stop in at the **Grant House Folk Art Center** (☎ 360/694-5252), which is named for President

Ulysses S. Grant, who was stationed here as quartermaster in the 1850s. This building was the first commanding officer's quarters. In addition to the art center, there is a cafe that serves good lunches. Further along Officers' Row, you'll find the **George C. Marshall House** (☎ 360/ 693-3103), which is also open to the public. This Victorian-style building replaced the Grant House as the commanding officer's quarters. The Grant House Folk Art Center is open Tuesday through Sunday from 10am to 5pm, and the Marshall House is open Monday through Friday from 10am to 5pm. You'll find the tree-shaded row of 21 homes just north of Fort Vancouver.

A very different piece of history is preserved on the far side of Fort Vancouver from Officers' Row, at **Pearson Air Museum,** 1105 E. Fifth St. (☎ 360/694-7026). This airfield was established in 1905 and is the oldest operating airfield in the United States. Dozens of vintage aircraft, including several World War I era biplanes and the plane that made the first trans-Pacific flight, are on display in a large hangar. The museum is open Wednesday through Sunday from noon to 5pm, and admission is $2 for adults and $1 for children.

In the town of Washougal, 16 miles east of Vancouver on Wash. 14, you can visit the **Pendleton Woolen Mills and Outlet Shop,** 217th St., Washougal (☎ 360/835-2131), and see how the famous wool blankets and classic wool fashions are made. The store is open Monday through Saturday from 8am to 4pm, with free mill tours offered Mon through Friday at 9, 10, and 11am, and 1:30pm.

Railroading buffs may want to drive north 10 miles to the town of Battle Ground and take a ride on the diesel-powered **Lewis River Excursion Train,** which has its depot at 1000 E. Main St. in Battle Ground (☎ 360/687-2626, or 503/227-2626 in Portland). The two-hour excursions run from Battle Ground to Moulton Falls County Park, where there is a 20-minute stop for passengers to view the falls. There are also dinner train excursions. Call ahead for the days and hours of scheduled trips. Tickets for the regular excursion are $10 for adults and $5 for children.

North of Vancouver 23 miles in the town of Woodland are the **Hulda Klager Lilac Gardens,** 115 S. Pekin Rd., Woodland (☎ 360/ 225-8996). Between late April and Mother's Day each year, these gardens are burst into color and fragrance of lilacs hangs in the air. The gardens are open daily from dawn to dusk and admission is $1.

Ten miles east of Woodland off NE Cedar Creek Road, you'll find the **Cedar Creek Grist Mill,** Grist Mill Road (☎ 360/225-9552), the only remaining 19th-century grist mill in Washington. Built in 1876, the grist mill was restored over a 10-year period, and in 1989 once again became functional. When the mill is open, volunteers demonstrate how wheat is ground into flour. Hours of operation are Saturday from 1 to 4pm and Sunday from 2 to 4pm. Admission is by donation.

5 Mount St. Helens National Volcanic Monument

Once it was regarded as the most perfect of the Cascade peaks, a snow-covered cone rising above lush forests, but on May 18, 1980, all that changed when Mount St. Helens erupted with a violent explosion.

Today the area surrounding the volcano is designated the Mount St. Helens National Volcanic Monument. The best place to start an exploration of the monument is at the **Mount St. Helens National Volcanic Monument Visitor Center** (☎ 360/274-2100), which is located at Silver Lake, five miles east of Castle Rock on Wash. 504. The visitor center houses extensive exhibits on the eruption and its effects on the region. Summer hours at the visitor center are daily from 9am to 6pm; winter hours are daily 9am to 5pm. Admission is free. For a closer look at the crater, continue to the **Coldwater Ridge Visitor Center,** which is at milepost 47 on Wash. 504, only eight miles from the crater. This center features interpretive displays on the events leading up to the eruption and the subsequent slow regeneration of life around the volcano. Hours are the same as at the main center. Here at Coldwater Ridge, you'll also find a picnic area, interpretive trail, a restaurant, and even a boat launch at Coldwater Lake.

Though these two centers can give you an idea of the power of the explosion that blew off this mountain's top, you need to drive around to the monument's east side for a close-up view of how the eruption effected the surrounding lands. It is here that you will see the forest that was blown down by the eruption. For the best views, take U.S. 12 east from exit 68 off I-5. In Randle, head south on Local Route 25 and then take Local Route 26. The Woods Creek Information Center, on Route 25 just before the junction with Route 26, has information on this part of the monument. Route 26 travels through mile after mile of blown-down trees, and though the sight of the thousands of trees that were felled by a single blast is quite bleak, it reminds one of the awesome power of nature. More than a decade after the eruption, life is slowly returning to this devastated forest. At Meta Lake, Route 26 joins Route 99, which continues to the Windy Ridge Viewpoint, where visitors get their closest look at the crater. Below Windy Ridge lies Spirit Lake, which was once one of the most popular summer vacation spots in the Washington Cascades. Today the lake is desolate and lifeless.

If you are an experienced hiker in good physical condition, you may want to consider climbing to the top of Mount St. Helens. It is an 8- to 10-hour, 10-mile hike and can require an ice ax. The trailhead is on the south side of the monument and permits are required between May 15 and October 31. Because this is a very popular climb it is advisable to request a permit in advance (summer weekends book up months in advance). However, you can also try your luck at getting an unreserved permit on the day of your climb. These are issued at **Jack's Restaurant and Store** on Wash. 503 five miles west of Cougar. To request a climbing permit, phone 360/750-3920.

On the south side of the monument, you can explore the **Ape Cave,** a lava tube that was formed 1,900 years ago when lava poured from the volcano. When the lava finally stopped flowing, it left a two-mile-long cave that is the longest continuous lava tube in the Americas. At the Apes Headquarters, you can rent a lantern for exploring the cave on your own, or join a regular ranger-led exploration of the cave. This center is open daily from late May through September.

Hikers who aren't doing the climb to the summit will find many other hiking trails within the monument, some in blast zones and some in forests that were left undamaged by the eruption. Ask at any visitor center for trail information.

For more information, contact the **Mount St. Helens National Volcanic Monument,** 42218 NE Yale Bridge Road, Amboy, WA 98601 (☎ 360/750-3900).

6 Oregon City and the End of the Oregon Trail

When the first white settlers began crossing the Oregon Trail in the early 1840s, their destination was Oregon City and the fertile Willamette Valley. At the time Portland had yet to be founded and Oregon City, set beside powerful Willamette Falls, was the largest town in Oregon. However, with the development of Portland and the shifting of the capital to Salem, Oregon City began to lose its importance. Today this is primarily an industrial town, though one steeped in Oregon history and well worth a visit.

To get to Oregon City from Portland, you can take I-5 south to I-205 east or you can head south from downtown Portland on SW Riverside Drive and drive through the wealthy suburbs of Lake Oswego and West Linn. Once in Oregon City, your first stop should be just south of town at the Willamette Falls overlook on Ore. 99E. Though the falls have been much changed by industry over the years, they are still an impressive sight.

Oregon City is divided into upper and lower sections by a steep bluff. The nation's only free municipal elevator connects the two halves of the city and affords a great view from its observation area at the top of the bluff. You'll find the 100-foot-tall elevator at the corner of Seventh Street and Railroad Avenue. Service is available from 6am to 8pm daily. It is in the upper section of town that you will find the town's many historic homes.

Oregon City's most famous citizen was retired Hudson's Bay Company chief factor John McLoughlin, who helped found Oregon City in 1829. By the 1840s, immigrants were pouring into Oregon, and McLoughlin provided food, seeds, and tools to many. Upon retirement in 1846, McLoughlin moved to Oregon City, where he built what was at that time the most luxurious home in Oregon. Today the **McLoughlin House,** 713 Center Street (☎ 503/656-5146) is a National Historic Site and is open to the public. The house is furnished as it would have been in McLoughlin's days and includes many original pieces. The house is open Tuesday through Saturday from 10am to 5pm (4pm in winter) and on Sunday from 1 to 4pm. Admission is $3 for adults, $2.50 for senior citizens, and $1 for children.

Several other Oregon City historical homes are also open to the public. The **Clackamas County Historical Museum,** 211 Tumwater Drive (☎ 503/655-5574), houses collections of historic memorabilia and old photos from this area. The museum is open Monday through Friday from 10am to 4pm and Saturday and Sunday from 1 to 5pm.

Admission is $3 for adults, $2 for senior citizens and $1.50 for children. The **Stevens Crawford House,** 603 Sixth Street (☎ 503/655-2866), is a foursquare-style home and is furnished with late-19th-century antiques. The house is open Tuesday through Friday from 10am to 4pm (Monday from 1 to 4pm in summer) and Saturday and Sunday from 1 to 4pm. $3, $2, $1.50. The **Ermatinger House,** on the corner of Sixth and John Adams streets (☎ 503/657-8316), is the town's oldest home. The hours are Wednesday through Sunday from 10am to 4pm. Admission is $1.50 for adults and 75¢ for children.

The story of the settlers who traveled the Oregon Trail is told at the **End of the Oregon Trail Interpretive Center,** 500 Washington Street (☎ 503/657-9336), which is located beneath a senior citizens center in the upper town neighborhood. The center is open Tuesday through Saturday from 10am to 4pm and Sunday from noon to 4pm. Admission is $2 for adults $1.50 for senior citizens, and $1 for children. A new interpretive center is currently under construction, so call to find out if this center has opened yet when you visit.

Each summer the history of the Oregon Trail comes alive in Oregon City with the staging of the *Oregon Trail Pageant.* Music and dancing, romance and drama are all part of this production. Performances are held in an amphitheater on the Clackamas Community College campus, which is located a few miles southeast of downtown Oregon City. Performances are held Tuesday through Saturday starting at 7:15pm, and tickets are $8 for adults, $7 for senior citizens, and $4 for children.

Another interesting chapter in Oregon pioneer history is preserved 13 miles south of Oregon City in the town of **Aurora,** which was founded in 1855 as a Christian communal society. Similar in many ways to such more famous communal experiments as the Amana Colony and the Shaker communities, the Aurora Colony lasted slightly more than 20 years. Today Aurora is a National Historic District and the large old homes of the community's founders have been restored. Many of the old commercial buildings now house antiques stores, which are the main reason most people visit Aurora. You can learn about the history of Aurora at the **Old Aurora Colony Museum** (☎ 503/678-5754). Between March and December, the museum is open Wednesday through Saturday from 10am to 4:30pm and on Sunday from 1 to 4:30pm (Tuesday 10am to 4:30pm June through August). January and February, the museum is open Thursday through Sunday from 1 to 4:30pm. Admission is $2.50 for adults and $1 for children.

Appendix

For Foreign Visitors

Although American trends have spread across Europe and other parts of the world to the extent that America may seem like familiar territory before your arrival, there are still many peculiarities and uniquely American situations that any foreign visitor will encounter.

1 Preparing for Your Trip

ENTRY REQUIREMENTS

Document Regulations   Canadian citizens may enter the United States without visas; they need only proof of residence.

Citizens of the U.K., New Zealand, Japan, and most western European countries traveling on valid passports may not need a visa for fewer than 90 days of holiday or business travel to the United States, providing that they hold a round-trip or return ticket and enter the United States on an airline or cruise line participating in the visa waiver program.

(Note that citizens of these visa-exempt countries who first enter the United States may then visit Mexico, Canada, Bermuda, and/or the Caribbean islands and then reenter the United States by any mode of transportation, without needing a visa. Further information is available from any U.S. embassy or consulate.)

Citizens of countries other than those stipulated above, including citizens of Australia, must have two documents:

- a valid passport, with an expiration date at least six months later than the scheduled end of the visit to the U.S.; and
- a tourist visa, available without charge from the nearest U.S. consulate. To obtain the visa, the traveler must submit a completed application form (either in person or by mail) with a 1 1/2 inch-square photo and demonstrate binding ties to a residence abroad.

Usually you can obtain a visa at once or within 24 hours, but it may take longer during the summer rush from June to August. If you cannot go in person, contact the nearest U.S. embassy or consulate for directions on applying by mail. Your travel agent or airline office may also be able to provide you with visa applications and instructions. The U.S. consulate or embassy that issues your visa will determine whether you will be issued a multiple- or single-entry visa and any restrictions regarding the length of your stay.

Medical Requirements   No inoculations are needed to enter the United States unless you are coming from, or have stopped over in, areas known to be suffering from epidemics, particularly of cholera or yellow fever.

If you have a disease requiring treatment with medications containing narcotics or drugs requiring a syringe, carry a valid signed prescription from your physician to allay any suspicions that you are smuggling drugs.

Customs   Every adult visitor may bring in free of duty: one liter of wine or hard liquor; 200 cigarettes or 100 cigars (but no cigars from Cuba) or three pounds of smoking tobacco; $100 worth of gifts. These exemptions are offered to travelers who spend at least 72 hours in the United States and who have not claimed these exemptions within the preceding six months. It is altogether forbidden to bring into the country foodstuffs (particularly cheese, fruit, cooked meats, and canned goods) and plants (vegetables, seeds, tropical plants, and so on). Foreign tourists may bring in or take out up to $10,000 in U.S. or foreign currency with no formalities; larger sums must be declared to Customs on entering or leaving.

INSURANCE

There is no national health system in the United States. Because the cost of medical care is extremely high, we strongly advise every traveler to secure health coverage before setting out.

You may want to take out a comprehensive travel policy that covers (for a relatively low premium) sickness or injury cost (medical, surgical, and hospital); loss or theft of your baggage; trip-cancellation costs; guarantee of bail in case you are arrested; costs of accident, repatriation, or death. Such packages (for example, "Europe Assistance" in Europe) are sold by automobile clubs at attractive rates, as well as by insurance companies and travel agencies.

MONEY

Currency & Exchange   The U.S. monetary system has a decimal base: 1 American **dollar** ($1) = 100 **cents** (100¢).

Dollar bills commonly come in $1 ("a buck"), $5, $10, $20, $50, and $100 denominations (the last two are not welcome when paying for small purchases and are not accepted in taxis or subway ticket booths). There are also $2 bills (seldom encountered).

There are six denominations of coins: 1¢ (one cent, or "penny"), 5¢ (five cents, or "a nickel"), 10¢ (ten cents, or "a dime"), 25¢ (twenty-five cents, or "a quarter"), 50¢ (fifty cents, or "a half dollar"), and the rare $1 piece.

Traveler's Checks   Traveler's checks in U.S. dollar denominations are readily accepted at most hotels, motels, restaurants, and large stores.

But the best place to change traveler's checks is at a bank. Do not bring traveler's checks denominated in other currencies, with the possible exception of those in Canadian dollars. Because of the proximity of the Canadian border, many hotels, restaurants, and shops will accept Canadian currency.

Credit Cards   The method of payment most widely used is the credit card: **VISA** (BarclayCard in Britain), **MasterCard** (EuroCard in Europe, Access in Britain, Charges in Canada), **American Express, Diners Club, Discover Card,** and **Carte Blanche.** You can save yourself trouble by using "plastic money," rather than cash or traveler's checks in most hotels, motels, restaurants, and retail stores (a growing number of food and liquor stores now accept credit cards). You must have a credit card to rent a car. It can also be used as proof of identity (often carrying more weight than a passport), or as a "cash card," enabling you to draw money from banks that accept them.

Note: The "foreign-exchange bureaus" so common in Europe are rare even at airports in the United States, and nonexistent outside major cities. Try to avoid having to change foreign money or traveler's checks not denominated in U.S. dollars at a small-town bank, or even a branch in a big city; in fact, leave any currency other than U.S. dollars at home—it may prove to be more of a nuisance to you than it's worth.

SAFETY

General   While tourist areas are generally safe, crime is on the increase everywhere, and U.S. urban areas tend to be less safe than those in Europe or Japan. Visitors should always be alert. This is particularly true of large U.S. cities. It is wise to ask the city's or area's tourist office if you are in doubt about which neighborhoods are safe.

Avoid deserted areas, especially at night. Don't enter a city park at night unless there is an event that attracts crowds—for example, New York City's concerts in the parks. Generally speaking, you can feel safe in areas where there are many people, and many open establishments.

Avoid carrying valuables with you on the street, and don't display expensive cameras or electronic equipment. Hold on to your pocketbook, and place your billfold in an inside pocket. In restaurants, theaters, and other public places, keep your possessions in sight.

Remember also that hotels are open to the public, and in a large hotel, security personnel may not be able to screen everyone entering. Always lock your room door—don't assume that once inside your hotel you are automatically safe and need no longer be aware of your surroundings.

Driving   Safety while driving is particularly important. Question your car-rental agency about personal safety, or ask for a brochure of traveler safety tips when you pick up your car. Obtain written directions, or a map with the route marked in red, from the agency showing how to reach your destination. And, if possible, arrive and depart during daylight hours.

Recently, more and more crime has involved cars and drivers. If you drive off a highway into a neighborhood that seems threatening, leave the area as quickly as possible. If you have an accident, even on a highway, remain inside your car with the doors locked until you assess the situation, or until the police arrive. If you are bumped from behind on the street or are involved in a minor accident with no injuries and the situation appears to be suspicious, motion to the other driver to follow you. *Never* get out of your car in such situations.

You can also keep a premade sign in your car which reads: PLEASE FOLLOW THIS VEHICLE TO REPORT THE ACCIDENT. Show the sign to the other driver and go directly to the nearest police precinct, well-lighted service station, or all-night store.

If you see someone on the road who indicates a need for help, do *not* stop. Take note of the location, drive on to a well-lighted area, and telephone the police by dialing 911.

Park in well-lighted, well-traveled areas if possible. Always keep your car doors locked, whether attended or unattended. Look around you before you get in or out of your car, and never leave packages or valuables in sight. If someone attempts to rob you or steal your car, do *not* try to resist the thief/carjacker—report the incident to the police department immediately.

You may wish to contact the visitor information centers in either Portland or Seattle for a safety brochure. In Portland, contact the **Portland Oregon Visitors Association,** Three World Trade Center, 26 SW Salmon St., Portland, OR 97204 3299 (☎ 503/222-2223, or 800/345-3214); in Seattle, contact the **Seattle-King County Convention & Visitors Bureau,** 520 Pike St., Suite 1300, Seattle, WA 98101-9927 (☎ 206/462-5840).

2 Getting To & Around the U.S.

Travelers from overseas can take advantage of **APEX (Advance Purchase Excursion) fares** offered by all major U.S. and European carriers. Aside from these, attractive values are offered by **Icelandair** on flights from Luxembourg to New York and by **Virgin Atlantic Airways** from London to New York/Newark.

From Toronto, there are flights to Seattle and Portland on **Air Canada, Northwest,** and **United.** There are flights from Vancouver B.C. to Seattle and Portland on **Air Canada, Horizon, Northwest,** and **United.**

Airlines traveling from London to Seattle and Portland are **American, Delta, Northwest, TWA,** and **United. British Airways** flies direct to Seattle from London.

From New Zealand and Australia, there are flights to Los Angeles on **Quantas** and **New Zealand Air. United** flies direct to Seattle from New Zealand and Australia.

Some large airlines (for example, **TWA, American, Northwest, United,** and **Delta**) offer transatlantic and transpacific travelers special discount tickets under the name **Visit USA,** allowing travel between any U.S. destinations at minimum rates. These tickets are not on sale in the United States and must therefore be purchased before you leave your foreign point of departure. This system is the best, easiest and fastest way to see the United States at low cost. You should obtain information well in advance from your travel agent or the office of the airline concerned, since the conditions attached to these discount tickets can be changed without advance notice.

The visitor arriving by air, no matter what the port of entry, should cultivate patience and resignation before setting foot on U.S. soil. Getting through Immigration control may take as long as two hours on some days, especially summer weekends. Add the time it takes to clear Customs and you'll see that you should make very generous allowance for delay in planning connections between international and domestic flights—an average of two to three hours at least.

In contrast, travelers arriving by car, rail, or ferry from Canada will find border-crossing formalities streamlined to the vanishing point. And air travelers from Canada, Bermuda, and some places in the Caribbean can sometimes go through Customs and Immigration at the point of departure, which is much quicker and less painful.

For further information about travel to and around Seattle and Portland, see "Getting There" in Chapters 2 and 12, and "Getting Around" in Chapters 3 and 13.

International visitors can also buy a USA Railpass, good for 15 or 30 days of unlimited travel on Amtrak. The pass is available through many foreign travel agents and at any staffed Amtrak station in the U.S. Prices in 1995 for a 15-day pass are $340; a 30-day pass costs $425. (With a foreign passport, you can also buy passes at some Amtrak offices in the United States, including locations in San Francisco, Los Angeles, Chicago, New York, Miami, Boston, and Washington, D.C.) Reservations are generally required and should be made for each part of your trip as early as possible.

Visitors should also be aware of the limitations of long-distance rail travel in the United States. With a few notable exceptions (for instance, the Northeast Corridor line between Boston and Washington, D.C.), service is rarely up to European standard: delays are common, routes are limited and often infrequently served, and fares are rarely significantly lower than discount airfares. Thus, cross-country train travel should be approached with caution.

The cheapest way to travel the United States is by **bus.** Greyhound, the nation's nationwide bus line, offers an **Ameripass** for unlimited travel for seven days (for $259), 15 days (for $459), and 30 days (for $559). Bus travel in the United States can be both slow and uncomfortable, so this option is not for everyone.

FAST FACTS: For the Foreign Traveler

Accommodations   It is always a good idea to make hotel reservations as soon as you know your trip dates. Reservations require a deposit of one night's payment. Seattle and Portland are particularly busy during summer months, and hotels book up in advance—especially on weekends when there is a festival on. If you do not have reservations, it is best to look for a room in the midafternoon. If you wait until evening, you run the risk that hotels will be filled.

In the United States, major downtown hotels, which cater primarily to business travelers, commonly offer weekend discounts of as much as 50 percent to entice vacationers to fill empty rooms. Note that rates in Seattle and Portland tend to go up in the summer, when there is a greater demand. If you wish to save money and don't mind cloudy or rainy weather, consider visiting sometime other than summer, though these cities really are at their best when the sun is shining.

Automobile Organizations   Auto clubs will supply maps, suggested routes, guidebooks, accident and bail-bond insurance, and emergency road service. The major auto club in the United States, with 955 offices nationwide, is the **American Automobile Association (AAA).** Members of some foreign auto clubs have reciprocal arrangements with the AAA and enjoy its services at no charge. If you belong to an auto club, inquire about AAA reciprocity before you leave. The AAA can provide you with an **International Driving Permit** validating your foreign license. You may be able to join the AAA even if you are not a member of a reciprocal club. To inquire, call 800/222-4357. In addition, some automobile rental agencies now provide these services, so you should inquire about their availability when you rent your car.

Automobile Rentals   To rent a car you need a major credit card and a valid driver's license. Sometimes a passport or an international driver's license is also required if your driver's license is in a language other than English. You usually need to be at least 25, although some companies do rent to younger people but may add a daily surcharge. Be sure to return your car with the same amount of gasoline you started out with as rental companies charge excessive prices for gas. Keep in mind that a separate motorcycle-driver's license is required in most states. See "Getting Around" in Chapter 3 and Chapter 13 for specifics on auto rental in Seattle and Portland.

Business Hours   **Banks** are open weekdays from 9am to 5pm, with later hours on Friday; many banks are now open on Saturday also. There is also 24-hour access to banks through automatic teller machines at most banks and other outlets. Most **offices** are open weekdays from 9am to 5pm. Most **post offices** are open weekdays from 8am to 5pm. In general, **stores** open between 9 and 10am and close between 5 and 6pm, Monday through Saturday; stores in malls generally stay open until 9pm; some **department stores** stay open till 9pm on Thursday and Friday evening; and many stores are open on Sunday from 11am to 5 or 6pm.

Climate   See "Climate" in Section 2 of Chapters 2 and 12.

Currency   See "Money" in "Preparing for Your Trip," above.

Currency Exchange   You will find currency exchange services in major airports with international service. Elsewhere, they may be quite difficult to come by.

To exchange money in Seattle, go to **American Express,** 600 Stewart St. (☎ 206/441-8622), or **Thomas Cook,** 906 Third Ave. (☎ 206/623-6203). To exchange money in Portland, go to **American Express,** 1100 SW Sixth Ave. (☎ 206/226-2961), or **Thomas Cook** at Powell's Travel Store, 701 SW Sixth Ave (☎ 206/ 222-2665).

Drinking Laws The legal drinking age in both Washington and Oregon is 21. The penalties for driving under the influence of alcohol are stiff.

Electricity The United States uses 110 to 120 volts, 60 cycles, compared to 220 to 240 volts, 50 cycles, in most of Europe. In addition to a 110-volt converter, small appliances of non-American manufacture, such as hair dryers or shavers, will require a plug adapter with two flat, parallel pins.

Embassies & Consulates All embassies are located in the national capital, Washington, D.C. Some consulates are located in major cities, and most nations have a mission to the United Nations in New York City. Listed here are embassies and consulates of some major English-speaking countries. If you are from another country, you can obtain the telephone number of your embassy or consulate by calling **Information** in Washington, D.C. (☎ 202/555-1212).

- **Australia** The **embassy** is at 1601 Massachusetts Ave. NW, Washington, DC 20036 (☎ 202/797-3000). The nearest **consulate** is in San Francisco at 1 Bush St., San Francisco, CA 94104-4413 (☎ 415/362-6160).
- **Canada** The **embassy** is at 501 Pennsylvania Ave. NW, Washington, DC 20001 (☎ 202/682-1740). The regional **consulate** is at 412 Plaza 600 Building, Sixth Ave. and Stewart St., Seattle, WA 98101-1286 (☎ 206/443-1777).
- **Ireland** The **embassy** is at 2234 Massachusetts Ave. NW, Washington, DC 20008 (☎ 202/462-3939). The nearest **consulate** is in San Francisco at 655 Montgomery St., Suite 930, San Francisco, CA 94111 (☎ 415/392-4214).
- **New Zealand** The **embassy** is at 37 Observatory Circle NW, Washington, DC 20008 (☎ 202/328-4800). The nearest **consulate** is in Los Angeles at Tishman Bldg., 10960 Wilshire Blvd., Suite 1530, Los Angeles, CA 90024 (☎ 310/477-8241).
- **United Kingdom** The **embassy** is at 3100 Massachusetts Ave. NW, Washington, DC 20008 (☎ 202/462-1340). There is a **consulate** in Seattle at 999 Third Ave., Suite 820 Seattle, WA 98104 (☎ 206/622-9255).

Emergencies Call **911** to report a fire, call the police, or get an ambulance.

If you encounter traveler's problems, check the local telephone directory to find an office of the **Traveler's Aid Society,** a nationwide, nonprofit, social-service organization geared to helping travelers in difficult straits. Their services might include reuniting families separated while traveling, providing food and/or shelter to people stranded without cash, or even emotional counseling. If you're in trouble, seek them out.

Gasoline (Petrol) One U.S. gallon equals 3.75 liters, while 1.2 U.S. gallons equals one Imperial gallon. You'll notice there are several grades (and price levels) of gasoline available at most gas stations. And you'll also notice that their names change from company to company. The unleaded ones with the highest octane are the most expensive (most rental cars take the least expensive "regular" unleaded) and leaded gas is the least expensive, but only older cars can take this any more, so check if you're not sure.

In Oregon you are not allowed to pump your own gasoline, but in Washington "self-service" gas stations are common and usually are less expensive than full-service stations.

Holidays   On the following legal national holidays, banks, government offices, post offices, and many stores, restaurants, and museums are closed:

> January 1 (New Year's Day)
> Third Monday in January (Martin Luther King, Jr. Day)
> Third Monday in February (Presidents' Day, Washington's Birthday)
> Last Monday in May (Memorial Day)
> July 4 (Independence Day)
> First Monday in September (Labor Day)
> Second Monday in October (Columbus Day)
> November 11 (Veterans Day/Armistice Day)
> Fourth Thursday in November (Thanksgiving Day)
> December 25 (Christmas Day)

> The Tuesday following the first Monday in November is Election Day, and is a legal holiday in presidential-election years.

Languages   Major hotels may have multilingual employees. Unless your language is very obscure, they can usually supply a translator on request.

Legal Aid   If you are stopped for a minor driving infraction (for example, of the highway code, such as speeding), never attempt to pay the fine directly to the police officer; you may wind up arrested on the much more serious charge of attempted bribery. Pay fines by mail, or directly into the hands of the clerk of the court. If accused of a more serious offense, it is wise to say and do nothing before consulting a lawyer. Under U.S. law, an arrested person is allowed one telephone call to a party of his or her choice. Call your embassy or consulate.

Mail   If you want to receive mail on your vacation and you aren't sure of your address, your mail can be sent to you, in your name, **c/o General Delivery** at the main post office of the city or region where you expect to be. The addressee must pick it up in person and produce proof of identity (driver's license, credit card, passport, etc.).

Generally to be found at intersections, mailboxes are blue with a red-and-white stripe and carry the inscription U.S. MAIL. If your mail is addressed to a U.S. destination, don't forget to add the five-figure postal code, or ZIP (Zone Improvement Plan) Code, after the two-letter abbreviation of the state to which the mail is addressed (OR for Oregon, WA for Washington, CA for California, and so on).

Newspapers/Magazines   National newspapers include *The New York Times, USA Today,* and the *Wall Street Journal.* National news weeklies include *Newsweek, Time,* and *U.S. News and World Report.* For local news publications, see "Fast Facts" for Seattle and Portland.

Radio and Television   Radio and TV, with four coast-to-coast networks—ABC, CBS, NBC, and Fox—joined by the Public Broadcasting System (PBS) and the cable network CNN, play a major part in American life. In big cities, viewers have a choice of about a dozen channels (including the UHF channels), most of them transmitting 24 hours a day, without counting the pay-TV channels showing recent movies or sports events. All options are usually indicated on your hotel TV set. You'll also find a wide choice of local radio stations, each broadcasting particular kinds of talk shows and/or music—classical, country, jazz, pop, gospel—punctuated by news broadcasts and frequent commercials.

Safety   See "Safety" in "Preparing for Your Trip," above.

Taxes   In the United States there is no VAT (value-added tax) or other indirect tax at a national level. Every state, and each city in it, can levy a local tax on all purchases, including hotel and restaurant checks, airline tickets, and so on. In Seattle and King County the **sales tax rate** is 8.2 percent. In Portland and the rest of Oregon, there is no sales tax.

Telephone, Telegraph, Telex & Fax   The telephone system in the United States is run by private corporations, so rates, especially for long distance service, can vary widely—even on calls made from public telephones. Local calls in the United States usually cost 25¢.

Generally, hotel surcharges on long-distance and local calls are astronomical. You are usually better off using a **public pay telephone,** which you will find clearly marked in most public buildings and private establishments as well as on the street. Outside metropolitan areas, public telephones are more difficult to find. Stores and gas stations are your best bet.

Most **long-distance** and **international** calls can be dialed directly from any phone. For calls to Canada and other parts of the United States, dial 1 followed by the area code and the seven-digit number. For international calls, dial 011 followed by the country code, city code, and the telephone number of the person you wish to call.

For **reversed-charge** or **collect calls,** and for **person-to-person calls,** dial 0 (zero, *not* the letter "O"), followed by the area code and number you want; an operator will then come on the line, and you should specify that you are calling collect, or person-to-person, or

both. If your operator-assisted call is international, ask for the overseas operator.

For local **directory assistance ("information"),** dial 555-1212;
for long-distance information, dial 1, then the appropriate area code
and 555-1212.

Like the telephone system, **telegraph** and **telex** services are provided by private corporations like ITT, MCI, and, above all, Western Union. You can bring your telegram to the nearest Western
Union office (there are hundreds across the country), or dictate it
over the phone (a toll-free call, 800/325-6000). You can also telegraph money, or have it telegraphed to you very quickly over the
Western Union system.

If you need to send a **fax,** almost all shops that make photocopies
offer fax service as well.

Telephone Directory   There are two kinds of telephone directo-
ries available to you. The general directory is the so-called **White
Pages,** in which private and business subscribers are listed in alphabetical order.

The inside front cover lists emergency numbers for police, fire, and
ambulance, as well as other vital numbers (coast guard, poison control center, crime-victims hot line, and so on). The first few pages
are devoted to community-service numbers, including a guide to
long-distance and international calling, complete with country codes
and area codes.

The second directory, printed on yellow paper (hence its name,
Yellow Pages), lists local services, businesses, and industries by type,
with an index at the back. The listings cover not only such obvious
items as automobile repair services by make of car, or drugstores (phar-
macies)—often by geographical location—but also restaurants by
type of cuisine and geographical location, bookstores by special subject and/or language, places of worship by religious denomination,
and other information that the tourist might otherwise not readily
find. The *Yellow Pages* also include city plans or detailed area maps,
often showing postal zip codes and public transportation.

Time   The United States is divided into four **time zones** (six, if
Alaska and Hawaii are included). From east to west, these are: eastern standard time (EST), central standard time (CST), mountain
standard time (MST), Pacific standard time (PST), Alaska standard
time (AST), and Hawaii standard time (HST). Always keep changing time zones in mind if you are traveling (or even telephoning) long
distance in the United States. For example, noon in Seattle (PT) is
1pm in Denver (MT), 2pm in Chicago (CT), 3pm in New York City
(ET), 11am in Anchorage (AT), and 10am in Honolulu (HT).
Daylight Saving Time is in effect from 2am on the last Sunday in
April until 2am on the last Sunday in October except in Arizona,

Hawaii, part of Indiana, and Puerto Rico. Daylight saving time moves the clock one hour ahead of standard time.

Tipping   This is part of the American way of life, on the principle that you must expect to pay for any service you get. Here are some rules of thumb:

>   **Bartenders:** 10 percent–15 percent.
>   **Bellhops:** at least 50¢ per piece; $2–$3 for a lot of baggage.
>   **Cab drivers:** 15 percent of the fare.
>   **Cafeterias, fast-food restaurants:** no tip
>   **Chambermaids:** $1 a day.
>   **Checkroom attendants (restaurants, theaters):** $1 per garment.
>   **Cinemas, movies, theaters:** no tip.
>   **Doormen (hotels or restaurants):** not obligatory.
>   **Gas-station attendants:** no tip.
>   **Hairdressers:** 15 percent–20 percent.
>   **Redcaps (airport and railroad stations):** at least 50¢ per piece, $2–$3 for a lot of baggage.
>   **Restaurants, nightclubs:** 15 percent–20 percent of the check.
>   **Sleeping-car porters:** $2–$3 per night to your attendant.
>   **Valet parking attendants:** $1.

Toilets   Foreign visitors often complain that public toilets (or "restrooms") are hard to find in most U.S. cities. True, there are none on the streets, but the visitor can usually find one in a bar, restau-

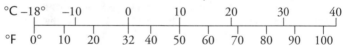

rant, hotel, museum, department store, or service station and it will probably be clean (although the last-mentioned sometimes leaves much to be desired).

Note, however, that some restaurants and bars display a notice that "Toilets Are for the Use of Patrons Only." You can ignore this sign, or better yet, avoid arguments by ordering a cup of coffee or a soft drink, which will qualify you as a patron. The cleanliness of toilets at railroad stations and bus depots may be questionable; some public places are equipped with pay toilets, which require you to insert one or more coins into a slot on the door before it will open.

AMERICAN SYSTEM OF MEASUREMENTS
Length

1 inch (in.)	=	2.54cm			
1 foot (ft.)	=	12 in.	=	30.48cm	=	.305m
1 yard (yd.)	=	3 ft.		=	.915m
1 mile (m)	=	5,280 ft.			=	1.609km

To convert **miles to kilometers,** multiply the number of miles by 1.61. Also use to convert miles per hour (mph) to kilometers per hour (kmph).

To convert **kilometers to miles,** multiply the number of kilometers by 0.62. Also use to convert kmph to mph.

Capacity

1 fluid ounce (fl. oz.)			=	.03 liters		
1 pint	=	16 fl. oz.	=	.47 liters		
1 quart	=	2 pints	=	.94 liters		
1 gallon (gal.)	=	4 quarts	=	3.79 liters	=	.83 Imperial gal

To convert **U.S. gallons to liters,** multiply the number of gallons by 3.79.

To convert **liters to U.S. gallons,** multiply the number of liters by 0.26.

To convert **U.S. gallons to Imperial gallons,** multiply the number of U.S. gallons by 0.83.

To convert **Imperial gallons to U.S. gallons,** multiply the number of Imperial gallons by 1.2.

Weight

1 ounce (oz.)			=	28.35g		
1 pound (lb.)	=	16 oz.	=	453.6g	=	.45 kg
1 ton	=	2,000 lb.			= 907kg	= .91 metric tons

To convert **pounds to kilograms,** multiply the number of pounds by 0.45.

To convert **kilograms to pounds,** multiply the number of kilograms by 2.2.

Temperature

To convert **degrees Fahrenheit to degrees Celsius,** subtract 32 from °F, multiply by 5, then divide by 9 (example: 85°F − 32 × 5/9 = 29.4°C).

To convert **degrees Celsius to degrees Fahrenheit,** multiply °C by 9, then divide by 5, and add 32 (example: 20°C × 9/5 + 32 = 68°F).

Index

SEATTLE

SEATTLE
ACCOMMODATIONS

SEATTLE RESTAURANTS

PORTLAND

PORTLAND
ACCOMMODATIONS

PORTLAND RESTAURANTS

NOTES

Now Save Money on All Your Travels by Joining

Frommer's
T R A V E L B O O K C L U B

The Advantages of Membership:

1. Your choice of any **TWO FREE BOOKS.**

2. Your own subscription to the **TRIPS & TRAVEL** quarterly newsletter, where you'll discover the best buys in travel, the hottest vacation spots, the latest travel trends, world-class events and festivals, and much more.

3. A **30% DISCOUNT** on any additional books you order through the club.

4. **DOMESTIC TRIP-ROUTING KITS** (available for a small additional fee). We'll send you a detailed map highlighting the most direct or scenic route to your destination, anywhere in North America.

Here's all you have to do to join:

Send in your annual membership fee of $25.00 ($35.00 Canada/Foreign) with your name, address, and selections on the form below. Or call 815/734-1104 to use your credit card.

Send all orders to:

FROMMER'S TRAVEL BOOK CLUB
P.O. Box 473 • Mt. Morris, IL 61054-0473 • ☎ 815/734-1104

YES! I want to take advantage of this opportunity to join Frommer's Travel Book Club.

[ ] My check for $25.00 ($35.00 for Canadian or foreign orders) is enclosed.
All orders must be prepaid in U.S. funds only. Please make checks payable to Frommer's Travel Book Club.
[ ] Please charge my credit card: [ ] Visa or [ ] Mastercard

Credit card number: _____

Expiration date: ___ / ___ / ___

Signature: _____

Or call 815/734-1104 to use your credit card by phone.

Name: _____

Address: _____

City: _____ State: _____ Zip code: _____

Phone number (in case we have a question regarding your order): _____

Please indicate your choices for TWO FREE books (*see following pages*):

Book 1   Code: _____   Title: _____   _____

Book 2 - Code: _____   Title: _____

For information on ordering additional titles, see your first issue of the *Trips & Travel* newsletter.

Allow 4–6 weeks for delivery for all items. Prices of books, membership fee, and publication dates are subject to change without notice. All orders are subject to acceptance and availability.   AC1

The following Frommer's guides are available from your favorite
bookstore, or you can use the order form on the preceding page
to request them as part of your membership in
Frommer's Travel Book Club.

FROMMER'S COMPLETE TRAVEL GUIDES

*(Comprehensive guides to sightseeing, dining and accommodations,
with selections in all price ranges—from deluxe to budget)*

Acapulco/Ixtapa/Taxco,		Italy '96 (avail. 11/95)	C183
2nd Ed.	C157	Jamaica/Barbados, 2nd Ed.	C149
Alaska '94-'95	C131	Japan '94-'95	C144
Arizona '95	C166	Maui, 1st Ed.	C153
Australia '94-'95	C147	Nepal, 3rd Ed. (avail. 11/95)	C184
Austria, 6th Ed.	C162	New England '95	C165
Bahamas '96 (avail. 8/95)	C172	New Mexico, 3rd Ed.	C167
Belgium/Holland/Luxembourg,		New York State, 4th Ed.	C133
4th Ed.	C170	Northwest, 5th Ed.	C140
Bermuda '96 (avail. 8/95)	C174	Portugal '94-'95	C141
California '95	C164	Puerto Rico '95-'96	C151
Canada '94-'95	C145	Puerto Vallarta/Manzanillo/	
Caribbean '96 (avail. 9/95)	C173	Guadalajara, 2nd Ed.	C135
Carolinas/Georgia, 2nd Ed.	C128	Scandinavia, 16th Ed.	C169
Colorado '96 (avail. 11/95)	C179	Scotland '94-'95	C146
Costa Rica, 1st Ed.	C161	South Pacific '94-'95	C138
Cruises '95-'96	C150	Spain, 16th Ed.	C163
Delaware/Maryland '94-'95	C136	Switzerland, 7th Ed.	
England '96 (avail. 10/95)	C180	(avail. 9/95)	C177
Florida '96 (avail. 9/95)	C181	Thailand, 2nd Ed.	C154
France '96 (avail. 11/95)	C182	U.S.A., 4th Ed.	C156
Germany '96 (avail. 9/95)	C176	Virgin Islands, 3rd Ed.	
Honolulu/Waikiki/Oahu,		(avail. 8/95)	C175
4th Ed. (avail. 10/95)	C178	Virginia '94-'95	C142
Ireland, 1st Ed.	C168	Yucatán '95-'96	C155

FROMMER'S $-A-DAY GUIDES

(Dream Vacations at Down-to-Earth Prices)

Australia on $45 '95-'96	D122	Ireland on $45 '94-'95	D118
Berlin from $50, 3rd Ed.		Israel on $45, 15th Ed.	D130
(avail. 10/95)	D137	London from $55 '96	
Caribbean from $60, 1st Ed.		(avail. 11/95)	D136
(avail. 9/95)	D133	Madrid on $50 '94-'95	D119
Costa Rica/Guatemala/Belize		Mexico from $35 '96	
on $35, 3rd Ed.	D126	(avail. 10/95)	D135
Eastern Europe on $30,		New York on $70 '94-'95	D121
5th Ed.	D129	New Zealand from $45,	
England from $50 '96		6th Ed.	D132
(avail. 11/95)	D138	Paris on $45 '94-'95	D117
Europe from $50 '96		South America on $40,	
(avail. 10/95)	D139	16th Ed.	D123
Greece from $45, 6th Ed.	D131	Washington, D.C. on	
Hawaii from $60 '96		$50 '94-'95	D120
(avail. 9/95)	D134		

FROMMER'S COMPLETE CITY GUIDES

(Comprehensive guides to sightseeing, dining, and accommodations in all price ranges)

Amsterdam, 8th Ed.	S176	Miami '95-'96	S149
Athens, 10th Ed.	S174	Minneapolis/St. Paul, 4th Ed.	S159
Atlanta & the Summer Olympic		Montréal/Québec City '95	S166
Games '96 (avail. 11/95)	S181	Nashville/Memphis, 1st Ed.	S141
Atlantic City/Cape May,		New Orleans '96 (avail. 10/95)	S182
5th Ed.	S130	New York City '96 (avail. 11/95)	S183
Bangkok, 2nd Ed.	S147	Paris '96 (avail. 9/95)	S180
Barcelona '93-'94	S115	Philadelphia, 8th Ed.	S167
Berlin, 3rd Ed.	S162	Prague, 1st Ed.	S143
Boston '95	S160	Rome, 10th Ed.	S168
Budapest, 1st Ed.	S139	St. Louis/Kansas City, 2nd Ed.	S127
Chicago '95	S169	San Antonio/Austin, 1st Ed.	S177
Denver/Boulder/		San Diego '95	S158
Colorado Springs, 3rd Ed.	S154	San Francisco '96 (avail. 10/95)	S184
Disney World/Orlando '96		Santa Fe/Taos/	
(avail. 9/95)	S178	Albuquerque '95	S172
Dublin, 2nd Ed.	S157	Seattle/Portland '94-'95	S137
Hong Kong '94-'95	S140	Sydney, 4th Ed.	S171
Las Vegas '95	S163	Tampa/St. Petersburg, 3rd Ed.	S146
London '96 (avail. 9/95)	S179	Tokyo '94-'95	S144
Los Angeles '95	S164	Toronto, 3rd Ed.	S173
Madrid/Costa del Sol, 2nd Ed.	S165	Vancouver/Victoria '94-'95	S142
Mexico City, 1st Ed.	S175	Washington, D.C. '95	S153

FROMMER'S FAMILY GUIDES

(Guides to family-friendly hotels, restaurants, activities, and attractions)

California with Kids	F105	San Francisco with Kids	F104
Los Angeles with Kids	F103	Washington, D.C. with Kids	F102
New York City with Kids	F101		

FROMMER'S WALKING TOURS

(Memorable strolls through colorful and historic neighborhoods, accompanied by detailed directions and maps)

Berlin	W100	San Francisco, 2nd Ed.	W115
Chicago	W107	Spain's Favorite Cities	
England's Favorite Cities	W108	(avail. 9/95)	W116
London, 2nd Ed.	W111	Tokyo	W109
Montréal/Québec City	W106	Venice	W110
New York, 2nd Ed.	W113	Washington, D.C., 2nd Ed.	W114
Paris, 2nd Ed.	W112		

FROMMER'S AMERICA ON WHEELS

(Guides for travelers who are exploring the U.S.A. by car, featuring a brand-new rating system for accommodations and full-color road maps)

Arizona/New Mexico	A100	Florida	A102
California/Nevada	A101	Mid-Atlantic	A103

FROMMER'S SPECIAL-INTEREST TITLES

Arthur Frommer's Branson!	P107	Frommer's Where to	
Arthur Frommer's New World		Stay U.S.A., 11th Ed.	P102
of Travel (avail. 11/95)	P112	National Park Guide, 29th Ed.	P106
Frommer's Caribbean		USA Today Golf	
Hideaways (avail. 9/95)	P110	Tournament Guide	P113
Frommer's America's 100		USA Today Minor League	
Best-Loved State Parks	P109	Baseball Book	P111

FROMMER'S BEST BEACH VACATIONS
*(The top places to sun, stroll, shop, stay, play, party, and swim—with each
beach rated for beauty, swimming, sand, and amenities)*

California (avail. 10/95)	G100	Hawaii (avail. 10/95)	G102
Florida (avail. 10/95)	G101		

FROMMER'S BED & BREAKFAST GUIDES
*(Selective guides with four-color photos and full descriptions of
the best inns in each region)*

California	B100	Hawaii	B105
Caribbean	B101	Pacific Northwest	B106
East Coast	B102	Rockies	B107
Eastern United States	B103	Southwest	B108
Great American Cities	B104		

FROMMER'S IRREVERENT GUIDES
*(Wickedly honest guides for sophisticated travelers and
those who want to be)*

Chicago (avail. 11/95)	I100	New Orleans (avail. 11/95)	I103
London (avail. 11/95)	I101	San Francisco (avail. 11/95)	I104
Manhattan (avail. 11/95)	I102	Virgin Islands (avail. 11/95)	I105

FROMMER'S DRIVING TOURS
*(Four-color photos and detailed maps outlining
spectacular scenic driving routes)*

Australia	Y100	Italy	Y108
Austria	Y101	Mexico	Y109
Britain	Y102	Scandinavia	Y110
Canada	Y103	Scotland	Y111
Florida	Y104	Spain	Y112
France	Y105	Switzerland	Y113
Germany	Y106	U.S.A.	Y114
Ireland	Y107		

FROMMER'S BORN TO SHOP
*(The ultimate travel guides for discriminating
shoppers—from cut-rate to couture)*

Hong Kong (avail. 11/95)	Z100	London (avail. 11/95)	Z101